52 Flowers That Shook My World

A RADICAL RETURN TO EARTH

Charlotte Du Cann

to David
with best wishes
and flowers
charlotte du cann
July 15
2012

TWO RAVENS
PRESS

Published by Two Ravens Press Ltd.
Taigh nam Fitheach
26 Breanish, Uig
Isle of Lewis HS2 9HB
United Kingdom

www.tworavenspress.com

ISBN: 978-1-906120-64-1

British Library Cataloguing in Publication Data: a CIP record for
this book can be obtained from the British Library.

Designed and typeset in Goudy by Two Ravens Press
Cover design by Two Ravens Press
Cover image: Mem Green | Shutterstock
Inside images: Charlotte Du Cann and Mark Watson

Printed in Poland
on Forest Stewardship Council-accredited paper.

About the Author

Charlotte Du Cann is a writer and community activist working in communications with the grassroots organisations Transition Network and the Dark Mountain Project. She was born in London in 1956, and worked during the 1980s as a lifestyle journalist, specialising in food, fashion and design. After travelling for ten years, mostly in the Americas, she settled in Suffolk in 2002 to write a sequence of books about reconnecting with the earth. She has published five works of nonfiction, ranging from a collection of essays about food, *Offal and the New Brutalism* (Heinemann), to the travelogue *Reality Is the Bug That Bit Me in the Galapagos* (Flamingo). She edits several collaborative blogs, 'This Low Carbon Life', 'The Social Reporters Project' and the 'OneWorldColumn', and is currently working on a low-carbon cookbook, *One Planet Community Kitchen* and a prequel to *52 Flowers, The Earth Dreaming Bank*.

You can find a selection of Charlotte's writings at:
http://charlotteducann.blogspot.com

Author's note

Originally this book contained the narratives of 52 flowers and was very long indeed. Rather than radically rewriting the content, we chose to reduce the number of flowers. And so the book is now, strictly speaking, 32 flowers, with the essence of the missing plants and trees threaded back into the text. You can see the original list in the appendix.

We decided to keep the original title however, for reasons you will shortly be finding out...

for the plants
for the places
for the people

52 Flowers That Shook My World

52 Flowers That Shook My World

INTRODUCTION
The Path of Flowers

It is deep midwinter. I am moving through the dawn, down the path towards the sea. The air is cold and I am wrapped in a long woollen skirt, shawl, coat, my boots tapping against the icy walkway. I walk through the wood, past the dark forms in the alder carr, past ghostly birches and wide-armed oaks, out into the marsh, through the tunnels of blackthorn and rose briars shining with red hips. Everything is edged with hoarfrost, even the tousled gold of the reeds. The whole world is held in suspense. At the crossroads I meet Mark and we walk together down to the shore. The sky is pale and clear except for a band of cloud at the horizon. At the sea's edge we pause, gazing across the milky calm, down an empty shingle coastline. Misty forms rise from the stillness of the water to meet the grey clouds that gather in the thick bar in the distance. We keep looking through the mist to the place where the sky meets the sea. We are waiting for the sun.

At some point we exhale and our breath plumes the air. We cannot see the red solar disc but we know it has come. The birds start flying past over our heads, the day has broken, the world is waking up. Everything that had been held in an icy grip has suddenly been released. The year has turned, and we head home.

It's the beginning of a new time.

Everything on earth is about return. In the winter you wait for the return of the sun. As snow falls, in the darkness of dawn, in the silence of birds, you long in your heart for the light and the warmth and the sound of singing. In that longing you feel the sun rising though you cannot see it from behind a bank of cloud.

The story of return is the story of this book. A return to the earth we once loved but then forgot. It is a remembering of the wild earth and the trackways we once took that lead us there – the trackways that still live inside our bodies and our imaginations, in deep time, that lead us toward the shining earth that exists beyond our ordinary sight, the sunlit world we inherit by right of being human, and yet our minds cloud over every day.

It is a personal story, but it is also the story of everyone who seeks knowledge, who creates, who sets out on a journey whose destination is not yet known. People have walked these tracks towards the sun and sea for thousands of years. Their shape lives in our dreams, etched within our ancestral bones, in the structure of our voices; they run in lines across England's chalky hills, through the deep forests and deserts and wild mountains of the world. Sometimes they come into our ordinary lives, like the tang of the salt wind, like a hare running across a field, like the skein of geese flying overhead as night falls, a flower whose name we have forgotten and yet whose urgent scent brings the memory of a child standing with the bud of a poppy in her hands, carefully unravelling the crinkly fabric inside, a flower dress she wishes to wear.

The mystery of this nature is all about us, and yet to discover it we must follow an invisible track that leads inside into the darkness of our unknown selves. That track leads in a different direction. It leads you through the door everyone told you never to go through, and yet you move towards it. Like the salmon, you cannot do otherwise. Our wild nature is to be free to return whence we came. Where do we come from? Some part of us remembers. When you find that part, you do not question: you start to swim upriver.

To know the nature of the earth is to know our own nature. To remember how to walk the track of return, to swim against the flow, is to know all things. This knowledge has not yet been written, it is yet to be experienced. Afterwards you find the words. You struggle within yourself to speak and describe what you find, forging meaning from the salty tears that run down your face, from the dead songbird in your hands, from the mountain you glimpse through the bus window, the fragments you collect in your coat pocket, the shards of deer bone, flint and cone, the thoughts that come as you wait in the stillness of a winter's afternoon, writing at a desk that belonged to someone you will never meet, the roaring of the night wind in the tree as you lie sleeping.

It is a story about return, but it is also a story about creativity – what being a writer really means.

Inquiry

How does this story begin? It could begin on a dark winter's night on the Suffolk coast, with a seawind blowing through the holm oaks and a moon sailing over the slate roofs of a boarding-school, as I step out into my own path, my own independent inquiry. It could start here, at this moment, as I sit sifting through the world's great literature in the small hours, looking for a point of departure, and come across a book by a French philosopher and another by an impoverished Englishman, living in Paris in 1929.

Jean-Paul Sartre is telling me that suffering, seen in a certain way, with imagination, has meaning, and that human beings need to make this meaning, otherwise they become like objects of no intrinsic value and so does their world. George Orwell is telling me that experiences of real life, the life he sees in the front lines of Spain, the slumlands of the north and the kitchens of Paris, teach us our common humanity and that this fellow-feeling is the key to our freedom. The doomed drawing rooms of Madame Bovary or Anna Karenina hold little interest for this passionate lover of books aged fourteen. Already she cares little for the bourgeois and the respectable. But the fates of the tortured young men of *Nausea* or *1984* speak urgently to her soul, a soul intensely interested in fairness, in liberty. And most of all these words speak to her heart.

The story of return is also a story of liberation, a revolution of the heart. It is our hearts that will return the earth to its former beauty and liberate all those who live bound in invisible chains. Revolutions in what we call history create upheaval and changes of order but they rarely bring social justice, and even more rarely individual freedom. Philosophers who have lived through such revolutions throw up their hands in despair and go and dig their gardens. The only way forward is for man himself to change his violent, self-seeking nature, they say, and do not tell us how we should proceed.

The revolution of the heart proceeds by shifting our allegiance. First in our imaginations, and then in our physical lives. It is a shift that moves our attention away from the civilisations that foster our violence and self-centredness and aligns it with the earth and our human hearts that know otherwise. The intelligence of our hearts and our real feeling natures are what civilisation and history push out of the door into the wilderness. It is not entirely our fault that we are so cruel and self-obsessed. For we have been trained in heartless institutions and set to work in heartless occupations and everything we look at, including the planet that gives us our sustenance and shelters us, is seen through heartless eyes. We have been encouraged to see each other as objects, to have little empathy for our fellows. The revolution of this book is about seeing everything anew with our hearts. It is not a historical or political revolution, but an inner one. A revolution that shook my own heartless world.

It is a revolutionary story of flowers because it was the wild flowers that showed me how to recognise the sun, even when it was hidden behind a bank of cloud. There are 52 world-shaking flowers but there could have just as easily been 500, or only one.

52 flowers tell the story.

The irrevocable step

I could start this story at the moment I first switched my allegiance, when I stood in a slumland garden, aged nineteen, in the red-light, sweatshop district of Birmingham and looked at the sooty amputated arms of a sycamore tree, and wondered how such a tree could ever find leaves. When a fellow lover of justice and literature called Tricia told me that everyone in her northern village went to work for ICI and only she had escaped. A shocking moment when I realised that everything I had been told about society was untrue: that 'lower class' people do not deserve the conditions they struggle in, that the snobberies I had been schooled in, our sacred knowledge of claret and music and houses, do not justify our superior position. What you see and experience in such a moment changes you utterly: you cannot afterwards go back to where you were before.

4

52 moments of changing allegiance.

52 ways of saying goodbye to one world.

52 ways of saying no to the illusions that define that world.

52 ways of crossing a bridge.

52 ways of leaving the past and entering the future.

52 steps I took where I never looked back.

Rise and fall

These men are definitely not bourgeois or respectable. Their destinies rise and fall with a spectacular brilliance. Like me, these men live on the edge, only as good as their last piece of work. Generous, spiky, outrageous, they are above all creators, and I like nothing better than to enter their extraordinary intense worlds with a tape recorder in my pocket. Here I am working as a journalist in the 1980s in London, conversing backstage with the shopkeepers, the pastry cooks, barmen, actresses, painters, chairmakers and hatmakers, all the brilliant creatures of the otherworld that provide the costumes and props for the theatre upstairs. For the show where there is always room for another hat, another chair, another way to toss a salad, or a new idea. Here we are talking over their drawing tables, meeting in a decade of parties and photographic shoots, while my life weaves a spidery pattern across dance floors, hotel balconies, drinking clubs and small flats in the small hours with the sounds of a taxi wheezing outside.

There is something not right about this. The way some of these young men disappear. Where one minute they are glorious and peacock-jacketed, dancing and laughing, and the next cut down. Some of them become forgotten, tossed aside when they take too many drugs or get sick and don't make everyone laugh any more. They don't flourish as they should. I don't like the endings to these stories, and maybe my own could begin here in my heart's disturbance, when I see how the wildness of these men is left out, trampled on, used, torn apart. We should all be growing, extending, gathering together. We should be breaking out but instead we are breaking down.

Along the shingle shore of Dungeness, Derek Jarman walks in a black coat through the kingdom of the *crambe maritima* and stunted blackthorn. As he walks he reels out a litany made of the names of English wild flowers. It is a song of farewell he is singing, like a nightingale in May, as the blood of life seeps out from his veins: scarlet pimpernel, red campion, red valerian, herb Robert, speedwell, forget-me-not.

The zenith

One thing I learned from these magazine years: you leave the party when you are having a good time. You leave at the zenith of your life. Why do you leave? Because the spirit that fires you only knows itself when it moves. You don't leave at the beginning because that would be meaningless. You leave at the best time because what you leave in your wake and the elegance of your farewell is what makes everything valuable. At the party, on the dance floor, how you move is everything. My fourth move, the one that really counted, was the way I left this successful world behind.

We are born into circumstances which are often the very opposite to our real natures. In our struggle to find this nature is the transformation of the world. My soul was deep but I was living a superficial life; my soul loved flowers and sunlight, but I was working in a dark and ugly city; my heart delighted in liberty and equality but everywhere I looked was bound by hierarchy. How could I be otherwise? As I paused by my typewriter to listen to the wind in the bamboo on the Greek island, in the quiet of a seaside town full of hollyhocks, as the winter rain fell in the Riviera garden and clouded the hills aflame with sweet chestnuts, my soul knew one day I would leave and remember almost nothing from these years, except sometimes the laughter of a friend whose address I will no longer have, whose face will appear in a dream. And yet I waited. Our story has not begun yet.

At the zenith something happens. You leave the party because you have found somewhere else to go. Because one day, aged thirty-three, a door opens out of the blue and the sun falls into your twilight world. And without thinking you run towards the light.

In the sun's doorway stands a man called Mark. Behind Mark is Mexico. Behind Mexico are extraordinary worlds conjured by magic mushrooms and behind them, out of the darkness of the void, comes a mysterious female figure, carrying an unknown plant in her hand that seeds in her wake, world upon world, galaxy beyond galaxy.

As I run towards the door the journey I will later call the solar path, the path of flowers, begins. The year is 1989. This is the moment when this story really begins. The moment when something I had never expected entered my life. And I began to let everything else go.

The losing throw

Everything in this story takes the shape of a sunflower. The 52 flowers each tell an individual tale, yet all 52 work together as a whole. The sunflowers come last in the evolutionary line of flowers. They are known as composites because each flower is actually a *collective* of flowers. So although the book is an individual tale, it is written from within the collective, as one among the many. These are 52 flowers that shook *my* world, but they also shook *our* world, and made me look at *our* evolutionary future as human beings living on the planet at a certain time, a time the ancient seers call the *kali yuga*, the dog's throw, the time of the losing throw. The time when we lose the game and have to start again.

The losing game is a civilisation of closed systems that keep us apart, not only from the living systems of the planet, but also from each other. In this game we do not speak as one-among-many. We are too busy drawing our battle lines. But the path of return leads us out of hiding, into the field, into the kingdom of the heart, back to the beginning. How each of us moves in this circular collective dance informs its whole direction, the way we start again.

To proceed in this dance, you have to move, you have to make the irrevocable step and throw the dice whose outcome you already know. You have to lose everything that keeps you reserved, superior, above it all, knowing the game but not playing it. You cannot do this with your mind, you can only do it with your heart, at the precise moment your soul gets a glimpse of its freedom, the possibility of starting again. When your consciousness becomes flooded with a sunlight you have longed for all your life. There are no words to describe this kind of freedom, to describe the lucidity of your mind or your feelings, when the bondage of aeons drops away.

This liberty is what the flowers brought when they shook my world, when I ran to the door and saw the track of the sun ahead of me, my life companion on that path and where it was going. When you see

7

that you don't care about magazines or parties, or even that your old friends don't recognise you any more. You have already forgotten that life of bondage. It has dropped away.

The solar path

There are two journeys the spirit makes on this earth, one illuminated by the blue moon and the other by the gold-coloured sun. The lunar journey of descent, sometimes known as the dark night of the soul, leads us down into the past, into the realms of Hades, lit with its lamps of asphodel, beyond the thrones of the mythological gods with their fennel spears and pomegranate bargains, where your father's shadow waits for you under the sighing poplar, into the realm of the ancestor bones, into the dragon's lair, into the seedstore of the earth.

The solar journey goes in a different direction: it goes outside into the wilderness, towards the unknown. Outside the town walls, beyond the school fence, through the wastelands, past the storm-cloud tyrants of the sky realms and into exile. This is the fiery path of spirit, edged with sunflowers, that leads out into the future, into the empty spaces of desert and mountain and tundra bright with lichen, towards the realms of the invisible workings of the sun. It is a path of action, a path of vision and a path of intellect. It is both a heroine's journey and a creator's task.

What instructs you on these metaphysical journeys are the beings who deal directly with the sun and moon, the flowering plants and trees who in their physical alchemy turn sunlight and water into the food that nourishes, shelters and inspires all creatures on the planet, including ourselves. In their radial structure, in their infrared scent, their ultraviolet colours, you will find keys for living on the earth in the future. The flowers are central to our planetary consciousness, to what may be called our spiritual or soul life. This is why at the mysterious heart of every culture you will find a flower: a lotus or a rose or a marigold.

These flowers live in a country you cannot always see but sometimes feel in your heart. They appear before us and call us to return to our original nature. Sometimes you sense this as you stand by your cooking pot with its scent of wild mountain thyme, or on a warm night in the city as you pause by a honeysuckle bush, or a rose. What happens when you dare to follow that primrose path into the wild places? Who is it who stands at the edge of the year, who waits to return, with the scarlet poppy in her hands?

The return

There is a myth about the flower path that underpins the whole of our modern world, a myth that I knew, even at eight years old, was mine: the myth of Persephone and a flower known in England as the poet's narcissus. In the myth the young Persephone, stooping to pick this wild lily, falls into the kingdom of Hades and becomes his sorrowful bride. But this is not the story that the initiates of the archaic worlds learned. For Persephone, who becomes Queen of the Underworld, is not a foolish girl but the personification of wisdom, the being the ancient seers and medicine men consulted in the deep wild places within themselves, who was once known by many names and resides in the depths of the night, in the darkness, in the still point of ourselves. In the traditional version of the myth Pluto makes a bargain with Demeter. Your daughter will live with you for six months of the year, he decrees. But Persephone never goes upstairs into the kingdom of the sun and earth. You find no reference to her return among the classical texts. She only exists in the land of the dead.

For the truth of the matter is that our world rests on the fact that Persephone never goes upstairs, and does everything in its power to keep her in her place. Persephone is supposed to return each spring with the flowers, when the narcissi emerge, and bring all the wisdom of the night and winter with her. Without her, her 'mother' Demeter is a foolish, weeping woman, incomplete, unwise, without any knowledge of the mysteries of birth and death that reside in the roots and seeds of the wild earth and in our own starry selves. The truth of the matter is that the world constructed by the philosophers and their inheritors, the scientists, could not exist if she were alive in all of us.

'The mother does not penetrate the mysteries,' says the mythologist Carl Kerenyi of the mystery rites of Eleusis. Persephone was originally the Kore, an aspect of a three-fold Moon goddess with Demeter and Hecate, and what is happening in these later 'official' versions of the myth is a splitting, a fragmentation of the female psyche in order that the patriarchal mindset can hold its invisible sway – the kind of myth

9

that psychologists like to use, while all the time keeping everyone inside the well-behaved drawing room worlds of Demeter.

Who is Persephone outside this myth? Is she happy to dwell among the dead, dark poppy-daughter to the mother of the golden barleyfield, or does she serve another purpose within our imaginations? Kerenyi, a perspicacious mythologist, writes that originally Persephone did not 'fall' but deliberately went down into Pluto's kingdom at the request of Rhea, her 'grandmother', the ancestor of the wild earth, to put the world of agriculture, the world of civilisation, back into balance. Once there she did not ally herself with Pluto but joined with her half-brother Dionysus, and their fall-and-return mysteries made a way through for human beings to remember their glorious origins and return whence they came, a way open to all those who journey into the wild, uncharted territory of themselves.

Persephone does not belong to the domesticated world, she is neither mother nor diva. She is as barren and as beautiful as the moon. Complete, autonomous. She is someone that our world makes no place for except as an untouchable. And so it was that I went to the wild uncharted places, to the barren places, to the deserts, to seek among the thistles and tares those parts of myself that were not subject to a bargain between matriarchy and patriarchy, the property of man or state; to treasure those parts of the female being, of the human being, that most people leave out or throw away on the garbage heap for the sake of a convenient life. It was not a spiritual system nor even an ancient mythology that finally led me upstairs, but the flowers that I found growing down in the underworld, in the wastelands, along the path that the Celtic poets once called the white track, the starry path of the Milky Way, that they saw reflected in the humble white clover among the meadow grasses, and praised above all other flowers.

It is not a new path, this path of flowers: it has been called the good red road, the pollen path of beauty, the path of heart, the way of the ancestors, the way of the fool, or simply the way. But whatever ancient or new names you call it, it is always the same path, the one that leads out of the city and into the woods. You might find it in the libraries, among folk tales and mythologies, and yet no one teaches you how to walk it. It was once called the path of the soul, and it is the one that will lead us all back to the earth when we follow it.

You are not the same person when you return on this path, nor

10

is the place you come back to the same. I remembered this the day I returned to the Suffolk shore and began this book. I stood on the collapsing seacliff with the marshland sighing behind me and the ghosts of the great mullein keeping watch by the tower. I remembered how it all began.

Sometimes I wish I could have written an ordinary book about plants: a nature-writing book about a city-dweller who went to live in the country and rediscovered her childhood love of wildflowers – but then that would not have been the truth of the matter. Because I was the kind of person who had read Sartre when I was young and knew that to treat the world and ourselves as objects was inauthentic, and the plants had not come back into my adult life as objects with botanical names, they had returned in utterly magical, metaphysical ways. They appeared in my dreams, in visions, out of the blue, in medicine ways and myths, in the lives of writers and in writing, and as I followed their track, leaving my old city life behind me, crossing the peaks of the Andes and the thorny deserts of Arizona, walking through the meadows and wastelands of middle England, through the forests and mountains of France, they called me home, back to the place I call the heartland, back to the apple grove, back to a seashore where the sea-kale grows, back to a world where nature is at the centre of life, and most of all back to myself, someone who loved to be light and at liberty, an independent female being at home on the earth. And that is the place that I want to tell you about because the flowers took me to this place for a reason. Because I was also once a person who had read George Orwell and knew that you don't suffer experiences in this world and write just for yourself. You write for your fellows. Because the path of the flowers is also the path of the heart.

Sometimes I wish this journey had only taken a year, so that I could have written a straight-forward book about plants as a travel book or a 'new-age' or ecological guidebook that could tell you that aligning with the earth, with your spirit, is something you can just get down and get sorted. But actually it took seventeen years. It took everything I ever had away, and it gave everything I ever loved back. It was a return journey. And that kind of journey is not really about travelling or ecology or the new age, it's about something else.

I
GERMINATION

No seed germinates without Spring. No journey of return begins until wild nature knocks at our city door and disturbs us. Until then, we slumber in our houses and offices, in our ordinary lives. Outside the wind howls, the sea crashes on the shore, eclipses of the sun and moon shake the sky. Like seeds kept in a drawer by a forgetful god, we are unaware of these tumultuous events, we remain quietly in our coloured packets, secure in everything we have been told about ourselves and our situation. But one day the elements break through the ancient casings in which our original beings are held. We are shaken up, thrown out into the light, thrown onto the earth, and the germ of our inner selves, after years of constraint, bursts out of its constriction. We have found the right conditions in which to flourish.

You go travelling. Not the small weekend at the hotel, not the vacation to the snows, the seaside holiday, the borrowed villa, but the long voyage into a vast and unknown country, in which your shell, your holding station of many years, is irrevocably shattered. One day, for no apparent reason, you start swimming up a strange yet familiar river.

One April day in 1990 I travel to Mexico with Mark.

Everything is disturbing in Mexico, India or Australia, this unknown country you go travelling through. The elemental worlds shake, tumble and turn you. The journeys are galling, and uncomfortable. Before, you controlled events to suit you; now, events act upon you. People do not conform to your needs, time goes to another rhythm, strange foods and landscapes enter your system.

Nothing is certain. The idea you have always held of yourself becomes less sure, less articulate. Some part of yourself however has broken free, sends green shoots into the open sky, small roots into the earth beneath. You stand by the ocean, untrammelled; an immensity fills your being. I am here! you declare. You take up a notebook, talk to strangers, take a bus to an unknown destination. As you move in these unpredictable ways, your city life, which depended on fixed routines and rituals, on reference to everyone else, on establishing yourself with houses and relationships, loses its implacable hold upon your imagination. You feel you could live forever in this small hotel room with the tropical rain falling, as if you could start all over again.

You return to Mexico the following year, with a suitcase and no plan: no longer possessed by possessions, no longer held in a position by your friends, pressured by society or work to conform. You can at any moment take a bus all the way down to Tierra del Fuego. You are at this moment on that bus. Others are on that bus with you, travelling for a year in South America. Most people are young and go back to the city. Some are not young. Some are like you, exploring the territory without a map. The man travelling with you is there for the long haul, going all the way down to the land of fire. Sometimes you meet people who have been on the road for a long time, living in the Arizona desert, in old houses, in bare studios with a small library and a woodstove. They are bitter-tasting and fierce, independent, non-conformist. They don't always like you but you feel at home with them none the less. Most of them love plants; all of them love the earth.

At some point you realise the river has become your life. At some point you realise that, though the beginning was about liberation, about swimming in fresh water, now it is also about work.

The solar path, though you do not call it as such yet, has made you aware of time. Now these people and places are here and tomorrow they will be gone. You have to make meaning now, live now, enjoy now, be in this moment. Before the moment could come again, you could repeat it whenever you wanted. You only needed a few super-ficial attitudes and contacts; you had no need of your heart or your creaturehood. But now to remember these moments with people and places, to flourish in this nomadic life, in this fluid world, you have to live intensely, really, deeply. To be alive your body requires movement; your imagination, space and time; you need to release yourself from the definitions civilisation and your history have given you, with their forms, their stories, with the images in which your friends and family keep you. Your values undergo a shift. You realise that this is not just personal: you are changing for a reason.

In the town squares of Bogota, of Quito, of Seattle, where you recognise no one, you realise you are one human being among many human beings. Your eyes, once bound up with the haughty images of glamour and architecture, now in wonder see the passing shapes of mountains, deep forests, the wild Pacific ocean. You sleep in small humble huts with roofs of leaves. You bathe in hot mineral springs and hear the wingbeats of hummingbirds and condors. The rough and beautiful language of the wild earth enters your being. Its rhythms, scents, sounds, colours – red earth, turquoise sky, yellow corn. You drink the juice of unknown fruits and sleep in a hammock; your bare feet touch sand and rock. Once you arrive, you do not want to leave. But you always leave. You may never come here again. You hold the moment in a photograph, in a picture you paint, in words that you write: you keep these places in your heart.

To go travelling across these continents is to know the poignancy of time. Before, your life was fixed. Everyone stayed in their places. There were advantages to that life because you were secure. Spring was spring. You held parties, kept to a deadline. You slept in the same bed for years. You had friendships that lasted a whole lifetime. Now you lack security, nobody knows you, your foibles, your tastes, the way you laugh. You sleep in a hundred different rooms. You are a stranger. You strike up friendships with other strangers. But one day they take a plane, go home, take another route. They always leave, you always leave. You hold the moment in a photograph; they send you a letter that takes six months to arrive; some of them stay in your heart.

The territory is a huge exterior geography that changes its shape, that enters your heart, but it is also an interior terrain. As you travel, something stirs within you. Something disturbing. You move always forward but the current is dragging you backwards. People have been crossing your mind, you are dreaming of past difficulties, you feel troubled, your body begins to ache. This is the beginning of alchemy. The *materia* of your life is presenting itself to be transformed. You have, though you did not know it before, embarked on a quest. From the world's point of view this has happened at a most inconvenient moment. From the perspective of your spirit it is the only moment. Your soul with its long memory has come with a heavy ledger, with its karmic record of what needs to be changed. A whole lineage of requirements. It tells you: now that you have the time and space, this is what you need to pay attention to, and this. Why were you born in such a city, in such circumstances? What does it mean that you are here in this place now? What is your destiny in this form you know as yourself? Who is it who is travelling by your side? You know at this point it is between you and the river. To get home, these obstacles need to be surmounted. To get home, you will need assistance.

At this moment the earth you have been travelling through becomes your ally. At times of extremity the flowers appear. Here is the pine tree in Sedona, Arizona, keeping me in its embrace when I am grieving; here is the persimmon like a glowing lamp in my hand in the Alhambra gardens of Granada when I have lost my way; here is the horse chestnut tree of Kensington Gardens in a dream, showing me how the people can shelter beneath her bountiful shade. Here are the women of the Southwest who tell me about the medicinal and magical properties of the bitter herb mugwort, who make inspirational elixirs infused by moonlight and sweet violets. Here I am alone in a forest in France collecting wild mushrooms, awoken by their strange and penetrating aroma at night to hear the sound of the wild boar roaring in the darkness.

The flowers that came during the germination years signalled the beginning of the alchemical work of return. These are the years 1991-1998, before our formal plant inquiry began, years of travelling through South America and Mexico, driving across America, taking trains across Australia; living in houses on Greek islands and on the Dorset and East Anglian coast. Years spent living out of suitcases, waiting in bus stations, arriving in small airports where the palm trees move in the breeze. All seeds require different conditions in which to germinate: frost, fire, the pecking of birds, the scouring by stones; I needed warm tropical rain and desert storms, long empty afternoons, intense dramatic encounters, world-shaking inner events. Some of these unsettling experiences came with flowers and trees – certain plants that brought with them the unmistakable signature of the solar path.

These alchemical flowers and trees did not bring answers,

they brought questions, dilemmas, unexplained mysteries, earth connections, glimmers of a different world that I recorded in a series of coloured notebooks and drawings. The first seven plants of this chapter all initiated shifts within myself and provided the framework for our subsequent inquiry. During this husk-breaking time we were writing travel books and poetry, performing and singing, and exploring the worlds of nature and spirit with fellow seekers in ways that were both modern and archaic. What were we doing in these meetings and exchanges? We were letting an old world go and entering another territory altogether. We were searching for the future.

The flowers were taking us there.

epazote
Notting Hill, London 1990

That night I had a dream. I was walking through a green land and an Indian woman came up to me and put some herbs in my hand. I have been having dreams about plants since I returned from Mexico. Men and women are appearing silently from nowhere and giving me sage tea to drink, or instructing me to plant bulbs, or I find myself walking through fields of wheat and maize and seeing how their growing patterns have been disturbed. This dream was unusual, however, in that this native woman spoke the names out loud: one was liquorice root and the other had a name I did not recognise, *epazote*.

In the dreams I know about the cornfields but I do not know about the herbs. I particularly do not know about this herb called *epazote*. That night I got up and sat at my writing table and looked at my hands. I have the familiar corn in my right, but in my left, I hold a plant I do not know. It is a stranger.

I am in my flat alone in the middle of the night, holding this strange herb from a dream. I am surrounded by everything I know: shelves of books, thousands of them, line the walls of this kitchen study. In the adjacent living room the treasures of a thirty-something life sit in the darkness: pottery bowls from markets, pearwood chairs from auctions, a long handcrafted table where people meet, an Indian mattress where people sometimes sleep. I could pick up every object in this room and tell you its story: who was there when I found it, what it means, how it defines me; how this jacket came from Paris, the paella pan from Madrid, the blue meshed larder from Athens, this stone from a certain beach in Wales, these cow bones from the New Mexican desert. I could tell you all the recipes that I cook in these earthenware dishes, with my junkstore utensils that lie in a drawer, in my alchemical workplace of words and cooking pots, my rooms with a certain atmosphere many people love to come to, even more than being with me. Charlotte's for supper, with its table and familiar objects, with its rough panelling, its windows without curtains, where you can hear the occasional sound of a bus passing, or a drunk reeling down the road. With its inspirational physical style.

In this moment I feel all the attention that I and others have placed on these objects dwelling in these rooms. I feel the way I move about them, write about them, handle them is becoming more important than my own living being, and something in me shudders.

I realise that my being is about something else that is not dependent on these objects. Life is not about things that others or I can handle. These objects are a replacement for a relationship with life. But nothing replaces that relationship, not really. It is a comfort, as a child is comforted in the night by a toy. But it is not the real thing. This plant I do not know yet is telling me this. It is having a certain effect as I sit and contemplate it. Everything I am surrounded by has become imbued with a different feeling, has become less secure in this moment. It as if these objects no longer have anything to do with me. They are losing their hold, unhooking themselves, as I hold this strange herb in my left hand.

The entrance of the stranger on the solar path is the pivotal point, the point when it begins. The stranger is something about which you know nothing, that you allow into your life. Sometimes this is a person and sometimes a new idea. But whatever form the stranger takes, it comes like a strange attractor and breaks the limit cycle of our lives, like a philosopher's stone that begins the strange alchemy of our souls. Our worlds are normally so circumscribed that we automatically do everything to keep this stranger out. We are programmed to defend ourselves, like genetically modified plants, to deport any visiting outsider as an undesirable alien, in order that we continue to conduct our affairs in the same small way, without questioning their validity.

But sometimes we let the stranger in anyway. Sometimes by accident, and sometimes fired up by an ancient curiosity, our native love of secrets and mysteries, our desire for keys and clues and signs. Our souls lie in wait for such a moment, the moment when our consciousness starts to ask questions and rouses us out of bed to look at our hands.

What has awoken me this night from my sleep is the memory of Mexico. This first germinating seed is a wild plant known as Mexican wormseed. Epazote is not a grand plant; in fact it is a common weed that flourishes by any highway, ditch or vacant lot from Sonora to Chiapas. Its name derives from the Nahuatl word for skunk, due to its unmistakable pungent aroma. It is a member of the goosefoot family, a whole tribe of flourishing weeds like tumbleweed and fat hen, all with small flowers and nourishing rich green leaves (beetroot, good king henry, spinach are all goosefoots). However, epazote's power lies not in its leaves but in its rank and bitter seeds, which are a formidable anti-parasitic and vermifuge. It was once cultivated throughout the world as a cure against the ravages of hookworm. It has been used for centuries in Mexican cooking to flavour and act as a digestive aid in beans. In fact, once you have tasted its strange and musty scent, you can't cook beans without it.

Once I had tasted Mexico, I could not do without Mexico either. Its strange and bitter flavours. When I had travelled there with Mark that spring I had gone without any references. It was unexpected, something I had not calculated for. 'No one I knew knew Mexico,' as I would write later in a book about this journey. Mexico did not exist in my library or my internal world, so its presence could act on my being absolutely. And absolutely it did. This did not just mean the unusual physical senses of the place: the scent of tuberose, the colours of the painted walls, the long bus rides through valleys of glow-worms, a hot turquoise sea – but also things of a deeper, more cosmic level. It meant taking hallucinogenic mushrooms that tore my consciousness open in the Mayan rainforest, and now, as I am looking at my hands, it means Carlos Castaneda and the warrior's path, a path of heart that goes through the desert. A certain desert of thorns and cactus.

When you start the solar journey, you hunt for ways to begin. If you are a writer, you start with books, and of all the many books I was reading at this time, it was Castaneda's account of his apprenticeship with the Yacqui seer don Juan in Mexico that spoke most urgently to me. While others I knew were fascinated by the book's description of power and the control of dreams, I was absorbed by its meticulous description of the energetic acts of the warrior, those strategic steps of the will that enabled one to live with fluidity in the world: the assuming of responsibility, the letting go of self-pity and self-importance, encountering the mysterious presence of twilight and the concept of impeccability.

The other 'new-age' works I looked at during this time had very little to do with impeccability. They concerned themselves with important gods and goddesses, family psychology and wounded healers, archetypes and temples. They belonged to the bourgeois city

19

parlours I recognised from my novel-reading days. But Castaneda's books were talking about something that did not originate in the city. The writer-anthropologist had left the city of Los Angeles in the early sixties in search of a plant called peyote that grew out in the desert chaparral that lay between Arizona and Mexico. There was something clear and autonomous and mysterious in his quest that resonated with my own being. His journey reminded me of the deliberate life I had come across in the works of Sartre when I was young. Don Juan's teachings spoke of a rigorous and affectionate relationship between man and earth that was both sparing and tender, that lived quite beyond this indulgent, acquisitive, objectifying world I lived and worked in. Because everything he spoke of worked within the framework of death.

Most of all Mexico meant death. Death is your advisor, don Juan advises Carlos Castaneda. We are all beings who are going to die. Every act you make as a warrior is your last act on earth, so you don't have time for petty moods or failures. You don't waste your time.

I had not considered death before, my death. Death is something you don't think about in the eternal shopping world of London or Los Angeles, but in Mexico death looks at you directly in the eye, rattling its smiling skeleton in the face of your artificial parasitic life, whose currency is inflated ten times its actual value. At a certain point, if you care about life, you turn to face death. You let go of the world you have been involved in constructing and start to work for the spirit of things. You realise you are not going to be on this earth forever and certain strategic moves need to be made if you want to experience this mysterious place while you are here.

In Palenque that spring I had realised my life in the world meant nothing. It wasn't worth a handful of beans. In the annihilating force of the mushrooms, I could hold on to nothing of this existence, not even my name. So I let them go. And what was left in its place was a relationship to life that now demanded my full attention, linked both with my own heart and with the mysterious man whose destiny now appeared inextricably bound up with my own. Mark.

One day shortly after this epazote dream, I picked up the telephone.

'Mark, Let's go to Mexico for six months,' I said. 'We can write a book together.'

'Oh, yes!' he said. 'But what about your flat?'

There was a pause.

'I'm going to sell it,' I said. 'I'm going to sell everything I own.'

When I left London I was thirty-five. The age when you let go of the corn you have been sowing in your right hand, and take up what destiny has given you in your left. When Death appears at your door, when the mysterious woman with her wand of wormseed comes to you and suggests you face another direction entirely. When you let go of everything you know and walk toward the sun, towards an unknown horizon.

passionflower
Merida, Mexico 1991

In the courtyard by a swimming pool full of leaves there is an alcove with a bare table and a large Remington typewriter. I have taken to going down there to break the solitude of my white-washed room. I share the typewriter with two Cuban poets, who smoke strong and fragrant cigarettes and talk Spanish so quickly I cannot understand a word they say. We take it in turns to hammer away at the ancient keys, so that the small courtyard rings out with our efforts, as if Vulcan himself was forging a new alphabet.

Our hotel is down a small side-street. In the evening, after wrestling all day in the smithy, I take a shower and go out into the streets of Mérida. The warm damp air is drenched with the scent of invisible jasmine. The women wear white dresses and hibiscus flowers in their hair, and walk on the arms of men elegantly dressed in the long pale shirts of the Yucatán, known as *guayaberas*, and panama hats. At the corner of the street I stop at a blue-painted stall, stacked high with pineapples, watermelons and giant papaya, and drink a long tall glass of coloured juice – orange mango, chestnut tamarind, crimson hibiscus, golden passionfruit. Everywhere is the scent of limes and guava. I step into the square where the people are gathering, where the night fills with the sound of marimbas and conversation, and small Mayan girls thread through the crowd with trays of gardenia flowers.

When I was twelve my grandfather began to perch on the edge of my life, like a sparrowhawk. And I was never quite sure, as I sat nervously before his cross-examination, whether I was lunch, or just learning, as all small sparrows must, how to avoid the attention of raptors.

I had written a thank-you letter for an uncharacteristic Christmas present and he had sent a reply in tiny crabbed script, formally inviting me to enter into a correspondence with him. Later he invited me to take tea with him at his club, the RAC. He was a formidable host: an entirely Victorian creature, with everything terrible and marvellous about that age. Domineering, formal, single-minded, ambitious, inventive, sentimental. What distinguished him was an unusual attitude towards women, perhaps because, an orphan from the age of three, he had been brought up in a convent. He was the first barrister at the Inns of Court to accept a female pupil, and once launched, aged eighty-seven, into a full-scale row with the doorman of the RAC because he wanted to show me the club's famous Grecian-style swimming pool which at that time was only open to men. A love of water was something we found out that we shared, as well as a love of words.

Surrounded by the formality of the club, he would launch into what he considered the worthwhile things of life, which went in the entirely opposite direction of everything I had so far been taught. Self-discipline, rigour, gnosis, was the basis of his creed, as well as generosity in important matters, such as clotted cream. Writing was life's greatest task; Arnold Bennett, who wrote two thousand words before breakfast, its ideal craftsman. Self-educated, he learned to write by becoming a journalist; he taught himself law while serving in the trenches, and he told me that life, and only life, can give you anything worthwhile.

'You must leave school,' he tells me, as I sit before the austere and shining battery of eating implements in the club dining room. Tea has now become lunch. 'School will only teach you how to read books. When you become a writer, then you can travel wherever you like and be able to earn your living.'

'But I am only fourteen!' I protest (I am fond of books, and also of my school companions).

But my grandfather does not change his position on the matter. He proof-reads and copy-edits my correspondence in red ink, informing me that *The Times* always expects a good margin from its contributors, and Life that we keep to the Delphic code.

Know thyself. To thine own self be true.

Each holiday, at the end of lunch or tea, he would take me to the exotic fruit section of Fortnum and Mason's and select a fruit I had never tasted before – nectarine, fresh figs and dates, persimmon, pomegranate, star fruit, mango – and tell me to try it out immediately in the middle of Piccadilly.

'Oh, it's delicious!' I say, awed and excited by the fruit as much as I am relieved that the ordeal by China tea or Vichy water is coming to a close.

'I told you,' he says. 'Never eat any grape but the Muscat because it is the best. Next time we meet you can try a passionfruit.'

And he would smile to himself, a smile that only he knew.

My grandfather does not write about his own true self. Of the self and the smile that only he knew. He keeps his feelings and his experiences firmly hidden. He writes biographies about writers he admires (George Bernard Shaw, Charles Dickens), about famous murder cases, and about the small shiny things he likes to collect – boxes by Fabergé, gold coins, diamond watches, cameo brooches.

How could he do otherwise, predator such as he was?

The fruit comes from a vine, a strong vine that grows along the walls of the town, in back alleys, along fences, rampant through the forest margins. Its flower is exotic, captivating, and somehow terrifying. It grows in different forms throughout the Americas, from the rainforests of Brazil to the deserts of Texas. In spite of its fragile and exotic look it is a tough climber and can grow even in the frosty polluted gardens of Europe. Its fruits are all rich and seedy. Wrinkled purplish sacs reveal red-coated golden seeds inside, that you bite into and suck as you do a ripe fig. It has one of those tastes that is always surprising, like rocket leaves or sharp mangos. Shocking, sour, sweet. It is the very opposite of the grey pavements of Piccadilly.

The flowers are complex and intricately made and rise in a series of discs: ten sepals and petals, usually greenish-white, with a eye-catching fringe that come from the calyx that is often purple or pink, followed by a ring of five anthers in the shape of hammers. The three stigmas that emerge from the top of the pistil stalk are dark-brown and stick out sideways, like cloves. Its common name refers to the passion of Christ, an association made by a Mexican friar who brought the flower to the attention of Rome in 1609. The petals are said to represent the apostles, the stigmas the nails or the Trinity, the stamens the five wounds, the tendrils the scourges – and so on. All passionflowers are arresting and scented. The common passionflower, the one most commonly grown in Europe, *Passiflora caerulea*, smells strangely medicinal, like Germolene.

The vine has been used as a medicine throughout the world for centuries and is a peerless herbal sedative, good even for children. A tea or tincture made from the leaves and tender stems of *passiflora incarnata* slows everything down in the physical and emotional body,

24

takes the pressure off, releases stresses and strain. Most sedatives are narcotics or nervines and have a 'downer' effect, like valerian, or make you drowsy, like hops or poppies. But the passionflower does not have these side-effects. It gently pulls you down two notches. Workaholics and those suffering from hypertension and insomnia love the vine. Some people take it in *extremis* as a legal high: they smoke the leaves or make a powerful decoction to experience the sensations of warmth, camaraderie and relaxation. However you approach the plant, it takes the tension out of everything and brings sweet dreams. You can drink a tea of passionflowers and their leaves and go calmly to sleep and wake refreshed the next day.

I don't know anything about plant medicine yet. I am just embarking on the path of flowers. To know the plant you have to know how to eat its fruit. And then you need to know the territory in which it grows. Then one day you find the flower. This is the way round. When I find the native wild passionflower of the desert, ten years later in Arizona, winding its way along a fence in the Dragoon hills, then I will know its medicine. I will look back at this time, the time of the fruit, the time of the territory, and remember everything about passionflowers. I will be able to answer the question it asks:

What are you putting yourself on the line for?

I will not be comfortable in front of the small white flower, or any of its large and showy town relatives. It is not a simple flower you can love instantly. It is complex, like the heart, fiddly almost to behold, with its wheels and spokes and different colours. I am not always comfortable in the small hotel room in Mérida and go out into the courtyard. The uncomfortable moment is when everything happens: when the pressures of your former existence have been taken off and you realise what really matters in life: not what your peers think, not what the country expects, but what your sparrow spirit has come here to do. You need the territory of the flower to do this.

The territory of the passionflower is an unknown geography, far from what is familiar, where there are no people who would bind you to them and their desires. A place where you can work things out on your own, where your spirit can make contact with you. Where in a relaxed state of warmth your heart can speak without interruption.

The hermits and sages traditionally chose for these reasons wilderness places far from their fellow men: remote Scottish islands, deep forests, deserts, high mountain peaks. I chose a city where I knew no one. Outside the city of Mérida the green peninsula of the Yucatán stretches in all directions, with its rich forest canopy, its spiky desert fields of agave and shark-infested Caribbean sea. In this flat and watery land live a people who have been here for thousands of years, famous in Europe for their astounding ability with time and for their former civilisation which now lies in ruins, dwelt in by iguanas with blue tongues, covered in vines.

You love the hut, this small hermetic space wherein you wrestle with demons. It is your crucible. You are the material, the agent and the result. You go in with black mud and come out with gold. When you walk out at the end of the day, the world is beautiful. When you return the next day you hammer out words in praise of everything you see and feel, in the heat of the tropical morning, scented with banana leaf and rain.

This is not the cell of austerity, of penance, of deprivation. Its bare lines of bed, table, chair, white wall, light and shadow, have their own clear lines of beauty. You enter this hermitage with joy – the shed, the cabin, the cave, the tent – from here seeds are planted, consciousness explored, terra incognita mapped. Without this inner sanctum you go nowhere. Where can you find this space in the drawing rooms and bedrooms of the world, with their parties, and furniture and curtains, with their endless meals? With their pursuits of pleasure and their avoidance of pain?

One thing is certain about the hut. Your endeavours will not bring you riches in the outside world. Inside this bare space you find out ways to transmute all things into treasure of another kind. The quality and the intelligence of the self you experience as you engage in this task is worth more than gold. Why would you need palaces and pleasure when you hold the philosopher's stone?

In the forest where the passionflower grows, where its leaves have been used as a poultice for thousands of years, the Maya sit in small straw huts and weave patterns of extraordinary complexity, the most beautiful fabrics of the world in all the colours of the quetzal bird. In their imaginations and in their hearts they hold calendars of equal complexity, that rotate at different speeds like the stars around the sun. They have held these complex patterns inside them for thousands of years – patterns of time, of colour, of beauty. They held them before the cities came and after they fell into ruin. The temples did not hold them. The temples never do.

The territory of spirit is as impossible to describe as the flower itself. *Who can describe the Tao?* ask the ancients – the wind you cannot see, the water you cannot grasp? Who can describe the fire that burns and yet does not burn? It is the elemental hardship of the hermitage in which you seek and encounter the self. To seek is to ask the question: for what purpose do I come? It is a dangerous question. The passion-flower is a dangerous flower, a new world flower. To eat its fruit is to taste the oasis. Once you have done that, only the desert life will satisfy you. You cannot go back to your old world. I do not know this yet, like all seekers, all travellers who go without a plan. I am sitting in the square, eating *sopa de lima,* talking with a Mayan man with a sleek head like a jaguar. Mark will come from Guatemala tomorrow. We will go swimming in the *cenote,* and then down to the sea.

To ask the question is to sit in the hermitage in the centre of complexity. To understand the flower is to sit in the centre and understand at a deep level your own suffering, betrayal and doubt. The discs of the passionflower move and grind you like a mill and you cry out in the night. By morning the sky is clear. You are refreshed. It is the agony of moving stiff and rigid things within yourself. Your feeling in this undertaking is everything. It is the last thing you wish to admit; all your training tells you never to admit feeling. Go into your mind and escape! it shouts. Keep a stiff upper lip, be superior, be victorious. Be a hawk! And yet your feeling, your child feeling, your small sparrow feeling, is what will liberate the world.

The passion of the flower is not the passion of desire, but the passion of suffering. There are two sorts of suffering, and they need to be distinguished. One is meaningless and the other has many meanings. To suffer without awareness is the first kind. It is to suffer the unkind institutions and the history of the world. The second kind of suffering, conscious suffering, is what liberates you from them. The institution – church, school, the family – bullies and pressurises small sparrows and turns them into hawks. The hawks keep the institution in place. To free yourself, to access your heart, your spirit, means you have to go into the passion. When you *consciously* suffer, recalling all the feelings you were not allowed to have in your sparrowhawk position, you find out what really matters and what does not, what is natural and true to your living form. *To thine own self be true.* This takes off the unnecessary pressure. You start not bullying yourself to write two thousand words before breakfast. You are not Arnold Bennett, nor even your grandfather. You write only because you love to, because it is, as you find out, the only thing you want to do.

The passionflower is complex. The heart is complex. Writing is complex. It can hold many things and goes in many directions: fringes, stigmas, petals that look like hammers, hand-shaped leaves, tendrils that curl about a bush, a tree, a house. Most of all it can take you back to yourself. *Know thyself.* It is a way that your spirit can talk to you. I am learning this. My notebooks are full of green leaves, parrots, hummingbirds, blue caves. I treasure dreams and fleeting memory. In the alcove, the two young poets and I cannot say many things to one another but we can laugh as we pass each other by. Strangers and writers such as we are.

I do not write the book of the sparrowhawk travel writer. I do not write to praise the establishment or history. I do not go, like the Victorian conqueror, into *la selva* and bring back dates and facts and information. I do not visit the Maya to document their medicine and spiritual ways. I do not write of churches, or wars, or museums. I sit in the square and listen to marimba players. And I try to write what it feels like to be in a place where men and women walk arm-in-arm and eat rainbow-coloured ices. Where the houses are pink and green. Where time does something extraordinary that has nothing to do with the twenty-four-hour clock. What kind of effect this has on your physical and emotional being, on your imagination. I try to write what it is like to give up everything just when the going was seemingly good.

My grandfather was a formidable collector. I am an uncollector. While my contemporaries are following his path, building up dynasties, reputations, bank accounts, houses with drawing rooms, joining clubs, I shore up nothing. I am letting go, leaving houses, people, complexes, opinions, learning to live on rice and beans and a simple cot in a bare room. I am undoing the unnatural work of the establishment, of the institution, as it impressed its own stricture, its artificial shapes, on my own being – centuries of church and school, of law and science. I go searching beneath my grandfather's murder trials looking for the nature of justice, and in his cameo brooch or necklace of jet for the natural beauty of the shell or stone. I roam like a vine, hands outstretched, scrambling over the temples of my deserted world, searching out for clues, seeking what real spirit lived here before. How the passionflower was before it was given over to the sacrifice required from an alien god.

Outside in the hammocks of the Yucatan, I swing, I swing, I move, I let go. Out of my sparrowhawk claw I release position, habit, circumstance, social ritual, the traffic of Piccadilly and the knives and forks of the RAC; in the space they leave behind comes feeling, memory, intuition, dreams, a notebook of colours, Cuban poets and a watery land. In their place comes passion.

Who are your ancestors? The ones who went before, who tell you about the path of return before you have even begun the path of flowers, who tell you about the nails, even as you taste the first fruits. If you are wise, you forget what they tell you. If you are wise, you remember everything. Under the stern invisible eye of my grandfather, I began my first journal. I did not become a librarian, I became a journalist. I relinquished my cello-playing and my school companions. I wrote two thousand words before breakfast like Arnold Bennett (though not every day). I sallied forth on my thirty-fifth birthday to know myself, carrying an Olivetti typewriter in my hands. Could I have avoided this? Or was it always going to happen? No one else gave me these instructions: about the struggle of writers, about the perils of the hermitage, about the advantages of drinking one glass of watered cider only, with meals. And yet as I wrestled with the demons of a lineage, as all writers must, with the workhouses and army camps of my grandfather's world, with its law courts and music halls, with a culture that only values its collections of shiny objects, and afterwards went out and refreshed myself with the fruits I had once tasted at his behest, it felt like the only way of life that was worthwhile.

When I wrote, I wrote with all the feelings of the small and insignificant city songbird. I sang *cheep cheep* from my humble eyrie made of leaves and bamboo. I will write like this for three years, as I travel though the vast landscapes of the Americas. In small whitewashed rooms. In small mud-floored *palapas* on the coasts of Ecuador, in the valleys of the Andes. Outside I listen to the roar of

29

the Pacific, the roar of these unknown cities, the wind in the banana leaves, the rain rushing in torrents down the streets. Inside me the unwritten legacy of a hundred years stretches back through time and turns like a knife in my heart.

I do not always write well. I can no longer write with the clear calculating eye of the raptor but with the foolish engagement of the sparrow. I write about pavements and eaves, of buses, of city squares, of people I meet as I flit from hotel to hotel. I write of common things. The ancestors sit invisibly behind us, beyond us, as we make our small moves along this living path. We are their second chance. They know everything, but cannot do anything. The sparrow chirps and talks. He is a merry bird. He engages with his fellows, full of hope and expectation. He can taste the fruit put before him and still delight in it. He can make mistakes. No one is watching. Everyone's eyes are on the hawk. The shadow of his scimitar wing makes all creatures below him tremble.

Why are we writing in the desert, wrestling with the demons of ourselves, that are not just ourselves? Why do we endure these spikes and torments? Because when we do we bring with us the sleep of the oasis, the sleep that the flowers bring. We bring sweet dreams and fellowship.

It is hard to love the sparrowhawk, if you love songbirds. To know sparrowhawks is to meet them eye to eye and know the business of elders.

'When I wanted to be a journalist I asked Lord Northcliffe for a job,' my grandfather repeated to me. 'If you want something in life, go to the man at the top! Don't bother with the people in between.' He was right of course, about being a journalist. But writing of the passionflower is not the same as writing about crimes of passion, or intricately wrought *vinaigrettes* of silver and gold that the superior classes held to their nostrils to avoid the stench of their fellow man.

To write of life you need to be in the position of the passionflower. No one wants to be in this position. I don't want to be in this position. I have been writing for years from the privileged view of the hawk, from the vantage place of the observer and collector. Everything can be funny, interesting, weird up there. You can be as smart as hell. You can earn money and be ambitious. But something is missing. You are far away from the earth. And your shadow has begun to scare everyone from the tree.

If you are not a Christian, the traditional desert of the spirit has become forgotten territory. You have pushed it from your mind. If you are English at the end of the twentieth century, you have especially pushed it from your mind. You are a rational creature, a defender of the Enlightenment. The business of dragons and demons does not concern you. Privately you fear you will be sacrificed, forced to your knees to pay penance for crimes you did not commit, made to worship an alien, hectoring god. You don't want to play the saviour, or the Magdalene; you shudder at the history of martyrs, of genocide, of inquisitional fires, the quiet cruelty of religious institutions. At school while my fellow choristers take communion, I secretly read the literature of Christian heretics and doubters within the scarlet folds of my robe. In the intensity of their poetry and prose a passion is burning. These writers are full of fire. In the school chapels, halls and dining rooms there is no fire. They are cold and cramped. When I flee the institution, I embrace the warm and spacious outside world, a profane world where you can be who you want. I am a resolute unbeliever.

And yet how can we find our spirits if we do not enter this territory? How will we find the true passion of our hearts? After so many years in hedonistic pursuit our gnosis has become the stuff of books, we dally with esoteric beliefs, we try on costumes. We are left with the shards of ancient cultures, of pyramids, a pile of knowledge, of dead things. This does not lead to the fire. What we need is the hermitage, the place wherein we can know ourselves and the truth of the matter.

You have to make the fire yourself, hew and forge a new path. Find it your own way. *Be a writer.* That's what my grandfather was telling me. To taste the fruit you have to endure the desert, my bearing down on you. This is the paradox: when you know the oasis, you can cross the desert; to eat the fruit of the passion, you have to suffer. We are not taught to suffer. Everyone teaches us to escape from suffering. We live encased with history books, with superior attitudes, amusing ourselves with entertainments, with little black dresses and cocktails. With our small cheap victories over others. The world gets harder and harder. Our lineages become poisoned, all the way down the line. We forget the passion of our hearts, we forget the way home.

The elders once taught us about suffering down in the kivas, in the dark forests, in the sombre rooms of the RAC. As they advanced towards us with their fierce bird faces, with their talons sharpened like knives, their eyes blazing like the sun, our hearts thumped. If you were wise you forgot everything they told you. But one day you remembered. You remember everything as if it were yesterday, as you sit in the room with the typewriter, as you sit in a bar in Mérida as night falls and drink the juice of a fruit, known as *maracujá*, the shocking sweet fruit of the passionflower.

liberty cap
High Wycombe, Buckinghamshire 1991

Returning to London, at a turning point, changing flights from Mexico City to the city of Quito, I find I no longer fit the description I once had of myself. *You haven't changed!* my former friends cry airily, as they turn away in restaurants and on street corners from my travelling tales, from the coloured notebooks I hold in my hand. *You're just the same.* But I do not feel the same inside. Standing outside the dress shop in Kensington, awaking in the small basement room in Notting Hill, I feel unnaturally constricted. I cannot stay. I am taking the evening train towards the Chiltern hills. Outside the air is damp and misty.

The change happens without your knowing. As you move through the land, speak with the people, struggle with words, you undergo a shift – what Carlos Castaneda once called the moving of the assemblage point. The point is the position from which you see and comprehend life. Tiny is your life as it revolves around this point with all its accumulations. The world will not reveal itself until you move beyond its hold. The voyage and the hermitage can shift you from your familiar position. But nothing moves the assemblage point quite like hallucinogenic plants.

Castaneda's sequence of adventures begin with three hallucinogenic plants: peyote, psilocybin mushrooms and the root of the sacred datura, or Jimson weed. Don Juan, who instructed him in the correct handling of these plants, favoured the mushroom that he called 'the little smoke'. Mushrooms are often favoured by modern *vegetalistas* because they are the lightest on the physical body, their effects lasting only a matter of four or five hours. However, they are fickle. After the lengthy endurance tests they exact you might never forget a peyote or datura encounter, but you could easily forget a mushroom one. Fast-acting and riotous in their effects and requiring no preparation except perhaps a judicious boiling into tea, it is hard to communicate the experience after the event. You find yourself chuckling knowingly, winking like a seaside postcard.

'What happened?' I asked one veteran explorer of his adventure. He looked at me in exasperation, and after a protracted silence, cried: 'Have you seen ...?' as his hands flew above his head and drew an elegant pair of deer's antlers in the air.

I laughed. Of course I had. Everyone sees the deer on magic mushrooms. They are the spirit messengers of the wild.

Mushrooms are not truly plants; they inhabit another biological kingdom entirely, and yet their relationship with the plant kingdom holds a mysterious key to our own evolutionary symbiosis with life. Mushrooms are deeply interconnected with human beings and with the plants that keep us alive as well as inspired, catalysing and transforming them into our cultured foods and drink: changing grapes into wine, wine into vinegar, corn into bread, barley and hops into beer. Inside our bodies they can fight infection in the form of penicillin and balance our internal flora as the agency in live yoghurt. And not just in our physical forms: they also wreak a similar alchemy in our consciousness.

You will find mushrooms at the beginning of nearly all human cultures: in the ancient sacred groves, in the Neolithic caves, in the Mayan rainforests. *Soma*, the elixir of life that brings divine consciousness to the Aryan people and is endlessly praised in the Vedic texts, is often considered to be the hallucinogenic mushroom fly agaric. I have not ever taken fly agaric, but once, sleeping beside this scarlet and white toadstool, I dreamed a small fierce man was pounding across the planet, across the blue winds and the northern lands. *Your mother has made a right mess!* he shouted, and as he did alphabets were pouring out of his mouth. The only letter I remember was a 'y' in the shape of a forked tree.

The pursuit of *soma*, the food of the gods, takes us back to our origins on earth. Mushrooms take you back to where all alphabets begin. The mushroom kingdom began our linguistic quest into the flowerworlds. They came into our lives in these travelling years as catalysts, so we could forge a new language in which to talk with life, with the earth and with ourselves. This autumn, as I travel into the interior of the misty kingdom, I am about to be pointed in a new direction by a tiny mushroom called the liberty cap, the magic mushroom of England.

All hallucinogenic mushrooms bring words, because you need language to form consciousness. When you eat magic mushrooms you find yourself speaking effortlessly, you are effortlessly witty. Everything you say can have ten or twenty subtle meanings, echoing on many levels at once. Because in ordinary reality we are governed by what things look like, by images, or by words that describe these images; most people tend to talk about what they see. But actually it is what you *feel* and *speak* that is more interesting and valuable. Mushrooms liberate your consciousness from its rational chains, and enable you to perceive and speak of things in their essence, in their original form, in the alphabets of stars and trees, in many dimensions at once. You find yourself oracular, sibylline, archaic. Everything you speak of is connected. The whole world bursts into a thousand meanings.

Beyond the delight of this experience lies the intelligence of the planet and its deep mysteries, a way of seeing the earth that radically alters the way you experience life thereafter. Catalysed by the mushroom, you can perceive the ur-pattern or ancestral blueprint of each form, behold everything as it was 'created' in the beginning, how all things are connected in a web of infinite correspondence. The water you thirst for is The Water of Life, the beech tree you lean against is The World Tree. The wood, a small copse beyond a housing estate in High Wycombe, is The Wild Wood, all forests on earth. The door, an ordinary back door in a council house, shifts out of the daily monodimensional context in which your consensual thinking mind holds it and suddenly becomes the multidimensional door that exists in all space and time. It is The Door. The door between life and death, between you and the Other, the door that leads out of city and on to the planet, the door that liberates your heart.

It is the ability to see life in this ancestral, original way that shifts your assemblage point away from the concerns of the city and into the life of beechwood. It is a small move and a small mushroom. But its effects catalyse a great leap inside your imagination. You realise you are changing because it is your nature to change. What you undergo with the liberty cap is the kind of alchemical conversion all mushrooms instigate by their presence, within whatever medium they find themselves. The shifting of your own references affects everything you are surrounded by. Among the beech, a tree whose name is synonymous with 'book' in the north, I am about to find out how this is connected with a writer's task. It is the business of creators to shift the assemblage point of the collective, to transform what is fixed, to keep life fluid and moving. They do this in their own protean imaginations, with their own Promethean struggle, and in their adeptness as communicators. Their ability to communicate with other beings, to be in touch with all life-forms on the planet, all ancestors, all trees.

Mushrooms are formidable communicators both with human beings and with other dimensions. They do this naturally in their ordinary lives, living underground, breaking the dead matter down, forming complex symbiotic networks with other life-forms, making connections. The ecosystems of woods are kept in connection by fungi that live among the roots of trees. Many plants cannot function without their catalysing presence. In the damp weather in October and November in England, these hidden networks throw up extraordinary forms in meadows and woods all over the land. The scarlet fly agaric is symbiotic with the silver birch and the Scots pine. Its relationship with these trees is everything. It is not a parasite. On the earth the trees come first. Life comes first. And then the mushrooms appear, emerging overground, with their strange and dangerous fruit. Beloved by deer and a curious humanity.

What we call mushrooms are in fact only the fruiting bodies that eventually burst and spread their spores into the atmosphere. The mushroom itself is an interconnecting web known as a mycelium. If you find a ring of fairy mushrooms in a field or green you can sense this mycelium as you stand in its centre. You can sense the circles of the mushroom kingdom under your feet, as they work and expand in the dark, the planet's secret service.

Liberty cap mushrooms have a particular relationship with cows, and grow in profusion in damp pasturelands, especially in the west of England and Wales. A tiny delicate mushroom with a characteristically nippled bonnet cap. Like many mushrooms, liberty caps are common but not always commonly found. Once you have found one, you can usually find a great many. But sometimes you come home empty-handed. The liberty caps we took that day were a gift that appeared, in the manner of mushrooms, out of the blue. There were four of us, Blanche, Andrew, Mark, myself. In high spirits, laughing and singing, we wandered one late afternoon into a dark wood, a beech wood in the Buckinghamshire hills. It was October and the beech leaves were full of coppery gold light.

We entered the wood just as the mushrooms began to take effect. Our passage through its interior became, in the manner of all hallucinogenic voyages, equally mythical and physical. We were penetrating this mysterious wild place, moving through its snares and thickets, through every inner confrontation that lay in our path. It was not just an ordinary wood, it was a beech wood – the trees that provided the wood on which words were first engraved and recorded, into whose bark every child and lover has inscribed their names. Whose lithe and graceful forms crown the hilltops of England, our ancient groves.

We moved into the wood together, we moved away, flitting between the great cylindrical columns of the trees, following the snaky paths through the brush. There were peacock eyes everywhere looking at us as we passed by. Sometimes the women met up and sometimes the men went their own way. Sometimes we were alone and sometimes searching for one other, locating and navigating ourselves according to a laugh we heard in the dark. We looked into each others' faces and sometimes we saw Native American chieftains, and sometimes we saw visitors from the stars, and sometimes we found ourselves standing close to one another, lost in the beech wood, but together.

'How are we going to get back?' asked Mark. 'It's getting late.'

'I've got it!' I said. 'It's in my pocket.'

'What is?' they turned and asked me.

'The key!' I said triumphantly. 'The key to the back door!'

At some point our high spirits waned and I found myself alone amid the tall sinewy trees. I felt unusually nervous. Instinctively, I looked back over my shoulder. And then stood stock still. There among the pillars of the beeches was an extraordinary walled garden made of light. It had a domed building at the end and fountains in the middle, and formal borders full of colours and shapes that shimmered and sparkled in the darkness. I could say it was Arabic or Egyptian, like the gardens of Babylon, but that would make it mundane. And it wasn't mundane. It was a garden from another world. I couldn't believe my eyes. I very rarely hallucinate, but this was definitely a hallucination. It had a force of its own that was palpable, pulling me, luring me into its field. *Come! Come!*

I realised at that moment I was looking at a trap. I have been looking at traps all my life.

When I am young I am obsessed with all creatures' escape from captivity. I can hardly bear to think of the Jacobite Lord Nithsdale as he dresses as a woman and, aided by his wife and her friends, escapes from the Tower of London. Every time I read his story my heart beats. Will he be discovered? Will he get past the guard? And oh, the sense of freedom he must have felt as he stood in the fresh air on the deck of the ship as it sailed to France! I am particularly obsessed with Houdini. I struggle with him as he is bound in wooden cases, weighted down with chains, as he slides through all constrictions and padlocks like an eel. Freedom from prisons and from small boxes in particular obsesses me. All my dreams are of places that require all my wit and resolve to find a way out. As I sit before my friends listening to their dilemmas, their entrenchment in the world's karma, my mind is furiously working out their escape route. Now, as a writer, I am finding a way out of the closed artificial systems of my old world. Here in the wood I am looking at a manifestation of the greatest obstacle that lies in my path.

One of the most dangerous traps in the human world is the cage of illusion. Illusions are powerful things because they promise you freedom from the reality of earthly life. Once you have agreed to their terms you are at their mercy. Our archaic poetry and folk tales are full of warnings against entering their worlds, the worlds of fairie, the worlds of eastern promise.

Shimmering oriental cities and palaces are often seen with hallucinogenics. They are recorded by Robert Graves in his essay on mushrooms, *The Poet's Paradise*; by Terence McKenna in *Food of the Gods*; by William Burroughs in *The Yage Letters*. However, this otherworld is not where you want to be if you want to be free. I had been a fashion editor for a long time by the time I entered this beech wood. I knew all about being pulled into shiny glamours: how you can be trapped in an actress's face, in an object by Fabergé, in an organza ballgown or patisserie cake from Paris. In the fairy lights that are not really lights.

I shut my eyes. The garden was beautiful, alluring, but it also felt dangerous, like a seduction that would have fatal consequences. *You are not real!* I said out loud and I turned away and went to seek out the others.

'You look like Byron,' said Blanche when we met on the path. I began to cough so violently, I though my lungs would burst.

'Or Keats!' Mark laughed.

But I did not want to be *like* a dead male writer, no matter how fine. I was about to embark on a journey that led towards the wild lands, towards the altiplano, toward the volcanoes and lakes of South America. I did not want to be coughing my life out, dying on Greek battlefields, drowning in Italian bays like the Romantic poets. The small liberty cap was showing me what it means to dwell in those secret wonderland gardens, enclosed in the merciless grip of *la belle dame sans merci*. The exit from the world's illusions will not go via Kubla Khan, but by another route entirely.

'I want to be real,' I said.

We moved out of the wood and found ourselves in a field of cows. It was dusk and almost winter. Blanche sat down and laughed.

'We are in a muddy field at the end of the day,' she announced, and in the way of mushrooms, hearing the words in several dimensions at once, we all laughed.

We were in a muddy field at the end of the day.

If you look up the liberty cap mushroom in a field guide it will tell you that its name refers to the style of cap worn first by emancipated slaves in Rome, and then by French revolutionaries: a Phrygian red cap, later adopted by the initiates of various arcane schools and worn by William Blake in defiance of the chartered world he opposed. You will find this cap on all kinds of seals and banknotes to symbolise democracy. But mushroom books tend not to be written by those who actually take psilocybin. Anyone who has eaten magic mushrooms knows are they are called liberty caps because they liberate your mind, They free your imagination from its shackles, they liberate you from the constrictions of consensus reality, so you can see and experience the cosmic fabric of life on earth. They take you out of the manufactured replicated images of our cityworlds, and key you directly into the planet's living systems. And if, like me, you are ancestrally linked to this mysterious earth, configured to break illusions of every kind, they will present to you the situations in which you need to do this.

Mushrooms are not, as I will find out later, like hallucinogenic plants. They do not instruct you in your purpose on the solar path. Like most human communicators, mushrooms are completely amoral. They act as bridges between consciousness, as metaphysical catalysts. So you have to know how to handle them, and not to stare reverently at what they show you. Mushrooms are not reverent; that is not their nature. They are game players, master tricksters, inventors, forgers of new alphabets. If in their presence you see an illusion, it is not there necessarily to be believed. What is to be believed is something the mushrooms cannot tell you about. It's there for you to find in yourself.

When I return to the Americas I will learn many things about hallucinogenic plants. The small liberty cap of England was showing me the first rule about navigating the world under their influence, which is this: if you voyage out and return together, you will return with riches. What you need to have is an agreement with your fellow travellers. Once you have a common base, a home, you can go anywhere in the universe, explore everything, articulate every experience and bring back treasures in your hands. And home is not necessarily where you think it is.

'What are we going to do now?' I asked.

There was a silence as we looked at each other: human beings, hills, trees, cows, England, almost winter. Here after so many urgent journeys, lost, alone and now together, in a late time, in the encroaching darkness. In a muddy field at the end of the day.

'It's time to go home,' said Mark. 'And you've got the key.'

red geranium
Santa Fe, New Mexico 1994

I am sitting on the steps of a hotel in downtown Santa Fe, waiting for our friend Jan to appear. Santa Fe in 1994 is a busy place, a mecca of new-age culture and Big American Art. There are new cars pulling up to this hotel and letting out white-clad women who move with a sleek kind of purpose, holding large shopping bags, fashionably late for appointments, spa treatments, lunch. I am in the confluence of this stream of activity and feel unusually unrooted and strange. Jan is an immigration lawyer and is taking part in a legal convention held here, and it's not the kind of hotel where you sit on the steps. It has the same pink adobe colour as the rest of the town, but it lacks the warmth of the old curved dwellings of the Southwest. It feels hard. I haven't been aware of this hardness before. Nor of this sense of myself being *lesser*, somehow *in the way*.

We are not staying in this hotel but in an international hostel on the outskirts of the town, an hour's walk away. This morning I made breakfast in the communal kitchen that smelled of old garlic, and went outside to sweep the courtyard, as part of the hostel duties. Mark went to empty the dustbins. It seemed a long way from room service. It was a pristine blue day when I stepped out, cold, sharp, with the scent of winter. Two large black birds were jumping and talking loudly to each other on the garden wall and making me laugh.

'The Don Juan crows are here,' a man remarked dryly as he passed by carrying laundry.

'They're not crows,' I said. 'They're ravens.'

'Same thing,' he said.

But they are not the same. Crows are law birds, keepers of the laws in the medicine of these lands and most northern mythologies. Sometimes they are not to be trusted. For Native Americans, crowtalking is double-talk, the kind of talk government land treaties are made of. Ravens, on the other hand, are creators, sun-stealers, hoarders of shiny objects, and famous for their acrobatics and for seeing into many dimensions at once. I know the difference between crows and ravens because a year ago in this courtyard I met a woman called Jamie Sams, creator of the 'Animal Medicine Cards'. I saw her sitting in a truck one snowy evening and went up to her:

'I dreamed of you last night!' I told her.

'Come to dinner!' she replied.

In her house outside Santa Fe, the three of us had a noisy and very merry time. I cooked chicken and lemon meringue pie. Jamie was part Cherokee, part Seneca, and well-known for her medicine cards and workbooks based on Native American teachings. We gave each other card readings, exchanged our life histories, read out loud from our manuscripts. We were intense, nonstop for three days. One night I slept in her moon lodge, surrounded by drums and feathers. It was an exciting time. I liked to hear her talk about dream lodges, elders, directions, the good red road. Most of all I liked her big bold voice. The way she would suddenly speak with the authority of mountains. No one fell here by mistake, she boomed at me. *Walk your talk.*

Outside our last breakfast stop, just before we parted, she leant over the wheel of her truck, and let out a deep sigh:

'It gets worse,' she said quietly, and gazed at the snowy track that lay ahead.

I leaned on my broom, remembering Jamie, and watched the blue-black ravens jump on the wall and talk. In England ravens are mostly rare and shy birds, dwellers of mountains and cliffs. But in London they are public tricksters: the famous keepers of the crown jewels, the sovereignty of the land. They were once feared for their gruesome prank of pecking traitors' eyes out. I watched them soar up and wheel in the sky and felt the mountains in the distance pulse in the pure clear light. For a moment I felt I was flying with them in all that vastness, in all that free air.

Here outside the hotel, however, I am feeling increasingly hemmed in, uneasy. That's when my eye catches the bright red of the geranium flowers.

In Santa Fe in 1994 the book of the moment is called *The Celestine Prophecy*. It is a new-age adventure in which the American hero goes to Peru in pursuit of a secret text. The text contains nine insights, steps of transformation that modern human beings need to take in order to ensure their future on earth. It's the kind of book everyone likes to dismiss as badly written, 'cheesy', like the rest of the new age, but nevertheless reads. We all want to find out what the great secret is. The insights are primarily to do with the energetics between people and the planet. The third insight concerns our relationships with the living systems of plants and old-growth forests. I had not taken this novel any more seriously than anyone else, but at this moment of unease I am letting go of my critical faculties and remembering Insight Number Three. The hero, in tight spots, connects with the energy fields of flowers, especially those of colour and beauty. I am turning my attention towards the red geraniums in a tub by the entrance. I have always loved these flowers. They remind me of the Mediterranean, of sunny days. I like their sharp scented leaves and their shocking reds and pinks; even these parking lot hybrids make me feel light-hearted. I cannot remember how you are supposed to connect with these energy fields of flowers, so I speak to them as I would anyone else, *Hello geraniums,* I say softly.

As I do this an unusual and subtle shift happens. One moment I am under duress, the next I feel there is space all around me. I realise I am not just on the hotel steps, I am at a crossroads in my life. Mark and I are about to change direction, to get on a bus and head into Arizona, to a place we do not know. We used to sing with Jan when we lived in Mexico. *By the Rivers of Babylon,* we sang in an orphanage chapel; *Wild Mountain Thyme,* we sang in a crowded night-club. Tonight we will sing together for the last time. We will drink tequila in a downtown bar and reel about a deserted moonlit square, roaring like drunkards in perfect three-part harmony. *Here Comes the Sun. After the Gold Rush.* And then we will be gone.

As I look at the geraniums I am aware everything is about to shift. The world moving around me is part of that shift. The hotel, Jan, myself, the shiny cars, the women with their shopping bags, the memory of ravens and brooms and Jamie, the sharp air, the red of the flowers, all have significance and in this split second I become aware of them. The plants have given me a root, an anchor of stability, so I can find my bearings and *see* this moment in space and time when things diverge. Everything after this moment will be different. I will no longer look at Santa Fe in the same way again. I will never look at flowers in the same way. Or singing, or lawyers.

I am also, suddenly, no longer alone. Sitting with the geraniums, I find I am no longer at the whim of the situation, at the behest of, *under* this hotel reality, but in command of my experience, sitting in my down-there position on these steps. My unease has completely vanished. In its stead is a thought that has jumped into my mind seemingly from nowhere.

You are not going any further than this hotel.

The red geranium is a hybrid. It sits in the hotel basket and knocks out its flowers month-in, month-out, as it does in all the windowboxes and parks of the world. Its wild ancestors live scattered in the dry and balmy slopes of southern Africa. Later I will come across wild geraniums: the pink-flowered storksbill known as filaree on the roadsides of America; the hairy herb robert in the English woods. When I learn about plant medicine, I will discover they are all superlative communicators. They hold their seed pods aloft like tuning forks, like small antennae, sensing the air, catching its subtle messages and vibrations, and they accentuate your own ability to perceive in a diagnostic way. They help you see into any matter in hand, as a car mechanic might look into the engine of a car. You can look into whole systems and scenarios and predict how things are going to turn out.

Our civilisation is not going to get any further than this lawyer's conference in an expensive pink hotel. It's a prediction that comes to me, sitting here by the red geraniums. Our imaginations have become thwarted. The menu will change, the girls at the bar will change, the film will change, we might take more drugs, have more appointments, our crow empires may rule the world, but we cannot go beyond that numbered room at the end of the corridor. It is always the same room, whatever town you find yourself in. Something is being demanded from us at this point, and we are offering up mere words and promises. The truth of the matter is that human beings have to change for a future to happen. And change for real.

This change has nothing to do with words, with secrets, priests or ancient texts; it has to do with leaving the room and going back to the land, toward the origins of things, back to our ancestor forms, away from our hybrid selves and these cities of enchantment. It is a move I am being required to make myself on this bright blue day.

Because I am not just a girl sitting on the steps. I am someone who has been writing about hotels and room service for years. Who has stayed in all the tip-top places in Tokyo and Paris and Madrid. A daughter of the crow empire, who is now changing her allegiance. The red flowers are signalling a communication shut-down, part of

44

a disenchantment. Although I left journalism three years ago, I have sometimes still written articles for magazines and newspapers, travel pieces, interviews with actors and performers. I have been writing a book commissioned by a major publishing house. I have thought, like everyone else, that you can play the game both ways. But now this is going to change. I will no longer predict changes on the hotel menu or the colours of the girls' dresses. I will no longer work for the Wizard of Oz. I am going to use my skills for something else. This move will cost me my name, but it will lead me back to the earth. And will give me the dubious gift of ravens, of all creators, which is this: the ability to know what is hybrid and what is real.

Because I am not just a girl sitting on the steps. I am someone who in the last five years has investigated and written about the 'shift in consciousness' which many people believed signalled the dawn of a new time. During this time of inquiry I have worked with bodyworkers, psychologists, channellers, astrologers; I have investigated ancient texts, prophecies, mythologies, ethnographies, game theory, chaos theory. I have known celestial horoscopes and crystals, the meaning in a pack of tarot cards, and the lines that cross your palm. I have met people who have told me they are reincarnations of Egyptian gods, the dwellers of Orion and Sirius and the Pleiades, who are so evolved, so chosen, so special, they no longer live in the third dimension. I have met Jamie Sams and been warned that it gets worse. *Walk your talk.* Oh, I know a lot of things about the new age. What I don't know is what this has to do with red geraniums.

Now I do. Some of this old and new knowledge had validity and intelligence, gave us tools and techniques we lacked, but none of it had real meaning while we were operating in a hybrid world. At one time there were all kinds of energetic and experimental forums in the western world, about the future. Everyone could take part, rich and poor, natives, outsiders. Now things are about to swing way back into conventionality; 'spirituality' has been co-opted by the shopping-world élite, which is, in this moment in 1994, about to assert its hard, old-style supremacy. *We* are in the hotel. *You* are in the hostel. Your job with your bodyworking skills, your native medicine, your ability to predict, your entertaining hippy style, are there to serve and amuse *us*. Until this moment I have been protected in my passage into the new age because I have gone along with its enchantments. I have got along with people who believe that you create your own reality, that we are all Aquarians and we are all singing the same song, but a split is about to take place because some of us are crows and some of us are ravens. And the new age is not what it says it is.

Because I am not just a girl sitting on the steps. I am someone who has read and studied hundreds of texts and I know, in spite of not wanting to dismiss anyone's work or a good idea, that there is something not quite right about *The Celestine Prophecy*, bestseller though it is. The Peru of the text has no bearing on the South American country I once travelled through: none of its resonance or colour, the sense of the people or the land, the uniqueness of the city of Lima shrouded in fog, or the towering emerald Andes. It is a Peru that serves as backdrop to the action, like a film set or a theme park. The forests and mountains are presented as existing for our convenience, rather than as beings in their own right; the flowers sit controlled and observed in gardens. The heroes are American scientists. The baddies are conveniently foreign and Catholic: zealot priests and soldiers. The insights are all right, but they are not leading us to the rainforest. The animal cards are all right, but they are not leading us back to the animals. They are certainly not leading us back to the relationship Native Americans once had with wild creatures, who were both their food, their clothes and their spirit medicine. The real animals and the real mountains have been relocated into this enchanted realm and have lost their power to connect us with the earth. They have become subject to the fantasies of our minds. On sale like everything else in the hotel, talismans and totems to boost our self-importance, a spiritual gloss over our materialistic lives.

Because I am not just a girl sitting on the steps. I am a female being who wants to return. A hybrid flower in search of her original form. Seven years ago I came to this adobe town as a journalist: I was in search of Southwestern style and shopping. I was looking at turquoise, strings of chillies, the colour of adobe, paintings, leatherwork, Navajo blankets, black bean soup, Georgia O'Keefe. One morning I went with the fashion team into the desert, to a ranch, so we could shoot some pictures with horses. It was a morning like this, cold and sharp, but I was heedless of it. I was transfixed as I stepped into the largest space I had ever experienced. The desert stretched for miles, oddly punctuated by shrubs and boulders. We were surrounded by mountains. The light was everywhere. Sky was everywhere. I was exultant. The cowboy in charge of the horses brought me a dead red-tailed hawk in his hands, its breast full of speckled feathers. 'Look!' he said. I had never seen anything more beautiful in my life. It seemed more alive in death than any person living.

This kind of energy you do not find in the shopping plazas of Santa Fe, or the lobby of the El Dorado hotel, among these lawyers and crystal-sellers and the women in white, but within the living systems of the land and sky. 'It was New Mexico that liberated me from the present civilisation,' wrote D.H. Lawrence, 'the great era of material and mechanical development. The moment I saw the brilliant proud morning shine high over the deserts of Santa Fe, something stood still in my soul and I started to attend.' That morning I walked into the desert in search of bones. The models laughed as they galloped past on their horses into the emptiness of the land, far out of the reach of the camera. Out of a location bus at the end of the day, I craned to watch the last light surge on the Sangre de Cristo mountains and some part of me paid attention. One day I will come back I said to myself, to the land, to the red-tailed hawk: 'It will itch you for the rest of your life,' said Georgia O'Keefe, the great desert artist of flowers and bones.

I have in my bag the last fashion article I will ever write, an interview with a rising New York supermodel called Jenny. When I reach Tucson I will ring the magazine office in London and tell them to remove my by-line – something I have never done in my life. The model agency has censored what I have written and I don't want to work for a world in which model agencies are in charge of editorial. I want to live in a world where the writers are in charge of editorial. The next day I will take a bus to the borderlands, to a desert town where skunks sleep under the houses and tribes of javelina trot across your path, where rattlesnakes sunbathe on the garden wall and coyotes howl by night. Where one day I will pick up a desert tortoise, its back ridged like mountain, walking down the interstate highway. I will look into its ancient eyes and feel an ancestral kinship between us I cannot put into words. In Phoenix, in a half-built shopping mall, waiting to interview the star of a science-fiction film, a location manager told me about this place. There are a lot of artists there, she said. It's funky.

One of the first things I will do when I arrive in the town of Bisbee, Arizona is to buy a red geranium. After this there will always be a red geranium by my side, in a terracotta pot, on the blue-painted porch, on my writing table in the spare desert hotel, on my urban kitchen window sill, in great profusion on the island balcony in Greece. The red geranium in England will grow long and leggy by the glasshouse door and bloom all winter, all spring, all summer. It will never stop flowering. And it will always be there, holding a certain vibration, an anchoring point, an intersection in time and space, keeping me in touch with what is going down.

juniper, saguaro, cottonwood
Arizona 1994/6

I was in Hawaii in the summer of 1994, and alone, at the beginning of the second journey. The first three years had been sheltered between the covers of our travelling book. This journey was already different. It promised the difficulty that all second stages have, of any undertaking or creative work. The first journey is an adventure: you rise to meet your experience, like the morning sun, new and full of expectation. Everyone greets you. Luck and fair winds are with your voyage. On the second journey you face everything that pushes against the ascending light, against your successful passage. The storm hits the rigging. You are becalmed for years. And then suddenly without knowing it you enter the third journey. You are weary, and older, but you realise you are coming home. There is a great joy when you discover this. But this sense of return will not come for many years yet. For here is the twilight, the stormy ocean, the desert before you. The second stage of the solar path is the longest and most demanding. The reason most people back down, give up travelling, go back to their old lives.

I am in Hawaii, beautiful Hawaii of the tropical breezes, the ridge-shaped mountains, of frangipani leis, of blue caves and swaying palm trees. For all this outer ease and beauty I could be travelling the first journey, but I am not feeling at ease inside myself: something is telling me I am not in the right place. I am staying in a hut next to a big wild boar in a pen. The hut's owner, an equally large and formidable artist, has a collection of intriguing tin sculptures. One of these is a mirror in the shape of a hand.

'It's the hand of God,' she explains. 'When the big wind came to Hawaii last year, it destroyed all the hotels built on the ancestors' land. The other houses it left. That was its message: transform or die.'

Transform or die. It's a hard decision to make when you are living in apparent paradise. Every day as the big tropical rain falls down and double rainbows span the green hills, I hitch a ride down to the local town for breakfast and groceries. Several times now people have asked me if I have been to Sedona in Arizona and I have told them politely no, I am spending the summer here in Kaui. Today, I have decided to experiment. I have said out loud to the universe, *If*

I am supposed to be in Arizona, I want a sign. Before twelve o'clock, I add.

Instead of buying papaya and mineral water at the market, I find myself next door in a mineral and gem store, surrounded by crystals and rocks and geodes. I pick up one of these stones. It's an ordinary piece of quartz, with an intriguing shine. The owner, another big woman, stands at the end of the store, holding a big book of mythologies in her hand:

'Let's see who you really are,' she says and opens the book.

We look at a picture of Anubis, jackal god of the Underworld. I frown. I am not best pleased at being a dog, let alone a scavenger dog-god from ancient Egypt.

'I don't feel like a weigher of hearts,' I say rather defensively.

'Opener of doors,' she corrects me, and laughs. 'And closer of doors.'

'Could you tell me where this crystal is from?' I ask her, changing the subject.

'Arizona,' she replies. 'That's a good one.'

It's eleven-thirty am.

Sometimes you are not in the right territory and sometimes you have to make bold decisions. Sometimes even though you are three thousand miles away from your apparent destination, you have made a pact with yourself, with the universe. Sometimes you just have to go and open the door.

Up on Airport Mesa in Sedona, Arizona, I am looking all around me, waiting at sundown. The mesa is a vortex, one of the great energy centres of these red rock lands. There are four vortexes in Sedona and each is a different shape: one is a giant rock, shaped like a bell jar, where in spring its tiny crevices are filled with anemones and cliffrose; another is a valley with a river running through it, fringed with willow, known as Red Rock Crossing, and with an edifice of rocks sculpted like a cathedral. Another is a narrow canyon where the wind sings, whose entrance is guarded by a rocky figure known as Kachina Woman. Airport Mesa is the most central and easy to access. Up there you can see the whole valley and the town lying before your feet.

I have climbed the mesa with Robert, aged twenty-two, who has just left the army. I am thirty-eight and have just published a book.

We are strange birds of passage, drawn together by the winds of circumstance, and have become firm friends. In the day we work our keep in a round house made of adobe just outside the town, down by Oak Creek. I water the garden, he chops wood; I vacuum, he collects laundry. We sleep next to each other on rolled-up mattresses on the floor, along with all the guests of this natural healing centre. Robert is extremely smart and knows about astrology. He has twelfth-house karma to work out, he tells me. I know about being twenty-two. Karma is a concern for thirty-eight-year-olds, I tell him. Go and have some fun first! In the afternoon, while he listens to Jimi Hendrix, I go for a swim in the creek, let my body slide down the stones, and immerse myself in the running water. It is June, the heat is fierce. The water is cool and fresh, like a balm. I love to be in these elements of sun and light and water, in a way I cannot yet explain to myself. I watch the ravens fly overhead, the crayfish move among the dark stones. I can spend hours here down among the willows and the oak.

I can spend hours with Robert, too. We are Gemini twins, he has told me, black and white, male and female, talkers to the max. At the mesa we are sitting next to each other, bare feet on the rock. 'Have some tobacco,' he says. We sit there in silence, smoking the tobacco. Before us the valley shimmers. It's six o clock: the heat has just lost its intensity and the light has begun to turn red-gold and fire all the rocks around us. We have emerged from our afternoon positions, panting in the shade, swimming in the creek. Out here in the open everything is vast, the great red sentinels of Arizona surround us, holding us in their immensity. Below in the town, you might notice only the store fronts and the cars. Here something else is going on. The light on the rocks increases its intensity; the energy in my body suddenly surges, as if the voltage of all my circuits has been accelerated. The rocks move forward. They feel alive. I feel alive, physical, fired up, in a way I have no words for.

Behind us is a tree. I don't know this tree yet. I won't discover it until I return to this mesa almost a decade from now. But it is still there, at the beginning of the transforming time. As the vortex turns on a switch inside.

It is a juniper. The pale wood of its trunk and branches have been sculptured by the wind into a dancing form. All along these rocks the junipers contort into weird and fantastic shapes, the energies of the Sedona vortexes famously spiralling their branches into helical form. In the grasslands they remain round and dark like sentinels. The junipers are tenacious trees: their roots cling to rocks and dry mountain, hold fast; their tiny scented needles are economical and tough. Their fruit is a berry that sometimes takes years to ripen from green to black. Everything about this tree is slow and sure. Its sweet-smelling wood is a prime fuel; its tart berries are a prime medicine for the kidneys and its resinous oil, like all sun-plants, can chase out all colds and rheums from the body. But it is most well known as a tree of the spirit: its branches make the ceremonial brush that sweeps the logs for the temascal; its berries once covered the Egyptian dead; its smoking leaves chase the spirits away from pueblos of the land, throughout America, Europe, the temples of Tibet, everywhere it grows. It deals with what needs chasing out. *Transform or die.*

A juniper grew beside a National Monument trailer where a young ranger called Edward Abbey spent two summers in the red rock country. He built a ramada underneath its spiky shade and slept under it, as it pointed its weathered hand toward the vast and starry skies of Arizona. He sat beneath the juniper tree and began to shape a fiery treatise on the wilderness, a practical and poignant hymn to the red rocks. *Desert Solitaire* brought wilderness as a human birthright into the modern imagination, just as the later *The Monkey Wrench Gang* inspired a new generation of ecological activism. Abbey was not a nature writer in the way it is normally understood – a naturalist who describes the workings of flowers or insects – but a writer who had no time for the industrial way of life and spoke out fearlessly on behalf of the land. Anarchist movements such *Earth First!* were born of his life-long defence of the wild against exploitation by corporations and governments. I don't know anything about Abbey or ecology in this moment, yet still I am here, in the place where radical ideas, uncompromising ways, are nurtured in the shade of a slow-growing tree, in the rocky land of transform or die.

Sedona is known among native peoples as a place of emergence. In the creation myths there are a succession of worlds. Because the people neglect their spirit and the spirit of the earth, they fall into materialism and their worlds corrupt and are destroyed. The Grand Canyon, the vortexes of Sedona, are places where the people emerge as they are recreated by the ancestors. According to native prophecies, we are at the end of the fourth world and entering the fifth. Modern industrialised people, looking for a new world, take their storefront crystals from their pockets and tune into the stars as they sit at Airport Mesa at sundown. Maybe they feel their ancestors originate from shiny space ships. But some of us don't think that way. We sit in the old earth places and we wait. We sit with a stranger who feels like ourselves, almost a twin, and we smoke tobacco in silence.

Sometimes you go to a place because you have to start again in the right place. So things can emerge you did not know were there. You have to know what kind of time you are in. And even though you are not aware of its presence, there is a guardian there behind you, a tough old guardian, a tree that can grow out of rocks, weather the storm, the drought, and never give up. A tree of the sun and wind, a heart tree, the heart of the ancestors tree. The tree of a radical beginning.

saguaro

Two years later, on the second journey, you are restless: your spirit requires thorns, rocks, stormy weather, challenging encounters. You can't find these in the old places. People are indifferent to your struggle. You roam around Europe, looking up old acquaintances in Spain, staying in empty London apartments, sit on a Greek island, on the Aran islands. In a caravan in a muddy field just outside Lyme Regis, lighting candles at the end of the day to keep warm, you sit in front of the typewriter with gloves on. You are in a corner and you could be in Mexico! you say to yourself. In colourful warm dry Mexico however you are still on the run, zigzagging from Guadalahara to Mazatlán, waiting in old hotels, listening to the Pacific ocean, feeling like a tourist. Then one day the running stops. You are on a plane from Tepic, heading back to Arizona. And you find yourself in the perfect place, though from the outside it would not seem it.

The sky island rises above the desert floor: a ring of mountains known as The Mules. The town within its rocky arms appears, at first glance, unremarkable: a collection of small wooden shacks scattered up a red hillside, down a gulch, with narrow steep streets, skinny metal staircases, a red-bricked main street with a few old-fashioned storefronts; an alternative café, a co-op store, a library with oak floors, a parking lot shaded with ash trees and desert willow. Just by the highway that winds through the mountains there is a gigantic 'hell's hole', an open pit where European immigrants once mined for copper; in the abandoned gardens their trees still grow covered in the fruits of paradise – crimson pomegranates, white mulberries, black figs.

Everyone that lives now in these shacks and old hotels has been somebody somewhere else. One day they woke up in the city and the desert called them. They got sick, or cried too much, or had a dream, or met someone on a film set who said it was a funky place full of artists, and now we are all here: angry, offended, haunted, brilliant, neurotic, in a corner, askew, full of thorny attitude. We came a winter ago and felt at home, for reasons only my mysterious heart knows for sure.

There is something that calls you: in this luminous space that surrounds the town, in the mineral mountains, in the prickliness of the people. The way they read poetry out loud for three hours in the park. The way everyone is an astrologer, a medicine person, a sybil, and cannot help predicting how your life is going to turn out. How everyone wants to get away from each other, and from each other's predictions, yet none of us can. We are strangely bound to each other here, in this underworld place, this old mining town full of ghosts, full of strange night winds; come to learn some lessons, to be tempered in the alchemical furnace of the desert. To look at the stars that burn each night in the obsidian sky, to start again. Outside the town the thorn bush and cactus keep their independent positions in the flat lands and in the canyons. Keep your distance! they say to each other with their formidable spines. Stay out of my way! And yet standing among them you have never felt so together in your life.

On Friday nights in Brewery Gulch when the karaoke is in full swing, there is a great crescendo as the bar is about to close, and someone inevitably starts to sing:

'I did it m-I-I-I-I-I-I way!'

In Bisbee everyone does it their way. Peyton, a one-time famous stage actress from New York, now in organic farmers' overalls, puts on her scarlet lipstick and turns toward us:

'Fuck!' she says with all the power of off-Broadway.

We laugh and buy her heirloom tomatoes, okra and dahlias. Someday we will perform the songs of *Mahogany* together, we all say. In the original German. But of course we won't.

I am sitting on the porch of our blue and white shack, reading a poem called 'The Miner's Hotel'. Mark is walking down the dark hotel corridor and remembering a friend singing loudly in Soho on a chilly night. In the days when you did sing loudly, and her Polish mother who told him: *Life is like party. Sometimes you dance closer to people than others.* And there is a poignancy in these small lines that tugs at my heart.

Julianne and Susie have driven across America to visit us in the desert. It has taken them three days from the cool climes of Minneapolis and by the time they arrived they were wearing bikinis. It was late May in the desert, the beginning of summer, and our small house has no air conditioning. We sit for a long time on the porch under the cottonwood, spraying ourselves with water scented with peppermint.

Today we went to visit the Desert Museum, a piece of pristine wilderness on the edge of the city of Tucson. Bisbee is in the Chihuahua desert, a rough bush desert of scrawny ocotillo, creosote and mesquite. We drove two hours through its red and granite boulders, its scrubland and dry washes, down a long straight road towards the blue horizon. Tucson marks the beginning of a lower quite different desert, called the Sonora, that stretches way down into coastal Mexico. Its floor is pink and sandy, with clear forms rounded rocks, glamorously studded with cacti and prickly pear. It is the Arizona everyone expects; its most distinctive feature are the titans of the cactus world, the saguaro, who hold their councils here on its slopes and in its valleys, hundreds of them with their arms held up to the sky, tipped in this almost-summer with rounded buds, just before their large white flowers open.

We are walking down the red road of the museum in Indian file, past these green, thorn-studded giants, among the flowering cholla and palo verde, Mark, Susie, Julianne and I. It is 103 degrees. Occasionally a jack rabbit crosses our path. Three years ago we walked like this down a street in Mexico City together and Susie made a film about us, as we travelled in turquoise taxis, talked around a fountain in the cool shade of a square. It was a very different time. And I am feeling this now, as we have all become silent, in our own thoughts.

The fine tendrils of our lives are crossing, making a pattern we cannot see. 'We are meeting in a cosmic kitchen!' laughed Julianne, as we cooked supper last night at the back of our wooden house and talked about the deeper meanings of our lives. We have visited thrift stores and found ourselves flowery dresses, and eaten Mexican breakfasts across the border, but other factors are at play now in these dry and spiky borderlands. America is the women's native land. Mark and I are no longer travelling in the gay way of the early '90s. Disturbing patterns are being brought to bear and our relationships are not going to last.

The solar path is exacting. It is a moving path and because it is moving and you are changing with it, you cannot hold on to people in the same way you could when your life was more fixed and stable. *Sometimes you dance closer to people than others.* You have to acknowledge when things change and be able let each other go. You would like to do these things with grace, in the way these women are graceful, as we laugh together in our thriftstore flowery frocks, in our misted peppermint rainwater, in our cosmic kitchen. But sometimes it is not possible.

We are not on neutral ground any more in the colourful holiday town of ice-cream parlours and rooftop concerts. In Bisbee we are scowly, difficult as everyone else. Nightmares, alien conspiracies, sexual confusions, dark feelings, underworld feelings have entered our once light-hearted conversation. The territory has changed. We're on the second journey.

So in my confusion, as we walk about the Sonora desert on this hot afternoon, I have turned away from my companions to face one of the saguaros, the largest cactus in the world, that can live to be two hundred years old. It is a big plant, with several arms either side of its trunk that soar into the cobalt sky. The saguaros dot the hillside as you slide past in the car. You get out and take the photograph that everyone takes. It is *so* Arizona, you say to yourself, carefully boxed up and shielded from any kind of exchange. Standing next to one of these giants close to is a different experience. The saguaro is huge, towering, fierce, unexpected. You feel humbled, an idiot with your camera. It is so alive and stern. You want to throw your arms around the cactus, and yet you cannot, deeply ridged, spiny as it is.

The saguaro waits there, pulsating in the glaring heat. You are a being! I realise with a shock. Something inside myself is pushing to make contact with this being. How do you make contact with a cactus? I carefully put my arms in a circle around its thorny central pillar. Immediately I receive back a bolt of energy, *wham!* directly into my heart. I feel like bursting into tears and laughing at the same time. A wild reckless joy rips through me as I stand immersed in the saguaro's field. It lasts about two minutes.

When I move away, the cactus stands before me shimmering and green, distinct, its arms extended. Now I know: plants are living conscious beings. This force did not come from myself. My own heart made the unexpected move and the contact with the saguaro happened.

Later I will find out that cacti are famous in these deserts as heart medicines, and that many plants transmit heart energy. People are embarrassed to talk about this force they feel from plants, from the places in the desert they find themselves; they want to call it something else. They will say things in Bisbee like: the saguaro's got a father energy, good vibes, you feel real safe and protected. We are all trying to avoid the 'L' word. The love word.

You do not think of the heart as a tough spiky thing or its energy as powerful; you think of it as soft, gentle, childish, almost unworldly. But it is not: it is giant, like this saguaro, and barbed. In the second territory you have to get to the heart. It is a great struggle. Perhaps the greatest struggle you can make as a human being. The heart is not what you think it is, a squashy pink thing, a new-age thing: *open your heart! love yourself!* It contains a massive force. How else can you get to your vast spirit if not through its fierce, stormy crucible? The heart is like the cactus: it flourishes in the hardest places, flowers in the hottest moments of the year, at home in the vast rocky spirit lands of Arizona. In the toughest times of our lives, the heart comes into play. It has to. How else can we survive these moments of unease? This moment with Julianne and Susie? How else can we be bold, jump in a plane, travel thousands of miles, switch course, let people go? I wanted it still to be light-hearted and free between us, but it couldn't. What but the heart can burst through all restriction, all difficulty, all pain, and still find joy? The heart has to make contact with its fellows. It is its nature. You put your arms around this being, round this spiky town, these spiky moments, in spite of everything. That's when everything turns around. When life starts again.

You could falter as you enter the second territory. You could falter in Arizona, in all that vastness and impersonality and dryness. That uncompromising light. But some of us starting again have nothing to lose. We are not, like Julianne and Susie, going back to our old lives in the city. We are not on holiday. We are not twenty-two. We are in the second territory. *Transform or die.* The ancestors are standing behind us though we do not see them, like the juniper, nurse tree for the young and tender saguaro.

The heart changes things, Arizona changes things. The saguaro changed my afternoon. It was still awkward between us but I could let everything be, stop controlling our time together, trying to make it other than it was. You can destroy your life trying to make something other than it is.

The heart is independent. It loves space in which it can be itself. That day we walked apart: there was space between yet we were together. Just not in this time. As we drove out of the museum we saw a huge long-eared owl sitting on a saguaro, watching us. It was getting dark.

Who knows who we are really, Mark, Susie, Julianne, myself, walking a red road in Indian file, sitting under the shade of the cottonwood tree. Who knows what our souls' meeting at this point of intersection really means, along the corridor of time? We came together once in a place called Mexico. We had a picnic under the bamboo. Julianne plaited Mark's hair and Susie made a record of us as we lay in blue watery pools together, a moment of harmony that happened between four people from England and America. And in the end that was what remained in my heart. It felt as if that was all that mattered. Hold that moment, said the desert, as we moved towards the highway. When you can hold that moment, you can let the rest just drop away.

Against the fiery sunset sky of Arizona, the very large array of saguaros held up their green arms to begin their nightly transmission to the stars.

Sometimes you dance closer to people than others.

cottonwood

No one would tell me what to do about the moths. Their caterpillars were hanging in strange ominous webs from the cottonwood tree outside our door, and I felt disturbed when I saw them there. The tree soared above the little miner's cottage with its five blue doors and tiny scrub garden, a huge imposing tree that cast its great shade over our heads, always rustling, moving, shifting. At night in the spring wind you could hear its heart-shaped leaves whispering together, like the riverside poplars and aspens of England. You could hear voices in those leaves that were not necessarily from this world. In Arizona the cottonwood is the spirit tree of the Hopi and they carve their Kachina dolls from its deep roots.

So I went to the town library and read how tent worms can decimate forest and fruit trees. Like the more notorious gypsy moth caterpillars, these worms devour a tree's leaves and without the leaves, the trees weaken and die. I don't like to read about this scenario. Go and tell your landlord, advise our friends. But our landlord lives in California and we are in a town where everyone does things for themselves. I feel I should take matters into my own hands, but what is the done thing around here? It depends, say the old hippies, on whether you want love or war in your garden. I don't want a metaphysical debate, I want action, so I go to see Peter. Peter is a stern gardener, a 'Hopi' gardener, sparing with water as he conjures rocket leaves and peppers and marigolds out of his terraces in this dry land. He says I can borrow his stepladder and secateurs. He is obviously not going to do the job for me.

'Why not ask the tree?' says Mark.

I had not thought of that.

So one windy night I stand and smoke some tobacco on the porch, and I speak to the tree. *Please come into my dreams and tell me what you want.*

That night I dream I am the cottonwood tree. I inhabit the tree as if it were my own body. Its bark fits like a coat, and I can feel the leaves like my hair, tossing in the wind. Then I feel something revolting on my skin, slurping and sucking my being, and everything in me wants to throw this parasite off myself. I throw my branches into the air in a powerful gesture of rejection.

59

When I wake up the answer is clear. I borrow Peter's tool and we cut down the offending worms. You could almost hear the tree sigh in relief.

'Now what are you going to do?' asks Mark.

I am reluctant to kill anything, even squirming caterpillars that are going to wreak damage. But I already considered what I should do when I awoke. I asked myself: if I were going to die, by which element would I choose to relinquish myself?

'I am going to drown them in a bucket of water,' I said calmly.

'I am sorry you have to go like this,' I told the worms, 'but there are too many of you and this thing has gone out of balance.'

The cottonwood tree grows down by the river, by all the waterholes. In a dry world, the desert world, these are the great water trees, the trees of life. And as you drive out from the town and head towards the Huachuca mountains, you can see the great cottonwoods like a green shimmering ribbon snaking across the desert floor, as they follow the San Pedro river, winding north towards Utah. For the Hopi who live in the north, the Kachinas are the spirits who live in everything: in butterflies, birds, rocks, planets and clouds. They are the spirits of the land and sky who keep everything in balance, the ones who bring the water, who live on the peaks of the San Francisco mountains. In the monsoon season they come in huge zigzag strikes of lightning, coloured pink and blue and green. As the rain floods the dry lands and brings it to life again.

The Hopi are striking among the North American tribes, because they are not warriors. As a people they put all their attention into their spiritual world. They are formidable balancers of life on the planet, and renowned for their prophecies which declare a bad end for all those who walk the crooked path. Many of their ceremonies centre on water, on the rattlesnakes who bring the rain for the life-giving corn. Their whole year revolves around the life-cycle of these plants, beginning at winter solstice when the seeds gestate in the depths of the kivas, in the matrix of themselves. You hear a lot of tales about the Hopi when you live in Arizona, especially if you are interested in plants. One of them is about the anthropologist who asked them: why are all your songs about water?

'That is because it is rare and precious in our land,' the elder replied. 'How come all your songs are about love?'

The Hopi are well-studied by academics because of the complexity and coherence of their world-view, which is still rigorously maintained in spite of the government's attempts to destroy it, and also for their language in which time is not linear but goes out in circles, and nouns act more like verbs. For the Hopi, who conjure life from one of the driest places on earth, speak in entirely fluid terms. Two of their terms, *koyaanisqatsi* and *powaqqatsi*, have entered our modern vocabulary as the titles of two documentaries by the director Godfrey Reggio. *Koyaaniqatsi* means 'world out of balance'. *Powaqqatsi* means 'world constructed by a negative sorcerer who lives at the expense of others'. The films show how our alienation from nature and the artificially created worlds we live in are devouring the planet like worms.

These documentaries have no words, only music. You perceive what they show and come to your own conclusions. At the beginning of *Koyaanisqatsi* you fly like a bird over the mesas of Hopiland. Time is slow and ancestral. The rocks are grand and beautiful. You then become caught up in the replicating worlds of modern cities. Everything is ugly, small-minded, mechanical. Time goes very fast. You know that something is needed to reverse this process, but you feel powerless. We are Bahannas, terrible white-skins. What can we do?

The Hopi, austere wisdom-keepers, remain in the northern mesas, in our imaginations, like a spiritual measure: they remember how we need to be. It is a bargain they made hundreds of years ago with their creator ancestor. They are keepers of the way in one of the most difficult terrains on earth. The prayer feathers they place in the wind's path are not just for themselves. What happens in the daily life of the village, in the ceremonial kiva, in the Kachina dance of the plaza, is happening in the world. This they seek to rectify, to bring into harmony. What happens in the documentary you need to rectify. It is clear, beholding the rocks and then the city, that you need to slow down and live at a different pace. You need to rekindle a relationship with all living forms, with your own being, know your breath as the breath of life, like the wind that blows through the cottonwood leaves. Somehow you have to learn to be fluid, not hold on to things, experience time in a different way. Most of all you can no longer live like a parasite, at the expense of others. When you see something is out of balance you need to act: reading, asking other people, is not enough. *You have to take responsibility into your own hands.* At some point you have to make contact with the tree.

The summer advances towards the town like a panting beast. The air is so dry the bedclothes crackle and spark with small blue lightnings. You realise you are thirsty and not just for the rain.

'Spirit' is a word you wrestle with under the shade of the cottonwood tree. You don't like this word. In the cityworlds it means ghostly, otherworldly, holier-than-thou, god-worshipping, superstitious, moralistic, insincere; it means religious rituals, secret societies, invisible almighties, moon-faced goddesses. You are smart and don't want anything to do with it. Outside of the city, 'spirit' means native tribal ways; the shadow of genocide falls across your conscience and you falter; you feel somehow inferior to the Hopi who sing to the tobacco and the squash flower, who breathe life into the corn as they grind the kernels against the stone. You are excluded from their dances and would feel a fool anyway if you attended, a tourist. You don't like judging yourself as 'wrong', as crooked, crow-talking, two-hearted, fallen. We grew out of such things centuries ago! you say to yourself. Now we feel superior to these ceremonies, though we are still empty and restless inside, incomplete without this relationship the Hopi so clearly possess. We wrestle with this spirit and its demands for expression in the springtide winds, in the soaring temperatures. I am a double outsider, double invader, white-skin and foreigner, and yet here I am in the borderlands, at home. Who can tell us where we belong? I sit with my back against the deep-furrowed trunk of the cottonwood and smoke tobacco. The wind rustles its great crown, and I breathe outward. The Great Spirit of North America blows through the tree: the spirit that moves in all things on earth.

Down the valley the sun is falling, igniting all the rocks with fire. Above the red hills, the turkey vultures are spiralling and the fire flashes under their wings, flames the trunks of white oaks down by the creek where they roost, shimmers in the creek water and charges through me, as the birds soar into the blue sky, hundreds of them, wheeling together higher and higher. This fire has a language all of its own. I will learn it one day from these rocks and creeks, from these trees and birds, from the sun.

I will not speak with the people of the kivas and the cornfields who have kept a sacred dialogue with the earth in spite of our world's profanity. History and culture lie between us. Maybe we will never cross those old borders, red and white, citydweller and pueblo dweller. But Arizona is vaster than all our differences. It lives in ancestral time, in all times. Slow as the juniper, stern as the saguaro. The cottonwood speaks to us all. Under its shade we are all brother and sister.

Soon the cottonwood tree outside our door, in the manner of all female poplars, will flower and form its seeds. They will appear one day, like small puffs of cotton, and these fluffy seeds will depart the tree and float about the town. Down its dry gulches, through the parched dry throat of the land, the seeds of the cottonwood will float looking for a damp place to nestle and wait for the monsoon rains. I will think of them floating by as I empty an old house of its heirloom contents in London, and remember a scene from a film by the Russian director Andrei Tarkovsky, called *Stalker*.

A man and woman and their crippled daughter sit at the end of the world in an empty apartment, as the seeds of the poplar trees from the Russian countryside drift through the windows with all the quietude of snowflakes. The man is silent: he is the stalker, the one who crosses the line, the one who opens the door. He has taken two men, a writer and a scientist, across the city's well-guarded border into a land where things are not what they seem. The territory has been revealed because of an apocalypse that has befallen the world. He has guided the men to a room wherein they can know themselves, but they stopped before the door and gave all the reasons why they should not enter. He despairs. Who will go into the room? What is the point of knowing the way if no one chooses to know themselves? How will the world turn around?

As the seeds of the cottonwood float by, Catherine Bailey will drift into our lives one evening in London, tall and gracious as a white poplar tree. She will arrive in a silvery car and tell us about making a documentary film in Russia and I will ask her: had she seen the poplar seeds float across the land? Yes, she said, the air was filled with their dispersal. She had just been there. We sat there with those vast geographies inside of us, the Russian steppes and the Arizona deserts, as we remembered the seeds of the ancestral trees drifting by. Outside the traffic droned and the light in the drawing room grew dim. It came to me in that moment that the only way forward lay in an imagination we could share, no matter what tribe or country we came from – an imagination based on the real places, on the mysteries of life itself. Only then could we live together in a new and harmonious way. It seemed as we sat, the three of us, in that summer twilight, with all that immensity inside us, that the borders between us no longer existed and the city had disappeared.

It felt as if a seed from the cottonwood had settled in my heart, and would never go away.

II
BUSH SCHOOL

On the solar path there are two directions: the first travels across an uncharted territory, the second explores the interior. Both moves involve breaking away from a known and familiar world, and often happen at the same time. The second move demands some kind of initiation, a deliberate breaking up of personal internal structure, in order that an expanded worldview can be embraced.

Initiation is almost a taboo word in modern civilisation. If mentioned at all it is within an academic context, as a barbarous or obsolete ritual – tribal elders breaking in young warriors, or the pagan rites of ancient worlds. Real-life initiatory experiences are studiously avoided in conversations. However, this does not mean they do not occur.

Initiation is any rite of passage or encounter with the nonhuman world that connects a human being with the mysteries of life on earth. Its effects are always life-changing and dramatic. Sometimes called 'breaking open the head', these transcendent events are a vital step on the solar path because, as modern people, we are indoctrinated to see a world dominated by human reason. Other cultures have always sought out non-ordinary states of consciousness, so the earth and our presence upon it can be fully comprehended; western rationality vehemently denies them. Instead, we are schooled to have minds like

Alexander. Our 'educated' eyes gaze upon a fixed world, in which everything is named and controlled and priced, where the wild and the natural have no function – except in terms of our use. We look at property and roadmaps, mutated plants and conquered mountains, and dismiss any other way of seeing the earth as superstitious or inferior or the product of a mental or behavioural disorder. As a result it is hard to perceive the planet and ourselves as a free-flowing and complex living system in which everything is related.

The truth of the matter, however, is that though reason is *one* way of looking at the world it is not the *only* way, and it is perhaps one that should be regarded with a good deal of scepticism, since its logical goal is the construction of a global city-state ruled by an elite that is served by millions of slaves (ourselves) all struggling for survival on a denatured planet we once called home. The monoculture of reason takes no notice of anyone's heart or feelings, let alone the kingdoms of nature or the mysteries of life. So if you want to learn about these things you have let something outside your control interrupt your fixed gaze and break open your rational mind.

Sometimes this internal collapse happens by accident – we fall by hazard into an encounter, fired up by our love of nature or ancient knowledge. Sometimes we suffer a *katabasis*, an illness or misfortune that shakes us out of our narrow-minded perception. But most people, like me, find themselves one day with a hallucinogenic plant in their hands, and instinctively let these plants take them into their world.

As soon as you do, you find yourself on a very different planet from the one that you have been so far living on. The world which up to now has been restricted by your reason has been by-passed with the help of the plant. Instead of living in a place where everything is subject to human control, dumb, inferior and non-conscious, you are now in a place where everything is conscious and communicating – birds, plants, rocks, rivers – where everything has meaning, order and intelligence. In order to handle life in these dimensions you have to access and use very different parts of yourself. You have to learn quickly and be endlessly inventive. You are no longer in a place or time in which you are mentally apart from what you are experiencing, but negotiating a multisense stream of images and feelings. You are in the thick of it. In this territory you need to 'speak' a different language, one that is not made from your linear word-based vocabulary. It is this language that plants are only too happy to show and teach you. We may not have mystery schools and shamans any more in our modern rational world, but the bush school remains open in the bush.

All people who work with plants in an other-dimensional capacity, that is beyond their existence in five-sense reality, see them as teachers. This is because in their myriad forms, shapes, emanations, positions, they teach the ABC and arithmetic of life. They don't teach history and geography and science, so you can dominate and control life, so you can live in the mind and turn yourself into an administrator of the city worlds. They don't teach you how to be more powerful than your neighbour or your enemy. They teach you how to interact with, respect and love without boundaries, the fabric of life on earth through your unique planetary being. They teach you rigour, feeling, insight, command, creativity, inspiration, intuition, perception. They will teach you how to handle the solar and cosmic forces that operate within all living things, how to journey inside yourself and find your own wisdom, your own medicine way. Some plants are natural teachers and have had exchanges with human beings for millennia. Some are particular to you and your individual expression of life. But all of them are exacting, and demand that you work together on the basis of cocreation and free will.

Most people want plants to be on their terms. They don't like the idea that a plant can 'speak' or that a relationship with them can go two ways. But if you want everything to be on your terms, you won't learn anything from the plants. You will just learn what human societies tell you about plants: taxonomy, farming, medicine, gardening, forestry, science i.e. plants as property, as objects of use. If you want to find out about those other subjects you have to go down into the place where their roots and seeds live, where all our roots and seeds live. You have, like the ancient poets and initiates, humbly and courageously to grasp the mistletoe key and the spear of giant fennel and you have to go down into the dark.

All initiations begin in the dark because life begins in the dark. Dark is where gestation takes places. All creatures on this planet begin their earthly life in a dark resonant ocean, floating within a giant egg, just as all flowers begin in the seedstore underground in the darkness of soil. In this watery dark you are still connected to the cosmic state before your individual being entered this form-creating matrix. Here you remember that you came from somewhere else and that there is a reason why you are here. Only the dark can teach you this. Plants take you there because during their lifetime on this earth their roots never leave this place. They have always been there.

When I began my solar journey I began also to dream at night of certain plants, of herbs and flowers and trees. *Epazote*, the Mexican goosefoot, led me on the outward journey that left a whole cityworld behind, but the plant that led me inward towards the mysteries was the poppy. The poppy is known throughout the world as the flower of the underworld. Sometimes this is the scarlet field poppy, sometimes the mauve opium flower, but the way-showing poppy I dreamed of was a celestial blue.

In those travelling years I kept many notebooks and would draw diagrams of the dreams or visions I had. They often looked like the kind of stick-drawings or shapes you might find on rock petroglyphs or figures in a cave. The blue poppy dream was depicted in a three-tiered drawing in blue ink. On the top level was a small stick girl dancing, and below her were three tall beings. Between them were three pictographs, the first a picture frame with the little girl's question: *What is behind the picture?* The second two were the answers the tall beings give her:

Behind the picture is a small door.

Through this door there is a secret room in a hidden house.

'How strange,' I thought of the blue poppy dream when I first drew the pictures. At that time I did not know about the blue poppies of the Himalayas that grow in the mountain meadows of Tibet and Nepal. The little drawing became significant only later, when I realised that the small door was referring to the door of perception. In order to see beyond the world of five senses, into the realm of the spiritual earth where everything is connected, you have to go through the picture, the *maya* of this world, and pass those beings who manifest it – the shiny actresses, the autocratic directors, the powers in charge of its production. You have to resist all these things and not be either seduced, distracted or overpowered by them, or waste your energy fighting them.

The small girl dancing is a key to this passage. In order to find the knowledge on the other side of the door you have to move and ask a question. Without movement, without a valid question, you do not find the door. The question is the question all curious children and seekers ask: *What is behind the picture?*

You also have to grow small enough, like Alice, to fit through this wonderland door. 'Grown-up' cynicism and know-it-all attitudes will not help you. What helps you is connecting with the wisdom of the tall beings (your ancestors) and having enough discipline to handle the energies and visions you encounter on the other side. In short, you have to maintain enough consciousness in those realms to find the secret room (yourself) in the hidden house (the earth) in order to remember them when you return to 'ordinary reality'. Power plants help find you that door very quickly indeed. But like many fast tracks there are downsides, especially if you go unguided into these realms – which most modern people do. One of these is that when you return to the 'real' world you are none the wiser.

Hallucinogenic plants may hurtle you into the otherworld dimensions where you see wonders, but you might not remember a thing afterwards, or be able to articulate what you have found. You might even not find your way back properly, and spend fruitless years yearning to return to a place that has in fact given you everything you have ever needed. This is why traditionally taking these plants was considered a 'sacred' task, and preparations were required before taking them. Because your intent in these realms is everything. You can take these plants for recreation but you won't gain any knowledge that way. Having a life-affirming question, however, anchors you and provides a point of departure. A certain flexibility and fluidity of movement enables you to negotiate your way. Because the earth dimension you access is governed by fire, by light and colour and frequency, and goes at a very much faster pace than five-sense reality, you need to keep up with it in order for things to make sense. That way, when you go back through the door, you can remember what you have experienced.

Returning and remembering is what the second inner track is all about. When you return you realise you are keeping a certain door open between the fleet world of spirit and the slower world of the five senses. You realise that for life to happen for human beings as it should, that door needs to be kept open. Once you understand that, you start living your earthly life according to the spirit of all things and letting go of all the glamours and promises that the picture deludes you into thinking is the point of your reason-based existence.

The truth of the matter is that in order to be fully human, the spirit – the solar-fire body – of each human being needs to move and change and grow. This spirit needs the archaic things, the earthly things, the encounter with the nonhuman, with the ancestors, in order to do this – otherwise we remain only half a person, unrealised, like stunted trees. On the solar path we walk toward the interior of ourselves as much as we travel outwards, because the sun is where we are from and where we are going. All mysteries teach you this. The sun resides mysteriously within the dark space of each human being as it does within the solar system. It is our inner selves governed by our hearts, and it is toward this solar intelligence that the plants lead all initiates. This inner life is rarely given any credit in our daily goal-fixated world, and yet it represents the majority of our lives – how we feel, what we remember, what thoughts arise within us, our inspiration, our originality, our love of all things. Very little of this life is expressed outwardly, unless we find a creative outlet for it, a way to describe our own song and dance. The outer world of materialism and success and power occupies all our attention. The solar path reverses this process. The inner life becomes everything, and as a result the outer ceases to have such a restrictive hold on the way we move through life.

When you go down into the underworld part of you never returns. That's the deal. You eat the six seeds of the pomegranate and that action seals a certain bargain with life thereafter. It's a deal nobody signs if they think about it, and yet those who do sign never regret it. If you don't go into the underworld you never find out what it means to go home. That's why no one ever regrets initiation, however it comes. It makes your upperworld life very hard thereafter, but your inner life becomes immeasurably rich. You have roots in the earth and you have a place to go to when you die. Those things count for everything. They make you bold and free.

During the archaic age these connections were an essential part of tribal life, a way of being on the earth that remained stable for over ten thousand years. Everyone was initiated into them. Then, when the first conquering cities appeared, those rites of passage were marginalised and turned into mystery schools. These schools ran alongside civilisation and outlived them all. The most famous of these took place outside Athens at Eleusis. Originally moon-based and female, these rites became solarised and male. Apollo took command of the Delphic oracle and the half-gods Orpheus and Dionysus took over from Demeter and Persephone. When Dionysus was trampled on the mountain like his sacred vines, his 'sacrifice' became institutionalised as religion, and those mythic transcendental events which kept us in touch with our origins and made meaning of our presence on the planet became derided as pagan and superstitious.

No one knew what happened in these initiation schools. It was assumed that terrifying punishments were meted out if you 'told'. But anyone who has worked with plants or dreams knows how difficult it is to talk about these encounters. This is partly because the reason-based educated mind will reject everything you say, thinking you are touched or have become some kind of drug fiend, but mostly because knowledge, what was once known as wisdom, does not exist in words or numbers or symbols. Those things can be *signs* of knowledge but they are not knowledge itself. The only way to gain knowledge is to experience it first-hand. Only the real thing gets you home.

When LSD was synthesised from morning glory seeds in the late fifties it was hailed as the liberator of mankind and was used with great success in experimental psychology at the time. Gordon Wasson, the writer who discovered the ceremonial use of *Psilocybin cubensis,* in the same year invited its inventor Albert Hofmann to Mexico, where they unearthed a third sacred hallucinogenic known as diviner's mint. In their book *The Road to Eleusis: Unveiling the Mysteries*, they concluded that the *kykeon* imbibed by the initiates of the ancient world contained an entheogen (a word they invented, meaning a plant that inspires a 'divine experience'), most probably the ergot fungus that grew on Demeter's sacred grains.

The effect of all entheogens is to transport one from the personal into the transpersonal realms. The price it exacts for this passage is what is known as the 'death of the ego', a dramatic internal event documented throughout the spiritual history of mankind. Stanislav Grof, a psychiatrist from Prague who conducted over four thousand sessions with LSD in the 1960s, noted that the initiatory feelings of terror and loss of control often led to encounters with mythical realms and archetypal beings. Many followed the same pattern: a primal state of oceanic bliss and unity; experiences of no-exit, struggle and annihilation of all known points of reference; and finally a sense of redemption and a rebirth into a world of light, love and liberation. The modern world, he conjectured, was a reflection of this process on a collective level. As a species we could either keep projecting and acting out its destructive phases, or we could internalise them and reach an extraordinary leap of consciousness.

After suffering all kinds of mental and emotional torments, the first explorer of LSD walked through his kitchen door and into the glorious morning outside. 'It had been raining in the night,' Hofmann told Grof. 'I had the feeling that I saw the earth and the beauty of nature as it had been when it had been created, at the first day of creation. It was a beautiful experience. I was reborn, seeing nature in quite a new light.'

For Hofmann, his medicine was 'a tool that turns us into what we are supposed to be', and he was dismayed by its recreational use as a psychedelic in the mid-sixties and seventies. In spite of Grof's assertion that the human drive for transcendence was stronger than sex, most people didn't make it into the morning. And official research on the effects of hallucinogenic plants on human consciousness was suppressed.

But the door had been opened, and the modern *kykeon* carried on unveiling its unofficial mystery schools in the underbelly of the western world. During the Summer of Love in 1989 I took, like thousands of others across the dance floors and disused warehouses of London, a small blue pill that shook my small inner-city world.

When Mark and I left England and travelled through Mexico and South America we explored the entheogens that have opened the eyes of human beings for millennia. We studied the effects of cacti, mushrooms, morning glory seeds and hemp flowers, in our bodies and imaginations. Some fellow travellers called these power plants, some psychoactive substances, but we knew them as plant hallucinogenics, because since that first encounter with the tiny liberty cap mushrooms among the beeches of the Chiltern Hills, they made us realise in shocking and extraordinary ways that the only real hallucination is the one we call modern civilisation.

san pedro cactus
Vilcabamba, Ecuador 1991/3

'There are two kinds of person on the earth,' said the stranger in the
bar in Quito, Ecuador. 'One is here for the beer, and the other is here
for something else. You, I can see, are here for the something else.'
    'What are you here for?' I asked.
    He laughed ruefully, the stranger, as if his life meant nothing at all.
'I am here for the beer,' he replied and then said nothing more.
    I thought about that moment when I returned to Ecuador with
Mark and Robert and Karen and we went to the valley they call the
valley of immortality. It is said that those who dwell there can live for
over a hundred years because it is so peaceful, so verdant, because the
water that flows from the Andes is so pure. But most of all because it
is the place where those people who are looking for something else
go when they can no longer find it in their glass of beer, or in the city
of Quito, or any city of the world. And they go to the valley because
the key to that 'something else' grows in great abundance there: the
San Pedro cactus.
    The San Pedro cactus is named after the saint who stands beside
the door of heaven, because it holds the keys to other dimensions
and allows you to see the earth in its true colours and know it for
what it truly is, a paradise.
    The cactus itself is tall, fast-growing, towering in luminous green
columns that sometimes reach fifteen feet. The flowers grow directly
out of the top of these columns, like floral loudspeakers: white, shiny,
scented, mostly in June. San Pedro flourishes in Ecuador, Bolivia
and Peru, as well as sunny locations outside its native territory, such
as residential Southern California. You can sometimes see it in
Quito where, like the saint, it guards the entrances of rich suburban
gardens, sometimes lopped in half by a passing thief. The form it
is traditionally taken in is a reduced syrup, sometimes mixed with
other plants, such as datura. After its prodigious spines are removed
it is brewed down for several hours. The resulting mass is strained
and a dark brown brew remains, viscous and vile-tasting. Apart from
peyote, it is the most unpleasant bitter thing I have tasted on this
earth, and makes you want to throw it up out of yourself as fast as

possible. However, you learn not to do this – at least not until an hour afterwards, by which time the plant's potent hallucinogens have entered your bloodstream and are already working their botanical alchemy. By this time the nausea has usually vanished. If not, then your throwing up becomes part of what is known as *la purificación*.

You take the cactus without knowing anything, sitting in the small hut on the hillside, overlooking rice fields and the river, bare feet on the bamboo balcony. You wait.

The first thing you notice is that you can see the valley in a state of pure transcendence. Everything is illuminated in the most beautiful colours. Everything is moving and converging in a vibrant pristine state, and you are beholding the harmony and beauty of all things under the morning sun – the breeze moving the green papaya trees, the sound of the women washing clothes down by the river, the donkey laughing on the hill, the turkeys talking as they pass by, the clouds passing by the mountains, reflecting everything below them. It is like a song that ripples in endless waves through the valley. Underneath this song you can hear the earth as a great heart beating and everything is in rhythm with this beat. You see this heart like a giant queen bee, see how all living beings bring the fruits of their collective labours, the sweet nectar of their gathered lives, home to this rainbow-coloured core that is also the core of yourself – your heart. Everything is made of the slanting hexagonal cells of a honeycomb – leaf, wind, feather, stone, your skin. You see the mountains take the forms of ancestral beings. One is shaped like a man's head, turned upwards to face the sky, which radiates an extraordinary light that dances with the movement and sound and forms of the green valley. The sky fades slowly from day into night, the frogs start to sing, the fireflies flicker, the men come back from the fields, the stars come out one by one as the mountain keeps gazing upward towards the Southern Cross.

The second thing you notice is that not everything is aligned and in harmony with this valley. The road, for example, looks like a scar as it rips through the belly of the land. You feel the poison that comes from this road and what it brings from the world beyond. Then you notice your fellow visitors from Europe and America. How strange and foreign and disjointed everyone looks, as if introverted into

74

themselves and bedevilled by their nation's history. The German man is as stiff as a board and looks bright red, as if he were embarrassed to be alive. The French man is wearing air plants in his ear and talking nonsense, like a courtier from the court of Louis XIV. The Jewish girl from England is laughing on the outside but sobbing underneath, crying tears that are not even her own. A group of Israelis are shouting angrily at each other and ignoring the rainbow that stretches across the horizon. You notice how your own insides don't feel at all right. As if you haven't paid attention to yourself in the right way. When you look into the clouds you see doctors peering down at you and you shudder. At some point you realise you can see into people's bodies. I can see into Mark, and notice how one side of his body is lopsided. We sit down by the wasps he is terrified of and look instead at the condors spiralling up the mountain, and the fear that was not his disappears. Mark touches the scar on my belly and tells me to ignore the sky surgeons. It was a bad dream from a long time ago.

San Pedro has been used for thousands of years by native *curanderos*. Singing songs, they look into people's bodies and they see what blow, what cruel or malign thought, has entered their souls and contorted the natural rhythm and harmony of things. Here in the valley we find we can do the same for each other. We keep spitting out the poison of this world, realigning my womb, my guts, our hearts, our minds.

No one can tell you how awe-inspiring and humbling these experiences are, how they put you back in touch with life, how you can hold your destiny in your own hands, how clearly you understand the extraordinary transformative nature of this planet, the something else that it offers your soul, as you turn to face all eternity. A space in which you can make moves and bring to light places within yourself, that is not just your self.

San Pedro, like other hallucinogenics, scours and purifies the body so, as William Blake once wrote, the doors of perception may be cleansed. To see something else means you need to *become* someone else. For Europeans this is a painstaking task, for our five senses that let us behold the world are as cobwebbed as a telescope kept in an attic for a thousand years. You can become obsessed by this *purificación*, by its peculiar personal and collective details. But this is not the main purpose of these encounters. This is just the beginning.

San Pedro is the beginning. The real story of the hallucinogenic

75

plants is the story of remembering. It is to remember how it is to be really human on this earth, part of its living systems: how it is to laugh and move without the constraint of history or politesse, what it feels like to be free, how it is to fly with eagles, to be a jaguar, a snake, a well, a tree, how it is to breathe together with Robert with the breath of whales in an ocean of sound and light, how it is to rock with April as she howls and keens and roars for the ancestors, how it is to dance with the volcano of Hawaii inside you, with the bones of Australia, to see the endless riches that live inside the void of your own being in a beech wood in England. What it feels like to sail through the night with your fellow voyagers until the dawn comes, as it always does, with the sound of birds singing and children laughing invisibly, at the beginning of a new day.

When we returned that year to the valley, I took this bitter brew for the first time at night. Night travelling is very different from day. Colours and sounds are replaced by a monochrome stillness. Silence descends on the valley. Beholding the sunlit earth you observe, take part, you laugh, dance and sing; by night you listen, feel, intuit, sense, inhabit the physical breathing world like a creature. The glittering stars wheel in the immense sky above your head. In this dark feeling mysterious world you speak from the interior of yourself; you become part of what you understand is the universe. While everyone sleeps in their straw huts on the hillside, I sit beside Karen on her veranda. A bat flickers past. We can feel the immanence, the shapes of the mountains in front of us, and a cool wind in our faces. We feel the presence of each other, the unknown parts of ourselves, now meeting under the stars at this time. We are almost strangers to one another by day, and yet at night we are not. Invisible banana leaves on the hillside shift and rattle. The moon is almost full.

We first met in Antigua, Guatemala in 1991 where Mark and I were living in a white-washed studio, surrounded by volcanoes, working on our travelling book; Karen was travelling through the town. One day she came by and told us how she had given up being a counsellor of 'inner-city' problems in New York and instead had begun to teach people creative writing. 'I realised I was part of the problem,' she said. I liked her directness and intelligence. It is rare to meet people who have a clear sense of direction, who change course and can give you the reasons why. Not the rational, practical reasons but the energetic ones. Energetic moves are what count in this world. San Pedro teaches you that. Talking from the rational mind gives a reason for everything in the western world, but when you begin to see energetically, you realise these flat, dull words mean very little. Talking explains, but it doesn't get life moving in the right direction.

To move in the right direction, you need to get your feet on the ground. That's the first step, really – what we concentrated on when the stars began to disappear behind the clouds that summer night. You feel the person you are sitting beside differently in the darkness. No longer dominated by appearance, by the unsolvable problems of the world, you can access the deeper things, what matters to the soul. That night in the valley we looked at our feet in the moonlight, our child-dancing feet, my ballet school feet and Karen's that were all snarled up from years as a champion roller-skater. We knew that somehow our feet had to get out of those artificial shoes, those red fairy shoes, and back on the earth. Because it looked as if every-thing that had been bottled up in those skating boots, like a kind of footbinding, even though she had thrown them down in rebellion when she was sixteen, still held her in a spell. Suddenly she jumped up. 'This is going to be my last cartwheel,' she said, and performed a perfect acrobatic arch; her bare feet whirled through the night air like a shower of shooting stars.

Afterwards we looked into the sky without saying anything. The clouds parted and revealed the shape of a woman in the void, made up of hundreds of stars. We looked at that shape in the clouds for a long time. It looked as though she was carrying something in her hand, like a torch.

'It needs to be whole,' said Karen.

'A hole?' I repeated.

Karen laughed. 'No – *whole*,' she said. 'With a W.'

You needed the hole to be whole. It was the kind of paradox you understood with San Pedro. The door needed to be open. The problems happened when the door shut and closed us in, when we no longer felt the movements of life within us.

Hallucinogenic 'trips' are many things, but energetic movement is essential in all of them. Sometimes you get becalmed in all sorts of places, in time, in spells, in corners, in clouds, in the lens of someone else's camera. San Pedro helps you see and feel your way out of them. It opens the door. Sometimes these corners are yours and sometimes the other person's, but really they always belong to both of you, because that is what you are doing there together in the valley they call the valley of immortality, working out ways to proceed forward at this moment of time, in 1993. Not being part of the problem, being creative, female, free.

At the end of the night, just before dawn, we go into the small straw cabin and lie in the narrow beds in the darkness. Although it is warm in here, it feels uneasy for some reason I can't quite define. Though we have been talking all night, we are now suddenly silent, but it is not the kind of silence that brings peace.

'I feel as though I'm aboard the boat,' says Karen.

'Is it your boat?'

'No, it's his,' she replies, and there is a another silence then as we feel the boat creaking in the night, ourselves caught in sea-hammocks like nets around our bodies, as it lies in the bay outside Long Island, not going anywhere. The door of the cabin is guarded by shadows.

'He used to call me Pearl,' she says.

I remember at this point, the time Latin America calls the *madrugada*, just before dawn, thinking of my old friend Blanche and how the words *she is seeking reparation* suddenly came to me. And how strange it was that these words provoked a wild kind of jubilation inside me. It was not that her fury had gone, but because, after all these years, I could suddenly see this female anger *energetically*, distinct from myself and therefore something I was no longer subject to. I could see that it didn't matter who I was, she was going to seek reparation for wrong that had once been done to her. I was just someone in a long line of someones who would serve at that moment, so she could vent her spleen as a release. I was seeing this because this is the world's bad sad story, the myth that binds our young female feet and keeps us trapped in places where we do not feel at home. The rageful Demeter after Hades' blood, and taking Persephone's as a substitute.

Seeing the energy behind the form, the stars beyond the cloud, is the key to liberation. Once you have seen something in the underworld you know what to do. The problems of the sense-bound world are always with what you can't see: the invisible forces that hold us captive, the hostility you cannot name, the feelings that bind you to a place, to a room, to a relationship, to a culture, the hell you know but cannot speak of to anyone. Hades is invisible. You don't see him. That's his power. The absent landlord, the invisible god, the nameless one. You can spend your life wishing you could find the man in charge of the underworld to ask him what to do, without realising he was there all the time. Just behind you, his blood running through your veins. You could spend your whole life longing for that man who is your gaoler, the holder of your heart, because his was ripped out thousands of years ago.

If you do realise it, you might then spend the rest of your life being angry, furious with him, and that too keeps you in this moment. The fury is all right if it liberates you, but sometimes it turns into rage and keeps you down in the underworld forever, in a boat that never moors, in the darkness that never becomes dawn. You have to transform the poison that anger brings – the wailing Demeter and the silent Hades-who-is-also-Zeus, whose archetypal drama plays out within your own being. You can't jump it. It's the worst part of the underworld. It blocks everything. You can spend your whole life worrying about this part, but this is not what being on earth in human form is truly about. Seeing this is part of the purification. Once you have dropped this story, life can begin again.

That small moment before dawn is the treasure the night brings, a detail you might not notice in daylight reality. San Pedro showed me all the glory of the valley during the day: how the earth and the sky work together, the shapes of the ancestors in the mountains, the turkeys that spoke, and all the wonders of this rainbow earth that lie just out of reach of our five senses. But the key it bequeathed me from itself was the ability to see in the dark. It was a thief's key, a skeleton key with which I would be able unpick every lock and combination that lay in my path. To leave the underworld you have to open many doors. To find that something else you have to move in a direction that only your night-eyes can discern; to move though your own history, through your nation's history, past the shadows, past Demeter, past Hades, towards morning. You have not to become part of the problem. Because the door that opens to paradise is also the door that leads out of hell.

peyote
Real de Catorce, Mexico 1993

The first thing I noticed was the cat. A stripy marmalade cat sitting on the cobbles in the sun. We had entered a side street and found what we were looking for. Travelling down to Mexico from Santa Fe, our driver had suddenly taken a detour down a long tunnel that had brought us into this old silver mining town. 'I've just met one of your compatriots,' he told us outside the hotel. I did not know this at the time but this detour was going to change our whole lives. The cat was pivotal. Above the cat was a sign painted with a jaguar. The Nagual Café, it said.

'Oh, she must live here,' I said to Mark. And indeed she did. The owner of the Nagual Café was an Englishwoman who was also part Italian and had lived abroad most of her fifty-something life. The café served a delicious green soup made of chard and had a small esoteric library and a collection of arrowheads on the shelves. We sat down and talked immediately. It was Teresa who told us about peyote and the nagual. The 'nagual' is a term used by Carlos Castaneda. It means the seer who leads a party of apprentices, and it also means the place he leads them to. The tonal, Don Juan once explained to his modern-world apprentice, is the table we are sitting at. Our description of the world is what is on the table. The nagual is everything that surrounds the table. The tonal is the orange cat; the nagual is the jaguar. The peyote takes you to the nagual. But it could be years before you knew how to navigate its territory. 'That takes work,' said Teresa and she smiled enigmatically.

'We will be back,' we told her, 'as soon as we can.'

Peyote is a small cactus that grows in the shape of a pincushion in the dry deserts of northern Mexico and Texas. Its flowers are candy-striped and sweet. In spite of its size and appearance however, it is one of the most powerful and demanding entheogens known to man. Every year, as they have for thousands of years, the Huichol Indians make a pilgrimage to 'hunt the deer' of the peyote, the spirit that keeps their people alive. It is an arduous journey that crosses through the desert across the Sierra Madre mountains. This old mining town is the place of their destination. During this journey they remember the shining world that underpins this world, a world they depict in their brilliantly coloured yarn paintings, peopled by crosses and figures and animals, scorpions and birds and deer. Peyote is taken by other indigenous tribes, by the Tarahumara Indians of the Copper Canyon, and also by the Native American Church in their sweatlodges and ceremonies. But it is peyote's relationship with those who journey to the sacred mountain of Wirikuta wherein you find its most dramatic expression.

Peyote is famous now, thanks to the works of Castaneda and other ethnobotanical explorers, but it is infamously difficult to procure. In those days, if you wanted to do things correctly, you had to go down to the desert to gather it yourself. You had to find someone to take you down the unpaved back route down from the town in a jeep. You had to negotiate for another person to drive you in a truck to find the cactus and then you had to cut it in the proper manner with a pocket knife, leaving the root to grow again. Everything that arises – the paranoia, the uncertainty, the squabbling between everyone, the typhoid you picked up from the rundown café where the bus stopped after a ten-hour journey from Mexico City, shivering, with a splitting headache, in a damp and uncomfortable hotel – challenge you at all turns. It is cold in these mountains, especially at night when the mists descend, and this is a strange foreboding place where you find other pilgrims stumbling on bleeding knees to repent for their sins at the Catholic church.

The desert is fiercely hot when I finally get there with Robert the next day, but it's a relief after the coldness of the cobbled town. This was before I had lived in Arizona, and it was unknown territory. But maybe because I had read Carlos Castaneda, whose descriptions of this dry and spiky terrain are so detailed and luminous, perhaps because it was my destiny to speak with deserts, or perhaps because as we left the truck that day I stopped our driver from killing a rattlesnake, the desert immediately became our friend. It felt as if we had known each other forever.

Robert was English too, a painter, and like many artists he had a natural sense of self. He had been travelling for five years when Mark met him in a bar and ordered him to join a play we were acting in at the time. 'You can be the porter!' Mark said, and laughed when Robert took up the offer, and then when he volunteered to come with us to find Teresa and the cactus we had been reading about for years. Robert was to prove the first and best companion we ever had. Kinship is an important criterion when you take hallucinogenic plants. You need affection as a base between you, otherwise things can fragment when the going gets tough. The best companions are creative, self-contained, loyal, and there out of their own sense of destiny. Peyote was going to change us all forever. After this Mark and I would stop living our travelling performance life, and take another path of inquiry entirely. Robert would return to England. I had been drifting, he told us, and he decided to go home. Peyote is not for drifters. It is for voyagers on the solar path.

We are about to find this out as the three of us step out into the mountains and walk all day without tiring, when we return with April the following month and sit under a blasted tree, the four of us in a cross that faces the four directions, and ask the pivotal questions that all seekers have to ask in front of the door: *Who am I? What am I doing here? Where am I going? Which is the way home?*

'I call it Mammon,' said Teresa in a dramatic tone as we stared at the gaunt tower looming across the valley. I hadn't noticed the mines before, so intent were we on our adventures up the sacred mountain. 'You don't have to look at it,' I said, feeling the prickles rise on my neck and imagining us falling down into some historical mining shaft that none of us had made.

What we decide to pay attention to in life is what we get. This is a new-age cliché but when you take peyote it becomes a living truth. You can focus on Mammon and you get a world ruled by Mammon, a world in which you are not in charge. Peyote in the synthetic form of mescaline was one of the most influential experimental drugs of the twentieth century, and sparked off some of its most formative ideas in literature and philosophy. It inspired Havelock Ellis while he formed his radical theories about sexuality, it inspired Aldous Huxley who wrote the first description of its effects in *The Doors of Perception*. But mostly it depicted the modern world as a world ruled by dark forces. It underpinned Huxley's late doomsday book *Brave New World*, and the existentialist visions of Jean-Paul Sartre's trilogy *The Roads to Freedom.* It showed the social world as a penitential madhouse in Ken Kesey's *One Flew Over the Cuckoo's Nest,* and as a devouring god, Moloch, in Allen Ginsberg's *Howl.* All of them dystopias, derived from investigations undertaken in cities, where the dominant imagery, like the mines, is of a hellish world. The world we were paying attention to among the mountains was the world of nature, the paradise of the earth.

'Everything is real,' remarked Teresa. 'Especially the monsters.'

April is our second companion. Large, blond-haired, Californian, a counsellor and rebirther with a loud hearty laugh. We were as a foursome diverse, but united in our intent to explore everything. We set forth in April's truck on our second trip to the mountains, like a warrior band.

Peyote is a sun plant and like most sun plants is a great chaser of the inner monsters, physical, mental and otherwise. Every kind of emotion, thought, physical symptom, energy block, denial, historical nightmare emerges under its brilliant all-seeing light. No vampire consciousness survives its unequivocal stare. It is a very taxing plant indeed and its effects can last up to eighteen hours. Quite apart from having to go into the desert to collect the plants and spend hours taking all their spikes out with meticulous care, you then have to eat several of them on an empty stomach – or drink them down, as we did, whooshed up with apple juice, in an attempt to mask its most fearsomely difficult taste. You then have to start walking very fast indeed up the mountain without throwing up, which, just looking at the huge liquidizer full of frothy green stuff, is all you ever want to do. Then after an hour of intestinal challenges, there is a palpable shift in your attention. It is as if rocket fuel has just entered your system. Physically you feel light, everything around you takes on an incredible hue and sharpness, the world feels alive, calling you welcome, and there is a palpable feeling of *belonging,* of coming home in yourself after an aeon. But sometimes it takes you a hell of a time to get there.

That stormy grey day as we climbed the hill path that winds above the town towards the plateau, I suddenly felt overwhelmed by a feeling of being left out. I found myself taking a solitary tack up one side of the mountain, while falling into a huge pit of self-pity inside myself. This became worse as I saw my companions below converging merrily by the cleft of a large rock. I moved miserably onwards, scrabbling up the stony incline to get away from their horrible jolliness. 'No one cares!' I thought. 'I am alone! I don't even feel the peyote!'

'There she is all alone on the mountain,' Mark yelled up, and they all fell about laughing. 'Come on, lonely Charlie crow!' And then they roared with laughter and rolled about again on the rock, mimicking me, sitting as I was all hunched up in a large black jumper, all beaky, and sad and cold. 'Caw caw, all alone! Ha ha ha!'

How I hated them laughing at me. How dare they, when I am in such a bad state! It seemed to go on forever. And then came another annoying feeling inside, a small but powerful desire to join them (*Why should I?*). I wanted to be with them and laugh too. To be warm! For what seemed like another aeon I battled within myself, with a huge monstrous desire to nurse my righteous apartness and sorrow, and with this other tiny indomitable contradictory feeling that refused to be ignored. In spite of the awesome power of my self-pity I found myself edging down the mountain and sidling up to them. 'What do you want, little crow?' they boomed at me, and stood up suddenly, all three together. They looked enormous.

'I want things to be different,' I said in a small pitiful voice.

'Lie down on the ground and get breathing!' roared April and she grabbed me by the arms and pulled me into her cavernous lap. I stared up at their faces towering above me, looking down, suddenly stern. Then Robert gave me a wink. 'Time to be reborn!' Mark declared, and they all blew their cheeks in and out and started to puff away like the wind. Mimicking them, I puffed too and in that moment I felt a huge elation rip through my whole being and I *burst* out of my sorry crow state and leapt to my feet, full of intense energy, another bird entirely. A raven and not a crow at all! I was small no longer. We were all the same size.

'We have to do something NOW!' I commanded. The three of them looked at me in astonishment.

'Oh, honey, can't we just stay here and enjoy ourselves?' wheedled April, as they all began to resume their jolly picnic positions. 'No,' I said, 'we can't. We have work to do. We need to take up the four directions. I will be in the south.'

Peyote can show you everything under the sun. Like all power plants it is a powerful teacher of perception. But because it is a plant

84

of the sun it goes the way of the sun and initiates an extremely exacting alchemy within those who take it. The exuberant San Pedro shows you the verdant valley that lies before your feet – the women laughing as they make a flower tea. It is lush, warm and sensual. You sit close beside each another and behold the marvels of the living earth. But the slow-growing peyote comes from a harsher terrain: it demands a warrior spirit and turns you to face each other. It does not cure, it calls you to account. Some people call peyote the grandfather, a stern taskmaster, the ancient one who keeps the people together. What it shows you is not personal story, but the impersonal forces of the world. The forces you need to transform within the furnace that burns inside you.

In this mineral fastness, in this windy territory of stone and scrub, you are taught how to perceive by experience. This means that whatever you see, you also experience, physically, emotionally, mentally. You do not just see images as you face each other; you feel the energy of those images and the effects they have upon your own being. You see the underlying forms that project those images, the forms that govern you as you agree to inhabit them or be subjected by them. How these images and forms hold you prisoner, how they set you free.

What did we see in each other's faces as we sat by the tree? In our voices, in the ways we moved? We saw and felt ourselves as tyrants and ancestors, crows and ravens, fairies and ghouls, priests and emperors. We experienced ourselves in myths and folk tales. We felt ourselves trapped in grey places, in dissolving cities, in faraway clouds. We sat in the four directions and this cross held us together in these myriad dimensions, as we brought each other out of those configurations that kept us captive and connected with those that liberated us and restored the place we call the earth. We were the vessels in which these forms and images arose and could be broken down and reformed in alignment with life. We could do this because underneath all these historical and mythological shows, under all the horrors of Mammon, there was something we found that was more powerful than their control: it was the power of our human hearts.

The peyote visits were pivotal on the solar path for many reasons. First, because I realised that the demon of self-pity, which rules our interior lives and thus our world, keeps us in a small sorrowful place, in which we endlessly replay the past. To break out of our self-imposed exile we need to remember something within us that is stronger than this sorrow. That day my solitude was broken by my desire to join in. The heart always wants to join in with its fellows. Unity is its ultimate strength. This is why the heartless monsters of Mammon will do everything to drive us apart from each other and keep us as miserable and separated as possible. And why, if we care about the planet, we should do everything in our hearts to join up with one another instead, and get on with the real business of being here together.

The second key lay in discovering the art of attention. Modern human beings are trained to watch and accept what is shown and broadcast to them. This is not a passive activity. As we focus our attention on the fabricated woes and wonders of the world, we also pour out our feelings, our life-force, as we react to what we are watching: laughing, crying, being fearful, furious, sad. These energies pour out of our physical and emotional bodies as we look at and recall these manufactured images and give them life. The main effect this has is to render us powerless. The art of attention is to focus only on that which you choose in your heart to see.

In the exacting light of peyote you become aware that these images and sounds make you react in a certain way, because your energy, your creativity and willpower, is required to uphold certain invisible forms. Letting go of these images and archetypes is what liberates you. You don't do this by battling with them, you do it by changing your inner structure so that these things no longer have any power over you. You place your attention instead on what you love, replacing the artificial with the natural, by connecting with the living systems of the earth – which are also your own living systems, your physical being, your imagination. You start walking up the mountain, going into the desert, sleeping under stars. Making your own pilgrimages into the wild lands. You start creating something else.

The third, perhaps most crucial aspect of these interactions was the direct contact with the peyote cactus itself and the territory in which it grew. It was to be a lifelong connection. Both the cactus and the mountain to which we journeyed would come into my dreams for years after we left Mexico, always in luminous ways, in startling colours of pink and green, accompanied by deer or wreathed in stars. I only had to imagine myself there laughing with everyone under the tree and the communication with the place and the plant would be as strong as if it were only yesterday. As if it were only last night that I went walking with Mark and Robert under the full moon and remembered the way home in the dark. Memory is everything: that's what the ancestors teach you, the plants and the mountain; the memory of your heart, your feet, your breath. What it means to be alive, here, now.

We took a lot of peyote that year and the year that followed: fresh buttons from the desert, vast liquidisers full, dried buttons ground up and formed into less challenging small balls. We laughed a lot and we did a lot of work. We worked with Robert from England, Aurelia and Cyril from France, with April and Tina and Jan from America; we took peyote in the Buckinghamshire woods and in the Arizona desert. We took peyote in the sunlight and in the dark. And then one day we didn't take peyote any more. It disappeared from our lives.

'Everything you learn here, you need to do in the world,' the peyote told me that day on the mountain. It was time to go back through the door.

The consciousness of everything communicating is what I brought back through the door. I returned to a world that believes itself to be separate and alone.

But we are not alone.

When the peyote was in my bloodstream on the mountain I became aware that another consciousness was actively inside me and our intelligences were interacting. The sentence was spoken as a voice that was distinctive from the voice I would normally associate as 'me' even though it was making itself known through my mind. The words 'spoken' by plants, I would find out later, always come like this. You know instinctively what is originating from or has arisen from your own being and what is coming from theirs. In the five-sense separated world this event would be reduced to a biochemical fact and this voice dismissed as hallucination, but in the cultures where it is recognised that the earth is a sentient being and all beings have consciousness, this transmission of information from plants to human beings is what is known as a teaching. If you ask, as many anthropologists have, where native people get their plant medicine information from, they will say, the plants told us. They came in a dream, or through ingesting peyote or ayahuasca, or any number of plants. And this process was exactly what happened to us, and indeed to everyone we ever spoke to concerning peyote taken in this spirit of exploration.

Sometimes the teaching came in things we saw in each other's faces, sometimes it came as an inner-sense knowing, sometimes as distinct words, in the shape of ravens flying across the sky, or yuccas waving in the breeze. But however the transmission came, peyote made us all aware that certain ways of being on the planet needed to be activated and remembered within ourselves. Our response to the peyote, to the intelligence that governs all planetary beings, was to show that in spite of the excesses of Mammon, human beings were willing to begin the path of return. We were not doing this by going down a traditional track, following the Huichols across the desert, because we were not an indigenous people. We were doing it in a modern way. So the peyote was not a teacher in the ordinary sense of the word because we were working with it as much as it was working with us. It was a cocreative partnership. The plant, through myself, showed us the four-way cross as a way of comprehending the dimensions we were experiencing, as individuals and as a group. It was an ancient invention, but it was also completely new.

This cross appears everywhere in Huichol art depicting peyote, and throughout the archaic world. It is the universal symbol for the sun. However, on that day it became something else. It became a living structure in which the worlds of spirit and the worlds of the five senses could interact in a new way. What created the bridge was the interdimensional dialogue held between four people of equal intent. This cross surfaced later as two communication games Tina and I simultaneously invented (unknown to each other, on separate continents) so we could explore this alchemical work with others. Later it formed the way Mark and I held dialogues with our dreams and with the people that for the next ten years would appear at our door, or we theirs. And it formed the basis of all our investigative communications with plants.

Why was the cat pivotal? Because when you look at the cat, you also look at the jaguar. You are a small alone person in the five-sense world but in the greater world of the sun you are infinitely connected. Every step you make in this place counts. To reach the nagual is an art and a task and peyote will take you there, just so long as you find your way to the mountain and know the reality of monsters. Teresa gave us the perfect directions as we set off down the path. But what I learned about peyote I learned for myself. That is the business of cats and jaguars, of alchemical creatures born under the sun. Finding things out for yourself.

blue mushroom
Norwich, Norfolk 2003

What is the ocean dreaming now? I asked Mark. It was a question I had just heard at a lecture. The lecture was called *The Aboriginal Dreamtime.* During the first half the speaker, an ecopsychologist called Stephen Eisenstat, had told us that the dreaming of the earth and all its creatures had been formally declared a vital part of our planetary future at the Rio Earth Summit. *Dreams are beings in their own right,* he had said. In the second half, he talked about Australia. But he did not tell us what the ocean had dreamed.

So I asked Mark. There was a pause as we looked at each other. It was a rainy dark December night in Santa Barbara, California. You could see palm trees outside the motel window, shrouded in sea-fog. We had just driven 12,000 miles across America and were looking for a point of departure. *Let's find out,* he said. You can look at the dream in five ways, I told him. You look at it in terms of your daily reality, as part of your whole life, as part of the human world, as a myth, and as a communication from the earth. The next morning we began a dialogue about dreams that lasted ten years.

We called it *the dreaming practice.* Like all spiritual or creative practices, we did it everyday. Dancers and musicians exercise their bodies, mystics move their minds. We explored our night dreams by engaging in a dialogue, based on the kind of inventive interchanges we had enjoyed with hallucinogenic plants. One person told the dream, and the other asked questions. The practice lasted about two hours each morning.

The dreams were complex, but their essential meaning was clear and simple: all of them required movement of some kind. Unless you move, you cannot contact the spirit, or dreaming, of yourself or any other living being. We discovered it is not what you think or believe in a dream that is crucial, but how you act, what position you take, how you *feel.* The fluid motion of the heart, your feelings, is what connects you with your spirit. Because the spirit needs to move in order to know itself.

What is the ocean dreaming now?

The practice, though hermetic, began to affect the way we looked at things, how we felt about our positions in the human world, our relationships with mythology, and most especially how we experienced the earth. The dreams and our ordinary lives began to interweave. The more we paid attention to our dreams, the more we found ourselves paying attention to life. Even though we were often immersed in the biographical and social levels, in people and past events, the physical presence of the earth made itself known from the beginning. Shortly after the practice began we travelled to Australia and our dreams through the red lands brought animals, fish, Aboriginal elders, rainbow snakes and waterholes and a blue mysterious ocean full of dolphins and giant rays. Returning to England they brought foxes and toads, birds and salmon, woods and rivers and seas. But most of all they brought plants.

Unlike the animals and the mountains, these plants did not simply appear within their natural habitat – the palm trees by the shore, for example – they penetrated the shadowlands of our dreams. They appeared as spots of light, as beacons in the dark cities and rooms in which our nightmares took place: a luminous pansy appearing at the crossroads when I did not know which way to turn; the scent of sweet violets inspiring me to find my way out of a dangerous house; the arms of belladonna directing me to shift dimensions. The vibrant flowers and assuring presence of trees acted as signposts, directing us out of the horrors of history, out of the maze of our cityminds, into another kind of living on the planet.

By the time we began working with dreams and plants at the end of the nineties, our intense exchanges with botanical hallucinogenics had come to an end. In many ways, these new dialogues replaced them. Sometimes someone would give us some mushrooms, or direct us to where they grew: dried blue mushrooms from Oregon, liberty caps in a field outside Oxford. But these were chance encounters. The mushrooms, when they came, always appeared out of nowhere, at a certain crossroads in our lives, when we looked back – points in time where we were just about to take another path.

Going down another path is a key move on the solar return journey. By force of habit you go down the known path – in your thoughts, in your behaviour, in your life. And then suddenly for no reason, except that you suddenly see it opening before you, you take another route. You come to different conclusions when you go down that path. Taking a detour is what led us to the Nagual Café that day. Side-stepping the ruins at Palenque and following a path into the trees, we found a man who gave us a jar of *Psilocybe mexicana* immersed in honey ('A queen bathed here once,' he told me as he swam naked in the forest pool). Down that path you find the stranger who points the way. These paths appear suddenly, as if by magic. When you look for them, you do not find them. When we looked for mushrooms, they did not come.

But in 2003, when we least expected it, the mushrooms arrived in force.

A flash of blue, out of the blue.

It was the night of the autumn equinox when I dreamed of datura. This is a flower I have dreamed of perhaps more than any other since our practice began. Datura is an intoxicating strong-scented power plant that grows all over the world – India, the Americas, Europe – and its presence is always alluring, often shocking, appearing both sacred and profane, ugly and beautiful at once. That night I had put some seeds under my pillow. I didn't think much about this, as I often invited flowers into my dreams this way. I didn't take much notice of the time either, as in those days I paid small attention to the key turning points of the solar year.

However, the seeds and the time mean everything, whether you choose to notice them or not. The datura is dark-leaved, night-flowering, poisonous. Everything about the plant is hallucinogenic. It is sometimes called Angel's Trumpet, the one that heralds change. The autumn equinox is the time when all things go down under, when the light cedes to the dark. It was at this equinox that the female mysteries began at Eleusis. September 23 is the day Persephone descends into the underworld and all her initiates follow in her wake, inspired by the hallucinogenic *kykeon*.

That night I dreamed I was with a raggedy troupe of young people gathered merrily around a plinth in a Mexican square. We are all taking peyote. I am slightly alarmed that we are doing this so blatantly in the open air, but nobody else seems to care. I take a small girl by the hand down a side street, and come across several datura plants and a peyote cactus in cages for sale in a shop.

The following morning Mark and I go to Norwich to see a film

92

called *Whale Rider*, about a young Maori girl who leads her people back to the ancestors. I enter the market from the north, a different direction than the one I normally take. The market was an urban rabbit-warren then, that reminded me of the narrow labyrinths of ancient cities, like Fez, or the old Walled City of Hong Kong, full of leering tramps, swinging light bulbs, steaming pots of food and tottering piles of merchandise. I loved the way it did not conform to the grid of well-lit, well-behaved high streets of everywhere else in England. Navigating an unknown alley, I come across a notice board: MAGIC MUSHROOMS! it declares. PEYOTE. SAN PEDRO. DIVINER'S MINT! Astonished, I go around the corner to investigate and find myself in a tiny stall full of clothes and objects in psychedelic rainbow colours, adorned with a familiar five-lobed green leaf – it's a head shop. The staff are very relaxed, at least twenty-five years younger than me, standing behind a glass counter. In the counter I can see a tiny peyote cactus in a pot. I realise, though I cannot quite believe it, that I am standing in my dream.

'Is that really a peyote?' I ask them.

'Oh yes,' they inform me quite nonchalantly, as if I were asking about geraniums.

'And your magic mushrooms, where are they from?'

'From Amsterdam,' they tell me. 'They are *Psilocybe mexicana*.' And one tall young man leans into a fridge and brings out a Tupperware box. My heart jumps. It's a kit, he explains, the instructions are inside.

Before I know it I have bought the peyote and the Tupperware kit and we are all merrily holding forth on the finer points of taking hallucinogenics – they with psilocybin, I with peyote. I haven't felt so free with people in years. Afterwards I set out towards the cinema. If I had been a whale I would have been leaping through the ocean, all the way down to New Zealand.

Having taken the mushrooms from the tank I observe them, lined like rows of soldiers in companies of ten. They are all different ranks, shapes and sizes: some slim, some large and carbuncled. All of them are streaked with inky blue, a sign of their great potency. Their energy is palpable.

I remember in that moment standing with my old friend Carmen Megeath in Bisbee Arizona. It was in her kitchen and we were looking at one of Peter's old paintings from the days when he worked out of a studio in New York. It was an extraordinary canvas that, close up, was intensely marked by millions of tiny intricate lines – but when you stepped back, from far away, it hovered like a vision of the light and colour you sometimes behold on mushrooms. It was like looking into the workings of the universe.

'Gurdjieff says that the real problem for human beings is they cannot handle the planetary forces that daily bombard them,' she is telling me. 'We are pushed and pulled both from within and without and so are entirely at their mercy, blown about like chaff in the breeze.' I am thinking about that sentence when I look at the mushrooms in their serried rows. It had intrigued me for years. In those days I had not read the deeply complex works of the Russian magus. Now I have. In his system of universal harmonics, there is a point at which something needs to come in from the outside and give you a necessary boost. That pushes you one notch further, up into the scale of things.

I am sitting in the Chair, Mark is standing in the Door. From the Chair's position you are in the thick of things: you are in a sea of feelings, sensory impressions, colours, vibrations; green plants swim are all around you. You experience everything. You don't necessarily know where you are going, except that you *are* going. Moving is all-important when you are here. You don't necessarily know the meaning of what is happening, you are too busy doing, responding, listening to what the Door is telling you. The meaning, you reckon, can wait. The thing is to be in the experience. You could say you were an actor, but everything feels too real, too alive, too urgent. The show is real! you tell the Door, who sometimes looks like a god.

The Door knows everything, except one thing: how to be in the Chair. The Chair, it observes, is uniquely itself. It is almost jealous of the Chair: how innocently it sallies forth! Sometimes you get irritated with the Chair for being so neurotic, when you know everything is so perfect, on time. All the Chair has to do now is change from that old position, turn its head from that obsessive slant. You need to forget about those Mayans and Egyptians, you say, and stop thinking. I'm seeing something interesting, the Chair insists. It's really *not* interesting, it's way off, you say. The Door is the director. But sometimes it doesn't know everything. Sometimes it feels left out.

The Chair, for instance, can make you laugh. It answers you back in surprising ways. You who know everything in the universe! With your great wisdom, from your great vantage point! In that surprise, the Door moves, a ripples passes through: stars shift, whole civilisations fall down, angels descend and become human. Something else is happening on planet earth.

I am the Door, Mark is the Chair. In the conservatory, all life happens inside the glass room. Mark is a certain shape like a wave, all the plants follow his shape and extend their arms towards him – hummingbird sage, sacred datura, jasmine tobacco, coral bean, Mexican marigold. He has grown all of these plants from seed, watered them, tended them, and now they follow his song. 'It's Shiva's garden,' I laugh. It feels as if an aeon passes and another one begins. The seed pod of the datura bursts and spills out onto the floor.

In the natural world there is a movement known as 'the pull to climax'. The climax is a condition in which natural systems become complex and symbiotic, interweaving with one another in a web of remarkable intricacy. In his essay *Poetry, Community and Climax*, the poet and activist Gary Snyder writes that in a climax situation, such as a mature oak or rainforest, a high percentage of the energy is not gleaned from the living biomass, but from the recycling of dead matter – dead trees and animals – that lie on the forest floor. This 'detritus energy' is liberated from these dead forms by the transformative actions of fungi and insects.

'As climax forest is to biome, and fungus is to the recycling of energy, so "enlightened mind" is to daily ego mind, and art to the recycling of neglected inner potential.'

Transforming old thoughts and feelings, composting our past becomes, in short, the life-energy that fuels our present lives. Both within the personal life and within the collective, the individual and the creative writer and mystic act like mushrooms. We liberate energy from what is dead and give energy to the living, and thus become symbionts rather than parasites within the collective consciousness of the earth.

Snyder sat doing *zazen* for ten years in the Zen monasteries of Japan. He then worked the land and wrote in the mountains of his native California, travelling out to read his poetry out loud in the cities of America each spring. His intense mix of spiritual discipline and creativity, his engagement in what he calls 'the most archaic values on earth ... the fertility of the soil, the magic of animals, the power-vision in solitude, the terrifying initiation and rebirth, the love and ecstasy of the dance, the common work of the tribe' demonstrate the way of life necessary for this human-nature symbiosis to take place.

The mysterious mushroom teaches you about symbiosis, about the pull to climax: you merge with the mushroom, and the mushroom show you how to merge with that which is not human – trees, animals, ancestors, planets – so you experience the transformational nature of the human being. When you merge, you learn what it means to liberate energy. Afterwards you fuel your life in a different way, you fuel the community in a different way. You are not struggling for survival in a wasteground, competing against everyone: you are a vibrant and vital part of a complex interconnecting exchange.

Merging is not possession. To be possessed is to forget yourself, babble incoherently, be a medium for any kind of proud and malevolent idea winging its way around the airwaves, looking for expression. Merging is holding the position of the chair and the door. You don't lose consciousness, you don't control. You take turns, holding the anchor, letting go. You are both there, independently, inter-dependently, working within the fabric of life.

When you merge you learn that everything is perfect but you have to change a position, an old position, and that the show is real. The chair makes the move that liberates the energy from old forms. The door asks the question, so the chair knows what to do. Afterwards you both work to make sense of what you see. That's the artist and the mystic working in the community, hidden within the detritus of the forest floor.

I am standing by the open bathroom window one winter night, look-ing out. A moment apart from the mushroom dialogue around the table downstairs. The land is covered in cobwebs. My mouth is full of cobwebs. Outside there are webs everywhere, like a thick white blanket of mist, covering the barley and beet fields, the sheep and cow pastures, hanging from some of the trees. It feels as if the whole countryside has fallen asleep. But in front of me the apple tree stands perfectly clear: there are several apples still hanging from its branches, golden-coloured, like beacons of light glowing in the deep cold night. Oh, I say softly, you are awake! And that's when I notice other small lights in the hawthorn hedge, coloured jewels in the darkness – the hearts of tiny birds and butterflies. And then I hear the foxes calling to one another, *yip yip yip*. All of us diminished and yet all of us still here, shining our small lights, keeping awake. I look for a long time at the apple tree glowing in the darkness. And I think that was the moment in cold December when I decided to do something about the webs.

When Gordon Wasson sent Albert Hofmann some *Psilocybe mexicana* from Oaxaca to try in Switzerland to see if he could make an analogue of psilocybin, the chemist decided, as he always did, to experiment on himself. He had made a breakthrough with LSD in this way because unlike his fellow scientists who experimented with rats, he used himself. His instinct told him that certain plants had a relationship with human beings that was particular, and only humans would be able to communicate their astounding properties. The experience with these mushrooms, he would relate to an audience in California several decades later, was unnerving. His colleague, who had volunteered to keep watch over him, turned into an Aztec priest and he became terrified that the man wanted to cut out his heart. It was an entirely Mexican experience: patterns from Mexico swirled about the room throughout the trip. This is perhaps not surprising, you might say, because the mushrooms were, after all, from there. What was surprising was that Albert Hofmann had never been to Mexico.

When we took our first Mexican mushrooms I just couldn't understand why I only felt at home in the conservatory. Why the outside garden and the land beyond looked so irrelevant. Then I realised the mushrooms had been grown in a fishtank in a plastic container. All they had known was the confines of glass and plastic walls, and the artificial light and damp heat we had carefully given them over the course of ten days. Unlike the liberty caps of the Chiltern downs or the wild mushrooms of rainy Oregon or the Mexican rainforest, they had had no contact with the earth. Where these other mushrooms had brought with them the earth-human shapes of Hopi, Mayan or Aboriginal design, these patterns were unusually otherworldly, *stellar*. It became clear that if we wanted to get in contact with the forces of other planets, these mushrooms might be the vehicle by which we could explore them.

However, something was odd about their character. In that first trip, I found I was in a strange position of being aware of the intelligence of the mushrooms inside me, and finding 'me' pushed aside. I didn't think much of that at all. Merging is one thing but a takeover bid is quite another. These 'earth-ships' obviously required a firm hand! When the anthropologist Michael Harner first took ayahuasca he encountered dragon-like beings who told him 'We created everything!' and showed him the whole history of the earth, in which human beings were their definite inferiors. 'They always say that,' remarked the shaman drily afterwards. At one point Harner felt these 'rulers' were malevolent and his humanness was what he cared about most. At that point he took command.

This is a crucial moment on the hallucinogenic voyage. Encountering the other, you realise that what makes you human, your heart, is the most important thing you posses. Sometimes you have to go to the ends of the universe to know this, right until the breaking point, and the vine, the cactus, the mushroom will take you to that point, just so you get it, once and for all. As the trip is coming to an end I find myself-as-chair, turning my head and looking into the ornate oriental head of the *Datura metel* seedpod, and almost jump out of my skin. It is like staring at the mouth of a *naga*:

'Feed me!' it growls furiously.

'Certainly not!' I reply, rather tartly, and then roar with laughter.

I don't know how we stumbled on these structures originally. It seemed they had always been there: the sun cross, the dreamer and the visitor, the door and the chair. Maybe it was because Mark had worked as an advisor and I had worked as an interviewer that we immediately took up the dialogue as a structure for every trip, one in which we would take turns. And maybe it was because we were dramatic in our natures, loving to sing and dance, that everything that arose within in us we embodied and turned into a performance. Most people's accounts of psychedelic voyaging happen in an interior space within themselves, or are projected outward into a kind of screen, manifesting as voices or visions. We played them out, saw them, questioned them, loved them, put them to the test.

What was vital was to remain creative, at play, to keep a sense of the fact we were forging a work together in which we ourselves were the vessel, the material and its mysterious alchemy. Looking back at these years, this is what made the hallucinogenic part of our research coherent. Engaging in these sessions was like an intensely serious and intensely hilarious game of charades. The play and the sense of equality, of taking turns, was crucial. Any time we took the role of shaman or psychotherapist with ourselves or with others it didn't work. You can't go into those power games on hallucinogenics. Things can go badly wrong when the heart is not in command – the atmosphere becomes grim and manipulative and you can fragment and lose the plot. There's enough of that kind of experience in five-sense reality. Your heart is the only part of yourself that can handle the extremity of the voyage.

Why do we voyage into this extremity? Because you don't want to know yourself as a person who just came and went through life to remain comfortable and have a certain amount of money in the bank. You want to know more. Something tells you you are more magnificent than these mundane concerns. The peyote button, the San Pedro key, the blue mushroom opens the door of other possibilities inside. You go about life differently after you have merged with their worlds and gone through that door. You make very different choices, not those directed by your perceived need for comfort or money. Your world changes: the whole world changes as you move through it, as you liberate energy from dead forms, as you move towards climax.

You seek extremity because as you face the howling darkness, you find the strength and the wit inside you to go through the door. In those moments you are working with eternity. Most of human life is spent keeping eternity at arm's length. In ordinary reality people are breezy about death, as if they can handle it by appearing not to take life seriously, but on hallucinogenics no one is breezy, annihilation is coming your way and, if you care about your spirit's integration, you throw overboard everything you no longer need. *Transform or die*, as the big wind in Hawaii told us. Those are the kind of options your ego has when you face the great hurricane of the invisible worlds.

You have to put yourself through the wringer because our modern desire for security is very strong. We have to be shaken up by deserts and mountains, by great winds and seas, by a blue mushroom that brings into our consciousness huge and sometimes terrifying forces our ego cannot handle. This is how you learn to weather the planetary forces of the universe. You do not handle the storm when you are at sea in a boat, you handle the boat in the storm. You don't go with the flow, one step at a time, when you face these kind of energies. You would be mashed in a second. You make sure the boat, the structure for the trip, is sound. Then you set sail into the ocean, all systems go, come what may and make everything up as you go along. You find within yourself everything that is magnificent because when that stowaway ego is no longer playing with the tiller, the real captain of yourself can take charge.

When Stanislav Grof worked with people who faced these forces on LSD he found a universal pattern that emerged out of their struggles: that of rebirth. This discovery led him to develop what he called 'rebirthing', which is a system of breathing that induces the original experience of being born. The four stages of the biological process of natural birth, he observed, paralleled the four stages the participants struggled through within their interior hells. What was happening in this birth process was the destruction of the ego, which is also the world's ego. The breaking down of old forms. Grof and other pioneers thought hallucinogenics were important because they gave modern people, from the industrial age that offered no spiritual guidance, an opportunity to 'slay the ego' and find transcendence on the other side of the door. Because the western world, constructed out of a monstrous collective ego that champions only its own demands for comfort and money, and projects all its negative energies outward onto others instead of transforming them, is driving us all downhill. In the opposite direction to climax.

Though we had often been challenged by hallucinogenics, our experiences with the blue mushrooms that winter came nearest to Grof's clinical descriptions of ego collapse. As soon as we embarked on our investigation of the planetary forces, all kinds of poisons coursed through our bodies. Mark was overwhelmed by the state of the bleeding heart of England, I was overwhelmed with meaninglessness at winter solstice, we were bombarded by the whirling detritus of the shopping malls, of night-clubs, by the desire to fall asleep for ever, to fall into fossilisation, to become trapped in mechanical frequencies that crushed the fluidity of our natural forms, in a merciless dark cold that sucked the warmth from our beings. We found ourselves conversing with aliens, with monstrous aspects of the human psyche, with strange beings that appeared as if from the pages of *Alice in Wonderland*. Our mouths were full of cobwebs. These shrooms were definitely not recreational.

And yet at the end of these difficulties, there was always transcendence. Great waves of butterfly colour rippled through the room. Light burst out of our hearts and the powerful forces of love coursed through our veins. We felt ourselves connected to all beings, on the earth, in time, in the universe. The planets emerged as luminous energies and intelligences within us; we showed each other our Jupiterian thunderbolts, our Venusian beauty, our ancient moonfaces, our earth dance. Who are the gods of the mysteries? They are ourselves. That is the great mystery. Apollo, Hermes, Persephone. The sun, our star, in human form.

By the spring of 2004 we had worked with all the planets of the solar system. In the light of the summer we went outside. We began work at a local arts centre, ran a flower exhibition at the local museum, went swimming most days. At the following autumn equinox I found myself in Norwich market once more. It was already a different year. The market was under reconstruction. The wooden labyrinth and its narrow alleyways were being pulled down, and the underworld that once lurked within its dark warm embrace was being driven out. The loophole in the law which had allowed the sale of the *Psilocybe mexicana* was about to tighten. A door was closing. I bought a handful of fresh gangly-looking mushrooms and some dried diviner's mint from the young tall man who no longer recognised me. Mark had wanted to try this hallucinogenic sage from Mexico for many years.

Whirling, whirling, whirling. I am walking down the stairs. Far too many mushrooms tonight, and not from the small glasshouse in our blue room. The walls are fragmenting into cells of light and energy. 'Stairs!' I command as I peer into the dissolving space, and focus on walking down them, one by one. The living room is collapsing. Nothing is solid or real. Everything is up for grabs. Mark is laughing like a lunatic. There is no structure and at that moment it feels impossible to remember anything, or even imagine such a thing.

That's when I notice the table. The table around which all our dialogues have taken place. An old painting table made of pine deal. While everything else is expendable in this chaos of breaking and whirling form the wooden table is still, present, and warm. Its fabric is coherent, intensely alive. It still has the memory of trees. I put my hand on the table and then I know what to do. 'You hold on to what is dear,' I say, and take Mark's hand. 'You are dear to me,' he says, and becomes in that moment sober.

It is a long trip, that last trip we took with the blue mushrooms at the second Autumn Equinox, a voyage from the light into the dark. A point at which everything becomes balanced, clear, exact. Eventually the whirling stops, everything calms. The walls cohere. The stars outside burn fiercely in the cold night. We go to sleep. When I close my eyes I see the earth spinning like a top, faster and faster in space, powered by an intense fiery core. As it spins, energies and forms that have no earthly root, who have ventured too far from home, are thrown off into outer space by its centrifugal force. There is an incredible hum that emanates from this spinning globe, that sounds like a thousand bees. *Feel the sun inside you,* whisper the departing blue mushrooms in my ear. *Hold on to what is dear.*

III
PLANT COMMUNICATIONS

In the spring of 1999 the plants entered our lives in a dramatic way. They were always entwined about the borders of our travelling lives, but it wasn't until we came to live in Oxford that we began a formal exploration into their green universe: to enter the doors of perception ushered by the red geranium and cottonwood tree, to access our deep memory of the earth, initiated by the hallucinogenic mushrooms and cacti.

Our communications began one rainy afternoon by the river Thames in a small patch of commonland called The Kidneys, where a young activist called Heather placed a small shiny leaf into my hand. 'Put it in your mouth,' she said. '*Crataegus monogyna*. Bread and cheese, we call it,' and then she handed me a dog violet: ' Look!' she said. 'They're everywhere.' And as I looked at my feet I saw these small flower-faces glowing in the wet spring grass and felt a sudden jolt inside. It was as if someone had turned on a switch. After that day we started to notice flowers everywhere we walked – ivy-leafed toadflax on ancient walls, sky-blue speedwells on kerbsides, the leaves of the city whitebeam, limes and beech trees unfurling themselves into a washed blue sky.

Shortly after this radical flower encounter I came across a book called *Plant Spirit Medicine* in a local bookstore, which stated that anyone could speak and dream with plants. All plants had 'spirit medicine' and most especially the native wild weeds that grew just outside your door. Intrigued, Mark and I walked out of our front door with a wild flower guide in our hands, and went to meet the plants. We began a dialogue with them and with each other about them. We called it *plant communications*.

Communicating with plants, like the solar path itself, entails two explorations: one goes outward, finding and observing the wild plant in its natural habitat, and the other goes inward, exploring its inner workings by employing a technique used since the archaic times to contact the hidden worlds of nature. This is variously known as *shamanic journeying* in plant spirit medicine and *iatromantic* work in the ancient world. Although we adopted the modern version of this practice by lying in a cave-like dark and stilling our consciousness with the sound of a drum, we did not follow its usual procedure. Rather than entering the imaginal dimensions by a chosen path or gateway and meeting the spirit of the plant as a separate entity in a (typically) humanoid form, we placed our consciousness next to the plant we had visited and received a readout of how its dynamic, form and intelligence interacted with our own. In order to give our findings the correct attention, we spoke to each other out loud about our experience, following the same principles we had when holding a dialogue about our dreams.

Plant communications, like all nonhuman encounters, require that you bypass your well-schooled rational mind and use instead the wild, open territory of your imagination (as perceived by the right hemisphere of the brain). You have to do this because the rational mind (or left hemisphere) is a ferocious editor of experience and will only see the other dwellers of this planet as subject to its dominance. Even the most radical ecologist, happy with one-world concepts such as the sentient earth, Gaia theory or quantum mechanics, will remain separate from what they are speaking about. As a result the communication is all one-way. The human being is in control, the talking observer, while the earth remains the silent observed. However our ancestors did not have this kind of relationship with nature. Their dialogue was two-way because the world they accessed was one that is held in common by all living forms. The plant, the animal, the rock and ourselves are living in the same dream of the earth. It was to re-enter this dream that we started our inquiry.

Oxford is a city full of green spaces, and its meadows, canal banks, riversides, wastelands, university parks and gardens became our open-air botanical laboratory. We began an active *visiting* of plants around the city and making a record of how these interactions affected our lives. Back at the house we initiated a series of *plant dreamings* (later known as *seeings*), imaginal and exploratory dialogues with the plant world. These inner world investigations not only provided us with an 'alphabet' of flowers, so that we could develop a lexicon in which to exchange information, but also provided an unexpected bridge in our communications with other people.

In the beginning we set forth with our new companions in the creative spirit of adventure to meet with individual plants: the herb robert that sprouted between the pavement stones, giant Russian sunflowers in the allotments, Mexican tree datura in the botanical gardens. Often our fellow investigators had spent time in places which had not lost their link with the wild – Australia, Africa, South America – and had taken hallucinogenic plants. As a consequence they were open and receptive to these kinds of outdoor seminar. We were often surprised by the ease and coherence of our communications. Even though we often sat separately beside different plants or trees, the material we gathered always made sense in a composite way.

In 2000 we began to visit certain flower territories in small bands. We walked through city wastelands abundant with St John's wort, an abandoned quarry by the river Thames fringed by hawthorn, and in an ancient hornbeam wood in Kent. Later on our travels, we would explore a yucca-dotted mountain pass in California, go walkabout in a fossilised 'rainbow' forest in Utah, swing up into ancient forest trees in France. After these events we coordinated our findings in a series of dialogues and built up a composite picture of the territory. We called these events *earth dialogues*. We were holding a discourse with the fabric of the earth: not just with the flowers, but also with the creatures and elements that moved through these habitats. The key plants that grew there acted as anchors or coordination points. We investigated these wild places with their layers of time, of geographic and geological time, of what some call the dreamtime, the ancestral lay of the land.

As we journeyed beyond our preliminary field work in the green-skirted city, we found that the land held the memories of the people who had interacted with these territories through time. We walked into dry lands where people held branches of desert rue and could find what they had lost, who cooled themselves with the yellow sap of poppies; into wet lands where people carved walking sticks from a blackthorn or spindle tree, who wrote poems in praise of the humble weeds of the fen, who walked through the bluebell woods in May.

We followed their tracks.

What is an inquiry? A voyage into a unknown territory; an engagement without a goal; a space in which a place, a person, a flower may appear and reveal their innermost secrets. The knowledge of the earth has to be discovered and experienced. That is its nature. If you do not seek, you do not find. The plant inquiry was a practice, something we did on a regular basis so that we could allow this kind of experience to happen. It was based on our former dreaming practice. Following those hermetic contours we went into the field, we went into ourselves, we held dialogues, we wrote everything down. It was a committed look at about one hundred flowers. We were looking for correspondence, at structure, shape, taste, meaning, colour, memory. There was no limit to our enthusiasm. In this academic time, the time of the inquiry, we developed certain methods and terminologies (see appendix) which enabled us to share these communications with other people.

In the beginning, you look at everything. You look at the flowers in the places, with the people, in the creative work of writers and explorers. You consult Nicholas Culpeper on wormwood and borage, Edward Thomas on southernwood and aspen; you study intensely the black and white pictures of thistle heads and yarrow stalks photographed by Karl Blossfeldt. You talk with the seed collector of the Botanical Gardens about the members of the Solanaceae family; with the Yugoslavian man who gathers sorb apples from the green autumnal floor. You ask the woman who works at the local apothecary about the meaning of ash leaves. Your eyes scan all flower guides, so that you recognise every flower in Britain, even though you have not yet found them; you yearn to find the obscure and rare, those plants that grow in far locations. Their names shift about your imagination: the scented bog myrtle, the brilliant blue viper's bugloss, the extinct thorow-wax. You learn to speak botanical Latin; you drink the leaves of wayside plants, boil up hedgerow jams, suffuse oils with petals, burn tree resins, collect cones, put apple twigs on the fire. You carry your notebook, your camera, your sharpened drawing pencil everywhere you go. There is not one tree in the neighbourhood you do not recognise; not one wall you have not scoured for small ferns and lichens. You immerse yourself in the fabric of the plant world that spreads like a carpet before your feet: fallen petals, winged seeds, rough barks, sour fruits, shiny nuts. Everything fascinates you. But most of all you love your original research. You love the world the way all nature-lovers do, extravagantly: you look at the sky and say, Today is a good day. You walk out of the front door in search of the wild, the beautiful and the free.

dandelion
Port Meadow, Oxford 1999

I looked at its sunny face in the tangled grass and laughed. We were walking through Port Meadow, searching for a plant to begin our dreamings with. It was April and small flowers were springing up everywhere – henbit, speedwell, dog violet, ground ivy. In the streets the cherries were flowering. But wherever I looked this yellow spiky flower disc caught my eye, pushing up through pavements, walls, cracks in car park tarmac, railway sidings. Everywhere hundreds of small suns with their ragged urchin leaves were shining forth. *I can cope with everything but not dandelions,* boomed a loud invisible voice as we walked home. I peered through the hedge and saw a North Oxford matron, standing outraged by her invaded garden path.

'I think we'll start with dandelion,' I said.

At the beginning we called our interior journeying *drumming and dreaming.* Listening to the beat of a *bodhrán,* we lay in the darkness and allowed whatever images and messages came to us in the space of half an hour. How did we know these images came from the plant? There was the presence of another intelligence which you could discern, an intelligence that was distinct from your own. You recognised this from your visit to the flower you held in your memory, when you noticed something striking, something original about its form. People who watch birds call this the *jizz:* how each bird moves, stands or inhabits the space. Black specks are flapping across the horizon, out of the corner of your eye a sharp wing flashes past; knowing the jizz of crows and hawks you see the specks are jackdaws and the flash is a sparrowhawk. It cannot be anything else. You know a flower in the field by its unmistakable colour: only the scarlet pimpernel is that kind of red; only the larkspur that kind of blue. There is something particular in its shape, emanation or scent, its presence, the way it appears, that makes you know instinctively, before you know in your mind, that it is a beech and not a hornbeam, a sow thistle and not a hawkweed. You know these images that appear in the seeing belong to the flower because they contain the essence of the spiky dandelion: they are not the kind of images you would make up yourself.

I am remembering goldness, ragged leaves, bitter sap, entering a deep space within myself, the way all creators do, 'so that imagination can meet memory in the dark,' as Annie Dillard once called it. Dillard, a peerless observer of nature, wrote in lonely shoreline huts and deliberately shut out the view; Chinese sages dwelt upon the complexity of the *tao* by retiring into the deep recesses of mountain caves. In Oxford, after looking at the sunny faces of dandelions in Port Meadow, I go home and lie down on the wooden ship that is my bed, next to Mark. We close the curtains and we close our eyes.

You close your eyes, turn away from the world to access your own abilities to perceive at depth, to see beyond five-sense reality and behold the energy that lies behind the form, the inner sun of the dandelion. Here in the interior of ourselves, as we begin the enquiry, we search for subtle signs, clues, words, images, nuances of meaning, a shift in awareness, a change in temperature. In the dialogues that follow we explore and bring together the form and dynamic of our interchanges. In contrast to the dramatic all-encompassing experiences of peyote and San Pedro, our work with plants in Oxford goes at a modest grammarian's pace. It is slow, thorough, paved with small triumphs. As we look at the individual flowers we begin to see how each plant fits into the living fabric of the earth, how its energies relate to our own. How the plants make us feel is always the key in our communications. Good communication depends in great measure on an ability to feel another's presence, to know their jizz, their original form. Fellow feeling, whether for plant, people or place, is what brings about a meeting of the heart.

The heart takes you into the spirit of things, takes you to the place where everything is connected. We realise that no matter how the plant makes us feel when we behold it or sit beside it – joyful, or at odds, energised or depleted – that feeling will be a way through into the dialogue. The dandelion that spring day made me feel unaccountably happy, liberated. When I heard the offended gardener, I loved the plant for being an upstart, such a terrible commoner, growing with abandon everywhere it could, pushing through the stones of civilisation come what may. It was reminding me of myself, my real self, not the hybrid self that was trained to feel cowed by autocratic high-bred matrons. Wild plants always remind us of our true forms because they themselves are true forms. It is what they are doing, their relationship with the human world, keeping us on track, in touch with the life that really matters.

I did not see the flower's sunny face that day in the seeing, but all its other parts. They came in the form of a royal family who were not on speaking terms, a family rather down on its luck. The seed was a king who was very melancholic, the root a French queen who was haughty, the sap was a crown prince who only cared about his dandy looks, and the leaves were frisky young princes who played without a care. In fact, no one really cared about anything or anyone. They were a most *disunited* family.

I related everything to Mark.

'But what does it mean?' he asked.

'How do I know?' I said rather snappily.

'Is that you or the dandelion speaking?' he said.

We looked at each other in a kind of shock.

Why was it shocking? Because I don't normally snap. Because it had *worked*. We had set out to have a dialogue with the plant and the plant immediately had spoken back, not just by showing a composite image of its workings, but with words that jumped out of my own mouth. This is what we found out at the beginning: plants 'speak' by resonating with the parts of yourself you are not necessarily in touch with, which you then voice out loud; they speak by showing these parts in a kind of pictorial language, in which subtle things are touched upon and made apparent, which you then find words for.

The dreamings of flowers, as we had found earlier with night dreams, did not respond kindly to interpretation, to meanings imposed on them from the outside. We realised you need to behold the images and feelings you receive and let those images work in your imagination without organising them according to your rational mind. You need to make connections you would not normally make, cross-reference, translate, imagine, invent, find words. The solar workings of plants are like a dance that needs transcribing in our daylight consciousness. Not because you are unable to *understand* the seeing on its own terms, but because voicing these connections and creative links out loud are how we communicate with the earth. It is part of our consciousness making meaning in the world.

When you look at a flower you look at everything, from all angles.

The essence of the information will be similar for most people, but the images will differ according to each person's intent. Although I had approached the plant as a medicine person might, my interests were metaphysical and evolutionary, so the 'information' I received from the plants took this form. It answered my own inquiry into consciousness. This was not just medicine for the body, it was the stuff of paradigm shifting.

The family were disunited (I will find out later that its Latin name *taraxacum* means remedy for disorder). This, however, did not mean that the plant was showing me that unification was the order of the day. Quite the opposite. The relationships within this severed family and their disputes were old and outdated and needed to be overthrown, while retaining the positive qualities they exhibited.

The dandelion is a principle medicine herb. Like other common weeds gardeners throw out of their kingdoms – horsetail, nettle, yarrow, burdock – it is an excellent tonic for the blood, keeping it pure, rich, flowing (just not necessarily blue). Northern Europeans have sought out its bitter leaves for centuries to keep themselves in balance. It is a great equaliser of the system. Its roots are particularly useful because they are full of building-block minerals. The king is a miser because the plant itself is a great hoarder of iron and copper. It is also one of the most effective urinary herbs (the king is pissed off) and a spring tonic for any system that has become stiff, cold and mean.

But the dandelion is addressing other issues that affect our physical beings here. The hierarchical systems we uphold in society are stiff like this dandelion family. You can see this in the static forms we seek to emulate, in political positions and religious statues, in our worship of form and ritual, in our hoarding of money and metals. The stiff-upper-lip élite are trained to be rigid: rigid manners, closely kept traditions, closely guarded secrets and bank accounts, clipped speech, clipped hedges. As this hierarchy extends its influence throughout the collective, everything stiffens up, seizes up, not just our manner with each other but also within our bodies. We live in a collective of creaking bones and joints. The fluidity and spontaneity of our feelings dry up and we become pissed off and bitter and self-obsessed. Dandelion releases these crystallisations in the body, caused by the accumulation of uric acid. It cures our jaded livers and kidneys. And, if we let it, it will cure our minds of our terrible worship of hierarchy.

The seeing was simple and yet it was complex. In fact, the more I looked at the dandelion images, the more complex they became. The sunny flowers had seemed simple as they shone in the meadow grass, our visit to them that day almost inconsequential, but the more attention we paid to their presence, the more composite the picture they presented. I felt there was never enough you could say about dandelions. This phenomenon of *seeing* I recognised from the dreaming practice. The more you observe a particular dream detail, the more the observed object will reveal itself. This is a quantum quality the soul brings when it pays attention – quantum seeing, if you like. The *idea* of quantum seeing is often talked about. The concept of the observer and the observed is almost a cliché, but very few people actually live their lives and see reality according to the quantum paradigm. When it comes to *being* the observer, rather than talking about it, Newton and the Rational Mind still hold their separatist sway.

However, plants require you to see in this quantum way. They require that you see the world in relationship, not, as the king and queen are, in isolation. You are not seeing with a closed mind that is cut off from, not on speaking terms with, what it is looking at, but with an open mind that is making connections and in communication. The mind here is the interface, not the controller of perception. You have opened this mind to the intelligence and communication of the flower so it can reveal its components, both in intricate detail and as part of a cosmic pattern. Which also includes yourself.

What was the royal family saying? I saw that dandelion is above all a *common* flower. It is a born proletarian. We found it on common land. It grows everywhere, showing its sunny head almost all year round, through every crack and cranny, even in the gardens of the high and mighty, causing them great exasperation. *I can cope with everything but not dandelions!* Why dandelions? Because they are uncontrollable, unpredictable, throwing their seeds wildly and joyfully into the wind. Because they are named after the regal lion who says no matter which house we were born into we are all born with the same hearts. And those hearts have teeth. They snap and bite when they are controlled, and most especially by the mummy queen, daddy king, son prince archetypes that dominate us, the *ancien régime*. The *dent-de-lion* dandelion is telling us to show our teeth, to show our mettle and most of all show ourselves.

Because the dandelion is also a flower of the sun. When I went out with Mark in those early pioneer days we took a wild flower guidebook with us and learned to recognise the plants using the Linnean system of taxonomy. It is a good way to identify plants, though I never liked the snobbery that goes with knowing the botanical Latin names. When you know the flowers you can drop the system. However, these flower groupings or families can sometimes contain useful hints as to the plant's characteristics. For example, the dandelion is a member of the sunflower, or composite, family. It possesses the qualities that many composites have of breaking up the negative effects of the old order and establishing new conditions on all kinds of levels – mental, emotional, physical. Echinacea, for example, is a composite medicine *par excellence*. It chases away the colds and flu and inflammations that are so prevalent among the collective when the establishment holds its clammy sway. The popular composite herbal remedies – chamomile, marigold, arnica – all have these simple and yet complex actions. Chamomile will make you go to sleep, calm your digestion, soothe inflamed gums, clear hay fever, combat all kinds of allergy, everything that is caused by an over-controlled unnatural existence.

Botanically, however, the composite flower is most striking for another reason: its structure takes the form of a group of flowers. You can see this most remarkably in the sunflower itself. The flowers open by radiating from the outside rim and moving towards the centre, a spiralling host of tiny sweet-scented golden flowers that invite the bees to join their circular solar dance. The composite flower is last in the evolutionary line of flowers, signalling that the highest development on earth is within a group structured on the workings of the sun.

In the seeing, the dandelion was displaying its composite signature. It is a group flower but the group it was showing was not one that it favoured. It was a royal family in need of a revolution. And I, as the observer, the one looking at the observed group, was the revolutionary daughter in the family, about to overthrow this hierarchy so that a very different kind of group could begin to form.

Egalité, fraternité, liberté! shouts the dandelion from every lawn in the land.

It was then that I realised the sunny flowerhead that had been absent in the seeing was my own.

113

Some people say that the basis for a whole relationship takes place in the first fifteen minutes of a meeting. Initial conditions are always key. This was certainly true of the plants. The first plant became the signature for all the other plants that followed. Our meeting was simple, direct, witty, complex, demanding, iconoclastic and pragmatic. The plant communications established with dandelion were all like this. It was a radical relationship from the start.

agrimony
Botanical Garden, Oxford 1999

That summer the botanical gardens became one of our principle places of study. At the end of the millennium these were one of the planet's greatest living libraries. An old-fashioned walled garden, formally laid out according to the different flower families, shaded by mature trees and harbouring some of the world's most extraordinary plants. A perfect reading room for the plant practice. During our early explorations hardly a week went by when I did not consult our green archive, entering the gates with my heart beating, not knowing what new plant may have bloomed in the night, or tree acquired fruit. When you learn about plants, there is a joy in their discovery that is hard to equal. Like first love. Even now when I come across a plant I do not know, an exuberance about life I can hardly name fills me. It's a feeling John Fowles describes in his great essay on plants and perception, *The Tree,* when he stumbles upon a rare military orchid in France and responds by falling rapturously to his knees.

We entered the gardens and sat before the plants, learning how to interact with them. On cold days we would go into the glasshouses to sit among the potted cacti of Arizona and Mexico, or in the warm tropical heat by the lily pond, surrounded by banana trees and papyrus grass. By the quiet beds and rockeries, we would lean against the yews and dawn redwood, linger in front of poke root from the Deep South, euphorbias from Africa, before old world plant medicines like mandrake and henbane, rare natives like pasque flower and herb paris.

Most of our early work took place in the wild green corridors of the city, but some common English flowers we could not find there. Here in the gardens we encountered the soft leaves of marshmallow years before we would find them in the marshlands of East Anglia, or the green flowers of hellebore in the forests of France. One of the very first we came across was agrimony.

Agrimony is a midsummer flower that grows on grassy banks and roadsides. Country people call it 'fairy's wand' or 'church steeples', botanists call it a typical rose specimen, herbalists a useful astringent, historians a folk remedy for poor eyesight and loss of memory. Like all roses you can call it by many names, but always it is itself, a plant remarkable for its soft intricate leaves and spikes of pale yellow petals. The lemony fragrance of its flowers and the tannin in its leaves make a tart and refreshing *tisane*. I find it among the sprawling burnets and cinquefoils one day in June, the great month of roses.

I stop in my tracks before the rose bed, recognising the flower from the guide book. As I gaze at the plant everything around me suddenly takes on a sharp quality of its own. All the sounds in the garden seem amplified. I am aware of people's voices as they come in through the gate, the gardener as he moves around the peony bed, the song of an invisible blackbird, the sunlight filtering through the Persian ironwood tree. All these elements are distinct, yet form an overall pattern. Before I had just been wandering about looking for a plant, unaware of anything. Now I sense my body, my feet on the ground, alert, grounded in this moment in time, part of the picture.

The presence of the agrimony flower has shifted my awareness, keyed me into *the frequency of the earth*. All living beings hold and maintain this frequency: the singing of birds and whales, the movement of aboriginal dancers, the colours of flowering plants. The industrial modern world, however, operates according to a lower, artificially constructed frequency, kept in place by the mechanical mind. Our natural access to the earth's frequency is blocked by our thinking. The vibrant energy fields of plants help us overthrow the domination of thoughts and become part of the picture, so long as we allow ourselves to be shifted in this way.

We are, of course, shifted by plants all the time: by tea leaves, hemp flowers, coffee beans, willow bark. Our bodies respond as the roots and leaves of plants and the fruits of trees enter our systems, as food or medicine. Our hearts beat when the cherry bursts into bloom and the bluebells shimmer in the woods. Now in the plant practice we watch for the moment, sit cross-legged in front of the plant, notebook in hand. Standing alongside agrimony, we ride the subtle shifts that happen and we pay attention.

Entering the emanation of the plant, your thoughts stop. You enter the present moment, no longer trapped in your mind, thinking about the past or the future; you snap out of your separated 'watcher' position and merge with the natural world that surrounds you. A door opens. The trees lean their branches towards you and dance in the wind. You feel lifted. The inner beauty of the flower is shining forth and the garden appears pristine and new. Before, these shifts of frequency happened by accident: they were caused by an extreme emotion, by an unusual sensitivity (nature writers or poets often write about such 'magical' moments). Now you do this deliberately. Still, these moments come unexpectedly. You cannot force them. Sometimes their effects linger for days.

At the beginning of the inquiry all these flower shifts are observed and catalogued. Moving quietly through the greenhouses you notice what your mind, intent on information, searching for buzz and sensation, never notices: how differently it feels to be among the frondy ferns than the dry stern cactus and African euphorbia. How you peer longingly through the locked glass door at the mysterious orchids. Among the rainforest trees and lotus ponds, the air is saturated with the breath of plants. You inhale their fragrance and exhale your own; your breaths mingle like lovers.

You remember so many places as you sit by the still warm water: arriving at dawn in Venezuela, in the singing rainforest in Peru. You become a connoisseur of shade: the shade of the weeping pear, the storm-tossed black pine, the unfamiliar foxglove tree. How this proximity brings you warmth, coolness, stability, refreshment. You become aware how some plants invite you to touch their leaves; how the sweet violets impel you to kneel down to catch their evanescent odour; how by the poke root you instinctively step back to appreciate the structure and colour of its bold pink stems. How some flowers reveal their essences immediately, while others take time. The plants of the garden taught us everything about physical presence: how presence manifests and communicates itself in the world.

Standing by agrimony, the golden rose of the wayside, I found out about active seeing, how to perceive the world afresh. The presence of the flower had an astringent quality that acted upon the physical sight, as well as the sight of the inner eye. I became aware I was seeing from a joint perspective. Everything was intensified, brought into sharp focus. I could see all the details of the garden, I could see from a 360° perspective. As if all the tiny flowers on the spike were conducting a survey readout and sending an input to my consciousness.

Afterwards, in the dialogue with Mark, I found myself articulating the exact procedure for plant visiting that would allow others to locate themselves in time and space, and join in with the plant communications that were to follow.

It was an initiating herb.

In the seeing that evening something extraordinary happened. Just as the drumming tape began and I was about to revisit the scene in the botanical gardens, a figure came into view. It was a giant, dark shape that seemed strangely familiar. For some reason my heart started beating.

Many people meet 'guides' when they travel towards the interior of themselves. They enter the 'spiritual realms' and are greeted by all kinds of teachers: wise men in hoods, imperious goddesses and fairies who tell them what to do. I am sceptical about these interdimensional know-it-alls, especially the ones who declare they are in charge of plants. I am, particularly in 1999 at the beginning of the plant practice, leery of anything that appears 'Celtic'. Not because I am leery of the lands or the people (most of my human ancestors are Cornish, Irish or Scottish) but because every time I mention our inquiry, people would start muttering about Druids and looking meaningful about mistletoe, as if Celts (by which they meant one of the ancient tribes who once ruled Britain) had the eternal intellectual rights to the plant world.

'What about the sacrifices?' I would ask men dressed up in skirts at East Oxford parties and they would stare at me defiantly, as if I were some kind of terrible Saxon, or even worse, Roman. 'How can they go into such denial?' I would fume at Mark when I returned home. And he would tell me I was throwing the baby out with the bathwater.

So you see I knew it was for real when Bran the Blessed appeared in the dreaming of the agrimony.

'Who is Bran?' said Mark after the seeing.

I looked at him.

'I don't know,' I said.

But some part of me did.

Bran is an ancient god, the god of barrows, the archaic chthonic god whose rule in Bronze Age Britain was usurped by the worshippers of Bel, the deity of the sun. When I went to look him up in the library I found he was an oracular sacred king of the alder grove. The Welsh legends sing of his great deeds, when his body lay across the sea like a bridge, and his speaking head lived on after his death, first at Harlech castle, and then in the White Tower at the Tower of London. Bran's bird is the raven, which is why, even though his prophetic voice fell silent thousands of years ago, his talking birds still protect the kingdom's crown jewels. His planet is Saturn, the planet of structure and form, the planetary influence that governs matter, and perhaps most importantly, time. Bran rules the ancient year at the Spring equinox, the beginning of the light half of the year, as the plant world stirs and trees begin to extend their forms into space.

When our dialogue with our native land began, Bran appeared: he was a dark figure, like a tree or a mountain, a presence you could never quite define and yet you felt at home with. In this presence you felt you could know all things without one word being uttered. He came, in the manner of ancestors, to initiate the structure of our inquiry, our interactions with the natural world and its mysterious cycles of time.

In the agrimony seeing Bran showed me the circle of the year. It looked like a round table made of black and white spokes, one for each day. Like Bran, the agrimony plant appeared in the position of the Spring equinox, in the west of the circle, at the beginning of the planetary cycle.

When you work with flowers you work with time, the time that lives outside the linear dates of personal and collective human history, the mechanical wheels of the 24-hour clock. These cycles of time are linked with the sun and moon, with the tides, with the growth of plants and trees, with the planets and the stars, our bodies. This is the time that gives rhythm and meaning to our human lives. Without a deep root in this earth time, you can be held ransom in a superficial world in which your presence on the planet becomes an arbitrary event. It is this deep knowledge of time that was initiated with Bran's table.

Agrimony was the initiating plant for all our future plant work, for both *visiting* and *seeings*. The 52 flowers would be our main helpers in this task. Agrimony appeared in the botanical gardens that day to *gain my attention*. It is the plant of attention for the outer and inner eye, for visiting and visioning work where rigour and tightness, *astringency*, are required. Bran put this flowery spear into my hand, as a joust. When you *see* the fabric of life, you need to expand your vision in order to perceive the whole picture, but you also need to knock off any opponents that stand in the way in a firm but friendly manner.

The opponents you unseat are the interferences of the clockwork mind.

In the presence of Bran, I entered into the ancestral time of the earth. This time is not bound by the historical past and future apocalyptic thinking. It happens in the present moment, in which archaic time, the memory of our beginnings, and the imaginative future, are held. It is in this 'now' that contact with what some call the ancestors can happen. The mind does not like this time because it is not in control of it. It belongs outside its sphere, so it does everything it can to block our access to it. It particularly does not like the sound of the ancestors, who come to remind us of the correct way to live upon the planet. The mind is like the upstart conqueror, razing rainforests and diverting rivers according to whim, cutting Gordian knots, deriding mysteries and oracles and poisoning every wild thing that holds a different frequency and appearance from its mean-faced cities and artificially powered machines.

The mind, instead of being the clever messenger it really is, has declared itself God, an Alexander of the whole world. A mighty ego – I against Them. The wild earth and all those who love to dwell in its sphere (including our own hearts) are, in short, its implacable enemy.

This is a particularly difficult thing for modern people to deal with. And yet we have to deal with it. Because it is our story. To liberate our consciousness from our own tyrannical mind-sets and move instead towards the fair government of our earth-loving hearts is our challenge. For this a small inner revolution, a sea-change within ourselves, has to happen.

For me this sea-change lay in my recognising Bran and the workings of the agrimony flower. I needed to recognise that, modern city people though we are, industrialised to the maximum, the ancestors of our native lands are still here with us in this 'now' of time, if we go to meet them in the ways they originally taught us. Our minds, suspicious, superstitious, all controlling, tell us these things are dangerous and idiotic, not real. But if we trust our hearts, we can trust any knowledge that comes to us in this way, as we sit by flowers or enter the dark spaces of ourselves. The clue lies in our relationship. *Is it creative? Is it free? Does my heart beat?*

I can write this because I distrust any kind of self-proclaimed teacher or god, in any reality. I wouldn't be seen dead worshipping anyone, especially invisible entities with rules and regulations who consider me inferior. Considering how opposed I was to Otherworld helpers, it was extraordinary that Bran appeared at all. However, sometimes someone comes into your life, in a land in which you are a stranger, and they point you in the direction in which you need to go. And you always love them for that. Bran was a way-shower. He showed me how to move out of tight spots and to value strategy. Once I learned how to negotiate the territory of plant *seeings*, he went. He did not come back, though sometimes when I passed along the canal path down by Isis Lock, I would feel his presence as the wind blew among the alder trees. I would stand and feel the water as it flowed beneath the bridge.

Bran came because he grabbed my imagination. Ancestral knowledge comes when your imagination allows it access and in a form that will make sense to you. The beings that hold this knowledge make your heart beat when they appear in the inner worlds because their energy is like your own, so you make them welcome *without thinking*. I had always loved the crow family. No matter how resistant I was to gods and Celts and kings, I could not resist those funny, noisy black birds, just as I could not resist Bran's loyalty or his mysteriousness. These were the keys that opened the door of my mind.

In inner-realm travelling you need to negotiate your terms. Because what you ask for, you get. If you want entertainment, there is plenty available in the invisible realms, all kind of devic shows and parties. But if you want to communicate with the inner worlds of plants you need to deal with them directly and ignore any faery pageants. Most of all you need to be straight with yourself. I wanted something real and evolutionary from our exchanges. I didn't know *what* exactly, but I knew it needed to be friendly to the earth and human beings. I wasn't interested in power. If you want power and control, whether in the otherworlds or this physical one, you have to be prepared to be controlled yourself, because that is the deal.

What I learned in my encounter with Bran is that those whom we might call the ancestors, or original creators, do not want to remain in the libraries, temples and museums where we keep them. They want to have a vibrant and free exchange with fellow creators. They want to be in communication, so they can bequeath their knowledge to those of us that live in this dimension. And in this, they are as discriminating as we are ourselves.

Bran did not 'guide' us in our flowerwork; we undertook everything ourselves. However, he would sometimes come as an informing presence in those preliminary *seeings*, as we observed and experienced the inner workings of many native flowers –meadowsweet, watermint, forget-me-not, yarrow, dandelion, musk thistle, burdock. Once or twice he showed me how to deal with the 'interference' that occurred – how to bundle historical figures into sacks, how not to get waylaid by mythical horror shows. *Forget the rape,* he would say. *Keep in the present. Take command. Tighten up.* By the late summer, as different trees began to enter in our research, I realised that the round table was in fact a map for a circle of trees. Bran was the rememberer of this circle, just as he was a bridge between the worlds. When I went to visit this tree council in the *seeings*, Bran would appear where he had once placed the agrimony lance in my hand, on the edge of Port Meadow, and ferry me across the lake to the imaginal island of trees.

There are 52 plants, he told me in that first seeing, and 365. At the time I thought he was referring to the numbers of weeks and days in a year. No fan of numbers, I dismissed them. However these were prophetic. 52 was the number I dreamed of in Mexico City in 2002, when I awoke with the idea for this book. 52 is the number of tidal waves of light I dreamed in Oxfordshire would shake the world. 52 is the number of hertz in the earth's resonance, the planetary frequency which we hold in our hearts, a frequency no machine can ever mimic or control. And when I went to count how many plants we found in our Oxford inquiry years ago, they were 365 exactly.

Some things you just can't fake in life.

A rose is one of them.

st john's wort
Railway bank, Oxford 1999

Some things you understand instantly. Nobody tells you how to love your best friend, but the moment you see him you know how to love them completely. Nobody teaches you about boats, yet when you jump into a boat and feel the oars, you know how to row, just as you know how to wrap the dead, bake bread, how the scent of roses lifts your spirits. How do we know? It's mysterious. It belongs to a part of us that is not written. Plants contain this kind of invisible knowledge. Sometimes when you find a plant, when you look at the shape of its leaves or gaze into its flower face, you just know. This is because you are understanding how it works in a particular kind of light.

When I first saw St John's wort at the railway gate on that summer's day, it flashed a brilliant ladder of light across my consciousness. I knew *everything* about this plant. I didn't have to visit it again or work with it in a seeing. It was complete vision. All I ever had to do, from the moment I saw it, was bring this plant into my awareness, and it would tell me everything I needed to know. However, our inquiry was based on communication, and consciousness is not just about knowing. It is expressing what you know and passing that knowledge on. The speaking out loud of what we know inside is part of our human experience on this planet. As vital as birdsong, or the roar of the sea, or the wind that blows through the willow trees.

'What did you see?' Mark asked when I returned, flushed with excitement from my discovery.

'I saw light.'

He looked at me sceptically. Light! Give me a break.

'What kind of light was that?' he asked.

'Oh, you know!' I said, rather irritated at having to explain myself.

'No, I don't,' he remarked.

I started to huff and puff. Nobody ever likes to say what they *just know*. You want other people to just 'get it' too. But plant communications require speaking. So I started to stagger about to find words and getting very frustrated, trying to put a peerless abstract design into an understandable narrative structure. What kind of light was it? It was the structure of light in all things, the interdimensional radiance that extends throughout the worlds and governs consciousness. As I started to talk about the solar architectural effect of this plant, I felt everything was expanding, reaching out in the darkness of myself, making sense. There seemed to be no limit to the extent of this solar intelligence. *There is no place where I am not!* I boomed out at some point and shocked myself.

'Oh, that's *very* exciting!' exclaimed Mark. 'I want to see that plant!'

This was our first *energetic readout* – a speaking out of the plant's inner essence as perceived and embodied by ourselves. It is an art, this kind of speaking, and it formed the creative basis of all our practices. It also took a fair deal of practice to get it 'right'. We are not used to speaking in this way, but the plants helped us rediscover this archaic oracular art. And not just in ourselves. When we began working with other people it formed the principle part of our flower dialogues. Everyone was always surprised by what *just came* out of their mouths, by what they *just knew*, but had not articulated until that point.

Just-knowing but not expressing impedes our participation in life on earth. Thousands of books and knowledge systems get in the way of our direct engagement with the planet. Our small minds are made busy with maps and theories and expert views and scientific studies. But these things do not satisfy our heart and soul. For that we need to leave the maps behind, to invent new ways of relating with nature. To get creative and open our mouths.

Generations have loved before us, written about love, sung about love, but this does not stop us from wanting to experience what love feels like for ourselves. To explore the territory as if for the first time. The knowledge of flowers is the same. You can never have enough of this kind of knowledge. It expands through the universe of our consciousness, seeking out what is not yet expressed, shedding its light wherever it goes.

At the beginning of our inquiry the places where we found the plants informed the meaning of our visits. Dandelion we discovered on the common land of Port Meadow, agrimony in the academic Botanical Garden. St John's wort grew in the city wastelands. Its distinctive branched form and its signature dotted narrow leaves and star-shaped yellow flowers flourished down every rough and abandoned trackway. At high summer you could enter the wastelands between the allotments and the railway station and be inundated by a shimmering cloud of gold: the vibrant shine of St John's wort, the deep yellow of Oxford ragwort, and the lemony hues of evening primrose and great mullein. St John's wort even spread onto the tracks themselves, like a flowery carpet of sunshine.

It was here that I first saw how the wastelands of the earth would be restored by the flowering of ourselves. We would not be able to regenerate anything outside ourselves unless we regenerated our own inner landscapes, until our true wild natures had burst through the broken rubble and tarmac of our own artificial city-based worlds.

It was here, surrounded by gold flowers and the scent of buddleia, that I became inspired to make tinctures and salves and flower essences. I collected the flowers of St John's wort in a jam jar of sunflower oil and put it on my sunny kitchen windowsill for two weeks, and watched how the red blood of the plant seeped into the oil (a superlative remedy for kitchen burns). It was here that I began to write a series of short monographs on plants, so others could connect with their 'medicines'. I started to put these plant essences and tinctures into small brown bottles, printed up instructions and give them to anyone who was interested. Generosity was one of the influences you felt down in the wasteland, in the company of those sun-infused plants.

The monographs contained each plant's energy *readout*, its mythological connections, and its physical uses. Each plant had a key word. St Johns' wort was *expansion*. Its ladder of light, its interdimensional radiance, expanded everything I looked at, and as I engaged in communicating what I 'just-knew' my life expanded like a vast network into the collective. Like the flowers that grew towards the path of the commuter trains, shimmering in front of the tired faces of the passengers as they stared out of the windows, at a figure standing there behind the fence among a blaze of golden-coloured flowers.

St John's wort is a major herb of the European pharmacopoeia. It has been used for centuries as a nervine, as a sedative, analgesic and anti-inflammatory, a powerful tonic for the whole nervous system, for those suffering anxiety and hysteria. Recently it has been extensively employed as a herbal remedy for depression. Before industrialisation St John's wort was understood as a plant of the spiritual realms. Its Latin name *hypericum* means 'over an apparition', referring to the flight of spirits who found it obnoxious. It was used in exorcism to chase ghosts and malignant spirits from the possessed and the 'mad'. Even though most people don't 'believe' in spirits any more, it is still used to calm those suffering from nightmares and for frightened children who wet their beds. One of the main properties of St John's wort is that it blocks the actions of certain conventional chemical drugs. It was this quality of preventing the conventional and the artificial in ourselves in order that the intelligence of the sun may properly shine through, that formed the basis of the plant card:

ST. JOHN'S WORT *is one of the great sun plants: a supreme universal connector. If* MUGWORT *is the doorway for the moon or intuitive, oracular self,* ST. JOHN'S WORT *is the doorway to the sun or radiant self. This radiance may illumine and release even the darkest conundrum within yourself and by extension bring lightness and a sense of liberty to everyone you meet.*

The radial structure of this plant is a clue to its effect upon the energy body: a sort of inner 'architectural' expansion. Its own energy is fast and dynamic and can accelerate the frequency of whomsoever comes within its field. From this perspective it is easy to understand why St. John's wort is used by herbalists for depression. However, if you wish to go deeper, to work at the root cause of this depression – rather than just 'fixing' its symptom by giving yourself a sunshine boost – you will find it is related to a lack of interconnectedness with the living beings of the sun and earth, and the alienation and isolation felt by most human beings when cut off from this primal relationship.

I realised it was by aligning ourselves with the workings of the sun in the natural world that we could put life back into our hands. As people appeared who took part in our flower work and spoke out what they just-knew, I saw how these activities restored a sense of self in everyone and released them from the unnatural constrictions of their social and biographical roles. There was something about the *abstract* intelligence of St John's wort that enabled us to see ourselves as part of a moving and meaningful pattern, rather than an accidental appearance in a story or dynastic drama we did not create. As we stood together in the wastelands, we connected with the field of St John's wort all around us – the sun in our faces, our feet on the earth, feeling ourselves like beacons of sun in an earth body.

The greatest work with this solar plant, however, did not happen in the wastelands or with other people but within myself. St John's wort traditionally banishes nightmares, but when I took the tincture I had made from its flowers and leaves, it *gave* me nightmares. At the time the plant communications practice ran alongside our dreaming practice, and the appearance of flowers in our dreams informed an intrinsic part of our work with flowers. We would often put a flower or bunch of leaves by our bed, and notice what dreams would occur the following night. St John's wort never failed to come up with some 'dark conundrum'.

People respond differently to the energies of plants, especially when they are taken as a physical medicine. The nervine plants – skullcap, poppies, valerian – all have a distinctly downward effect on my own energy. Instead of making me feel relaxed, I become agitated. Plants work to keep us in balance. If you are highly strung and tense, nervines will calm you down. If you are sufficiently unwound, you don't need to go down any further.

I was not in pursuit of plant remedies, however, but of plant knowledge. So I took the tincture anyway. Curious to know the structure and content of each plant's world, I followed the tracks of St John's wort in my dreams. They led me down into subways of the dead, into terrifying shopping-centre worlds where no green things grew, into building complexes, into broken lifts where you could be incarcerated for aeons. I moved through administration offices and crowded stations, where tramps and ghouls slept in corners. Sometimes I recognised an ex-colleague surrounded by mounds of paperwork, fixed in front of a computer. Sometimes I would find myself in the operations centre of these underground interdimensional places and cause great commotion. The alarm bells were always ringing. What did I do in these nightmare situations? I looked for ways out. I looked for the door where the sunlight fell. I found those doors and I ran out of them as fast as I could.

This is the mysterious action of the St John's wort herb. It helps us find our own ways out of dangerous artificially constructed realities and back onto the earth where the sunlight is. It is our incarceration in the mechanised world, the repetitive world of the mind, that makes modern people so depressed. Cut off from the revivifying earth-sun dynamics of nature, from natural interactions with one another, our spirits entropy, our hearts fail. St John's wort can show us the way out of these unnatural places, both as a physical medicine and as a spiritual presence. It is a key that opens a door.

There are often great blocks to taking this exit into a greater freedom, not just because we are used to living lives encased in architecture and surrounded by machines, but because in the darker recesses of our imaginations there lurk ancient fears we sense but cannot name. We are held back in all ways in ourselves: from exploring our own mysterious nature, our vast spirits, the intriguing and beautiful planet on which we dwell. Something stops us and keeps us quiet and in the shadows, hiding in subway corners like outcasts. Something stops us from going through the sun's door.

St John's wort, herb of midsummer, is connected to the 'King' mysteries of the summer solstice. In the Celtic year this is the day on which the oak king, ruler of the ascendant year, 'loses his head', his crown, to the dark reign of holly or holm oak. In the manner of all sacred pagan kings he dies on behalf of the goddess. He dies on the sun cross of the year, so that life on earth can continue. St John's wort is named after John the Baptist who supplanted the oak king in the Christian era, and lost his oracular head to the 'goddess' Salome.

These mythologies still resonate within us because they make sense of being human in partnership with the land, in a way our materialistic and scientific focus on the planet will never do. But instead of finding what they really mean beyond these barbarous acts, we push them away and so they remain in the dark conundrums of our dreams. Sometimes they terrify us. We could engage in them as modern people, in a way that does not demand our worship or sacrifice to any god or goddess, but first we have to face our cultural fears of being torn apart in the sun's name for the good of the tribe, that if we prophesy or speak of our own divinity we will be betrayed and lose our heads to those in secular power.

Everyone I ever met was trapped in some way by these terrors. The nightmares of sacrifice that haunt us all and prevent us every day from speaking out what we just-know. That keep us from experiencing the ancient mysteries of the sun and earth that still move through our blood, through the arteries of the land, that will regenerate us all.

St John wort is not about losing your head. It is all about finding it.

In 1920 Alfred Watkins, merchant, amateur archaeologist and inventor of the pinhole camera, stopped his horse on the brow of a hill in Herefordshire and saw in one flash the tracks and leys that spread across the islands of Britain, like a golden interconnecting web. He was sixty-five and he spent the rest of his life charting those leys, working out their meaning and their origin, and communicating them to everyone he met. His book *The Old Straight Track* is a meticulous account of what he saw that day: a network of paths and beacon mounds, water places and mark stones, the workings of an ancient people who once aligned all their routes of exchange across mountains and lakes and moors, according to the mysterious workings of the sun. These paths once existed everywhere on earth. They are the songlines of the world.

Sun visions are like that. You stand one summer's day and look at the hills, or the plants, or the inner workings of yourself, and suddenly you just know. You only see this vision once, in a flash, though you might spend the rest of your life working out what you have seen. Once you have seen the pathways of the sun, you see them in everything. It makes sense of everything you experience, every relationship you have, every communication you have. The light extends into all parts of your life, expanding the knowing of yourself in this life on this earth, beyond all stories, all dramas, all nightmares. *There is no place where I am not.* Once you are aligned with these pathways in yourself, you are walking your way home. I could happily spend the rest of my life showing you the solar tracks of the universe I once saw in a humble 'weed' growing in July by a railway track in Oxfordshire.

sycamore
Cowley Road, Oxford 1999

Sometimes, cycling down Aristotle Lane, I would pause on the canal
bridge that led from Port Meadow into the well-heeled streets of North
Oxford. I would look down at the shining water of the canal, at the
narrow boat going by and the children waving, at the ducks cocking
an eye up at me as they all glided under the bridge together. There
was a calm here at this crossing place. A feeling of lightness, airiness,
possibility. It wasn't until later that I realised that this emanation
came from a tree obscured by the canal's great willows.

The sycamore is a lovely tree. Maligned as a foreigner, as an alien
invasive weed without a noble native history (except for the famous
Tolpuddle Martyr tree in Dorset) it has, in its full glory, with its
smooth reddish trunk and soaring arms, a presence in which you
can feel entirely at home. But you can never quite *know* it. There is
something mysterious about the tree. Something you can't quite put
your finger on right away.

Looking back, I realised it was the sycamore that gathered everyone
and influenced the style of our flowerwork with others. The action of
looking back, I realised too, was part of its medicine. In the beginning
of our inquiry we had worked with plants by ourselves, but always
felt a strong desire to share our findings. When we opened out the
plant practice with other people, the presence of the flowers changed
the nature of our interchanges. In the practice you did not talk from
your head about abstract theories or ideals, but from your heart,
transmitting your physical experiences and feelings and inspirations.
You paid attention to each other in terms of the living systems, rather
than the constructed world. The flowers sat in the centre of the
pine table, like the sun in the solar system, and we talked in turns,
discovering all our relationships with the flowers and ourselves. Our
communications took a circular form. As we looked back at our visits
and *seeings*, we found ourselves more intelligent, more fluid, less
bound by our egos and psychological hang-ups. We felt less impelled
to download the latest drama of our lives on each other, and got down
instead to the more interesting debate of the mysterious nature of life.

Who were these plant companions who sat around our table?

They were the young women of the sycamore. The sycamore is above all a female tree, a light and airy tree, and our first fellow investigators appeared at our door like her spring leaves, full of lightness. They brought their drums, their dreams, their dances. We shared meals, held sessions, made tinctures and flower essences. We were not friends in the conventional sense, nor even colleagues, but in the company of flowers we knew each other and what we were doing. In a mysterious way you could not quite put your finger on right away. Looking back, years later, I called our first companions the A girls because all their names ended in A. They had quite different characters and backgrounds. In the conventional world they appeared unremarkable, almost like misfits, but in the imaginative realms they were all extremely articulate and adept.

The sycamore in Oxford is an urban tree: green-barked, straight up, its signature maple leaves turning gold and russet in the autumn. It grows profusely in the wastegrounds, down by the fields, along the canal banks. Here we are on our bicycles passing under its leafy summer canopy, the A girls and ourselves, as we set out to gather mugwort by full moon, sit by the herb robert, stand in the botanical gardens before heartsease and marshmallow, make a tincture of tansy at the solar eclipse We are laughing sometimes. But not always. The A girls find it easy to access the flowerworlds as we sit in the summer meadow together, around the table, but when the flowers bring their challenges, they falter. It is a difficulty I had not bargained for.

I will not know the sycamore's mature form until much later, when it changes its shape, becomes red, gigantic, its arms soaring into the air, the sturdy guardian in the woodland, the companion of the upland farmhouse. Perhaps if I had known it, I would have considered maturity. The girls are in their twenties, Mark is thirty-seven, I am forty-three. Time makes a difference between us. I have the discipline of a writer, the experience of the world, and the rigour of a practice behind me. The practice brings commitment and an impeccable attitude: it deals with all difficulty as material, as an opportunity for expansion and knowledge. You need this rigour and this commitment, because the practice dismantles all false structures, all ideals and illusions, to make space for the new and the real.

The difficulty I face is that no one wants to go down this particular path right now. The practice demands that the girls look at their families and at their social karma, and in spite of their new-age style they are quite conventional in their 'other' lives. They are waiting like Cinders for a prince to arrive in their lives, and are too young really for the solar path. I don't know this yet. I am assuming we are all comrades in pursuit of freedom and enlightenment and that age doesn't matter. I am sallying forth with these communications in the same way I did with peyote and mushrooms with fellow seekers in my travelling years. Except this is not Mexico, or South America. This is Britain at the turn of the millennium.

Everyone who comes to the house enjoys the sessions when things go their way. We are happy to meet around the table with glasses of limeflower tea in our hands, talking about beauty and inspiration and the future of the planet. But to make a place for the new, you need to deconstruct the old. To be in the lightness of the sycamore, you need to transform that which is heavy. The old clings on: it gathers its heavy archetypal vestments around us and drags us all down. I know the practice; we need to divest ourselves of these costumes, get past those deva shows. But the A girls don't think these things are real. They like the *idea* of moving energy. Illusions, maya, ego – these are spiritual terms that trip lightly from our tongues, rather than powerful inner forces that keep an old world in place.

In the practice, we are engaging in an original dialogue about our place on the earth. The flowers key us into its living fabric. It requires a certain attention, an *alchemical* attention. The flowers, orchestrated to the sun, disturb that which is artificial in our natural beings: as you dismantle these unnatural forms, your own ego rises up in defence of them. To engage in this endeavour we need to be comrades. We need to trust each other implicitly. We need to respect this space. Everyone needs to bring each other back into alignment when the heavy weather arrives in the room, as it always does. But we are not schooled to have self-discipline. When the storm breaks the girls retreat into themselves, into their problems, throw a fit, search for emotional security, for comfort. Their minds wander outside the room; they don't like the feeling of what is being presented.

The feeling, however, is the way through to the spirit in all things. We are not smart in the matter of feelings. As soon as anything uncomfortable occurs, we look for someone else to take the flak.

The practice demands that everyone takes responsibility for their own difficulty and that we hold a harmonic within ourselves. Within this agreement, an alchemy can happen. What is going down between us in the room is going down in the world, I tell everyone. Everyone imagines they are innocent of the world's difficulty. They are not to blame. There is no blame, I say. We are all in a certain territory and we have to make energetic moves. It is not an idea. The girls look at me askance. At this point you need to engage with what is being presented in the room. You need to pull your weight. You have to work. If you don't, someone else will have to pick up the slack.

As autumn arrives in the city and the keys of the sycamore begin to spin through the air, I realise I have been picking up that slack too many times. Something key is missing. The practice had brought fresh air and possibility into our communications. It took us out into the summerland of flowers, brought company to the house, opened everything up. The presence of the plants gave us a stable base for a lighthearted and creative exchange between us. But what the practice could never do was *make* anyone a comrade. I realised that what was missing was the whole point of the exercise.

The mysterious thing I could never quite put my finger on: the affection of the heart.

Heather was definitely not a A girl. An activist and road protester and an expert on the wayward habits of wild camomile, she ran an unofficial meeting house for all the radical souls passing through Oxford at that time. We had met at a Spring Equinox gathering. What are those flowers? I had asked her, seeing a banner with flowers bursting through the tarmac. 'Buttercups, poppies and snake's head fritillary,' she replied. Heather was smart and fragile and tough, and in spite of her limited resources, extremely generous. Like her beloved rolling stone camomiles, she longed to live along a green track, one of those wide grassy roads that wind their way across the land.

I liked Heather because she did things for real. She wasn't playing. She was passionate about wild plants and on principle only grew wild strawberries and Jacob's ladder in her practical vegetable garden in East Oxford. Climbing barefoot into the ancient yew of the Iffley churchyard, we exchange plants: she talks hedgerow botany and the wild places of England; I talk medicine and desert plants of Arizona.

She tells me what life was like living in the oak trees at Newbury, working for the ecological protest group The Land is Ours, and I tell her what life was like travelling and writing on the road. It was Heather who showed me the real difficulties about human-plant communications. Unlike the A girls, she had experienced huge resistances in the *seeing* we had done with a white foxglove. 'It's my mind,' she told us, as we held a dialogue about this tall mysterious flower.

One day we went to the wasteland and I asked her: *Do you want to talk with the great mullein?* We were sitting cross-legged before a roundel of these tall plants with soft greyish leaves and honey-scented flowers. And she frowned, looking at their spikes, and said firmly: *No!* I laughed. It was quite shocking. But at least it was clear.

After the great mullein encounter, I wised up. I had assumed that everyone *must* want to communicate with the earth – *surely*, especially those who said they loved it. *Visiting* was a technique that was simple and easy to learn. What I had not bargained for was the nature of communication itself. That communications, like relationships, are not always two-way things. Mostly they are one-way things about power and position and getting what you want. People, I found out, like to be in control of the earth they are saving, in the same way that one-way lovers like to be in control of what they are 'loving'. But you can't communicate and be in control at the same time.

There was often a struggle in a plant exchange between the mind that likes to control and the heart which desires to communicate. The heart has to be in charge for right relations in the dialogue. But sometimes the inner forces are too strong. You just don't want to let your control go.

I learned a lot about human communication from plants. I realised in spite of my hopes and desires for exploration and expansion that the A girls came to see us because we kept a welcoming house and they felt at home in our company. However, in spite of their lightness and creativity, our meetings were very one-sided and lacked a comrade-like engagement. *It all makes sense here, but when we go out we just forget everything*, one of them once said to us. Because we were older and directed the sessions, we were often treated like parents. Sometimes I would feel disquieted after our meetings, as if to blame for disturbing their peace, or ideas of themselves. Somehow *responsible*. Once, under duress after a plant visit, when I suggested to one of the A girls that perhaps the flowers were presenting something she needed to look at, she shouted: *I don't care what the flowers say, I just want to the bad feeling to go away.*

I thought in my foolishness that people who paid me for a session might engage in the communications in a more sober way. I was not correct. However, unknown to me, the sycamore was about to make its own calm and mysterious appearance and make all matters clear.

John Rose was an irascible man, one of those men who challenge princesses by talking loudly about sex. I have learned, however, that some ogres like to test you, and that once you have passed through their thicket of thorns and not been offended, you often find they are the kindest of souls.

'Oh, I am *far* too old for that kind of thing!' I exclaimed, and handed him my copy for an advertisement.

'Plant communications,' he said, looking at the text. I was hoping to place it in the events broadsheet he published from his house, an extremely idiosyncratic communications centre in North Oxford.

'Talking with plants,' I explained.

'I've heard of talking with plants,' he retorted gruffly. 'What I want to know is do they speak back?'

'Yes, they do,' I replied.

'Ah, now that is very interesting. *That* is worth a free advertisement.' And he took the paste-up from my hand.

Plant Communications went out publicly into the streets of Oxford just as the leaves were beginning to fall from the trees. It flew into the bookstores and cafés, fluttered on the public billboards, and appeared briefly in the *Daily Information* broadsheet printed by John Rose. Bright green, with a background of a black poplar leaf. Not long afterwards I received a phone call.

'I want to speak with my London plane,' said a woman's voice. 'It is about to be lopped. Will you take payment in kind?'

I leapt at the opportunity and agreed the terms. When I told Heather about my first official dialogue she looked at me in that nervous and wise way she sometime did, like a hare.

'Beware,' was all she said.

Heedless, I set forth one bright cold October day to speak with the London plane and the woman from the Cowley Road. We sat in the quiet side street under its bare branches, its fiery leaves at our feet. Holding a professional dialogue was something I learned when I interviewed people for newspapers and magazines. Most journalists prepare for such events, and know what they want before they begin. But I always liked to go forth in the spirit of adventure, come what may, with one or two genuine lines of inquiry up my sleeve.

When interviews are not controlled, people let their guard down and say things they wouldn't normally admit, not even to themselves. However, it's a risky style: sometimes the surprises that emerge are not the ones you might desire. Tempers sometimes fly, walls come down, silences ensue, and you have to weather these moments and get out of all kinds of tight corners. You usually have to lose your cool to get good copy in life.

Not that I had reminded myself of this truism when I set out.

The London plane was a tree I knew well. I had spent my childhood playing under these tolerant beings of the city squares and gardens. Mark and I often visited the great London planes of the colleges and university parks and sat beneath their dappled shade. Their transmissions often concerned the business of transmutation and government. So, assuming this was the tree, I launched confidently into a dialogue about roots, as my 'client' was also originally from the city.

But all the while we were talking about Hampstead, something was not happening. I was trying to connect with the tree but there was no response. The woman started to talk about lopping the branches of the tree (which was her responsibility since it was on her land), about disputes with neighbours, with the town council, with the tree surgeons, with the academics of Oxford, and how *she* just liked to leave these leaves to rot down and become compost, and all the time I was looking at these *keys* hanging from the branches – and to my horror, I suddenly realised we were not sitting under a London plane at all but under a *sycamore*.

I had to backpedal fast and switch our attention toward a tree I knew but had not worked with. Of course, this mistake is part of the proceedings, I claimed blithely, and veered away from our heavy duty London plane discussion about The Patriarchy into what now felt like the airiness and lightness and allowance of the sycamore's vibration. Suddenly I found myself full of inspiration, and talking about letting go of guilt and connecting with the female spirit.

But I had lost all credibility. The mood, which had been friendly up until this point, turned unpleasant and cold. I was distrusted. A fool who did not know her trees! The tree surgeons and I were totally responsible for misnaming the tree and somehow for everything that had ever gone wrong in this woman's life.

Mistaken identity, as I will find out, is part of the sycamore's medicine. Sycamore often appears like another tree – an oak or ash or beech – and even its name *Acer pseudoplatanus* means 'false plane maple'. It leaves look very like a plane's. Encountering trickery is the kind of experience you can have in her field. She is is a formidable presenter of *what is.*

What is is a key quality of the heart. The heart, unlike the mind, can see what is really going on – not what you think is going on, or would like to think is going on. In this clarity you can act on what you see. *What is* is seeing directly what is staring you in the face. Beware! No! *What is* was this uncomfortable moment when I realised I was not there to have a plant communication, I was there to give *spiritual* permission for the tree to be cut. I was there to take the flak.

The civilised world operates by covering up *what is* with all kinds of shows, by party tricks and princess ballgowns, while something quite different goes on. Sometimes our own trust in human goodness, our hopes for a better world, are the greatest illusions we hold. Sometimes we are the greatest fools in keeping illusions going. Under the sycamore I came to realise that, in spite of my desires for interesting two-way conversations, dominating one-way power exchanges between people need to seen for what they are. I saw that those cold unpleasant feelings meant I was taking on a burden that wasn't mine to take.

I am wondering if I can speak to you about something.

And what am I going to get out of it? I started to wonder back.

The sycamore taught me to be bold in the way of all fools. To say the reverse, to ask the unexpected question, to push buttons like John Rose and not give a damn about the consequences. To value *what is* above all things. *What is* did not bring me any more Plant Communications but it brought me space and freedom – the invisible treasure the practice brings. After the 'London plane' visit, I conducted a *seeing* with the sycamore and posted the plant card through the door in Cowley Road. Its main message was about freeing the mind, about not blaming 'Them'. Letting a new wind blow through all our old houses.

Two years later, passing through Oxford on a dark December evening, I went to a talk given by a Native American at the Quaker meeting house. He was talking about shooting arrows into the barricaded western mind, and had a familiar rueful look as he confronted the wall of silent anoraked people in the audience. At the interval the woman from Cowley Road came up to me and apologised: 'A lot of the things you said made sense later,' she said. 'I gave you a hard time, I'm sorry. I was just looking for someone to take my guilt away about cutting the tree.'

'Oh,' I said. (Because what else can you say when you are asked to let someone off the hook?)

I don't want to know what the flowers are saying, I just want the bad feelings to go.

At the end of the meeting the speaker threw back his head and roared a chant that shook the hall and rumbled through all the city's architecture, then floated calmly out into the freezing night air.

In winter the sycamore, like all deciduous trees, loses its beautiful fire-coloured leaves. Its sweet sap runs down to the roots and it stands dormant and still until spring. The morning after the meeting, I woke up and saw the world had turned into a wonderland. Everything was pure white with frost and sparkled in the brilliant clear air. I went down to Port Meadow. It was the time of the solstice and very cold. The hoar frost had sharpened every blade of grass, covered the hedges with rime, and small dark shapes were skating over the frozen lake that had formed in the middle of the meadow. On the way home I paused at the sycamore to collect some of its fallen sticks for kindling. There was no one about, the tree was bare, its branches edged with ice, the canal quiet and frozen, and yet the calm of this crossing place was still there. The A girls had departed from our lives. Heather had returned to Scotland, John Rose had closed his door. It is the same place, but I feel a different person. In a mysterious way I can't quite put my finger on.

Like everyone else, you never want to be a ninny – but you can't avoid it, because the solar path is the path of the fool. You march into situations where angels fear to tread and like all creators – ravens, coyotes and human writers – you get tricked. The joke is always on you. You enter the territory full of hope and good intentions, and you get your tail wet. But when you look back you find yourself smiling: *Well, at least I went in and had a go!* you say, and the shine you felt you had lost comes back tenfold. That is the recompense for creators. You are not prepared, you are not in control, but you are inventive. Because of your original move the sun can get through. This is how creativity always outwits the darkness of the world. And *you* get smart, very smart indeed, and free. You may have lost your cool, but you don't do the same thing twice.

What are most communications, after all? Why do people get so defensive and flaky when a dialogue begins? Because we have been told we are going to have a nice, cosy chat under the London plane, when in fact we are going to have something else entirely.

You could be held for eternity in these unfree dialogues, in these meetings around the table, picking up the slack, taking the flak. One day, however, you find yourself looking at *what is*. One day you say, I don't do flak. That's a good day. That's when the real lightness comes, all your natural airiness and allowing, and a new wind starts blowing through the door. That's when the calmness of the great maple comes to you one winter afternoon on Aristotle Bridge, as you laugh at yourself, at the folly of the world, and head home, carrying the firesticks in your hand.

IV
MEDICINE ROOT

Everything on this earth – each animal, each rock, each tree – has medicine. It is the power of its nature to affect the fabric of life and keep everything in balance. Though we are taught to think of the human form as a genetic machine, this is not our nature: we are ancestral beings of the earth and sun, kin with all planetary elements, each with our own medicine. The living systems of our bodies require us to be in harmony with the living systems all around us. In this crucial art of balance the wild plants come and assist us, as they do all creatures, as they have done throughout time. They enter our spheres and keep us in tune and in synchronicity in this world that is ever-changing, interwoven with the complex and mysterious fabric of life.

However, most of us are, by circumstance, also shaped by civilisation – a human-centric culture in which everything, including the idea that we are machines, is an artificial imposition upon our natural bodies and intelligences. All civilisations impose these restrictions upon living beings, and hold their life-force in artificial containers. None of these are in line with the energy shapes of the earth. The shapes of earth are round, sinuous, warm, fluid; they have rhythm and colour, depth and fluidity. They are shaped like clouds, like mountains, like snaking rivers, rippling grasses, undulating coastlines, our bellies, our hair. The shapes of civilisations, in contrast, are unforgiving and do not respond to our presences: they are hard-edged, geometric, superficial, exaggerated and cold; their colours are harsh and unreal. Of themselves they cannot move, have resonance. None of them bears relation to us, except to our indoctrinated minds. Every living being on earth has correspondence and is related by its kinship; the artificial shapes work within purpose-designed systems which human beings, forcibly separated from this kinship, are educated to believe are superior to the living systems of nature. These systems require huge amounts of energy and maintenance from both ourselves and the planet to uphold. Because they are mechanical, however, they are always entropic. At some point the strain they exert on the natural systems creates too much toxic by-product and those toxins begin to affect the whole.

If any parasite becomes too numerous within a living body it begins to destroy its host and thereby brings about its own destruction: when the management of nature becomes too drastic ecosystems collapse, species disappear, human minds dissolve and bodies break down. The borders of the Empire prove too difficult to maintain and our immune systems weaken. Within the collective new psychologies, new formulas and new illusions are introduced to deploy the effects of this stress and to 'detoxify' the people, so they keep serving whatever civilisation – Aztec, Roman, industrial, consumer – is controlling them. However, it is an uphill struggle against the ravages of time. Living in this heartless authoritarian way, the heart, governor of our natural selves, finally gives way, the population becomes senile, the link between what is proclaimed and what is real becomes more and more tenuous and eventually the city walls fall down. All civilisations, no matter how powerful, invariably collapse. Whether we, as individuals or a collective, undergo a cultural psychosis or what is known as a healing crisis at this point, depends entirely on our intent.

Within this context the plant medicine of the earth is not an alleviator of stress or physical break-down but a re-engagement with the living systems, so that human beings might transform themselves and avoid such a dramatic end-result. It was in this spirit that the medicine plant part of our inquiry proceeded. We wanted to know how an ordinary western person – male or female – might realign themselves with the earth. What did the plants have to say about our realignment? What part did they play in this process, on the physical, emotional, mental and spiritual levels? How do we, as earth dwellers, fit into the natural fabric of life? Do we contain a medicine in ourselves, as individuals and as a collective, and if so, what might that be?

The position from which you understand experience is pivotal. Medicine plants will affect the physical body, but you have to enter the spirit of the plant world for it to shake your world. Many herbs are used by modern people, but they are taken in the same way as an allopathic cure. We take medicine to get back to the place we were before, period. We are in control of this process. Plant medicine, on the other hand, gets you back to the place where you are in alignment with your real being and the planet that sustains you. This requires your participation: you may need to change the relationships within yourself, to drop habits, absorb new energies, live differently, think differently. In this relationship, we are not in control of the process, we *are* the process.

This shift of position is vital for an understanding of plant medicine, as it is in any exchange with the nonhuman living systems. The difficulty lies, as I had already discovered in plant communications, in our refusal to relinquish our mind's dominion over wild nature. Even to allow the possibility of any alternative way of thinking or interacting with life. The Swiss anthropologist may relate interesting data about Amazonian *vegetalistas* influenced by ayahuasca, but when he takes the vine himself and has similar experiences his report is considered invalid, even dangerous. OK for rainforest tribes, OK for aboriginals, OK for first world nations, but not for educated white people. White people are in charge, in control. They don't see visions on ayahuasaca, or talk to plants; those that do are deluded and to be avoided. The fact that most white people long to have a connection to nature, and are sick in ways they cannot heal because they lack such a connection, is deemed to be beside the point. We just don't do that kind of thing in Europe.

The medicine of ourselves as a result is hard to know. To understand the balance of life and the ways of the moving earth, modern city-dwellers need to radically adjust the way they allow and synthesise their experiences. To interact with life, you need to let go of control and submission and learn about reciprocity and relationship. You need to immerse yourself in the territory, learn how to receive and absorb many kinds of input like the earth, how to be active and invigorating like the sun. You need to rediscover the technology of your own body, your heart, mind and will, and no longer just put your energies into upholding fixed positions within the status quo, supporting its manufactured life-styles and belief systems. To undergo this kind of transformation you have to go outside the city and follow a path of self-discovery.

I discovered my own medicine way in dream. It was about medicine roots and a direction I needed to take:

I am standing in Kensington Gardens by Lancaster Gate. Behind me is the fountain garden, formal, made of stone, and in front of me, underneath a group of London plane and sweet chestnut trees, is a huge shed with shut-up windows, like a battery-hen barn. Above this is a configuration in the 'sky', like a mathematical diagram. This diagram shows intersectional points that make up an interdimensional map of the human form, powered by a purple crystal. The crystal is very far away. Below on the 'ground' are two roots next to each other. The shed, I am given to understand, is the prison of the human collective. In order to liberate ourselves from this prison we have to choose, I have to choose, between the configuration in the sky and the roots on the ground. The roots are called by the names of two tribes. One is called Nayum, which I do not recognise, but the other I do. It is Tungus.

The Tungus are a Siberian reindeer tribe, famous for supplying the modern world with the word and concept of the shaman. A voice was telling me I needed to use these two roots. In effect, I was being asked to choose between an esoteric knowledge governed by a faraway power, linked with the mind, and a shamanic knowledge to do with the earth.

I chose the roots.

I chose the world I did not know. I stepped out of the city park into the Siberian tundra where the reindeer move silently and very fast. Unlike the crystalline diagram, which was clear, this territory was not. It had no maps. When I arrived at its cold and windy edge all I had was my own intelligence and the courage of my own heart. And with these I set forth.

At the beginning of the solar path in London in 1990, I was thrown into a certain type of dreamworld. These were all places formed by the ancient and classical architecture of the mind – museums, art galleries, churches, underground chambers, spiral staircases, formal fountains, mystical symbols. I was given the Jewish Kabbala, I was told I was a renegade member of 'The Nine', a group of Egyptian deities. All kinds of mystical and arcane rambling went on. But there was always something sinister and gloomy about these dream places, and often there would be scenes of bloodshed and terror. I always felt trapped and wanted to get out. *What's the matter?* asked one museum attendant as he advanced ominously towards me. *Don't you like the Celtic section?* To tell you the truth, the Celtic section gave me the heebie-jeebies. *Run!* I would yell to Mark, and we would find ourselves outside in the fresh air.

So it was not surprising I chose the roots in the dream. They were at least in the fresh air. Though as I found out, these roots were not my destination. They were the way through.

I needed these ancestral roots because it is our allegiance to high culture that holds us captive within the shed. The mindset of the western world, founded on scientific rationality, is enlivened by its collections of knowledge and artefacts raided from the archaic and natural worlds. The intelligence of native peoples is not considered valid except under the guise of science or entertainment (i.e. from the viewpoint of its own dominance). However, as many arbitrators of western consciousness have realised, from Plato to Jacques Derrida, the city *logos* is totally dependent on the barbarian *mythos* to describe itself. It needs its stories and dramas, its dance and music, its colour, its mystery. It also has to control all these with its conquistador will, so no one will realise that *everything* comes from the *mythos*. The city of civilisation is dependant on the earth. It is not the other way round. But no one in control of this civilisation likes to pay this fact any kind of real attention.

The indigenous knowledge of the earth is therefore only understood as the intellectual *property* of civilisation. It reaches our imaginations via the reports of scientists or explorers who search for material in the rainforests or desert or tundra. Most of what we know about plant communication comes from anthropologists' and ethnobotanists' field studies of traditional medicine, especially of hallucinogenic plants. It comes from books like Jeremy Narby's *The Cosmic Serpent* and the work of Michael Harner with the Amazon *ayahuasqueros*, Gordon Wasson's seminal encounter with the mushroom healer,

Maria Sabina, in Mexico; from books by modern medicine men like the African Malidoma Somé in *Of Water and Spirit,* coworkers with traditional plant healers such as Rosita Arvigo in *Sastun,* based on her experience with the Mayan Don Jose Panti in Belize, or from accounts by individual 'psychonauts' such as Terence McKenna in *Food of the Gods,* with his original take on the matriarchal world that once existed in Turkey.

I started my own inquiry into medicinal plants inspired by these books, and later by my own inner and outer travels in Mexico and South America. I did not seek out instruction from any native medicine man or woman. Instead, I explored a series of hallucinogenic plants within what might be called a shamanic context, in order to reconnect with the ancestral spirit of the land. I did this with fellow explorers, learning from direct experience and our own original and creative work. When Mark and I began our plant communications in Oxford in 1999 we immersed ourselves in the 'language' of these plants and the study of herbal medicine. We were intent on knowledge, on practice, on encounter. We used our own bodies as our material, becoming both patient and apothecary; soaked ourselves in water scented with cedar and birch, burned juniper leaves and myrrh, inhaled thyme, drank decoctions of wild cherry bark, applied poultices of linseed and salves of great mullein, dried valerian roots, hung bunches of nettles from the rafters, rubbed our bodies with rose oil and chamomile. In the garden we grew rosemary, rue and angelica; in the wild places we collected skullcap and tansy flowers. We noted the effects of all these plants on our physical, mental and emotional bodies and dreams, and held *seeings* in order to find out how their structural make up could assist us in our pursuit of realignment. We pored over old-fashioned herbals and new-world research into flower essences, studied the elements of the Chinese system, the Ayurvedic spices. We came to know ourselves in terms of temperature, taste, humour and season. To recognise the value of bitterness, of deep sleep, of warmth, of breath.

One midsummer's day we picked a bunch of yarrow from the meadows and made our first tincture. It was a medicine to strengthen mental boundaries, to help differentiate between what was ours and what was not, to detoxify our minds from artificial environments. Like many of our medicine plants, it was a medicine that helped us reconfigure ourselves in accordance with the sun.

My intention in all these activities was self-transformation. I never had any intention of becoming a medicine person or healing other people. However in the years that followed I found myself working with herbalists, dispensing remedies, being called upon for spiritual and medical assistance and facing the kinds of demons shamans have had to battle with for thousands of years – the darkness of the human heart. Even though I never worked officially as healer, because our inquiry involved working with medicine plants, I encountered many people who expected others to take on their burdens for them. At times I found myself overwhelmed by their unexpressed rage, by their nightmares, by their family ghosts who pursued me down the corridors of time. The traditional shaman deals with the darkness for the sake of his tribe. But what if the darkness were of the tribe's own making? What if he were just being used to keep the same old invisible battles and power structures going?

The modern version of the shaman – the sin-eater, the transformer of poisons – I came to realise was one of the greatest blocks to our liberation from the prison shed and the enclosing architecture of the city mind.

As I held in my hands the roots of the dream – one called Tungus and another whose name was now forgotten.

hemlock
Port Meadow, Oxford 1999

You do not expect gentleness. But gentleness was what came with her green touch. Gentleness, joy, humour, warmth, affection. In short, everything you would want to experience in the company of another being. If I had to characterise the essential nature of my communications with the medicine plants it would be summed up in the meeting with this one flower. But if I were to tell you its name, you would probably recoil in horror.

In fact, most people did recoil in horror, for hemlock is a plant that inspires perhaps more dread than any other. Even professional herbalists turned their backs on it and shuddered. This is not necessarily because it is poisonous. Plenty of plants are poisonous and don't inspire dread. It is not even a scary-looking plant, appearing to the untrained eye just like cow parsley. Most people aren't aware of its very common presence and walk by it without a care. However, the name 'hemlock' will cause them to shiver. This is because its most common association is as the poison that killed the stoic philosopher Socrates, the hero of the rational mind.

Robert Graves, in his extraordinary work of seer- and scholarship, *The White Goddess*, looks at Socrates' crime from the perspective of the Goddess, an example of what happens when a city logos disrespects the earthly *mythos* and does not accord it its proper place in life:

> '... it was the male intellect trying to make itself spiritually self-sufficient. Her revenge on Socrates – if I might put it that way – was characteristic. She found him a shrew of a wife and made him fix his idealistic affections on the same Alciabades, who disgraced him, growing up vicious, godless, treacherous and selfish – the ruin of Athens. She ended his life with a draught of the white-flowered, mousey-smelling hemlock, a plant sacred to herself as Hecate, prescribed to him by his fellow-citizens for the corruption of youth.'

The *mythos*, which for Graves is the true root of all poetry, is the subject of his book. However, he writes this from a male historical and academic point of view in which woman is Muse and Goddess.

From the female perspective things sometimes look very different. And one's practical intuitive relationship with the earth and its plants are different also. Having that relationship is not hard, but to share its medicine with others is another thing entirely. The plant that showed me these challenges was hemlock. Hemlock made it very clear to me exactly why I, as a writer, was making such an effort with these medicinal plants.

In his introduction, Graves addresses the question of what is the function and use of poetry in the modern world:

> 'The function of poetry is religious invocation of the Muse; its use is the mixed exultation and horror that her presence excites. But 'nowadays'? Function and use remain the same: only the application has changed. This was once a warning to man that he must keep in harmony among the family of living creatures among which he was born, in accordance with the wishes of the lady of the house; it is now a reminder he has disregarded the warning, turned the house upside down by capricious experiments in philosophy, science and industry, and brought ruin on himself and his family.'

To find the wishes of the lady of the house was my intent as I set forth on my medicine root inquiry. But I had not bargained for the looks of exultation and horror that my own presence would excite, especially from my fellow female beings, as all manner of imagined witchery, spell-making, manipulation of reality, projection, and all the dark unspoken currents that go with the medicine way began to appear in my life. Women would look at me in a very strange way. Being naïve, I imagined they were interested in what I was saying. In fact, very few of them were. When you work with medicine plants, people become interested in a wild power that they imagine you have. They are not interested in you or the plant you are speaking of, but in securing their own position which they now feel to be challenged. You have become competition, and you need to be debunked. This is achieved by patronising you, or ignoring what you have to say, but mostly by projection: by projecting all kinds of dark and terrible imaginings upon you so that you falter, stop talking and withdraw your presence. It is this kind of poisonous projection that hemlock taught me to withstand, so I could begin to know the wishes of the lady of the house.

The difficulty you face in this task is that 'women', like everything else in the artificial world, are oddly distorted. We are hybrid creatures, bred to be sexually attractive, educated to be efficient consumers, child-raisers and office workers. All other attributes of our female beings are suppressed, especially our naturally creative and spiritual natures. This suppression becomes more keen as we mature. Instead of growing into wise and eloquent elders, we are encouraged to be silly and forgetful, autocratic gargoyles whose prime function is to uphold the male establishment. Smart young female beings often act like men to avoid this archetype; I was quite androgynous in my own city days, wearing designer pinstriped jackets and drinking with the boys down in Fleet Street. But at some point you can't do this any more. You have to become female. If you decide to align yourself with the earth, you particularly have to become female. The hemlock challenges everything that prevents its expression, everything we have left out, wittingly or unwittingly, in order to fit the hybrid form society wants its women to be. What prevents female beings from being female most of all is the projection of their shadow on each other. The one with the long nose and the broomstick.

This character I already knew. At the age of ten, dressed in long black skirts and brandishing a besom of birch twigs, I made a dramatic entrance as the Wicked Witch of the West in *The Wizard of Oz* at the Dorchester Hotel. I cackled and grimaced and whirled my broomstick around. The audience howled with laughter. They thought it was the funniest thing they had ever seen. I was mortified, but stoically carried on with my scary speech. Afterwards I hung up my tall pointy hat and had a rethink about my career as an actress.

But even if those heartless parents had not laughed that day, I would never have made the grade: I was a born iconoclast, a challenger of teachers and gurus, priestesses and wizards, an eschewer of all ceremony, talisman and altar. I had no more time for spells than I did arithmetic. What I liked was the great expanse of open sky and the wild rough elements of the earth, my own free imagination.

To speak of the earth's wild intelligence in the face of centuries-old control and censorship requires a great medicine. You can become skilled at herbal simples, knowing the ways of chamomile flowers, of gingko leaves, of valerian roots, all manner of their histories and cures – but in times of extremity, of paradigm shift, you need the big plants. To outwit civilisation you need to connect with the roots of the ancestors. Above all, you need a discerning and free-thinking mind, one that is quick to recognise the exception to the rule.

I was not alone in my endeavours. Some female earth-dwellers, like myself, were also seeking an independence of mind and heart. When we met we did not consider each other strange. Emma, a lover of lime trees and a formidable advocate for permaculture, told me she had given up on the local pagans in Port Meadow one evening when she found them reluctant to stray too far from the car park. Emma lived on a narrow boat and worked as a freelance editor for the Oxford University Press. As we sat on her deck talking about hawthorns and the lady of the house, I realised that the most intelligent 'plant people' were neither pagans nor herbalists, but artists, often immersed in the business of words. I had found out about hemlock and the archaic language of trees from an intense, complex book by Robert Graves. I discovered the underworld medicine of black poplars from Gerald Manley Hopkins and Seamus Heaney, of shivering aspens from Edward Thomas. The poets, inheritors of the tree alphabets, had access to the invisible worlds, without needing or wanting to turn their words into spells or manipulations. It was along these literary pathways that I first explored the language of plants. But after a while, I had to forge ahead on my own. Because I was a female being, and what was female and known about plants had not yet been written down.

The medicine comes when you make your own inquiry. When you go and stand by the plant and find out what your relationship is. That way, you find out what is real and what is a matter of make-believe. Many plants, especially the poisonous 'power' plants, are superstitiously avoided because they have been covertly used by human beings to influence the energy fields of other people. This is not because the plants have a malicious nature, but because they are agents for seeing in other realities and for finding connections. The traditional 'witch's brew', which contained all kinds of wildflowers – cinquefoil, henbane, hemlock, mugwort – allowed access to these hidden dimensions. How these dimensions were and are engaged in depends, like words, on those who use them. It hasn't always been pure. As a result, those very machinations that originated in the *human* mind are projected on the plants. This is like blaming the useful pocket knife for cutting you, or more pertinently, for your causing harm to another. No matter how poisonous the plant, none of them goes out of its way to poison human beings, or manipulate their reality. Besides, like the knife, these power tools have brought far more good to the human world than they have harm. Datura has helped more asthma sufferers breathe than it has ever sent people mad. Monkshood and belladonna are not only used in allopathic cures, but were the founding plant intelligences of the homeopathic system.

Hemlock is the least known of the power plants. It is rarely used as a medicine. It is not a beautiful cultivar that appears in showy gardens. It is a common 'weed' that flourishes wherever it pleases. It doesn't stand out; it looks like many other umbellifer plants. It's tall and gangly and smells of mice.

And yet, what an amazing plant! The first time I encountered hemlock was while taking a short cut through the allotments home from Port Meadow one summer evening. I brushed past some tall leopard-spotted beings with lacy flowers and became immediately rooted to the spot. I felt impelled to touch their shiny soft leaves. 'Don't touch them!' said Mark, who did not share my enthusiasm. 'It's hemlock!' I cried joyfully, although I had never seen one in my life.

When we got home Mark looked up hemlock in our small collection of flower books and started muttering darkly about Socrates, there being no antidote, how your mind starts to spin when you ingest it. 'Oh, Mark, that's true, I do feel a bit dizzy!' I exclaim. But nothing in me is afraid. One of my hands is tingling as though tiny electrical currents were going through it.

I ignore all Mark's warnings about washing hands. Foolishly, in the manner of all adventurers into the plant worlds, into the ancestor realms of once-upon-a-time, I am blithely entering a door to another dimension. The truth of the matter is I don't give a damn about health and safety, I am enjoying the sensation of seeing lights and spinning. It makes me feel light-hearted.

Later I lie down in bed, thinking about the plant. *Conium maculatum*. The spotted cone. Not immaculate like a virgin: something quite opposite. Spotted like a leopard, dappled like a deer; not still like a statue, but whirling, like a dervish, like a spiral. I get a sense of a tall hat of energy above my head. Then I fall asleep.

I wake up suddenly, it could be five minutes or five hours later. I'm not sure. The room feels full of invisible beings. I am super-aware of my body. One side is freezing cold and the other boiling hot. I am split in two halves. The hot side is the side of the tingling hand which I notice suddenly does not feel like 'my' hand at all. It has its own life and is stroking my face gently with great affection. As I let this happen I sense amusement all around me. In this moment I am connected with all the female beings who have loved this land and worked with plants, with all my green ancestors. Here we are, they say. They are not mean or manipulative; they are generous, full of heart and happy to give me a hand (as it were).

Then I fall asleep again. I try to tell Mark about this the next day but it is hard to put into words. I want to tell him how the ancestors came through my body and showed me how they are here. Energies often ran through our bodies at night, or we found ourselves half-awake between the crack of the worlds. But this was a different experience, because I *knew* the plant had initiated it. Hemlock was the first 'shamanic' plant I worked with. Plants ground your connections with other dimensions by being a memory holdall. They act like markers in time and space, so you can return to your original experience at will. Hemlock was a link, my line to the ancestors. It was through this ancestral lineage that I found the house of the earth.

This connection presented no difficulty to me, only to my fellow human beings. The business of the writer is, in archaic terms, to be a way-shower. Hemlock is an umbellifer, a member of a tribe of plants governed by the planet Mercury, and like Mercury it is a guide plant in the invisible realms. The business of the writer as seer, lawgiver, keeper of the ways and the ancient crossroads, was originally to remind the populace of the correct way to proceed 'in accordance with the wishes of the lady of the house'. This required him to balance himself within the visible and invisible worlds of nature. The true writer, governed also by Mercury, was in essence a metaphysical guide. Here, hemlock was reminding me of my own path, and that projections of 'witch' were not to be taken on board. Nor should I let myself become an entertainer, or, as Graves puts it with characteristic contempt, a *gleeman*.

The lady of the house, however mythology shapes her – a

moon goddess, a sheaf-bearing star, a wild woman archetype – is an intelligence that informs the fabric of the earth. This lady is everywhere in matter: the spirit of life in our own cells, the intelligence of all plants, especially medicine plants, which keep us in harmony with our fellow creatures. Her wishes lie in our hearts. This ancestor intelligence, however, was rarely in my experience greeted with the kind of respect or honour it deserved. And again, Graves points out why. In the patriarchal system devised by the Greeks (although not only by them) where the logos of the city holds sway, anything that calls for balance is pushed away into its mythical 'opposite', into the dark territory of the banished and demonised goddess. Even intelligent, pro-earth, pro-female people would react negatively to the medicine represented by hemlock.

'What are you doing here?' asked one woman at a crèche, as if I was about to push her children in a cauldron. 'You invited me!' I replied, bemused. Others would interrogate me for information and test it with 'reputable sources', shrink away from me at parties as if I were wearing that great pointy hat on my head, or ask me ominously if I 'had the Sight'. One man even refused to come to our house because he felt we were going to poison him with datura seeds. The amount of hysteria, superstition and fear really would make you think we were living in the Middle Ages and that the Enlightenment had never happened.

I would not have taken any notice of this nonsense were I not in the business of communication, nor if the shamanic path had not been part of my inquiry. I realised that the history of oppression of any kind of earth or ancestral knowledge (which is still perpetuated throughout the world, as indigenous ways are systematically destroyed) runs very deep in people. It can be combatted, but only if you really desire your own relationship with plants and with the earth. When you find these, you find yourself outside the henhouse door in a very different world.

One of the greatest barriers to this is the pressure from the domi-nator *logos* for vanquished *mythos* to take on its spiritual burdens. To succumb is to take an ancient sacrificial position that does not just belong to the Christian era. To speak of the metaphysics of wild plants is to put yourself unwittingly into this dangerous position: you can, if you are not smart, appear like some kind of *hijra*, an outcast from the 'normal' world: a magical strange being living on the edge of the collective, who inspires alarm by her appearance but also acts as a source of entertainment and a convenient dumping ground for any psychic garbage. It is a galling position when you find yourself there. And you need to get yourself out immediately.

I had to get out of it many times. The poisonous attitude women have towards each other, the repression and cruelty they wreak, is one of the most difficult aspects of human social life. Whether women actually do cast spells on each other, or get a local magician to do so (I know that when I lived in Guatemala such things did occur between jealous neighbours) or whether those 'spells' are simply malignant and unkind thoughts, superstitions, gossip, feelings of spite and envy, betrayal and hostility, makes no odds. They all damage and prevent not only a true and friendly intercourse with each other, but also a true and loving relationship with the earth. No matter how inspiring the white goddess may be to the male poet or seer, in the women's quarter she is a demon. And moreover a very hard demon to exorcise. Even with a growing number of intelligent books like *Women Who Run With the Wolves*, which uses traditional folk stories to illustrate the psychological dangers of female antagonism, which encourages every woman to stand up and be her own wildish self, to be creative, fiery and free, the real life challenge to withstand archetypal projection is immense.

In the social world, women are the genetic keepers of the intractable laws and boundaries that define community. This requires them to shame and denounce any individual, any creative artist, any free-thinker who wishes to challenge those boundaries, and most of all, explore and love the wild earth outside the town walls. They do this not consciously but unconsciously, out of fear. Because they themselves have been bullied to conform, and do not wish to be again.

So though I loved the big medicine herbs, those stars of every herbalist's shelf – echinacea, yarrow, angelica – my principle medicine was the inedible and despised English hemlock. To be able to withstand the projection of others and allow the earth to speak through me was my challenge. I did this by forging my own relationship with the natural world, by strengthening my inner being, and most of all by writing everything I experienced down. I spent years keeping notebooks, writing and drawing and photographing our plant encounters and dialogues – finding words, phrases, meaningful expression for the intricate solar workings I saw in all living forms. It was the way I knew best, my use and function, as Graves might have put it. The way I felt I could best inspire my fellows, especially my fellow female beings, to find their own feet on the earth, their own medicine, that lay outside the walls of the town.

In the end what one needs is one's own relationship with things. That is what really matters. The others do not matter. You can always be open to communication in which there is equal exchange and respect, but everyone has to make their own connection with the earth, as they have with their own destiny. Our civilised logos world is cruel because it depends on those who have wild and creative spirits to perform tasks of *hijra*, to play barbarian, tramp, loser, blighted one, the furious goddess, the *maculata*, so that the shiny Socratic people, the immaculate people, can carry on running the show.

It was hemlock that first told me my hands were there not to deal with others' shadows but to administer a very different kind of medicine. A medicine of words that would deal with the suspicious, superstitious modern mind, that would bring the heart to bear in places where it had never been. The heart is the only medicine worth paying attention to in the end. It's what being on earth is all about. To be human is not to aspire to an ideal, perfect, non-natural form, to engage in an arid Socratic dialogue in order to be a creature of pure mind like an immortal god. Instead it is to be a multifaceted moving creature of heart, to be dappled as light in a spring wood, to sing as insistently as the speckled thrush, to be as shiny as the mottled plant. To be human is to be *maculata*, blemished, asymmetric, a pied creature of sun and shadow, of winter and summer, at home, ever-changing, like the animals and the flowers. Like the moon and the sea.

To this day I only have to think of hemlock and my hand starts to tingle. For a long time I did not know what that tingling signified, and then I realised it was the electricity of the sun that is in all earthly beings, that keeps everything alive. I realised that the lineage of beings I felt in my room that night in Oxford were the ones who know what keeps everything alive. And do everything they can to keep it that way.

Later, my medicine journey led me abroad to meet herbalists and medicine people, all kinds of sick people, crazy people, and the unquiet spirits of many places, but my roots, my lineage, went deep into these islands. Hemlock is a native plant and it provided an anchor wherever I went. It provided a connection not only with the land, but also with the people who had walked the green road before me: an ancient knowledge, one not written; one that is sometimes found in riddles and dreams, in reeling dances and cross-stitches, one that came from the stones and our own bones, from sitting at the roots of pine trees and of a mouse-smelling plant with a spotted stem.

When you are going forward on the solar journey you need to feel supported by the earth on which you are walking, otherwise you could falter. You need to know you are backed by your many ancestors, by the trees and flowers. I was always backed by the plant world. And I was also backed by someone else.

Who, after all, is the lady of the house? Is she a poet-consuming, cold haughty goddess? Is she a raging monster mother of the deep, disturbing all our dreams? Or is she someone quite different? I went to the furthest ends of the earth to find this out. I climbed Cader Idris and sat under the hawthorn tree, I walked into the Sonora desert and slept beneath the palo verde bush. I brushed past a hemlock plant in Oxford and felt my hands tingle, and paused by a lady orchid in a dark wood in the south of France and felt my heart jump. And I found that this lady was someone no one had ever written about. Because when I went to all these places I heard a laugh there that reminded me of my grandmother.

I was reminded, when I sat with certain plants and trees, of a time in a sun-parlour scented with geraniums, of long quiet afternoons when time seemed to go on forever. My grandmother sat sewing a patchwork quilt: hundreds of perfectly stitched hexagonal shapes kept appearing from her basket in all the colours of the rainbow, crackling with last year's newspapers inside, like so many cells of a honeycomb. I sat beside her reading. We sat in silence together. A large industrious being and a small inquisitive one. Occasionally my grandmother would remark on the spotted woodpecker that flew past to feed at her bird table, or tell me that perhaps I would like to go to a boarding school in Suffolk. It's by the sea, she said, and they serve roast chicken once a week. And now I was ten maybe I was too old to be reading those comic books any more.

And so I began reading grown-up books and telling my grandmother what I thought about them.

And she would laugh, a deep mysterious chuckle that shook her whole body: *Bless your heart*, she would say. *Bless your heart*.

She was not a cosy, comfy grandma. She was a fierce and independent woman from an era that did not champion women: a student chemist, an apothecary, a wartime ambulance worker, a suffragette, a divorcee in the days you didn't get divorced, a single mother who worked all her life selling school uniforms in various grand department stores. She had a Scottish austerity mixed with a Celtic extravagance that I liked to be around. I liked her bathroom that smelled of lemon balm. I liked being treated like a grown-up, taught how to play cards and how to mix cocktails. I liked to be sitting there with her because she let me be myself. She did not want me to be someone else, something *for* her. Because there was in her house an atmosphere of unspoken affection. That kind of affection goes a long way in this world. Feeling at home goes a long way. Being allowed to be yourself goes a long way. And sometimes we have to travel a long way, a hard road, to find this kind of affection in ourselves.

Sometimes now I hear myself laugh my grandmother's laugh, my ancestral laugh, as I look back to where my childhood inquisitiveness led me, at the hugely complicated things I had to go through, just in order to return to the place where I began – to sit in another sun-parlour, by another bird table, patiently stitching together the stories of 52 plants, their colours, shapes and sweetness stored like honey in hexagonal cells. Memories of my earthtime that flit past, like freckled trout made of light and shade, fleeting like a dappled deer, like a flower with a spotted stem. Like my grandmother's quilt.

You want your medicine to be a powerful medicine. You want to be an important medicine eagle when in fact you are a woodpecker with a crazy laugh and an inordinate fondness for peanuts. You want your medicine roots to heal the world's broken heart, but you are a poisonous plant everyone wants to run away from. You desire so many things in the face of so much indifference. But something in you no longer cares what people think or say. You know that in the end affection is the best medicine, and that it only happens here on this earth, where you are. You are wise enough to know that what everyone longs for is to be allowed to become themselves, to feel at home, and that in your presence this can happen. You know that everything on this green earth will become all right, once all the comic books are gone, with their stories of goddesses and priests and philosophers, witches and witchfinders, and time stretches out once more to an infinite afternoon, and the one beside you can sit unafraid in your company, sometimes writing down what you show them, their forehead furrowed as they try to find the words. *Bless your heart*, you say as they tell you everything they see, *bless your heart*.

monkshood
Botanical Garden, Oxford 1999

At some point you have to deal with power. When you work with medicine plants you particularly need to deal with power. If not, like everyone else, you will be under its spell.

During these medicine years, I began to notice something strange that would take place during our dialogues about plants. There was a little glint in people's eyes sometimes, a pressure to get me to tell them what a particular plant could *do*: the old man who coveted the datura in his garden, the young man who fashioned wands out of English trees, the girl who sought to prescribe flower essences. I thought at first it was the look of a raven bird when he finds something light and shiny, something *very* interesting on his path. That will do nicely for my nest! he says and looks warily around. All fire-stealers are as wary as they are bold. They know, fools though they are, that stealing shiny things exacts a price and makes certain demands. If you hold a fire in your hands, you know it can never be yours to keep: you have to give it back. Otherwise it will burn your house down.

Fire-stealers, for this reason, are creators. They handle fire by practising their Promethean art. It's a risky business and you do not live a comfortable life. This is because when you hold the fire of the sun in your hands you are no longer loyal to the establishment. You are loyal to the ancestors and your creation. In a difficult time, you get your liver torn out.

However, those who covet fire are not necessarily creators. Most people, subject to the implacable will of the establishment, are on the look out for power – for power-bestowing possessions, shiny objects, interesting facts, big houses, famous acquaintances. Sometimes they are on the look out for important flora. Those shiny-eyed people, I soon realised, were desirous of the magical power of plants and trees. They wanted to feel in control of situations. They wanted to play Merlin and strike attitudes in star-spangled mantles with a retinue of girls, wearing the robes of high priests and weather-controlling shamans, in the same way non-writers like to imagine themselves as prize-winning authors, swanning into coffee houses, with the world at their feet. In *This Writing Life*, Annie Dillard tells of a sobering riposte to people who tell you they are thinking of being creative:

'Do you like sentences?'

Writing is hard labour: the coffee houses and the prizes may never come your way, so you have to like the work. I might have asked these power-plant seekers:

'Do you like dealing with the poisons of this world?'

It's a transformative business. The only way is through. You have to able to handle the fire.

All forms of establishment are challenged by fire, by the unifying forces of the sun, by the liberating, fiery hearts of individuals. If, by your presence and your art you bring these solar forces into play, you have to withstand the onslaughts of Empire and not be desirous of its powers. This is a certain task, one given to all fire-stealers, that requires an indomitable independence of spirit. First, however, you have to know what you are up against. And nothing on earth can make this more terrifyingly clear than an encounter with a power plant.

In Europe power plants are highly poisonous herbs which have, since antiquity, cured, inspired and at times intoxicated and destroyed man. These are the plants that appear in herbals with skulls beside the text and grave warnings, that grow in ruined monastery gardens, in graveyards and around middens, in all the dark places, lurking dangerously and beautifully: henbane, hemlock, belladonna, datura. In spite of their dangerous natures these plants have always been highly potent communicators. The visionary Rudolf Steiner, talking about the effect of bee poison on human beings, remarked that poisonous plants acted as accumulators of spiritual properties from what he called 'the cosmic environment'. 'Poisons generally are the collections of such spiritual elements,' he said, which gives them their curative capacities. The power of their poison is not, as some might imagine, to wield over others and cause harm, but to shift our awareness, so that we can see in the invisible dimensions, in realms normally hidden from ordinary consensus reality. In these dimensions, you perceive what requires a bringing into balance: the alignment of man with his environment, the core of all earth medicine.

Although I had taken power plants such as peyote in the past, those I worked with in Oxford I did not ingest. I approached them as I would any other plant, using our techniques of *visiting* and *seeing*.

160

As well as hemlock, I worked with datura and belladonna in this way. But the plant which showed us how to deal with power was the tall blue-flowered giant of the buttercup family. Monkshood.

Monkshood is a native of European forests and a rare plant to find in the wild in England. I once came across a large array growing on a remote road on the borderlands between Wales and Herefordshire. However, it is a popular garden flower, and in the Botanical Gardens it was the most striking member of the celebrated 1648 border, where it flourished in its non-hybridised (and therefore fully potent) form. This border is so called because it was formed to celebrate the publication of the Garden's first catalogue – an auspicious year, since it was the turning point of the English Revolution. All the plants that grow there now are the plants that flowered there then: foxglove, bear's breeches, purple mullein, rose campion.

Monkshood is an intoxicating plant to look at. It demands your attention: tall as a human being, with intricately laced leaves and shocking blue helmet-shaped flowers growing up a spire stem. In Germany it is called *Sturmhut*, storm hat. And it has something of the stormtrooper about it, something distinctly Roundhead. Something that challenges and shakes the cavalier soul out of any illusory position.

At the time I went to visit the monkshood a film had just come out called *The Matrix*. The film was set in a machine-run world fuelled by the energy of human beings. The humans were bred, like insects, in a dark hive with their energy centres attached to machines by wires, and kept ignorant of this state by being intoxicated by an illusionary world – the Matrix. In the story the hero frees himself from his machine incarceration and joins a band of warriors whose principle aim is to liberate the human race from their slavery. They do this by intercepting the communications network of the Matrix. Their greatest opponents in this task are the guardians of the system, who block entrance to any outsider. They are known as gatekeepers. The film was extremely popular among the modern-day levellers of Oxford who identified with this small band of liberators freeing mankind from illusion. Especially as it was full of all kinds of spiritual and right-on references.

I was thinking about this film as I walked through the Garden's ancient stone doorway. As I stood there in the fierce June heat beside the flowers, I felt an abrupt shift of awareness that was so powerful I almost lost my balance. I felt an uncanny knowing within myself, as if there were a tone in the air, informing the moment, like an ominous brooding film score. I felt agitated and wanted to move out of my position. Everything around me appeared dark and sharply delineated. Many plants shift your awareness, but power plants shift them more dramatically and more urgently and you have to pay rigorous attention when they do.

We will show you the Matrix, they said.

I left the gardens to go home, walking down the cobbled streets behind the high street, still influenced by the mysterious blue flowers. As I walked, the university buildings either side of me felt alive, as if they possessed a control over things that was absolute and unyielding, an ancient power that had a palpable malevolence. Everything was clasped by a dark line of energy, like a liquid metal band. It is easy to say that Oxford colleges are about power, about the elite, but it is another thing to fully experience the power that elite exerts. As I approached the gates of Oriel college I saw the burly energetic form of the porter and my heart jumped into my mouth: gatekeeper!

I started to shake. It happened in a split second, but in that moment I saw that what he blocked the entrance to was not just a building but something else entirely, and what it contained was not only not human-friendly but overtly hostile enough to make me shake. This hostility was not something that could be breezily shrugged off, or dismissed by identifying with hero-actors in a film. I shook for hours afterwards. It was a shocking encounter with power. The power of the will, the power of a certain world.

Monkshood is one of the most formidable plant poisons on the planet. All parts of the plant are poisonous, especially the root. Herbals and materia medica will warn you that one tenth of a grain of the poison will kill a rabbit in five minutes, one fiftieth a sparrow in a few seconds. However, they will also inform you that monkshood was cultivated for centuries in monastery and medicine gardens, since, in small doses, it afforded great relief from physical complaints such as neuralgia, pleurisy, lumbago and rheumatism. When the German doctor Samuel Hahnemann worked with monkshood in the nineteenth century it became - with belladonna - one of the founding plants of his radical new medical system, known as homeopathy, and did more than any other plant to abolish the established practice of blood-letting. Hahnemann noticed that the poison of monkshood produced the chill and anxiety and irritable restlessness that characterise the first stages of fevers and inflammatory states. Following the principles of 'like cures like' it was used with great success in an epidemic of scarlet fever. To this day monkshood is used in homeopathic doses for certain inflammations, and in particular for the sudden effects of a chill or fever brought about by being in situations over which you have no control, when held against your will by another of a superior force.

In the *seeing* that night I found myself in a graveyard. Men in black robes were gliding down vaulted corridors. As I watched these shrouded shapes questions began to appear in my mind: *What was held within these walls that surround the garden? What secrets lay within them, kept hidden for centuries? What was I doing here? Why could I not see these men's faces?* These corridors were operating in a certain band of linear time and the plant was acting like a direct line into this historical continuum (the botanical garden, I would find out years later, had been built on the grounds of an old Jewish cemetery).

This was not the flower asking me questions. The monkshood was prompting me to ask myself questions about what I was seeing. Not in a way that would provide rational answers, but in a way that would reconfigure my perception, actively *work* with what I was seeing: *Why do I recognise this dark corridor? Why was I raised in these institutions of power when I had no care for them? Why was I so carefully instructed in the ways of the French Revolution and the Tower of London and the Old Bailey?*

The solar path is an alchemical path. What you transform in yourself is the dark *materia* of your life and, most of all, the power structures that have governed your experience in whatever social environment you have arisen. You do this in order to put what you see as crooked, straight. You don't engage in this alignment by changing your vocabulary, or being spiritually or ecologically righteous. You don't do it by manipulating images. You do it by asking yourself questions: *Why have I witnessed first-hand the invisible oppression that institutions wreak upon people? Why had I spent my formative years feeling the terror emanating from these stone walls, the gloom of people who had been to these universities?* What you do is act on the answers.

In the second section of the *seeing* I found myself looking into a well situated in the garden. The well was dark and deep, like a stone well I had once drawn water from on an island in Greece. This was a perception that could look profoundly into the dark waters of the human soul, into ancient matters, and see them at a depth not normally experienced by modern people who draw water mechanically from a tap. In the plant's company I felt a gravitas. This gravitas was needed to secure my own being, so I could hold my own within these difficult scenes. You need the energy of your own will, your intent, to be in line with your heart, to see a crooked thing straight. Most of all you need your deep intuition, an intelligence that can see beneath the hostile 'gatekeeper' forces I had experienced earlier that day, and be in touch with the earth that lies outside the black-robed controllers of the corridor.

The monkshood was giving me an experience of what I came to call the power lines. Walking past the Oxford colleges, I had seen a dark outline around the buildings and around the form of the porter. Thereafter I could see these lines around the faces of people whose business was in the powerlines of the world. I saw them around official buildings, large country houses, around the faces of actresses, politicians, gamekeepers, the moving lines of a grid I saw in a dream of a friend trapped in the world of the city, the nuclear lines of power that *contain* form and hold it in certain heraldic configurations. They differed radically from the expansive solar workings I had once glimpsed with St John's wort.

Once you encounter that kind of power, feel what energies and obeisance it demands from you, you want nothing to do with it. In fact you do everything you can to liberate yourself from its domination.

In the film there was only one matrix. This was because the earth had already been destroyed by machines. But in reality there are two. The living web of life, and the power grid that obscures and seeks to tap and control its resources. In time I learned to dissolve this grid in the *seeings*, with its gatekeepers, its aristocratic parades, its devic shows and hunting parties. I did this not by confronting these images, but by seeing *through* them and placing my attention on the fabric of the living systems. All power struggles in the civilised world are over our collective agreement to see the world in a particular way, to go by its names and descriptions. The establishment teaches us to seek out the power positions of this world and to give all our energy and attention to them. To break the hold of this 'grid', so we might see ourselves in real terms, within the fabric of life, is both a task and an art, and goes in the very opposite direction of control. In spite of the film's emphasis on warrior action, the gatekeepers that held the Matrix in place were overcome by *seeing*. The hero avoids their bullets because he sees with his heart. This is not seeing with our physical eyes but our solar eyes, the eyes that see the workings of the sun in all earthly things. With our own free solar-powered energies rather than from an indentured position within a nuclear-powered elite, an elite which seeks to exerts its will over the whole world. This is the kind of seeing Monkshood was initiating that day.

Everyone who is sensitive, who is creative, whether poet, philosopher or a mystic, at some point sees 'the matrix', the powers of the Empire that engineer our brave new worlds, its gulags, madhouses, wars and slave trades. Free thinkers throughout history document the effects of its merciless captivity. By 1648, not only the visionaries but the populace of England had revolted against these powers, in an unprecedented confrontation of the *ancien régime*. Inspired by radical pamphlets published in a decade without censorship, a confederacy of Ranters, Diggers, Levellers, Fifth Columnists and Quakers turned the world upside down. In spite of the people's part in the first civil war, the military of the New Order decided that the rights of everyman would not rule the realm. The English revolution was about to go the way of all subsequent popular revolutions, and be taken over by the middle men. Where the first Civil War was about liberty, the Second was about power. Already the Army had taken over London. The dour repression of Cromwell's rule was about to assert itself, leading to a backlash and the return of the monarchy and the established Church seven years later. All those who had been fighting in the name of freedom, of men and women equal before god, would go the way of all dissenters and disappear underground. Many of them would flee to the wide, open spaces of America.

The black robed figures, detested centuries later by William Blake, would continue to flow down the corridors.

Among the populace today these power structures are known as The System, The Establishment, The Empire, or simply, 'Them'. Some pride themselves in knowing all their occult machinations, others are entertained by them in science-fiction and historical films. The monkshood showed me, in that small shocking encounter, that whatever names you may call it by, this system is not something you toy with. You cannot be cavalier about these matters. Power is a real force, and so is the heart and its desire for liberty. You have at this moment in the garden to choose between this liberty and power. It is the deciding factor for all those who hold fire in their hands. The two forces cannot exist in the same space within you. Do you seek medicine in the name of freedom for your fellows, asks the monkshood, or to assert your control? This is why you have the encounter with power, so you experience what you are allying yourself with when you choose. This is why you are standing at this border in 1648 at a pivotal point. These powers operate remorselessly through history like a machine: they take away all the oceans and all the room and keep all human beings prisoner, even the elite who are educated at Oxford. *Where has it got you?* asks the poet in the gulag. *Nowhere*. Power gets you nowhere.

The monkshood is equally remorseless. The powers of the world operate through everyone on the planet, through the fury of their egos, which seek omnipotence and revenge at every turn, rich or poor, male or female. You overcome them not by waging war on others, but by liberating yourself from your own power struggles. If you fight, rebel, criticise, make comment, have a fantasy within any system – political or religious or academic – you give it more power. You can't fight the world of the ego that is separated from the heart: it has too much negative energy. It is like fighting a nuclear submarine. What you need to do is disentangle yourself from the power lines that operate within your own being. What you need to do is connect with the living fabric of the earth and use the energies released by your own inner work.

All homeopathic medicine works on the principle of 'like cures like'. It was a principle that was discovered with the blue-flowering monkshood. When you convert your experience of the world into creative fire, you start to accumulate the spiritual properties Steiner was talking about. It's the paradox contained in all power plants, all kill-or-cure medicine. Monkshood is a formidable confronter of poisons because it itself is a poison. If you take your lineage, your terrible childhood, your former foolish life, your defective character, and alchemise all these 'poisons', those dark materials, your presence

166

will take on a certain transformative quality. This will affect everything you place your attention on subsequently, all places as you pass by. That's another kind of power, a medicine. *Why was I told stories about the French Revolution as a child, why did I spend my adolescence in the law courts, why did I work in the fashion business, walk down all kinds of corridors of power? Why did my student heart pound when I read of Winstanley on St George's Hill, Ravensborough as he rose to speak at the Putney Debates?* Because, when I answer these questions, I will be like curing like.

The monkshood was the instigator of what we came to call the homeopathic dose. This is a medicine way of walking through the world, that acts like a homeopathic medicine in the body. It is light, almost imperceptible, and yet emanates the pattern of your transformation everywhere you go. You are not submitting to the powers of the world because they no longer operate within you. You have undergone an alchemical process and now live within the governance of the heart. The powers of the world always move away from the heart, towards totalitarian control of the will. This collective will seeks to dominate the whole globe, but it is weak because it needs to have everyone's agreement. You do not agree, you are the exception to its rule. Its power is not absolute because of you. You are keeping another possibility open, the possibility all creators keep open, the possibility of freedom. *You left my lips and they shape words even in silence.* It's the power of the powerless. The dissenting powerhouse of the heart.

Monkshood was a formidable teacher of perception. It taught us how to perceive with the heart and not allow the dominion of the will to rule the world. It appeared at the beginning of our inquiry to herald a transformation that would take many years to undergo, perhaps our whole lives. It acted like a mark-stone for all our subsequent *seeings*, turning what had, up to then, been an investigation into the language of flowers into a creative, spiritual undertaking. Confronted by any difficulty, I could always imagine myself back at the Botanical Gardens and feel the presence and intelligence of these flowers, as they gathered in the 1648 border, a dark blue confederation. I would stand beside them, in consultation, and be able to see my way through any entanglement of the mind or will. The monkshood taught me about medicine, what it was and what it was not. Most of all they taught me about seeing: when you see in other dimensions, you dominate nothing, you manipulate nothing; you allow the fabric to inform you; you move only yourself, you ask questions, remain open, and then act on what you see.

One day that summer Mark asked me if I could see something on his behalf. The monkshood showed me what was happening from a bird's-eye perspective. I saw how he could see his stuck positioning within this energy field and make his liberating move. All I had to do was communicate my findings. It was this seeing that inspired me to conduct *inner realm travelling* on the behalf of others. It was the beginning of a rocky road of healing encounters during which I discovered that although Mark was willing to do the work himself, most people who ask for a hand expect you to do the work for them. It began one day with a phone call out of the blue from California, and an orange poppy that grew outside my room.

pine
Santa Inez mountains, California 2000

For the first time in a long time I thought of Eliot Cowan. I had a dream about peyote, a dream that took place on a golden hill dotted with juniper trees. A full moon was shining in the sky.

In the dream two unknown women bring me to their country house, and after supper I tell them I want to walk up the hill and contact a man I know who has peyote. One of the women takes me to where he lives. The man is dark, a stranger: he could be Hispanic or even Indian. When he goes into another room my companion leaves. For some reason I open my jean buttons so you can see my knickers. I say 'for some reason' because there is nothing erotic in this dream. When he comes back he looks at my open fly, and says hurriedly: I have to go to sleep now, because tomorrow I am shomon.

'Oh!' I say, 'how frightfully interesting, we call them shamans in my country.'

When I told Mark the dream this morning we both roared with laughter at my response. It sounded so incongruous, so *English*. I had been thinking about juniper trees before I went to sleep. Juniper trees often come in my dreams. They are big medicine trees whose leaves and berries are burned throughout the world to banish negative influences.

'Why do you think you had a dream about junipers?' he asked me.

'Oh, I don't know,' I replied breezily, not wanting to be pressed for details. 'Maybe it's to do with the sun.'

The dream was set in New Mexico, where these dark conifers stand upon the soft grassland mounds, like sentinels.

But for some reason I was thinking of California.

I am driving with Eliot Cowan through the juniper-piñon belt above Santa Barbara. On the way he stops the car to show me particular plants, bushes and trees: Californian bay, the dark benzoin bush, red-barked madrone trees, different coloured flowering sages, artemisias, figworts, the small red flames of the Indian paintbrush flower.

'Do you work with this tree?' I ask him at every stop. 'What is this flower about?'

'I call this mother's milk,' he tells me, as we walk through the fragrant wild lilac bushes that are growing everywhere on the hillsides. 'Yes, this tree I have a relationship with. I have a certain number of plants that I work with now. But I am not really into plants as much as before. I work with feathers instead.'

'What about California poppy?'

He turns and gives me a piercing look. 'That is a very *strange* plant,' he says.

After about half an hour we stop at a bend in the road. We walk up a mountainside and sit under a tall pine tree on its dry needle floor. We can talk here, he says. For a long time we say nothing. It feels strong and peaceful under the tree, as if we don't need to speak: two people who have spent time with wild plants, feeling at home in their company. The presence of the man is as palpable as the tree. My heart suddenly gives a great leap as I feel the vibration of everything in the warm spring sunshine, as we sit tuning into the mountain and the tree, the land stretching outwards towards the sea below.

I had come to interview the man I was now sitting next to because I was searching for a way forward, a way to turn our research into earth dreaming and plants into a creative project that others could share. I had decided to speak with the two people whose work had inspired us: Stephen Aizenstat with the dreaming practice, and Eliot Cowan with plant communications. When I found out that they both lived in Santa Barbara, I didn't hesitate. I just got on a plane.

Here I am sitting with a stranger who is not quite a stranger, since I have read his life story and engaged in his work. Before me the small piñon and juniper trees dot the hillside. The two are inseparable companions on the slopes of the hills, in the Rockies, in Arizona, in California. Conversations about nature with Americans are quite different than with English people. In England you are lyrical: you extol your love of beech trees and nightingales, you comment on the lovely morning and the rain. In America, you pay attention to the territory: you speak about great spirit and medicine. You don't mess around talking about the weather.

I sat under the pine tree wondering how to begin our dialogue, staring down at the woven bag round my waist, a Huichol bag I bought once in Tepic, bright green with embroidered fuchsia-pink scorpions, deer and peyote. So I began talking about peyote. I began to tell Eliot Cowan about the visionary experiences I had with this slow-growing cactus, what I had discovered with my companions in the mountains of Mexico. *It is a dangerous plant when it falls into the wrong hands*, he said sharply, interrupting me. *It needs guidance.* So I took another tack and talked about our activist work with trees in Oxford. *Forget it!* he thundered and made me jump. At this point he took over the conversation and began to tell me about the Huichol concept of peyote as the governor of life on earth, as the cosmic worlds were governed by what was known as the wind tree. He spoke slowly and deliberately and with authority. I listened. The wind stirred in the needles of the pine. Then the meeting suddenly took an abrupt turn, as he asked if I would consider being his apprentice.

I felt knocked sideways. One moment I imagined I was interviewing him and the next discovered *he* was interviewing me. And not as a fellow author. When Eliot Cowan had written his book *Plant Spirit Medicine*, he conducted a practice based on his own work with plants, but now, several years later, he had become a Huichol shaman. He was about to go to Mexico with a group of apprentices he was initiating into this medicine way. Did I want to go with him?

'What does it entail?' I asked, bursting with curiosity.

It was a twelve-year apprenticeship, he said. Each year you would make a pilgrimage to the sacred mountain which may or may not involve taking peyote. Each month you would light a fire at full moon and keep vigil. There were also detailed preparations for these events which included eating only certain foods and abstaining from certain activities. The key commitment was that you could only sleep with your partner, and also that your partner would back and support you in your various abstinences. I thought of Mark.

'Well, I already work with someone.'

'You have to have a committed man-wife relationship. Because twelve years is a long time,' he said. 'Maybe you will find a new partner after the first pilgrimage.'

I stared at him, speechless. Nothing in me wanted to abandon my work with Mark, nor to live or be with anybody else. But it was an intriguing offer. 'Can I think about this?' I asked him. 'Of course,' he replied. As we went back down the mountain my mind was whirling. Eliot invited me to have supper with his family, and then to go and meet some of the apprentices who were lighting fires that night of the full moon on the beach. 'You can ask Grandfather

Fire about the apprenticeship,' he said.

That afternoon I cycled to the cliffs above Butterfly Beach and tried to cohere my thoughts. The sea spread before me like a dazzling cloak, dolphins passed by, leaping, orange nasturtiums tumbled in the grass. Here, I reasoned, was an offer by a man with impeccable credentials. He had conducted his own original research into flowers and had a successful healing practice. He had trained in shamanic journeying with Michael Harner, in five-element acupuncture with the pioneer Professor J. R. Worsley, and been apprenticed to a Huichol medicine man for many years in order to become a fully fledged shaman. He had been chosen for the task in order that the old medicine ways could be translated into the new.

So why was I feeling so disorientated? I had come to speak in the spirit of exchange. But something else had happened under the pine tree. I did not know the tree's name, but I knew about pines: they concerned transmission. Pines are straight up trees, and emblematic in America. The white pine, Tree of the Long Leaves, represented the peaceful councils between the Native American Confederacy. The pine tree chiefs were non-hereditary leaders who negotiated for peaceful relations between different tribes. One of the laws of these meetings concerned listening. It insisted on equal exchange, straightness in all matters, on the correct conditions for transmission. In the stillness of the pine forest you listen as the winds of the world sough through their highest branches. What is spoken needs to be listened to in stillness. That way you can come to a peaceful conclusion.

However, on the mountain it had felt like a one-way dialogue and now my mind was whirling about and I felt agitated. I realised I was no longer in command. I had lost my bearings.

America is a citadel of conifers: spruces, firs, redwoods, cypress and pines. Along the west coast their range extends from the tiny piñons and junipers in the dry south to the giant sequoias and hemlocks of the rainy north. In England these trees stand unrespected in suburban parks and plantations. But in its native land the pine is a wild and ancestral tree, a world tree that grows in forests of great power and resonance. Under its totem branches the tribes of the Five Nations once gathered and made an unprecedented peace. It gave the people wood for shelter and fuel, pinenuts for food, leaves and inner bark and pitch for medicine. The resin from its sap clears the head and lungs, its smoke purifies the air. The presence of pine in the territory brings clarity within confusion.

In the British Isles the Scots pine is one of only three native wild conifers, with yew and juniper. This red-barked and handsome pine has an uncharacteristic tendency to quiff its topmost branch. The north was once covered with these trees, until their felling for turpentine, tar and timber (mostly for telegraph poles), leaving only remnants of this primeval forest in Scotland. There are stands of these pines on the sandy soils of England: they form windbreaks, or take position on ancient mounds and barrows. One of their strongholds is in coastal Suffolk. And it is here in a small cove in an estuary that I find myself, as I try to cohere my thoughts, on a clifftop where a line of Scots pine creaks in the wind. The cove is known as Little Japan because these quirky-topped pines look like the stylised trees in classical Japanese paintings. For years I had called them Japanese umbrella pines. Now I know they are nothing to do with Japan or paintings or umbrellas. They are our ancestral native trees.

You cannot work with medicine plants without encountering the glamour attached to other people's native traditions, especially when you are in America or Mexico. Glamour is a confusing business: if you are not careful, you can find yourself stranded in a realm far from home. To deal with glamour you need to be clear. You need to be straight with yourself, and not fall prey to fantasy, preferring foreign paintings to reality. Most of all you can't attach yourself to someone else's ancestral root when you have your own, humble though it may seem in comparison. You need to love what is native in yourself, your own small quirky Scottish root, and not to be attracted to another's because of its mighty forests. Most of all, you need to be real about the person you are talking with under the tree.

In Europe, people who work with herbs are not wild and romantic figures: they are mild-mannered therapists in white coats. But in the Americas there are still medicine men with feathers and power plants, and the mystique they hold within the modern imagination is very strong. You feel somehow that these people are the real thing, where you are not. Instead of making steps to discover the real thing in yourself, you imagine all kinds of fancies. Even though I had never actively sought out any medicine teacher, I had always secretly enjoyed the idea of meeting Don Juan in among the shelves of Safeway, imagining the moment when he would appear and say: You! Come with me! Be my apprentice!

And now it was happening.

So why, I asked myself sternly as I sat among the orange flowers, are you not now jumping with joy?

That night I go to have dinner with Eliot and his family. His wife is Mexican, graceful and light-hearted and a great cook; his two teenage boys are very laid-back and Californian, and we had a lively supper, laughing and talking about surfing and *The Matrix*. Eliot is sober among all this activity. He has other things on his mind. After dinner several people who had travelled from the Midwest to have treatments with him arrive, and we set off together into the night towards the sea. A full moon sails in the sky: my heart is beating loudly as we walk Indian file, silently through the trees, the live oaks and the pines. I can hear the roar of the surf in the darkness, the urgent expansive sound of the Pacific Ocean. Down on the beach, Eliot's apprentices have built big driftwood fires and are keeping a night-time vigil in three different places. We visit them all, exchanging greetings, while Eliot speaks to them about their experiences in his deep, slow voice. At the third fire we halt.

'Ask Grandfather Fire about the apprenticeship,' he tells me. 'Ask peyote.' I sit cross-legged by the fire. The full moon fires flicker like beacons in the night, the invisible sea laps in the darkness. Should I join them? It feels exciting to be here, with people who are envisioning a new future for the planet. People who go up mountains together, who keep vigil, who know about plants and peyote and the meaning of earth medicine.

I look into the flames of the fire and bring my concentration to bear on the matter. Inside myself I ask the peyote what I should do – the cactus that the Huichol people call the deer, shaped like the disc of the sun; I ask the fire made from the logs of driftwood, from oak, juniper and pine that crackles in the darkness and heats my face on this windy foreign shore. *Should I come?* I find myself thinking about Mark and our plant practice. I find myself on the mountain where we once took peyote with Robert and April under the tree, when Mark kept telling me to look as his fingers as they opened to reveal an orange, the colour of the rising sun: *It's in your hands, it's in your hands*, he kept saying. *What's in my hands?* I asked him, and laughed.

Suddenly, I look up from the fire. Out of the corner of my eye I see two small lights glowing in the darkness: the two men, master and apprentice, are sitting smoking large cigars, talking in the manner of all men when they talk of power. They have turned their backs to me.

Who am I, who sits by the fire, the stranger they have turned their back on?

In that moment everything becomes clear; my mind stops whirling; I come back down to ground. I realise I cannot be anyone's apprentice. I cannot be subject to any master or magus. I am no one's wife. I am an independent female being who sits in the night, and the sun is in my hands. I cannot follow an indigenous tradition. I have my own native medicine root, my own world tree. Everything on this mysterious earth I have found out directly from the fabric of the place itself: I taught myself knowledge, invented my own pathway, with the trees, with the flowers, with peyote, with my fellow explorers. On the mountain we had started with nothing. We went back to our origins and we started again. We did not follow an ancient road because we were here to create the new, the structure of which has to be forged within the smelter of our human hearts. It has to be re-imagined, re-dreamed, re-loved, re-felt. And this is a work we have to do together, men and women, red and white. As equals. As real people. As straight up people. Just as it was in the beginning.

poison ivy
Santa Barbara, California 2000

It was March when I arrived. I stepped into the warmth and light and space of California and the cold cramped English winter fell away from me like an old coat. I ran down to the beach towards the sea: sanderlings ran in and out along the shore, sea lions played among the rolling waves. I walked along the boulevards under wavy palm trees, under the scented eucalyptus, and everywhere flowers appeared at my feet: blue lupins, filaree, rosemary, scarlet pimpernel, purple morning glories. It was suddenly spring and glorious. You could feel yourself stretch in all directions, endlessly, on such a day.

I had first come to Santa Barbara in 1997, when Mark and I were driving down the Pacific coastline. The axle of our car broke just off Main Street, and we waited three weeks for a part. It is a laid-back ocean town of jacaranda trees and farmers' markets, surrounded by purple mountains. *Beautiful Santa Barbara!* a woman gushed at us as she jogged past. But sometimes Santa Barbara isn't so beautiful. One night under the subway of highway 101, a girl loomed towards us like a creature from beyond. *Is this the way to Skid Row?* she asked in a crepuscular tone.

'There is an amnesia in people,' said Gay, an ecologist I met soon after I arrived. It feels as if there is a lovely show on the surface, but something rather *underworld* is being left out. That first night I had a dream of a Jewish patriarch and I was cutting the shadow from the skirt of his robe with a giant pair of scissors.

I had invited Terry and his family to my motel room to look at the flower cards. I had met Terry the night before with Eliot Cowan sitting by the full moon fires and we had immediately struck up a friendship. Both of us were undecided about becoming Eliot's apprentices. The four members of the family had travelled across the country to have healing sessions, and they called themselves the Minnesota ground crew. They all perched on my bed and we took turns choosing cards, speaking about them, about ourselves. The flower cards were small coloured cards with the names of about a hundred flowers and trees and their key qualities. Sometimes I used them for my own inspiration, sometimes to initiate a dialogue with others. People open up with flowers. They spark everyone's imagination. Memories, associations, dreams, places appear as if from nowhere. You can look at people you have known all your life and see qualities you never articulated before; conversations between strangers become easy and flowing. Talking with flowers is like entering the balmy zone of California after a long winter in the northern latitudes.

When it was my turn, I chose ivy. 'Oh!' laughed Scott, 'Watch out! Once you meet ivy, you don't want to meet it again!'

For a moment I was perplexed, and then I realised why they were all laughing. For Europeans, ivy is the dark-leaved evergreen that climbs over walls and trees. But for Americans, ivy means poison ivy, the bushy understorey shrub or climbing vine of the sumach family. An unusual plant with oak-like leaves (known as poison oak in the east of the country) which, like many sumachs, turns brilliant scarlet in the autumn, and panicles of greenish-white flowers that become ivory-white fruits, covered with a papery shell, rather like physalis.

But that is just how it appears. Its touch is something quite else. Whereas in Europe we learn to avoid nettles as children and alleviate their mild stings with dock leaves, Americans skirt round poison ivy in a kind of botanical horror. Its poisonous sting can be excruciating and sometimes drives people to hospital. Once its oily resins have got into the skin, nothing removes them, not even bleach. Sufferers burst out in horrendous sores for days. Foresters can damage their lungs after inhaling its fumes in forest fires. Poison ivy's ability to stay in the skin is legendary. Its toxic effect can last up to eighteen months in dead branches, up to one year in clothes that have brushed against it.

Everyone goes round this plant, gives it a wide berth. It's a wake-up call from nature, the Minnesota ground crew tell me: after that you pay attention where you are walking.

After our lively conversation, Terry and his brother-in-law ask if they can have individual flower consultations with me. 'I like speaking with you,' Terry said. 'No one talks with me in the healing sessions.' I have not done any medicine dialogues with these cards before but, always keen for experience, always game to enter new territory, come what may, I agree.

Terry came to see me the next day and picked the lotus card from the rainbow-coloured pile. We also chose from a pack of animal dreaming cards I had made. Terry picked snake, and I picked cat. We looked at each other across the motel writing table, with the bright sunshine outside the window, holding our cards. The lotus of the quiet waters, the snake of transmutation. The scarlet-leaved ivy and the mysteriously smiling cat.

'Are you transforming something?' I asked him.

Terry began to tell me why he had come to California. He was suffering from an unknown condition and hoped Eliot Cowan would be able to help him. He felt as if his whole body was itching all over. He scratched himself until he was sore. He had been to all manner of doctors, specialists and healers but no one could tell him what was the matter.

'You see, I don't have anything wrong with me physically. I don't have a skin disease. It is invisible.'

'Why do you think you have got this?' I asked.

'I think it's something I did in Vietnam.'

My body jolted in shock. I had not met a soldier from Vietnam before. Mark had once been given a lift by a Vietnam vet in Arizona and been shocked by the man's fury. You heard stories in Arizona about hard men, mad men, broken men who lived in the hills with shotguns. Most people shook their heads when you asked about the war. They would mumble something about the Wall in Washington, and look at you as though it were a shameful, hippy thing to discuss. *Where have all the flowers gone?* they sometimes still sang, but did not necessarily remember all those young men who had died or committed suicide when they had returned. I had had another war. It had been my special subject when I was studying American modern literature. Vietnam meant Ken Kesey, Joseph Heller, Michael Herr, stylish and powerful journalism. I had never met anyone who had fought in those forests. It was like imagining you knew about the trenches because you had read Wilfred Owen's poetry. I suddenly felt shallow and inadequate.

Terry had been working in a hospital during the war, where there were political prisoners suffering from burns. He had been cruel, he said, to these enemy patients, rough with their bodies when he had changed their dressings. They had done such terrible things to his friends and he was so angry. These memories were torturing him now, and making his skin feel as thought it were alive. He had sought out

Vietnamese refugees and made a formal apology to them; he had travelled all over the country looking for a cure, talking to medicine men, seeking a spiritual path, but nothing so far had relieved him.

'It's my guilt,' he said. But even this knowledge was not freeing him from his torment. He was a man in a burning house without water.

I looked at him. At a man who had, like many people, been dealt a harsh blow by circumstance. His childhood had been marked by leather belts, alcohol and freezing Minnesota winters. He was seventeen years old when he was sent to Vietnam.

'You have a lovely smile,' he said. And suddenly I didn't feel like such a fool.

All skin diseases, whether real or psychological, are to do with fire, with spirit. If the body wants to purify itself, it will do so through the skin. It will shed itself of poison, like a snake sheds its skin. But skin diseases are also the diseases of the collective: scrofulas, sores, plagues and poxes that erupt from the unnatural way of life in civilisations and cities. The native tribes who lived in balance with the earth did not have these diseases that the European invaders brought with them. They killed them in their thousands.

I guessed that Terry was suffering not just a personal difficulty but a collective one. However, he had picked the lotus card. A flower of contemplation that brings a clarity, though it arises from the dark and toxic mud. Somehow these confessions, articulate, meaningful, urgent, shocking as they were, did not seem to make any sense in the face of this flower. They did not add up. It was as if these facts, talked over many times, were whirling around in the air but had no root. As he was talking I found myself thinking of Amsterdam, where his mother had come from.

'I think this poison stems from another war,' I said.

He looked at me as if he could not believe what I had said.

'What happened to your mother?'

Terry's mother was a Jewish refugee from Holland who had come to America during the Second World War. Her family had not survived the Holocaust.

'I think you may be carrying something from the past,' I said. 'I think the cause of your difficulty lies in a deeper place.'

It seemed the most obvious question to ask and yet no one had asked it. When you are having a lovely time in beautiful Santa Barbara, you don't want to look at what is lurking in the subway. You are not sure you can deal with it. I am not sure I can deal with it. I am holding a rainbow flower card on a bright spring day and suddenly find myself looking at Vietnam and the Holocaust. What can any one of us do when we face each other's ghosts? Can any of us go through those old traumas, those pogroms, the poverty and the cruelty, and find where our ancestors had once belonged to the earth? We are afraid to look one another in the eye. We start telling stories and confessions in the hope that those who listen to us will wipe the slate clean. We hold the unmentionable taboo in front of us, keeping everything at bay, shut off, shut down, unconnected to its ancestral root. Still the spectre of history stands in the shadows, watching as it wreaks its havoc through the generations – poisoning our lives with holocausts and horrors, histories that are never properly spoken of, beheld, honoured, made sense of, transformed, buried at a proper depth by ourselves. The past holds us to ransom down in the subway, while we live out our dangerous and superficial lives. Slowly the planet loses its leaves.

But sometimes you find yourself with a wild card in your hand, with a plant you do not know. Sometimes you are the stranger who doesn't know the rules and ask the question no one else has dared to ask us. *Where did you come from? What happened?* Sometimes you look directly at the answer that looms up out of the darkness and smile at the one who has crossed your path in this moment of epiphany.

That's a new kind of dialogue.

'At some point you hit a wall,' said Gay. We were walking, the three of us, through the redwood trees, through carpets of wild ginger, in the Botanical Gardens, talking about amnesia, about ancestral roots, how the lack of a connection to the earth caused so much illness and unhappiness in America. Gay was from Oregon, part Norwegian, part English. We were talking big time, we were talking everywhere: all along the western coast, in the moors of England, in the north, in the wild places, in deep time. We were walking around the manzanita bushes, through fields of orange poppy, past mugwort and desert bluebell, talking the forests of the world. Gay was talking about her forestry project with Native Americans, called 're-storying the earth'. Jeff was talking about his reclamation work in the pine forests of Siberia. I was talking about the Celtic alphabet of trees, about archaic and modern ways of being together on the planet. 'That's it!' Jeff says. 'What you say speaks to me. I can't connect with the Native American ways but I can with my Irish roots.'

He suddenly swerved dramatically away from us.

'What was *that*?' I called after him.

'Poison ivy!' he yelled. 'Don't go anywhere near it!'

In Santa Barbara you love to talk big time everywhere with everyone but the flowers don't let you go that way. You want to speak eloquently about ancestral dreams and ecopsychology but the dreams don't let you act like that. You want to talk ecologically about deep time and the forests of the world, but the redwoods won't let you get away with it. The mountains of California don't let you get away with it. Because you can't skip the poison. Nobody can skip it. The poison is where the memory is.

Sometimes you walk right into those scruffy, innocuous-looking oak leaves and let yourself get stung. Afterwards, you wake up and remember where you are.

That's a silent moment.

It was not until I returned to America the following summer that I realised what these encounters with dangerous medicine plants were showing me. They were giving me a key about poison. About the sting that breaks our illusions and reveals the underworld seeping invisibly into our lives. I picked the poison ivy because the people had forgotten: they had forgotten the history that was held in their cells, in their blood and skin and bone, the untransformed legacy that keeps the ancestors at bay and themselves from inheriting the earth. I came from that old Europe they were avoiding like the plague, strange as a Californian poppy, scary as a hemlock, rigorous as a monkshood. I sallied forth on a bright spring day to speak with the shaman, the psychologist and the ecologists. We sat by the sea, under trees, walked through fields of flowers. Somewhere in all the talking I hit the wall. They all swerved away. One man, however, looked me in the eye: an ordinary man who held an invisible poison in his skin, who held a card that said Snake in one hand and Lotus in the other. What was I doing, looking straight back at him, sitting like a cat in a motel room in California? I was discovering the oldest medicine in the world.

The snake is the universal transformer, the core of all alchemical process, the twisting life-giving helix that lives in all our cells. He is respected throughout all ancient systems, all native medicine ways. In the world beyond the five senses, the snake is the transformer of all underworld poison because he holds the possibility of death in his own jaws. The snake can look at life straight on and not turn away, not leave things out, no matter how difficult the subject. Not because snakes are pure or powerful, but because they know the way to skid row.

Today I look out from a desert window towards the sky islands that appear on the horizon. The window is framed either side by a sumach bush with small leaves, known as lemonita because its red sticky berries make a tart lemony drink. Like the fruit of its more famous relative, the mango, the taste bites your tongue. It is a frisson, an intensity you recoil from, yet immediately want to experience again. Out in the chaparral the poison ivy grows like a vine, nonchalantly, insignificantly, beneath bushes. No one pays it much attention. Everything poisonous takes its place in the desert: the rattlesnake, the tarantula, the scorpion. There are no illusions out there.

Terry has written me a letter and told me he is now following a Lakota medicine path. I am sitting before this empty land, writing back, telling him about a path I have been reading about, walked by people known as flower soldiers. Flower soldiers live by a code of self-responsibility that recognises that we choose certain, often very difficult, formative experiences which then become our 'battle Kachinas' or medicine.

With the letter I enclose a small bottle of lotus essence and a twig from a sun-scented bush known as snakebroom:

'I made it one gold and blue day at my friend Mimi's house in the desert. The white flower sat in perfect stillness in an oasis pond surrounded by desert willow and bamboo. A giant toad lives by this pond and several box turtles and sometimes at night the bobcat comes and drinks the water. While I made this essence I thought of you. I thought of how some of us old snake people have a hard time transmuting the poisons of this world. The lotus told me that instead of trying to clean everything all the time, getting rid of 'stuff' out of our pores, we need to bring all the poison *up* into our hearts and trans-

182

form it there. The lotus has its roots in mud that if stirred up would kill the gold and silver fish in the water. For the flowers however this toxicity is food.

How can our dark experiences, these physical torments, these monsters we fight be food? I wondered. *Focus on your intent*, said the lotus. *What did you come here for?* To live a comfortable conformist's existence, or to engage in a noble, extraordinary life for our spirit's sake, for the planet's sake, to become an essential part of a cosmic pattern that we in our human form can only glimpse in a fleeting moment? *Focus to catch that moment*, said the lotus, as I found my attention wandering towards the tick that was threatening to jump on my ankle. *And this too*, said the lotus: *include everything, save nothing. Then let that moment go.*

Until we meet again I wish you the best of good fortune for your travels on the Lakota path, dear Terry.

Please send *lots* of love to all the ground crew from me.

I remain your friend in flowers,

With love and a big smile.

Charlotte X'

tronadora
Bisbee, Arizona 2000/01

In the end you want a physical relationship. There is nothing that can replace that relationship. Whatever the modern world promises, all its technological allures and opiates, its shiny pictures, machines, its hypnotic music, its clever words, it cannot love like physical presence, the presence of people and places. It is that you miss in the end: how you feel when someone enters the room, how you feel when you are in that land. It's the last thing you think about, the least considered, the least important, something you take for granted while it is happening, but when it's gone, you realise that this presence is what you want more than anything. Just to be in that place, by that tree, among those flowers, in that spring light, by that winter fire, sitting beside you, to know you are there, to feel you close by.

When you know the value of presence, you treasure it more than anything else. Sometimes you don't know you are storing up this treasure. Sometimes, though you thought you were in a place for one reason, you realise when you look back, you were there for something else.

At the beginning of June, just as the jacaranda trees were coming into bloom, we came back to California. I had been fired up by all my spring time meetings and the project that had emerged from them called the Earth Dreaming Bank.

'We're going!' I had announced gaily when I returned. Mark was not enthusiastic. Nevertheless, we packed up our Oxford house and set out three months later. I had written a proposal for the initial work of the Bank, outlining how we might go about gathering material, collecting dreams, holding dialogues and seminars, and had sent it ahead to everyone concerned. However, things in Santa Barbara were not going to plan. Ideas on paper, in meetings, are not the same as physical reality, as people turning up in a place. We were swimming down in Summerland, among the dolphins, we were walking through the sidewalks of towering scented fennel. We were eating Mexican breakfasts, surrounded by morning glories. We were hanging out in paradise, in our blue motel room, reading books and waiting for the phone to ring. Waiting for the door to open.

One midsummer morning, we got up early to see the sun rise from a pass in the mountains known as the Sky Path. A deep fog had rolled in from the ocean and we lost our way along the back roads. As we wound about the misty hills Mark became furious, I became silent. After what seemed like hours, way beyond sunrise, we found ourselves back where we had started under the eucalyptus trees.

'We're not going anywhere,' I said. And we both began to laugh. We decided to go back to Arizona.

Today we are walking up a stony hill on a hot afternoon after the rains, in search of an elusive bush called tronadora. We are following Mimi, walking Indian file on this red earth path, wending our way through the prickly domes of rainbow cactus with sacks on our back, helping her collect herbs for an apothecary in New Mexico. It has been raining for some months now and the parched desert lands have burst into green. The craggy arms of the ocotillos have filled out and become vibrant green limbs, the spikes of the agaves have burst into honey-scented bloom. At our feet small flowers tumble around every rock, the shocking magenta petals of ratany, the dainty fairy dusters. The air is scented with white-flowered dogbane and kidneywood, and the bouvadia flames in all the crevices.

We find the tronadora by the gorge, after walking about an hour. It is a handsome bush with bright pinnate green leaves (sometimes called yellow elder). Its trumpet-shaped flowers are a deep and vibrant yellow. The feeling of the plant is very joyous. And we are excited to find it still in bloom and set about collecting some of its flowers and leaves and stems. Collecting herbs requires a certain attention. You do not just grab everything you see; you tune in, speak to the plants, ask their permission, listen to what they say, *yes* or *no*. If you are like me, reluctant to pick anything, this sometimes takes time. But at some point, your mind and your eyes let go and your heart chooses instead, and you find your hands just whizzing about taking what is needed. Tronadora was a generous plant but there was a rigour too in our collection. Some bushes we left completely alone. Afterwards we filed back to Mimi's house with full sacks on our backs and had a dialogue about our day, about the plant that we were sorting out on the kitchen table.

Tronadora is a traditional folk medicine for adult-onset diabetes. It is particularly valued because, unlike many chemical remedies, it has no toxic side-effects. Diabetes is a sugar imbalance and famous in the Americas for affecting the lives of indigenous people. Many tribes suffer from its debilitating effects. It is blamed on their poor diet, on their poverty. But really, like all diseases, diabetes is a result of an out-of-kilter relationship with the earth. It is a malfunction of the pancreas which, with the spleen, is the seat of the earth in the Chinese five-element system. The season of earth comes at harvest time, at Indian summer, when the summer's heat and rain swells the pumpkins and the beans and corn and makes them a sweet and nourishing store for the winter months. Diabetes is a white man's disease, where there is too much white sugar, too much white bread, too much white refinement and artifice. It comes from a consciousness that does not know the sweetness of the earthly life, that lives out of season and goes way too fast for its own good.

When the native people of America were forcibly removed from their homelands by the white invaders, something was taken away from them inside, a sweetness that once came from having a slow rhythmic relationship with the earth. Tronadora reminds the body of the presence of earth, of the sweetness of life, and helps sort the storage of sugars in the liver. It's a folk remedy that helps many people, and not just because it contains the right substances. We don't live in a time where anyone looks at these things carefully, to ask why these disorders happen. But maybe we should.

We should look at that whiteness, what it really does. What it does to all of us.

Tronadora belongs to the bignonia family, a botanical group of plants that does not exist in Europe. It is a flower that flourishes in the full summer heat and monsoon rains of the Americas. Its most well known member is the jacaranda tree, which is grown by the thousand in this continent's gardens and cities and is universally beloved for its purple, sweet-scented blossom. The bignonias of the desert are the graceful and fragrant desert willow trees and the startling orange trumpet vine that clambers over the fences of the town. All are powerful anti-viral medicines. Their most famous qualities lie in their ability to tackle the yeast fungus known as *candida albicans*, which can proliferate all over the body when it is under too much stress and impair the immune system. The bignonias rigorously put these 'whites' in their place.

That first summer in Arizona we started working with the bushes that flowered after the monsoon rains. We followed Mimi up and down many red paths, collecting, visiting, 'hanging out' with medicine plants and holding dialogues in her kitchen on our return. Bisbee is a town full of herbalists and plant lovers. I talk to everyone I meet about plants, about the dreaming of plants, about the Bank. Everyone has a use for the spiky wild inhabitants of the arroyos and canyons, the feral fleabane and fennel that shoot up in the sidewalks. The co-op store stocks large jars of wild leaves and roots, small home-made salves of grindelia (for poison ivy), tinctures of bearberry, dried bunches of echinacea from local gardens. Outside the town there is a school of south-western plant medicine run by the herbalist and writer, Michael Moore. Greta is one of his students. Sometimes I swing by Peter's studio and find her set about her tasks, chopping up ocotillo stems, peeling prickly pears, and we debate the noble qualities of the lowly *brickellia*, the indigenous use of tree tobacco, the bitterness of silk tassel, the sweetness of the saguaro fruit. One day, hiking up to the waterfall, she surprised me: *Do you know water hemlock?* she asked. *It's even more poisonous than European hemlock!* I stopped in my tracks and laughed. I had never met anyone who loved hemlock before.

Greta has written a paper about indigenous herbs and has designed a medicine garden for a Native American trading post out in the Dragoon Hills. Next spring we will go with Peter and look around the land where Greta's garden will be. Apache Ray, brought up in a Mexican neighbourhood in Los Angeles, has returned to his homeland and has opened up the store as a communications centre.

'We didn't make a good job of things before,' laughs Apache Ray. 'We're going to leave it to the women this time.'

On the hot spring day, in the shade of the ramada, Ray's brother will play a flute, Mark will chant. We will sit in silence together on the porch, the Dragoons rising behind us, a flowering tamarisk shifting in front of us in a small breeze. About us in all directions the gold California poppies will ribbon the highway, the blue lupines shine on the hillside; the evening primroses will cover the red earth. Like white handkerchiefs, waving.

In the town the dawn-tinted flowers of the desert willow throw their intoxicating perfume into the air. In the baking afternoons I go down to the small park and sit in their peaceful shade. Giant wasps crawl in and out of the flowers, greedily sucking their nectar. You cannot believe how such an elegant tree with its delicate flowers and fine willow leaves flourishes in such a rough place. But that is something I am learning, about medicine, about the flowers that cure all humans who have gone too far away from their roots. 'There were not many flowers; did we collect them too late?' I asked Mimi, as she cut up the tough stems and leaves of the tronadora. 'Everything is medicine,' she snapped fiercely, shaking her knife in the air, 'even these old sticks have medicine.'

In Arizona, I will learn everything about earth medicine, in among the red rocks, in this fierce outpost town fringed by desert willow. I will learn the difference between male and female ephedra bushes, how the best red roots grow in the toughest places, how sagebrush and juniper leaves will clear bad vibes, how ocotillo bark clears meridians. But most of all I will learn about flowers. The shocking beauty that comes out of the toughest places, the harmony that comes out of conflict. How they will bring you back together, remember you, no matter how far you have gone away. I will discover how the flowers of the *yerba de alonso garcia* make the best drink at the end of the day – not because they 'do' anything, but just because they are who they are. Just because if you are ever lucky enough to find yourself in the desert of south-east Arizona, and find these small sweet-smelling pea flowers, coloured cream and purple with a touch of red, infuse them in hot water for five minutes and drink the tea slowly. Then you will know what I mean. Some things you can't describe. The heavenly taste of flowers at the end of a long hard road.

At the end of the Indian summer we go down to Mimi's round house in the desert and help restore the garden, clearing paths when they have become choked with amaranth and pepperweed, watering the herbs that grow under the Mexican elder in the cool of the evening: hummingbird sage, catnip, Tarahumara chia, mugwort, indigo, *epazote*. The coyote melons lie everywhere on the ground. I am sitting by a piano, my bare feet on the bare earth floor. The piano is out of tune and I can't remember all the chords of a piece by Mozart I used to play. The medicine jars sit on the rough shelves in the dark cool adobe room: with their treasures of roots, bark, leaves, flowers, labelled with names that I now can recognise. My eyes scan them, and then look outside and scan the sky. The rain clouds have disappeared from the peaks. I go out and walk towards the study.

Here I sit at the writing desk in the straw bale house, with a cat sitting beside me and the desert unfolding before me. What can I tell you about my medicine time? What I held in my writing hands at the end of the day? I want to tell you about something extraordinary I found, something about sweetness: that when you start to walk that hard red road, something happens inside, in a place you did not even know existed, and it's to do with the flowers, to do with the place the flowers have taken you. Because all the time when you are there with the plants in your hands, winnowing tiny black amaranth seeds in the warm south wind, or sitting patiently sifting the pale-husked seeds of Syrian rue, while you slowly pour the Mexican sugar cane alcohol over the bright blue skullcap flowers as you make a tincture, steep lemonade berries from the sumach bush as you make a cool drink, as you bundle up the sharp-scented sticks of desert rue and burn the sweet mastic of the elephant tree, a great treasure is being stored up. While you take your breakfast sitting by the creek, by the waterfall, under false indigo, by the passion flowers, under the coolness of the cottonwood tree, something happens within you you cannot name. You start to belong. And I can't tell you what that feels like, because sometimes you have to experience it. You have to put your white feet on the red earth and start to walk, and when you walk, you realise you are going to a place where your heart has always wanted to go.

You are walking home.

V
Speaking Bush

Bushes are the trees of the high chaparral. They stand strategically on the dry plateaux, holding the fabric of life together. Their presence in the territory makes sense of everything. Their spiky forms orient the directions, and their flowering times the land like a giant clock. Every living thing, man, beast, insect and bird, finds sustenance within their thorny shelter.

To know these bushes is to understand everything about the desert. You think it is a dry land, full of thorns and hardship, but then the spring arrives and this bare world comes alive: wave after wave of flowers carpet the earth floor, every dry stick becomes a vibrant being. The mesquites throw themselves into honey-scented bloom, the scarlet tips of the ocotillos burst into flame in the flatlands, the urn-shaped manzanita flowers and the silk tassel transform the canyons, the soapberries bust out along the riverbanks, the puff-balled acacias, sumachs and condalias in the scrub. As the summer heat advances the heavily-scented creamy cliffrose and the scarlet pagodas of the coral bean defy the drought among the arroyos and washes. Just as it feels as if the earth itself will break up under the baking heat, lightning cracks among the peaks, the monsoon rains arrive and there is a second spring. A dry red world becomes green and lush. With the storm comes another wave of flowers that catch your eye along the highways: the golden petalled chaparral and tronadora, the delicate pink wild cotton waving scarlet-leaved arms among the great platoons of sunflowers.

In those two years in Arizona we made two sets of flower essences inspired by this second flower wave. The first I made on my own, called The Speaking Bush, based on my interaction with eight bushes within different territories. The second set, The Snake Sequence, came out of an experimental medicine dialogue with Mark and Mimi and six high desert plants. A joint production we called High Desert Speaks. All these essences shared the common theme of speaking. They concerned our communication with the ancestral forces that 'govern' planetary life, and addressed our native capacity for speaking out loud with one other, in the land in which we lived. They looked at what it would take for modern people to create a future in which we would be able to hold council – man, animal and plant – and live in harmony on our planetary home. I began to make these essences after a dream in which I was preparing for a gathering, taking with me three gallons of water, infused by a desert shrub known as creosote.

Speaking circles are a strong tradition in America, originating not only with Native American tribal councils but also from the inspirational nonconformist meetings of early settlers. These gatherings were held at local grassroots level to decide how communities were run. They had a broad spiritual base in which the virtues of our humanity and the balance of the earth were placed in the centre of debate, rather than the economic self-interest of individuals or corporations – which is the driving force behind most political meetings in the modern western world. Making flower essences with these bushes highlighted the process through which we needed to go to become the kind of people that could work together in this enlightened communal way, rather than from within an aggressive and individualist struggle for supremacy.

Flower essences were pioneered by the Welsh doctor Edward Bach in the 1930s. Unlike plant tinctures, which work to align the physical body, flower essences work with the feeling or etheric body. Dr Bach, diagnosed with a fatal illness at the age of thirty-one, did not turn to the conventional or homeopathic medicine in which he was skilled, but instead walked out into the East Anglian countryside and cured himself by energetically interacting with the vibrations of certain wild flowers. During this process he realised that diseases are often caused by rigid mindsets and stuck emotional patterns, which

191

the innate fluidity and wholeness of flowers could help to release. Inspired by this success, he applied the methods of homeopathic medicine to distil the subtle energies of thirty-eight plants and trees, infusing their flowers and twigs in the dynamic alchemical forces of spring water and sunlight.

All flower essences follow this original method, and the native flora from many wild lands has since been 'proved' all over the world – from the Australian Bush essences to the Flower Essence Society of California, from the Aloha essences of Hawaii to those pioneered at the Findhorn community in Scotland. Some, like the Alaska essences, also infuse the energies of planetary events such as high tide, full moon in reflection, and the northern lights, and distil them within certain wilderness territories – glaciers, bays and mountains.

The Speaking Bush essences made in the borderlands of the south-western desert were all 'live' essences. Traditional flower essences record the patterning of the physical forms of flowers separated from the plant and steeped in water; live essences hold the vibratory forces emanating from the whole living plant, as the makers tune into its energy field and hold a dialogue within its native territory. All essences work with vibratory or etheric forces (subtle energies which cannot be physically sensed or rationally determined) but live essences require you to work with their invisible energies and communications and not just rely on the physical medium as you might a medicine.

Flower essences are traditionally employed by practitioners to balance 'disorders' within the personality of individuals and the detrimental effect these have on health and wellbeing. They often work, however, within a conventional social paradigm. These live essences were made with the future in mind. They were not made to 'fix' conventional psychological profiles but to activate our evolutionary abilities to voice ourselves as one-among-the-many. They all were made as the millennium turned, and heralded a radically new way of being human on the planet. As well as the Speaking Bush and The Snake Sequence sets, I made several single essences – Russian thistle (or tumbleweed), soaptree yucca, sacred datura, desert rue – and a triad of cacti, the saguaro, queen of the night and the rainbow cactus.

The essences were made in response to the spirit of the times. It was clear, by the time we arrived in Arizona, that the earth required a different relationship with its human inhabitants if a life-affirming future was to happen in the next thousand years. This was not going to be a matter of economics or political engineering, or uttering spiritual truths, which is the common response to such a question, but the way we interact with life itself. As we followed the track of the bushes, we felt impelled to explore and restructure our communications with each other and the planet. A new and ancestral dialogue needed to happen, a dialogue that could begin out in the flatlands, among the mountains, or in any wild place you found yourself.

None of these essences, as a result, were made as remedies. They were made to provide a focus or intent in order that questions could be asked that are normally obscured by the distractions of daily life. Entering an intentional hermetic space and engaging in a 'work' are the decisions that bring the alchemical forces of life into play. All the high desert bushes in this chapter, as well as common wormwood, provided this interface so we could mediate on an inner level between the fleet worlds of spirit (the sun) and the slower worlds of matter (the earth).

The essences themselves acted as a mnemonic to remind us of the subtle and different dimensions of the earth. Driven by one-track mindsets and a false sense of survival, we rarely give ourselves the time and space to interact with the myriad energies and intelligences of earthly life. Working with these bushes opened the door and gave us access to this bigger picture. They quickened our senses, so we could understand our lives in an expansive, fluid, less personal way.

Rather than seeing these plants as *nouns*, as objects, we could see them as interactive forces, as *verbs* in the moving fabric of life. This allowed us to experience ourselves in terms of flow, change and movement rather than fixed items within an established structure. In our dialogues we were challenged to move from a noun-based, descriptive way of speaking about our lives (this is me in my world) to seeing ourselves as part of the changing fabric of life (my move in our world). We saw what prevented us from speaking freely and moving forward in an evolutionary way. In this we were challenged not only with the restrictive inventory of our own personal histories, but also the broadcasts of our civilisation, instilled in us by our education, our upbringing, and constantly reaffirmed by our cultural media.

The desert is where you go to get clear. Under its panoply of stars, in its emptiness and sparse beauty, these inner and outer broadcasts lose their hold and instead the small voice of your spirit begins to speak to you. As you gaze into the far horizon you can see your destiny written in the rocks and clouds. For thousands of years visionaries and leaders have gone into the desert to become inwardly clear so they can bring new ideas into the collective. As we worked with these bushes we realised that we needed to foster this ability to speak harmoniously together, so that we could co-create the lives we wanted to live.

These original bush and flower essences were made in order to address those separating inner forces that were hostile to such a cooperative future, and to realign our energies so these defences were dismantled within ourselves. The bitter-tasting experiences of these years showed us that it was vital that these meetings took place with our feet on the ground and the light vibration of the heart. For without a connection with the earth, without our heart's command, without the ability to speak to one another in a straightforward, warm and sincere way, the aeon of peace and fellowship, for which so many people longed, would never take place.

bearberry
Red hill, Bisbee, Arizona 2000

I was on top of the red hill above Bisbee. It was ferociously hot. We had just arrived in Arizona after having been in California to try to set up the Earth Dreaming Bank. I had climbed the hill to connect with the plants. Disoriented, exhausted by the heat and altitude, I sat down by an agave flowering by the Roman Catholic shrine. Its tall upright stem, like a giant asparagus stalk soaring skyward, felt like an anchor among the red rocks. For a week I had felt silently scrutinised by the thorny desert plants, as if they were testing me. Is she worth talking to? Is she for real? And now I was being addressed in a very forthright manner. But it was not the agave that was speaking.

I looked around. There in front of me was a strong-armed, handsome bush with sculpted red-brown branches, small leathery leaves and tassels of dark berries. I recognised this bush from the Botanical Gardens in Santa Barbara. It grows in great profusion all around the hillsides of Southern California. It was a manzanita, known throughout the world in its variety of forms as bearberry, *arctostaphylos uva-ursi*.

I didn't know what the bush was speaking about, but it was definitely *speaking* to me. I had made contact at last! That was enough. Suddenly full of energy, I ran down the hill to the desert hotel where we were staying, impostor and stranger no longer!

It was autumn equinox on the red hill. It felt strange somehow to consider the equinox in America. In Britain you can feel the turn of the year as the light equalises and the night draws in. The deer are about to rut, the leaves to turn, the mushrooms to appear. The mornings are tangy, full of mist. But here, though the hackberries and aspens have grown golden in the Huachuca mountains, it can still reach 100 degrees at midday. The monsoon rains have only just ended: the land is green and vibrant, the sky a pure cobalt blue. I would have to work to make sense of its energies: this moment when you leave the fields of summer and enter the dark kingdom of winter. It is the time of initiation, the mysteries, of the ancestors, when you contact the roots of life.

What are you going to do about the American dream?

At the time the bearberry spoke, I was focused on establishing our dreaming work with other people. I had not considered the American dream. Or even my own relationship with the land. Like most visitors, I had assumed my presence bore no significance to the place I was visiting. The Earth Dreaming Bank was founded on the principle that paying attention to our dreams, communicating with the kingdoms of nature, has an effect within the complex fabric of planetary life. All our small actions go recorded. This increased attention works to make the dream of the earth stronger than the industrial trance that holds us all to ransom. The American dream is the illusion of consumer freedom. In this dream everything is for sale: you can live in a world where you can be who you want to be, where your past does not matter and your actions have no consequence. It is a dream that runs entirely contrary to the ancestral dream of the earth. By 2000 it was turning into a nightmare for the whole of the planet.

What was the ancestral dream of America? What was I doing here, climbing towards these red-armed bushes on this clear fall evening? This moment bears no equivalence with the equinoxes I had already experienced: Bran and his bridge of alder trees, Persephone's ivy-wreathed descent into the seedstore of earth, the Saturnian world of form that governs the archaic worlds of Europe. It belonged to another order that was based on space, rather than time, to a geography ordered by the principles of the sun. In Europe our relationship with the land is gauged in a cycle of the solar year based on the seasons. The spokes of this calendar year are signified by trees and plants. In the Americas this relationship is governed by a medicine wheel of the four directions. The spokes of this wheel are signified by the wild animals and the mountains. This ordering principle was kept by the people who spent their lives in communication with the land, with clouds, stones, water, who called themselves after the animals they honoured, whose every action was done in relation with what is known as Great Spirit.

You cannot enter the territory of the Southwest without sensing the presence of the people that went before, without feeling these principles. It seeps into your own language, your dreams, the way you hold council, the way you walk up a hill. There were many ways of being human among the tribes, in their crafts and warriorship, but in their knowledge of right relation, their way of walking the land, in balance and beauty, they knew themselves as one nation, The People. The Okanagan word for human being means *land dreaming capacity*. The people recognised that the human ability to dream with the land was our primary function. Our language, our vision, the way we spoke, danced, made music, was the land speaking to itself, how the earth and sun and all beings communicated. This was not a preserve of the people of the tribe, but was intrinsic to all peoples' ancestral form, the reason human beings are present in the land.

The words spoken by the chiefs and elders in defence of America as it was invaded still resonate with modern people. In defence of our own wild places, we quote the great chiefs – Sitting Bull, Standing Bear, Black Hawk, Red Cloud. These words, spoken directly from the heart, have an authority and integrity which the shifting morality of the industrial western world does not have. Something of this language, this spirit, still lives in their territory even though they are long gone, in the rocks and the animals, in the plants that are named after the animals. In the wind that runs through their leaves.

I don't know this yet. But somewhere I do. The first wild creature to capture my heart was an American bison. Even though I was a small English girl watching these great beasts across a concrete divide in a city zoo, something in my own mysterious land dreaming capacity recognised them. Something deep within me brought me to this land, led me to scramble at the end of this day up a red hill with a jar of spring water in my hand.

The evening has a sharpness to its mood. The temperature is falling rapidly as the shadows lengthen. At the summit, among a group of manzanitas, I put the jar down and look up into the sky. The clouds above my head are huge, red-coloured. One of them is shaped like a bull, with lightening flashes inside its head. A wind whips through the bushes. And a hawk appears. Suddenly I am with him, looking down at the vast land below us. This lasts no more than a minute. When I return, I have a strong sensation the bushes are part of a council meeting taking place. My body jolts. It is as if there were a collective presence in communication, linked with the sky, with the mountains, with a hawk hovering on the breeze on an equinox day.

A door has opened. Everything beyond that door has consciousness, intent, communion. I realise I am no longer alone on the hill.

It was the moment I saw Turtle Island. Before, it was a word, a term, something glimpsed by chance, standing among the rippling prairie grasses of the plains or driving through the rain-washed faces of the Cascade mountains. Now I experienced it. Turtle Island is the ancestral name for America, its dreamtime. These are the red lands that bear no relation to the governments of the white settlers, their land claims, or their copper mines. This is the place that existed once and still exists now. The place which was fiercely defended by the tribes when the invaders came and still is, by both red and white Americans, and even by some visitors who climb a hill on an autumn day, who longed for the buffalo when they were four years old in a city on another island far away.

The bearberry opened the door into another America. When I had first come to Bisbee, I was immersed in the communal life of this small artist colony. I went down into the Sonora desert to see saguaros, took picnics up at Juniper Flats, and sat beneath the cottonwood tree that grew outside the door, but my main focus was on the creative and spiritual activity of my travelling years. When I returned five years later it was to a different place. The people were still there, but our plant inquiry and dreaming practice had shifted our attention. We were looking toward another horizon.

During those first weeks Mark and I would walk up this red hill, early in the morning. It felt good to be up there in the cool hours among all the bushes, under the diamond-leaved live oaks and the manzanitas, the coral beans and the junipers, gazing over into the immortal spaces of the Chihuahua desert – the empty quarter, as Carmen used to call it. We sat up there and looked at a blue haze that stretched for hundreds of miles. It is the kind of space that gets into your bones when you live in the desert. *It will itch you for the rest of your life*, as the artist of horizons and empty spaces Georgia O'Keefe once said. Your soul feels as though it could extend outwards in all directions. You feel older, huger, vaster, wilder. You are reluctant to return to your small domestic life, once you have felt all that space inside.

That equinox night, in a seeing, I felt this space inside me. I revisited the ridge where the meeting had taken place and felt strong sensations in my body and the inner forces that were driving its engine. Then I saw the white American dream pass by the shrine, where the bearberry had first spoken. It was led by the daughters of the American revolution, followed by English foxhounds, Japanese women in kimonos, Italian popes. As I connected with the forces inside my body and increased my vibration, this parade started to disappear.

That was the night I dreamed of the gathering and the creosote water. When I awoke I decided to make the essences that I would later call the Speaking Bush. Bearberry was the chief of the series.

Bearberry is one of the world's oldest kidney medicines. Its waxy pink and white flowers grow from February to June, and are in the familiar urn shape of the heather family. These turn to small wizened red-brown berries that are tough to eat but delicious. The heather tribe are famous for their berries – cranberries, bilberries, blueberries, whortleberries – and are much prized and collected, especially in the northern lands. But it is the manzanita's leathery leaves which provide its chief medicine, acting as a peerless diuretic, antibiotic and disinfectant for the kidneys and urinary tract. Native Americans also smoke these dried leaves in ceremony, either by themselves or mixed with wild tobacco and red willow.

To know the land is to know the body of the ancestors. It is to know our own selves. The earth and our physical forms have an indivisible relationship. We think the earth is a place outside ourselves. But its wild, fruit-bearing nature is our own nature, its rocks our bones, its roaring rivers the waters of our selves, and all our vitality and well-being depends on this connection. The relationship with the land gives us everything we need. Going up the red hill after visiting the manzanitas, I found I could run along the tracks, even in the fiercest heat, without tiring. This was extraordinary because I am not a runner. I never run, except upstairs. I am the least sporty person you can imagine. But as soon as I put those dried berries in my mouth, I felt full of life-force. I felt I could run forever among these hills, as fleet and sure-footed as a deer.

As a citydweller of the developed world you stumble by luck upon this elemental, ancestral part of yourself. You venture off-track into another country and are surprised by wildness and weather, the way your body responds. How you feel suddenly in touch with the nobility of being alive, your place within the territory, in touch with those who walked this track before you. You pull water from an ancient well, feel the rough bark of an old tree, awaken to moonlight, walk moors and mountains drenched in rain, pulled by the seawind in a small boat. This encounter with the elements is a rare and cherished moment. You find it on vacation, by accident, and then you lose it. You return, put on your cityclothes, shrink back into familiar streets and rooms and clocktime. Once people all over the world lived like this on the mountain. They kept hold of that relationship with the earth because they knew it as life, what our rightful place was, how we made sense in the landscape as part of the ancestral dream. The dream kept us all alive, kept us on track.

The bushes kept me on track. Sometimes they would call out as I ran past:

Whose arms rock you?

Bearberry opened the door to the country once called Turtle Island. Every time I went up the red hill, I was reminded of this place. My feet picked up the energy of the sky island that was also Turtle Island, and powered the energy forces in me. Imperceptibly, the 'American dream' stared to fade within me. I became less and less interested in the modern world, with its dramas, its histories and its parades, less involved with the activities of the town. I felt I could never have enough of wild spaces, of sky, and desert and storm.

I made the essence so I could remind myself of what happened on the hill. I took the spring water from the jar where I had placed it among the bushes, mixed it with some brandy, shook it, stored it in a brown bottle. I had already made a flower essence with the soaptree yucca, floated its giant scented lilyflower in spring water at full moon. But this was a live plant essence. It required a different attention. The water in the jar recorded not just the plant's energy, but everything that happened around that equinox walk: the visit, the seeing, the dream, all its medicine. When I planned to make the essences I did not know what bushes would make up the series, but I did know they would be about speaking with the land. I wanted to be able to speak of the earth, in the way the chiefs of the red tribes once spoke, and sometimes still do. I wanted to know whether you could, as an industrialised white person, recover the intimacy of that archaic relationship and make it your own. What its elements and requirements might be.

It began with water, because life begins with water. The bearberry essence, like all flower essences, used water as a conductor. The invisible vibrations of plants can be absorbed by water because it has a superlative memory. How you speak, what takes place, the feeling of the land, are recorded within its fluidity. Wild water holds the vibration of the earth, which is why bathing in rivers or sea or mineral springs recharges your energies. It is remembering you, bringing you back into alignment within the primordial medium of life. What governs the water of ourselves are our kidneys. In the Chinese medicine system the kidneys are the wellspring of the life-force, or *chi*. They are the seat of the ancestors, because it is the ancestors who remind us that without water, without life-force, we die.

To remember the value of water, you have to go beyond the human world and its civilisations into the elemental worlds, into primordial night, and listen to the rhythm of the year. The kidney rules the darkness and depth of winter, the time of going into the roots, towards the wellspring where you gather strength. This is the place where you remember that life itself, not your parents, your house or nation, has given you life and maintains you in this form. Once you are aligned with the forces that power the earth, your own body, this will sustain you, back you, hold you together as you go within yourself and let the nightmares go. The bearberry reminds you of this connection as you sit held in its strong mahogany arms, as its berries sweeten your dry mouth.

The red hill is part of the Mule Mountains, named after the mule trains that brought the miners at the end of the nineteenth century, when Bisbee was the largest urban development in the west after San Francisco. Originally, however, they were named after their many springs of underground water. You would not know there was water here, in this year of intense drought when the live oaks have died of thirst. You have to know the territory to find that water among the red rocks, in yourself. Once you have found this source you can run for ever.

The bear is a key. Our kidneys contain the medicine of winter, when the bear goes into the cave and hibernates through the cold months. This equinox tips the year: as the light drains from the land and sky we turn inward, take stock, become cave-bound and dream.

The bear holds us close in our dreaming, fierce animal of the mysteries. These are lands where bears still live, chew berries high up among the peaks of the sky islands. Something of their resonance lingers, reminds you of the mysterious art of being fully alive.

Archaic body. Bear body. You cannot know the earth without this body. When you inhabit this body consciously, you know how to absorb sunlight, take strength from rocks, cool from tree shade, energy from rivers. You know how to sleep in winter, what winter does to the land, to yourself. A door swings open. You know your land dreaming capacity. You know the value of everything. You don't know it intellectually, you know it instinctively, like an animal. You are using parts of your intelligence that the modern world, driven along rational, mechanical lines, does not even know exists, and would refute, deny, dismiss if you told it. On the hill you take no notice of this world. You have already run refreshed by the bearberries in your mouth. Already you have lived through the desert summer, cured your own malcontent with leaves and roots and flowers.

Who is the self who sits in the territory, without name or circumstance? Unbound to history, I am free to know this self. No allegiance in the town claims me, no culture or family or tradition shapes my feeling or my thought. This hill holds no nostalgia. It is a pure territory of rock and scree and bush. It exists in its own right. I exist in my own right, a creature of sun and earth, of bones and sinew and light.

As I sit I become this self who can sit in this territory, cohering all its elements, of rock, sky, bird and tree, the one who dreams with the land, held in the rocky arms of the ones who went before.

Where is your allegiance?

Whose name is on our lips as we plunge forward? Whose courage do we exhort as we leap into the unknown? There have been many commanders - captains, presidents, leaders of men - but the name on everyone's lips as they stand and face the impossible task, the one whose courage in the face of death is certain, is the name of a Chiricauhua Indian, the Apache commander, Geronimo. These mountains of hidden springs once were the homeland of the Apache. On the red hill as far as you can see are their traditional hunting grounds. The Apache are famous in history for being the

202

last tribe on Turtle Island to stand against the invaders. Formidable warriors, they fought to the death and only conceded defeat to the white man's army when their leader, the fearless medicine man Geronimo, lay down his arms, saying: *Great Spirit does not want war.* It was a pivotal statement, and condemned the man to imprisonment and exile for the remaining twenty-five years of his life. He never returned to Arizona.

He is a small man with a turned-down mouth. You could not romanticise him. He looks implacably at the camera, a rifle across his knee. The Apache have none of the high glamour of the plains Indian, with their eagle feathers and buffalo hides, their words of great wisdom. They ride in the opposite direction of the visionary, peaceful Hopi. They were raiders, tough and stealthy. They lived in warrior bands in these sky islands like mountain lions, red bands tied around their heads, men and women smoking the rough leaves of the wild tobacco. Everything they did was about action. For Geronimo to surrender was a highly unusual act.

I do not want to imagine a fanciful thing: the idea of a council of chiefs on the red hill. It is easy for modern people to romanticise such things, or hope for them. Except the territory is not romantic, and nor is this self that sits with the bushes on a fierce day to gather strength, to know about surrender. To live henceforth on the earth meant Great Spirit did not want war. It was a move Geronimo made. If you have allegiance to the earth, you cannot want war. War tears the people apart, and then the territory. It tore all the tribes apart in America. It always does. Red or white. We imagine we are peaceable people, but the western world is bound by war as it is by men in robes, by women in tight dresses, by dogs that kill the creatures of the wild for pleasure. America has been making war in the world since the fifties, when modern consumerism was designed as a way of life. Like all empires, it requires conquest and enemies. The dream, though it speaks of peace and brotherhood, is founded on conflict. To end the dream you have to end the conflict, lay down your arms. You have to place your allegiance outside the Empire.

What was I going to do about the American dream? I was going inhabit the real American dream and let the false one pass by and fade. The dream of the earth lies deep in the land: in this hawk, this rock, this energy under the rock, this mountain, these sky islands,

203

this vast plain spreading before me. The dream is this bush on a red hill where I sit, a visitor who also is not a visitor, connecting with ancestors, animals, plants and sun. A council of all beings that starts with myself.

When I am here, this self in this territory, I remember everything. I remember whose arms hold me, where my allegiance lies.

snakebroom
Bisbee junction, Arizona 2000

It was during the storm-time, at the crest of the second flower wave, that Mimi came one day to our apartment in the desert hotel and we found ourselves talking about the earth dialogues. 'I think I need to work with you,' she said.

I looked at her with curiosity and some misgiving. The dialogues had had their shortcomings. There was always someone unwilling to connect with plants, someone looking awkward in a tree, a girl nervously marooned on a cushion of moss or a man who was weeping about the past and turning his head away from the mountains, lamenting the damage of the quarry as it flourished before his eyes. It was not that these feelings were irrelevant, but there was a lack of intent to explore them.

But the person who had just appeared before us was unlike any of our former companions. She possessed a singular quality I had not yet encountered in anyone else: medicine attention.

For twenty-five years, Mimi had lived on the edge of this 'last outpost of the Roman Empire', making medicines from the plants of the Chihuahua desert. She had drawn them, photographed them, catalogued them, taught others how to make tinctures from their flowers and leaves. It was Mimi who had shown us where Indian snakeroot hid under river rocks, where skullcap sprawled in the scree along the canyon. Mimi thought nothing of driving her truck a hundred miles across the border to collect elephant gum, or sitting in the wilderness connecting with organ pipe cactus in 100 degrees Fahrenheit.

'We are plant people,' she announces, as if to seal a bargain between us. One thing is for sure: we are fellow workers. We can bring a technology, Mark and I – our *seeings*, flower dialogues, earth dialogues, working with dreams. Mimi knows this desert territory, rock by rock. She knows homeopathy, Chinese herbs, how to grow exotic vines down at Turtle Ranch, rare cactus, a field of mugwort. What we share is medicine attention, the ability to pay attention to what is going down in the room, to bring into balance what is so clearly askew.

'We need a structure,' says Mark, who is pragmatic and likes to establish the correct path along which to proceed.

'There is a craving for ritual,' declares Mimi, who is fiery, inspirational, keen to find a showcase for the plants.

'I'm for temporary set-ups, myself,' I say airily, wary of ritual, game for adventure. 'You know, an agreement for the flowers. We could throw it open and see what flowers wanted to come and speak with us.'

In the beginning we met to find out our elemental qualities, how our temperaments worked together, how we inspired each other, the three of us, the way we laughed. We walked out into the territory, along hill paths, roadsides and chaparral, and jammed around Mimi's kitchen table in her house in town. It was one of those ordinary clapboard houses you find in America, down a dusty suburban street: one storey, a screen door, porch, a front yard, a shade tree. The kitchen was the centre of the house: a pot of beans sat on the stove next to another of creosote salve, the crockery shelf was lined with Mason jars filled with macerating roots and leaves. In the middle of the large wooden table were sprigs and twigs in pots – hop tree, filaree, apache plume – a stack of notebooks, a bundle of pens and half-finished illustrations for a botanical guide. We would go round and sit here and talk plants: about queen of the night, morning glory, cliffrose, condalia, cocklebur. I talked about our encounters with people, Mark talked about the challenges experienced in medicine work, Mimi talked about a *curandero* called Francisco she was working with down in the Sonora desert. Sometimes a plant grabbed our attention more than another. There's a bush called Graythorn out there, Mimi would say. It's totally radiant. Mark wrote the name down, started making an inventory of names, flashes of our quicksilver communications. We ate the beans with a stack of tortillas, drank cups of tea made from the leaves in the jars. On the windowsill a jungle milkweed was opening, its wide zigzag petals like a Zulu shield. A faint stench of rotting meat pervaded the air. Outside the thunder rocked the canyons, the afternoon rain poured down the guttering of the house.

One day Mimi hands me a small box.

'It's for you,' she says. Inside are a row of small bottles. Each one is an essence made from cactus flowers. They are beautifully presented.

I study them carefully, the labels, the instructions printed on the underside of the lid.

'Do they work together?' I ask her.

'What do you mean?

'Do the plants relate to one another?'

We look at each other. Something is happening, forming itself, as we speak.

'Maybe we could do a kit,' I say.

'The plants will choose themselves,' declares Mimi.

'That's good,' I say, 'I like that. They will just come to us. What do you think about datura?'

'What about cottonwood?' asks Mark.

'What about noxious weeds?' says Mimi. 'The ones no one loves?'

We laugh.

'Seriously,' she says, 'the weeds are important, because they are successful where others are endangered. They appear when the land needs restoring.'

One morning I woke up and saw the kit in my mind's eye. It was going to be six plants that emerged after the monsoon rains, six end-of-the-season plants. There was a rattlesnake on the lid.

'We need to create a space to hold the focus,' I said. 'Here's a bottle, a container for our experiences. When it's held transmutation can happen. We just need an agreement to hang in there and let things pass.'

'You've got to trust the process rather than the goal,' said Mimi.

'The real work is not being done because of being too defensive,' said Mark.

'Everything,' I said, 'needs to be out in the open.'

Medicine plants are often 'tested' by a process called proving. Proving means taking a medicine and seeing what happens in your physical body, your feelings, your thoughts. By engaging in the plants this way, you experience their influence personally, so you know what you are administering to others when you practice. Medicine attention works in a similar way: you engage with the energies of the plant and recognise what comes up within yourself, between yourselves in the dialogue. The difference between the two is that with medicine attention you don't know what to expect. The pathway has not been taken before. It's original, 'on the edge' work. Whatever happens between you and the others and the plant makes the path. Your shared intent means everything in this endeavour.

We combined our skills – of proving, essence making, drawing, writing, dreaming – and we began to forge a work in those dialogues around the kitchen table. Contained in this space we found ourselves naturally oracular. Everything that came up between us – difficult feelings, dreams, nervousness, insights – was aired, explored, turned into material. Unlike the earth dialogues, which lasted about one or two hours and often felt like a one-off workshop, the three of us could go all day. That's what medicine attention requires: you keep going until something shifts. You weren't doing it to entertain yourself, you were doing it for real. You were creating a work that could transmit itself to others as much as yourself.

'It's about vibes,' I say, gazing into the iridescent petals of a portulaca, known as bearflower.

'That is a lazy word,' says Mark. 'People will think "hippy" and switch off.'

'Vibes are energy information in a field,' I snap back.

We began to be snappy as turtles around the table, scratchy as the ocotillo, thorny as a mesquite bush. We felt a hundred prickly feelings none of us wanted to feel. But none of it mattered because we had medicine attention. We had an agreement that kept us on track. It wasn't perfect. Our strong characters sometimes clashed. Mimi often had other commitments, went walkabout for days, disappearing down into Mexico. Sometimes the monsoon days were oppressive, put us out of the mood, the flowers shook us up the wrong way. But when we met, we got down to business. We make the difficulty of opening our mouths our material. We took turns speaking round that table, letting words come out from ourselves. We called ourselves Dandelion Productions in honour of the weeds and thought we were in for the long haul.

One morning we went to a canyon in the Huachuca mountains, just outside Sierra Vista. We had planned to have a quiet breakfast by the stream, hanging out with columbines and stream orchids. But when we arrived everyone felt tired and depressed. I refused to join in a conversation about a sick person in town. 'You are rigid and not allowing!' Mark shouted. 'You don't even care about this person!' I shouted back. Mimi was offended by our bad behaviour and clammed up. I waltzed off.

Bloody healing lark! I thought as I sat down at a pool under the cool shade of an Arizona plane.

The urchin-faced monkey flowers grimaced and grinned at me:
We've all heard the bad news, when's the good news going to start? they said.

I laughed. The plane leaves shook in the breeze. I didn't know why I had interrupted the dialogue. I had just had enough of all that talk of woe and suffering and other people. After a while Mimi and Mark came and sat down by the flowers and we got over ourselves. The argument shook us up, made us pay attention to the moment, to what we were doing together. We drove up the canyon in search of bee balm and false arnica; the sisters butterflies danced ahead of us on the track. I felt full of energy and free.

The monkey flowers had broken the ice. After that we could really get going. You can't be polite and pussyfoot around each other when you do original work with plants. Especially when you are in a canyon just outside the military base of Fort Huachuca. You have to consider the territory. You just have to let surface what is there and ride the storm. Sometimes you have to stick out your monkey-tongue and walk devil-may-care upstream.

'We should call ourselves High Desert Speaks,' said Mimi.

'I think it should be called The Snake Sequence,' I said.

'It could really be about transformation,' Mark said.

'Let's go down by the wash in San Jose tomorrow and look at some morning glories,' said Mimi. 'There's kidneywood down there too.'

It was the kidneywood that showed us what needed to be transformed. We passed several bushes en route to the wash, their fronded leaves bright green after the rains. Kidneywood is a member of the pea family and like other peas its flowers are arresting, bright white, strong-scented, and jump out at you like the shiny yellow of gorse or broom. In the Southwest it is not used as a herbal cure, but as an essence: the subtle energies of its flowers work directly with deep and buried emotions, what lies hidden under the surface.

'It's about *susto*,' remarked Mimi, as she cut a twig to take back and told us how Francisco's apprentice had had to confront the bullying he had suffered as a child at the hands of an angry father when he had come here the week before. 'It touched him in his wound place,' she said.

Susto is the Spanish word for shock, the kind of shock you have as a child when you realise that the human world is a hostile place. The kidneys represent the child as well as the ancestors in Chinese medicine, and kidneywood is sometimes used to help one confront what is known as *primary insult*, a traumatic event in which you find out that those who supposedly care for you dislike your real being and only want you to exist on their terms. At this shocking disclosure the real child that is you disappears and starts constructing an artificial self moulded on approval from the huge beings ruling its world – its parents and teachers. This false self then starts to run the show. Anytime you try to contact your original being thereafter, the fear and hostility experienced at the original *susto* surfaces and forces you back into the welter of neuroses, complexes and fantasies you have carefully constructed in order to defend yourself.

Primary insult is well-recognised by people who work with trauma. Our modern world is infamously full of shocked and traumatised children. However, it is rarely acknowledged that this traumatic self-censorship is how the institutions of the world keep everyone under their control. And that perhaps it is time we no longer allowed these hostile and intimidating forces to run through us and silence our hearts and each other.

When we returned from our walk we sat around the kitchen table, talking about childhood wounds as the kidneywood flowers exuded their strong vanilla-like scent into the dry morning air. Before we knew it, archetypal forces and primary insults were running riot. The *susto* happens usually very early in life, so these forces are powerful, inchoate, full of the shrieking terrors of babyhood. One of the principles of 'proving' essences is that you let the plant throw you into the very state it helps align, so you can look at these invisible forces and get clear. We looked at each other in shock and confusion as the furious winds of our collective feelings whirled about the desert kitchen.

'I think we need to move from defence into radiance,' said Mimi in that understated way she had of just saying things.

Mark exhaled deeply his breath moving the scent of the flowers around the room.

And then the whirling stopped.

It was always like that when we worked together. Big sentences would suddenly appear out of nowhere, one of us would respond, and things would shift. It was like that from the beginning. We had gone one winter's night in '94 to supper at Peter's studio and Mimi was there. At one point during the meal, she leaned dramatically across the rocket salad and told me about how the elder stands at the edge of the dark wood and can act as a bridge between the outer sunlight world and your deeper instinctive inner being. I just stared at her and said WOW!

It was the most interesting thing anyone had ever said to me about a plant.

'We collected these today,' said Peter as we departed, and showed us a wooden box with black seeds inside.

'You should try them,' said Mimi. 'They're neat.'

The seeds were from the night-flowering plant known as Sacred Datura. Mark and I took nine seeds each and the dreams we had that night were *anything* but neat. Mark dreamed he was not himself, and I dreamed of soldiers undergoing horrific sexual initiations at Fort Huachuca (datura is infamously connected with the army). But something in my imagination took hold that night. By the time Mimi reappeared in our lives six years later, we were game for all kinds of full-on encounters with *sustos* and insults. It meant the sequence could be tough – tough plants, tough subjects, tough going – and perhaps because it was so tough, it was to endure more than any of our plant work with others. The beauty of toughness is something you learn from the desert. We needed to be tough because the monster of self-pity we had once glimpsed with peyote had just came leering into view, out of the kidneywood fronds.

'What was going on in the room?' I asked.

'The plant triggered something old,' Mimi answered.

We had gone into lock-down. Our bodies registered ancient fears. We shrank from one other. Oppression and terror stalked the kitchen table, while we sat small and terrified inside.

Confronting childhood terror is a prerequisite for transformation. If we don't face this lock-down, dismantle our defences, none of us grows up and the world remains cruel. The oceans fall silent, the forest disappears before our eyes and we can say nothing. We are scared of everyone. We escape into anything that offers consolation. We rush after power, protection, attention, we vent our griefs and our grievances, but none of these things transform our world. Our inner territories have been constructed around these *sustos*. Engulfed by self-pity, we have every excuse not to be creative or in charge. With this Great Wound we can remain eternally insulted. If anyone challenges us, we instantly short-circuit, loop backwards into our traumas, into our control towers, and silently start transferring our introjected hostility with a vengeance.

Transformation begins the moment you are prepared to put yourself on the line and face the terror. It couldn't really happen before with the girl in the mackintosh in a tree, or sitting scaredy-cat in the woods, everyone in their hidey-holes with no agreement. You need a kind of long-term commitment to do that work together and you need to be tough enough, experienced enough, grounded enough to do it. Speaking circles, especially those to do with the future and the earth, are often poisoned by those negative *sustos*. This is why you cannot linger in your childhood hurts and shames, because you remain subject to the institutions of the world, defending yourself from those who did you wrong long ago. Through the door of your wound pours all the antagonism of Empire and prevents the future from happening.

To engage in the work of transformation means these hostile forces no longer have any hold over you, and by extension, wherever you walk on the planet. To be equal to the task requires you keep your own wound door firmly shut and know your allegiance is with the earth. We were English and American, from different houses, genders and classes, but the hostilities kidneywood brought out into the open were the same. The world's Empire stood on our heads, dictated our thoughts, ran through our emotional bodies, like machine-fire. We experienced everything personally, but it wasn't personal. Our fears were not psychological individual problems, but the result of being indoctrinated and intimidated into a particular perception of the world, and bullied for a lifetime into giving our vital life-force to uphold it.

In some ways we did not know what we were doing in this business of alignment, of closing and opening doors, and in other ways we all did. We knew we needed to shift from being small defensive creatures with stuck inner worlds to being bold, radiant individuals who could speak one among the many. We knew that the flowers would demonstrate these qualities of radiance as much as they would bring our energetic blocks to them to light. We knew the rattlesnake in whose territory these flowers grew was a master key. We knew that in our endeavours, however they turned out, we would find the tools for this transformation, what needed to be lightened up. And that whatever happened between ourselves, the flowers and the land would be recorded in these essences and become their signature.

In short we knew even before the flowers came we were embarking on what Gary Snyder, poet and activist, once called the real work, 'hard yoga for Earth'.

The six flowers were all weeds. You would pass them by as they stand, nameless, stateless, under threat by herbicides, growing with great abandon after the rains, out of overgrazed pastures, by the side of the road, with their irrepressible dusty thorns and rough green leaves. Already embarked on the regeneration business, we had learned to pay them respect. Already we know that the transformers of the wastegrounds will restore us. It was what the plants were doing there, when things had got out of balance.

The six flowers took the shape of the curled-up rattlesnake, sleeping as he sheds his skin. They appeared one by one as the Indian summer deepened into fall. At the snake's head there appeared a tiny morning glory, known as Arizona blue eyes; at the tail, a fragrant golden-haired bush called snakebroom. Each flower in the snake's body showed a move we needed to make so we could 'shed' our historical programming. Key to this process was activating the different earth energies represented by the flowers within ourselves. The smelly and hairy-leaved unicorn plant, devil's claw, reminded us of our physical life-force, the red-stemmed wild food plant, amaranth, our solar energies, the delicate mallow, desert cotton, our beauty and grace, the radiant spiky graythorn, our mysterious spirits. Arizona blue eyes opened our own eyes to seeing the world anew, the snakebroom swept the old one away to be consumed in the snake's mouth. We visited the flowers in their territories, in the washes, arroyos and canyons; dreamed with them, held *seeings*, kept a dialogue open as their spiky forms, flowers and roots lay upon on the kitchen table. Mark kept the log. As we connected with their qualities and dialogued about their effects in our ordinary lives, we realised we spent our time giving the qualities represented by the flowers away, that what we most curb in ourselves, what we most fear to express are those very things we are best at: the electrical energy of our heart, our magnetic attraction,

213

our bright ideas, the sounds of our own voices.

It was October by the time we worked with snakebroom. The five previous flowers had keyed us into the energies and intelligence of our physical, emotional, mental and spiritual bodies. The snakeweed came in with a great cosmic dance, with the kind of inner moves that could shuffle off an old cycle and begin a new. All the plants shook us up, but none as much as this sunflower bush. Shake-up medicine is what you need for transformation. The shake up was everywhere around us as we met. The violent monsoon weather wreaks havoc in the desert and disturbs its typically fierce but serene mood. The sky goes dark, the washes fill up with torrents of water, lightning crackles overhead for hours, the roads flood, your bones ache and, like the snake, everyone is hyper-alert, on edge, uncertain. You have to step carefully when the rattlesnake is shedding his skin: he is blind in these times and vulnerable, and will lash out at anything that threatens him.

We were threatened on all sides by difficulty, inside ourselves, between ourselves. The vigorous devil's claw challenged our inhibitions, the solar amaranth our lack of love, the beauty of wild cotton our sexual slavery. People stared at us as we sat by the roadside, border guards questioned us, lightning unnerved Mark, our car broke down. But when we sat at first by the soft haze of the snakebroom, down by the footbridge to Mimi's ranch, we felt at peace. It had appeared at the end, as the monsoon time was giving way to the clarity of fall, a myriad yellow flowers on rigid stems like so many eyes on stalks, imbued with a musty honey-coloured scent. It felt homely, dependable as we sat there. It's a famous folk remedy for arthritis and is sometimes used as a brush, hence its common name. Sufferers from all kinds of inflammatory states in the south-west and northern Mexico put bunches of snakebroom in their baths and drink cups of its golden-coloured tea to soothe their aches and pains. But they also take it because its snake dance livens everything up, makes sinuous all cramped and creaky conditions, warms up those cold inert places where we have become stiff and crystallised, shut down.

The Empire shuts us all down, keeps us small and silent and terrified stiff in its low repressive vibration. Stuck inside our interior narratives, we allow these old power structures to hold sway. Everyone tells us it is our problem, that we don't fit, don't succeed, don't feel at home inside our own skins. We feel overwhelmed by responsibility.

We close down all our options, recede ever further, protecting ourselves from the world's furious gods and its systems, while we wait for a magical elixir, for the paradigm to shift miraculously on its own. As we sat by the plant, we realised something else was needed. The snake was soothing at first, made us relax, be at ease in one another's company, but then it had another effect: you began to wriggle and move about. You wanted to get up and shimmy. The shake-it-up snakebroom was showing us how to connect with our cosmic life-force, the serpentine energy that runs down our spines, so we could vibrate at the same rate as the earth rather than be held down in the low frequency of the Empire.

Fired up by its energy, we encountered exactly what was going on with the snake. It was as if the six plants were converging in the snakebroom. It was shaking off the Empire, all those memories out of our cells, cracking up old forms, throwing out the old programming, bringing in new energies. Everything was on the move, up for reorganisation, the idols were falling – all the cold and heartless parts of ourselves, the madonnas and angels, emperors and generals. It was showing us how to slough off our old skins, like the diamond-back who lay sleeping now in the long grass, so that a small bird, a rock wren, could one day come and take it away for his nest.

Down by the bridge we sat down together around the sun-coloured bush. Afterwards we went into the straw bale cabin, and Mark sang a chant. We felt pain in our chests. Then we spoke:

'I felt the chanting aligned with the snake,' Mimi said. 'I went very quickly into a deep place, and the snake was pulling out old energies. It was uncomfortable – painful. Normally snakeweed takes away all the pain without processes, like a light sweep. But I'm sitting there going deeper and deeper. There is intense emotion, a lot of sadness – some guilt. So I say to myself "I'm just going to close my eyes and let go." A broom appeared in front of my eyes but it wasn't able to just whisk the pain away. The snake was coiled up inside my torso and starting to shake, shaking off falsities, as if the earth was shaking. I started seeing patches on the snake. The snake was made up of many segments that were breaking up and separating. It shook old patterns apart – then the soft, cloudlike soothing broom came and was sweeping them away.'

'I thought,' Mark said, 'why have I been so shy? This chanting is something I can do. I felt the energetic effect of lightning. I thought: If I hear lightning I will stay until Charlotte and Mimi are ready. Then I realised: I'm in it. I felt like I was here and was going to stay till I was ready. I felt the beauty of completion, of not running away before the end. I realised I didn't just want to be a notemaker. I was aware of snakes, of lightning. I realised that all the things I am afraid of are myself. Last night I heard the words: Re-initiate your spirit work. I'm not going to run away.'

'Last night I had a dream,' I said. 'There was a snake by this very bridge but on the other side. When I sat by the bridge, it was like my dream. When Mark chanted I felt everything come round in a full circle, that wholeness which pulls all things together. I saw a golden presence, a glowing being, radiating outwards. I heard the wind through the cottonwood, the sound of cockerels and dogs. The earth was golden. I realised we were going from number five to number six, going from human consciousness to form some cosmic pattern.

'The snake was activating me. I felt its energy in my solar plexus and my heart, moving upward and outwards. The cosmic sound was in my ears. The chanting brought the two centres together. The earth was calling other cosmic beings, the planets, to be of assistance in letting go and throwing off the old skin. When humans are fired up like this they can attract energies which give the earth a hand.

'I felt the whole high desert coming towards us because it wanted to attend. A strong sense of presence was key: it was not the "I am here" of the ego, but the "I am here" of the heart, so that all that is "I am" is here.'

We spoke: around the table, in the strawbale, in the territory. We were seeing ourselves with the plants. The plants were our bodies, our talents, the way we interacted with each other. We saw our strengths and our weaknesses, our serious sibylline selves speaking, our rude roughness coming up the path, how we could not be afraid of ourselves, how our energies worked in harmony. How our blue-eyed brilliance needed the love and warmth of amaranth, how our sober greythorn spirit needed the beautiful show of wild cotton, how the shattering snake-dance needed the humour and rumbustious nature of the devil's claw. We remembered everything. I saw Mimi in her desert cotton dress, I saw blue sparks flashing out of Mark's eye as he chanted.

'For a while the three of us were like snakes, shaking and dancing around,' Mimi was saying. 'We were spiralling around, with masks and headdresses on like Apache mountain spirit dancers. I felt like a deer. I looked at the ground. There was a shape made out of earth – round – with three bars across it. I reached down and picked it up. It was like a turtle and then it was a turtle,' she said.

Don't lose the thread to your wild self, said the wild cotton to Mark. The strength of the heart is something to be reckoned with, said Mark to us, as he held the amaranth seeds in his hand. The six plants were a cycle: you started with a blue spark, landed on earth in physical form, there was movement, growth, attraction and relationship, wisdom, then you shook off your mortal coil and went back to the beginning. It was life, really. The whole scene was in earth colours, said Mimi, ochres and gold, but the masks were blue, indigo, the colour of night sky. One thing, I said, about the snake. There is a gap between the beginning and the end. We cannot be a closed system. We have to consume the tail. At some point we have to open our mouths.

Out of nowhere he came, the feathered serpent.

'The earth is part of a cosmic event and the snake is activating everything.' I was saying. 'The snake does not exist on its own. It is ascending to meet something and that something is coming down to meet it. The snake and the bird need to merge. We need to go up.'

That was when the rift happened. The moment the eagle came into play. Outside everything was the same. The afternoon remained hot and still, the lizards were still sleeping under the rocks, a breeze stirring the cottonwood leaves, Francisco carried on moving past the cactus-studded window with a spade. Inside we sat in the same positions on the floor, on an old carpet, a spring of snakebroom in a pot. But something had torn through the strawbale house and thrown us all apart.

The feathered serpent is a mythological creature, a juxtaposition of bird and snake. It signifies the dynamic between the realms of earth and sky. It's an image found throughout the Mesoamerican world. In Mexico this eagle-serpent is known as Quetzalcoatl, and relates to the alchemical planet of Venus. In Europe and the Orient it bears the form of a dragon, whose elemental presence underlies all life on earth. All cultures interact with the fabric of life in consideration of this alchemical creature. But there are no dragons in America, at least none that are talked about, and for some reason the mention of this mythical beast has snapped the connection between us. There was a sudden drop in energy in the room. Everything slowed down. The snake is about earth, Mimi declared after a long silence, and didn't want to discuss the matter any further. Mark had no truck either with this sudden shift into the invisible realms. I kept talking about dragons. I was as earth-centric as the others and had no desire to indulge in any fancies about otherworlds or ascension, but I had seen something in the centre of the radiant snakebroom. I saw that something was being required as we danced from the fifth plant and into the sixth. We needed to make a dimensional leap, beyond our medicine attention and into ancestral imagination.

'We need to make a bridge,' I said.

Try as we might, however, we could not get back together again. We talked about the rift, about our resistances, and set a date for another meeting. But in the invisible place where vibes are energy-information-in-the-field we had become stuck and could not cross the bridge. Invisible power structures constrained us, and we needed our creative faculties to deal with them, our ability to see imaginatively, mythologically, in deep time. We found ourselves ill-equipped for this venture, no longer in the right territory.

Modern America, like all empires, is built on the repression of the *mythos*. But it does this in a unique and unprecedented way, by erasing its very existence. This denial gives it all its power, all its attraction, and all of its weakness. You become American by leaving your ancestors behind in the old country, by cutting your roots to the motherland. In many ways you are free, free from obligation, from mythology, free to start again. But this freedom comes at a price, especially in your imagination. As you become part of a streamlined monoculture you suffer, without knowing you suffer, from a great collective *susto*. You are living an existence outside ancestral time and place. This lack of relationship with what native cultures call 'the real world' has turned America into the most defensive nation in the world.

To return to earth you have, at some point, to come together in an ancestral way, in a collective way. To engage in this shift we had to let go of our 'little me' egos and become of one heart. The transformation that up to now had been based on our personal biographies, with all

218

their human trials and traumas, had suddenly became collective. The snakebroom, like all sunflowers, is a composite group of flowers. We were no longer just Mark and Mimi and Charlotte, we were all human beings in transition, part of a composite group, part of a mythological and cosmic cycle. We were being fired up so we could attract energies from other dimensions that would give the earth a hand.

For this task we needed to be bigger than our small selves. We needed to open our mouths and go up together, out of the world of the five senses and into our sixth sense. The rattlesnake is a creature of the sun, and like all sun-creatures – reindeer, cats, bees – has the ability to 'fly' to the sun with human beings on its back. This event can only happen on an ancestral earth in which all creatures are related. You don't access this earth with the rational mind, with the moral, monodimensional mindset of the industrial world: you access it with your creative ancestral imagination, in the way all peoples have done through time. As we sat by the bush by the bridge, I had felt the high desert coming towards us because it wanted to attend to this moment. We had attracted its attention with our strong presence and the sound we made together. But then the *susto* had happened. Something came in and diverted our plans.

Where shall we go from here? we were left wondering as the afternoon faded. But by that time Mimi had disappeared. She had gone to work with Francisco who was building a temascal down among the pepperweeds.

Years later, I will stand with a small box of rainbow-coloured bottles in my hand, their flower labels drawn by Mimi, the brochure inside collated from Mark's notes. On the cover there is a picture of a devil's claw seed pod. It looks like the horns of a deer, like a curled-up snake, like a womb. I am telling an audience of strangers in England how six weeds from the Arizona desert can transform your life, and words are pouring effortlessly from my mouth.

I have dreamed of this moment. Born tongue-tied, stammering, nervous, last in a long line of smooth-talking advocates, I have dreamed of being able speak eloquently in public. The Snake Sequence is giving me this chance. I am doing my snake dance and everyone is laughing. But as Mark and I show our slides of the desert plants, I realise that this performance is not really what the flowers were about. That the success I had hoped for for them was not really the success I had hoped for. We had planned to distribute the flower knowledge held in those small bottles, to put on a show and speak about our findings. But rattlesnake medicine doesn't happen in places where everyone is looking for entertainment or the soft forgiving touch of the broom. It happens in tough real-life communication. When you put yourself on the line and allow yourself to be shaken up, the way the flowers had once challenged us in those difficult monsoon times.

The truth was, I had already had that extraordinary dialogue. I realised as I stood there that though we had made The Snake Sequence for other people, it had been for ourselves. It was what we did, Mark, Mimi and I, when we met each other. I had to honour that, really. It is the hardest part of the solar path: because when you sit down together and decide to do things for real, you have to acknowledge that sometimes it doesn't turn out the way you would have liked it to, or thought it should. It was like that with our projects in those years. It was about doing them at the time, not where they led us, or didn't. It was like that in America too. Perhaps it is always like that. I met the most extraordinary people there, but we couldn't talk in the way I would have liked to, which is to say *freely*. Or rather we did talk but there were just too many *sustos* in the way. Personal *sustos*, collective *sustos*. I had to come to terms with that. It didn't mean The Snake Sequence was a failure. Because it was still looking at us all the time with its blue Arizona eyes and shaking us up seven years later. *Do your dance,* it said. Most of what it shook up was the feeling that we should have got it down somehow.

That day I did my dance and spoke about the sequence out loud I realised I wouldn't meet another person like Mimi and be able to sit around a table with a sprig of kidneywood and weather the storm in the way we all once had. I remembered then how she would always stop the truck if she saw a dead snake on the road and respectfully lay it on the side among the flowers. One time she told us she found a deer on the road. It looked dead but something made her punch it in the heart. Be alive! she commanded and the startled deer jumped up and ran away.

The sequence taught me everything about medicine, about *sustos* and shocks and what it will take for us to get back on track. It taught me that when someone punches you in the heart and commands you to be alive, you jump up and pay attention. Sometimes I think about those days when we sat on the roadside by the devil's claw or cooked up a bunch of amaranth leaves, or lay down together in the straw bale and spoke about the snakebroom with its golden flowers, when we stuck out our monkey-tongues at each other and wore mountain-masks the colour of the Arizona sky. They were the toughest times imaginable. But even though I have had easier encounters since then, easier relationships, and lived in easier places, I haven't found anything anywhere as good as those times.

red root
Highway 90, Arizona 2000

Along the borderlands there are two great tribes that hold position within in the territory: the warriors of the hills, the Apache, and the dreamers of the desert, the Yaqui. The Yaqui in Europe are known as the tribe from which Carlos Castaneda's teacher, the seer Don Juan, originated. But in Arizona they are known as the people who speak with flowers and dance with the deer.

Across the earth the people run alongside the deer. With his antlers in the spirit worlds, his hooves on the ground, the fleet-footed deer roams across the plains and hills of our ancestral lands – the white antelope of the African savannah, the red stags of the British Isles, the reindeer of the far north. In the neolithic caves of France the man-deer is the lord of the animals, the speaking bridge between all living things. In the deserts of Mexico the deer is the peyote, hunted by the Huichol, the door to their rainbow-coloured dreamtime. In the deer parks of India the Buddha gives his discourse on right action, on dispelling the illusions of the world. We are, in our zenith, a people of deer. All cultures, when they put the deer antlers on their heads, indicate that they are accessing the fleet worlds of spirit, connecting the people with the correct walking of the way.

For the Yaqui the deer is an animal of the Otherworld who comes into this phenomenal world to bring life to the people: who lives, dies, leaves his body for food, and then returns. It is a hunter myth and a teaching myth. For the deer is also ourselves. He is showing us how we come into this life to give sustenance for life itself. Each spring a man dressed as a deer dances the deer dance for the Yaqui people and for the land. I have not seen the deer dance but I have seen deer on this mountain: their clear gaze that holds yours for a full moment before they vanish into the air, white tails bobbing, small stones skittering down the slope. *You are an enchanted flower wilderness world*, sing the deer men. *You lie with see-through freshness.* The deer emerge from behind the live oaks to chew the leaves of the hillside bushes. One of their favourites is the fragrant wild lilac. It is known as deer brush.

I am sitting in a canyon beside the deer brush on a clear fall day. In gardens this bush is called ceanothus because of its cultivated blue flowers (from the Greek *cean,* meaning blue). 'Mother's milk', Eliot Cowan called it when he introduced me to the bush. I am not sure I would call it that. In fact, something balked in me when he said those words in California. 'Californian lilac' is another of its names, as it flourishes in the rocky coastal hills in all shades of blue and cream. In Arizona it is better known as red root, and is highly valued by herbalists. The first time I came to this canyon was with Mimi to gather some of its wintergreen-scented roots that colour everything red.

Red root is a medicine for the spleen, an organ little known by modern western people. In Chinese medicine it governs the earth element, and is sometimes called the organ of the mother. The spleen governs the lymphatic system that transports food and waste from the blood into the cells. By correspondence, it relates to the mind and the mouth. Imbalances of the earth element are often detected by 'singing', by the sound of people who do not stop talking.

The spleen works in dynamic with the stomach, organising what goes where. It is not the milk-providing mother, but the red-blooded mother who decides what is nourishing and what is waste, what should be stored, dispersed, refused. The organiser of all our transport systems. Without this director, all life in ourselves and on earth goes haywire.

The strict instructions of the spleen, however, are frequently destabilised by the mindset of the modern world. This mindset, intent on keeping all people infantilised, ignorantly sucking the planet dry, intimidates the part of us that would naturally restrict our appetite, tell ourselves to get real and grow up. The spleen, knowing the real sweetness of earthly life, has no time for the fairy cakes and fairytales of Empire. If our spleens were given a voice, they would remind us that the earth needs adults to keep the human world in balance. It requires a people who know what it means to kill a deer and consume its flesh, or wrench the roots of a bush out of a mountain.

The Empire silences the spleen, overloads it with false promises, threatens it to conform. The wild lilac brings the spleen's intelligence to our attention. It does this in its own way, gently, fiercely. You can take the sweet-smelling tincture to cure your swollen side, or you can go up into the mountains and sit by the plant to find the root cause of your predicament.

I sit beside the red root bush on a hot September afternoon, place a travelling Mason jar within its spiky branches filled with spring water. In March these small round bushes are fragrant, frothy with blossom, but now after the summer rains they are distinguished by long grey spines that stick out at right-angles beyond their small tongue-shaped green leaves. I am alone on a promontory above the highway that goes past the town, surrounded by the tall rocks of the mountain pass at the mouth of the canyon. A track winds behind me and disappears. Below me on a rocky scree is a carpet of skullcap, its flowers winking like little blue eyes. An empty container lorry stands in the lay-by. There is no one about, but I am queasy, filled with disquiet. Earlier I heard a dog barking further up the canyon, and then men shouting. Are they hunting? Are they chasing someone? It is quiet now except for the traffic that goes by below me, but I am still on edge, feeling I shouldn't be here, unwelcome. I don't like this anxiety, except I know this is part of the bush's medicine. So I keep still. The red root is a tenacious bush, it clings to the rocky land throughout the west. The more precariously placed the bush, the stronger its roots, the stronger its medicine. The more I can hold on, the stronger I will be. Even though I am jumpy, easily intimidated by shots, shouting, dogs, thoughts of attack, I am aware I need to go through this and not to budge from my position. When I decide to hold my ground, that's when the bush speaks out of the blue:

Do not feed them. Not this time.

The last time was a key moment in the history of America: the moment when the 'Red Indians' appear out of the woods and bring the Pilgrim Fathers nourishment from their larder after the harsh Massachusetts winter. Their English wheat has failed and they are facing starvation The indigenous foods the Algonquin people bring are the three sisters – pumpkins, beans and corn. By teaching them how to sow their seeds, gather medicine and build strong shelters, they help the pilgrims to survive. The original Thanksgiving was given in celebration of this exchange and the sweet sisters and the native turkey still form the modern version of this feast. But the settlers' gratitude was short-lived. The wars waged against the Wampanoag nation over natural resources were the most bloody of any conflict fought on American soil, and this intimidation continued as the 'savages' of all North America were hounded, displaced and their lands appropriated in a systemised genocide

224

that most of the pilgrim's descendants do not care to recall.

In 1676 the original native Americans had taken pity on the settlers, and their generosity sealed their doom. In 2000 the red root bush was telling me: *Do not feed them, not this time.* It was instructing the native red-blooded 'mother' of myself not to feel sorry for those who could not feed themselves. Not to allow myself to be intimidated and overrun.

I am intimidated in the canyon because like everyone else I fear reprisal. We are bullied from the moment we are born to remain within the confines of an artificially managed world, and our minds continue to bully us as we grow older. *If I don't do what I am told, death will come to me!* Everyone in our dreams, at our workplaces is after us to be other than we naturally are; we are hounded by our friends and relations to be kind, to be sweet, to be forgiving, to take the rap. Rarely do we set out and explore the territory of the earth. We have been taught to fear places that have no people in them. You need the discipline of the spleen to rid the emotional body of these childish and imaginary fears. Fear is the greatest obstacle to freedom, to enjoying the fruits of being alive. You shake this fear loose by walking in the wild places, by taking up position in the territory, by contacting your own authority.

As I sit in the canyon I become aware of the bush's roots, of my own feet. It feels as if we share an anchor between us, tapped into the earth's magnetic field. Even though the sounds have unnerved me, something stronger is holding me secure in my position. I realise that although my thoughts are jumping around in my head like terrified mice – *danger! leave! go home! death is coming!* – my body feels relaxed. As I sit there my field of vision expands and brings everything within the territory into view. I feel the presence of the other bushes and trees around me – catclaw, tree of heaven, black walnut, mountain mahogany – sense the sentinel rocks, notice two eagles circling in the sky, the sky's outstanding blue. As my awareness opens, a expanse fills me and in that vastness, my fear begins to disappear.

It was Alex who told me about the wild turkeys. A friend of his had kept turkeys in the north. He said that sometimes the wild turkeys came to visit the ranch, and sometimes his turkeys went with them, and did not return.

'Did it ever happen the other way round?' I asked.

Alex laughed.

'What do you think?' he said.

The wild turkey is a beautiful bird, startling in its colours, its great tail that fans out like its relative the peacock. To stumble across the wild turkey in the canyons of America is to behold the beauty and integrity of true form. Afterwards you don't think about turkeys in the same way.

When the real thing crosses your path is when you realise how peculiar your human life is. You start asking yourself the questions your upbringing threatens you never to ask. But it's too late. You realise that the domesticated fowl is a strange contortion of its original self. We are a strange contortion of ourselves. Thanksgiving is a strange contortion of the Native American *potlatch* given in praise of the harvest.

How do we return to our original selves, to become the kind of people who can celebrate our passage on earth with all our relations? One day the wild turkey comes and waits outside the door. You have to recognise the moment. You can't stay in your room when you see him standing there. You have to go out boldly into the wild by yourself, swing up into the tree, swim across the cold river, walk through the dark wood. You have to sit in a canyon for long enough for your own fears to subside and put a deep anchoring root in the territory. You have to sit by a red root and build up enough courage to walk out of the compound of your own bullying mind.

The second visit to the red root was with Mimi, when we climbed the track to consider the plant for the Snake Sequence. As soon as we sat beside the bush Mimi began to talk about flower essences and a patient for whom she had prescribed red root. I found myself becoming intensely irritated. The talking seemed to float about and not connect with the bush. I felt pinned down by these problems and syndromes and by Me and Her. I became so restless I thought I would implode.

When the white people first came among the Okanagan, the people noticed that they suffered from a strange madness. They walked around with a fixed stare, as if they were having an argument with themselves. The Okanagan called this condition *talking-talking in the head*, and avoided them. At some point, the flower essence talking disconnects from Mimi and becomes a voice that whines. I realise I can't move because 'it' is demanding my attention.

The voice goes on and on. It's going to go on until it gets its way. It seems as if this voice has been whining inside me, outside me, for aeons. Now it's Mimi talking-talking about her client whining to her. Later I could start talking-talking and whining to Mark about Mimi. Except I am sitting under the spiky red root and being provoked to do something else. First I have to listen and not react to what I don't want to hear. Then I need to act. I don't like the sound of that voice. It sounds sorry for itself, and wants you to feel sorry for it, to give it all your energy and time. *O woe is me living on this dreadful planet!* Behind that wailing and whining is a flash of anger: *Why should I be here?* And behind that anger is a demand: *You lowly life form, take this uncomfortable feeling away, give me your sweeties!*

And there it is, the civilised white world, the Empire, superior to all earth forms and yet utterly dependent on them for food and warmth and shelter and not one scrap of thanksgiving about it. Here it comes with its superior technology, its mind-control, its religions, its schools and universities, its know-it-all books, full of flag-waving nationhood and gilt-edged self-importance, with its high-maintenance penis and vagina. It cannot sit down for five minutes on this red earth without complaining about its condition, without bullying someone else to do its dirty work, to provide.

Do not feed them, not this time.

You could want Mimi to be different in this unbearable, spiky moment: how she was when you first saw her, a deer woman with horns in a mystery play down at the Old High School, the one who shares a kinship in your desert quest. But you knew she was not going to be, not that day anyway. We were sitting by a thornbush, beloved by creatures with horns.

You look at people with a certain attention in these moments. You have to, otherwise you would miss all their medicine in your great desire to get away. You want the canyon to be a serene and reassuring sanctuary. But it isn't. It is a medicine place that holds deep mysteries in its rocky core. A territory that can show you why the deer still roam in our imaginations, how the thornbushes keep us alive. The red root is a rigorously structured plant. Everything about it is designed for economy: small leaves, tough stems, strong root. It reserves all its beauty and sweetness for the bees. The protective grey spikes wake you up to what is going on. Wise up!

Part of you is irritable, wants to get up to go and look at the verbena on the other side of the track. Another part is wisely observing, aware of all the ramifications. Wait a moment, it says: the plant is giving you a *key*. How are you going to confront these energies? These are conditions in which you have to make an original move.

Do not feed them, not this time

You need your fluidity and your discernment. You can't get trapped in the mind, hemmed in by good manners, by imaginary fears of reprisal. You are not in the encounter to avoid the encounter. You are here to get out of the turkey farm.

I realise I don't like this flower essence talk. I like sitting here on my own and connecting with the territory. I realise I don't feel sorry for anyone, or care about their problems. That voice is really getting on my nerves. Enough of this bloody talking! I say to myself, and spring up on to my feet and go to look at the verbena.

It's a subtle medicine in an awkward place. One you might miss. Like the deer watching you as you climb the scree. The sweet juice of the red roots enters your system and imperceptibly awakens the electrical charge of the blood, quickens the transport of waste from the lymph. Everything clears. Life can go on.

The action of the world is brutal. Feed me! Give me attention! Do as I say! Your choices are limited: flee or submit. Shrinking from these hostilities you live in a contracted state, in a stagnant place that is also a state of emergency. You are unmoored from your own being, lacking any connection to time or place. Everything is disturbing, making you anxious. Unwisely you take on the burdens of others, your lymph system overloads.

Emboldened by the deer brush, however, you hold your ground until this intimidation runs out. You hear your own blood singing in your ears. Afterwards you relax and absorb your surroundings. Your intelligence returns.

The deer comes and shows you his enchanted flower world. The bushes he feeds delicately upon are doorways to an original earth. They exist in slow time, in big time; in low wave, in high frequency.

Where they do not exist are in the realms of fear. When you sit beside them, you do not exist in the realms of fear. You realise that all the fear lives in the constructed human world.

When I sat by the red root I remembered a dream. I am walking down the High Street in Oxford. There is a woman coming the other way with a bird cage on her head, with encrusted wires that go inside her head and hold her there. I am horrified. How will she be able to free herself? Then I catch sight of myself in the shop window. The cage is on my own head.

The flowers release you from the mind's captivity by activating what is called the etheric body. This body surrounds and influences our physical form in the same way the moon circles the earth and influences the tides and the growth of plants. It is the feeling part of ourselves that tunes into vibration, mood, atmosphere, rhythm, the soul of people and places. It is the body that moves us to dance and sing and write poetry and hold a dialogue with plants.

In industrial societies the interconnecting field of our etheric bodies is covertly manipulated to be non-aligned with natural life. We are programmed to be wonky, off-centre, out of tune, out of step with the rhythm of our own blood and heartbeat. We are trained to sit still and escape into our minds, into the feel-good places with artificial sounds and frequencies. Unconnected to our wild selves, we remain in our bird cages, behind the fence of the farm.

When you align with the flower worlds these self-restricting patterns of behaviour are interrupted. The wild turkey enters the field, and your real being responds. You are drawn magnetically outside the parameters of your restricted thoughts. Untangled from the mindset, you can open a dialogue with your spirit. You become conscious of the natural world. You feel inspired, connected, at home. You look up from the deer brush and see the deer. Sometimes this encounter changes the course of a whole life. People take a flower essence and are cured of 'incurable' states – diseases, allergies, depression, toxic relationships. They recover their souls, face their demons. In the presence of the real thing, the self-attacking forces lose their hold. If a negative pattern is not held within the etheric body, it cannot be held in the physical.

At some point in the encounter, your spirit moves away from the talking-talking parasitic mind and into a greater space. You gaze at the person talking to themselves inside a cage of words, and then you vanish, small stones skittering down the slope.

The last time, I went alone. I set out from the hotel, crossed the small park, walked up through Main Street past the library, following the creek full of late sunflowers and evening primrose, past white oaks and fences entwined with morning glories. After a mile the wooden cabins petered out as I headed to where the old road continued up towards Juniper Flats and a new one led towards the tunnel. I walked down the shoulder and crossed the highway, greeting the canyon as I climbed the ridge to where the bushes stood in the heat of the afternoon. There were no difficult feelings left. The lorry was still in the parking lot, there were still shouts, but I was no longer afraid. The dog was no longer barking.

It is not beautiful, this canyon, but it's where the red root bushes grow and I can sit alongside them. Alexis who has hiked all over these mountains tells me she doesn't like to come here. Something bad happened, she said. We look at each other, imagining bloodshed and rape, death stalking among by the skullcaps. It's true. You can feel bad things in the atmosphere. But it is part of the neighbourhood as much as the red hill, the creek of sunflowers, the Siberian elms that grow along the highway, the rocky pool up at Juniper Flats where you can slide a desert thirsty body into its bone-chilling arms. I have spent a summer and fall among these rocks, encountering these territories, these strange and shifting atmospheres, sheltering beside these thorns. Now winter is approaching, we are soon to depart. The trees in the canyon have already grown fiery and are losing their leaves. Next spring I will come back, I tell the bushes, I will come and see your flowers.

Something has happened between us this fall, with that Mason jar of spring water. The bush has become a keystone, a meeting place in the dreaming of the land. The bush has put down roots in my imagination. It will connect me forever with this place. Somewhere in the blue sky of Arizona, those eagles will always be flying above my head.

I had set out to make the speaking bush essences for everyone, but their real medicine was not to be found in those Mason jars, it lay in the experience. No matter how scary the canyon was, or how hot the afternoon, something was making me get up and walk out of the door, walk up the hill, run across a highway with a beating heart.

What was that something? It's what I learned with the red root, with all the bushes, as I set out in the car with its dancing necklace of devil's claw seed pods, as I walked up the steep gulch collecting malachite, noticing birds of paradise growing everywhere out of the corner of my eye. It was a relationship with the neighbourhood, with the borderlands, with Arizona, with the self that went into the territory. People kept telling me: the country is all managed now, the desert is overgrazed, the ancient forests have gone, the wild places are not there any more. It's all fenced in, they say. But one day the wild turkey comes and shows you his world. One day you hold the gaze of the deer and find you can see that wild see-through freshness everywhere you look. You realise wildness is a *quality* implicit within all living forms, no matter how contorted or caged in. It's in people and trees, rocks and deer. Once you find that wild original self, something shifts. You start seeing the world from the perspective of earth, rather than through the bars of a cage.

If you sit long enough by the red root, fill yourself up with enough rocks and cloud, you can see the wild everywhere – interpenetrating the squares of offices, the endless roads, the grey geometry of the human world. Before, those thoughts, all that disturbance, hid that colour and movement from view. Now you follow the wild turkey and see his track everywhere: the iridescent green flash of a hummingbird, the copper flash of a snake, the ravens dancing merrily on the mortuary roof. People are staring, moving mechanically in and out of buildings, while a host of swallowtail butterflies is fluttering down Main Street, the asphodels are pushing up through the tarmac of the parking lot, the rainwater is pouring down Brewery Gulch. The praying mantis swivels his eye and looks back at you. There's the moon glinting like a god's fingernail in the sky, the night wind is shifting around the cottonwoods, the coyotes are singing across the land. You haven't hiked a hundred miles into the pristine wilderness, you've just walked out of your front door.

In the canyon there is a bush that teaches you how to see this world, how to walk through a gulch full of ghosts and gunfire and not run away. The deer are easily frightened, yet they are the peerless creatures of spirit. To speak from our original selves, we need not be set into flight. Alone, it is hard not to back down and become silent in the face of the world's history. You can walk into the Chiricauhuas, into the Huachucas, into the Dragoons, into the White Mountains, and the vibrations don't feel good. Something bad happened here, everyone tells me. Something bad happened in the woods of Europe, in the misty valleys of the Andes, in the rainforest pools of Australia. One day you sit by the red root of Arizona and you find out what to do. You don't skip over the fear if it comes to you, but then you don't go down with it either. You hold it in your gaze and stand your ground because the earth is all around you. You are not alone. You have entered a dream that is not dominated by these human nightmares. You have aligned with the planet, rather than its parasite. The red root has opened a door.

In the rocky times, the plants provide a meeting place, bring the wild things into play, open up your world. They are what make you not give up or lose heart. I knew when I sat beside the red root that everything within the territory – deer, eagle, red root, red rock, sky, sun, wind – was with me, that we were all in it together. In that space, backed by nature, no longer hounded by your own mind, you can sort everything out, get clear, make bold decisions.

That's when you realise what makes you run across the highway. It's the sweet and intoxicating taste of liberty.

The speaking bushes gave me keys to unlock the cage. As I sat in the scrublands and juniper belts, immersed in light, in heat and earth, I was remembering myself – bone, blood, nerve, spleen, heart and eye – tuning myself up to the high frequency of flowers, to the spirit of the deer. As I did I felt invisible bars around my head fall away, the mask slip from my face; the earth releasing me from my own captivity.

'What is your favourite flower?' I ask Francisco, *curandero* and lover of flowers. He looks at me. 'I think the wild cotton,' he says – a speaking bush, like the deer-brush, with red medicine roots and white luminous flowers. Part-Yaqui, part-Apache, born under a cottonwood tree in Mexico from a long line of medicine men and women, he has returned to his tribal lands to dispense his plant knowledge. Like many native people called to be bridges between nations, between tribes, between the ancient and the new, he feels constrained by his own traditions, the dour it's-got-to-be-done attitudes that are reluctant to change and lighten up. The mountain does not belong to anyone, he says, neither to the white people, nor to the red. We belong to the mountain. He despairs too of his new-age patients who prefer to talk and talk and talk about their problems rather than take his red root medicine. But sometimes it happens that the white people appear and perform their own alchemy, bringing a moment of lightness that comes from another lineage that has learned not to take itself too seriously.

Climbing the stairs to our apartment, he looks darkly at the photographs of Aryan gurus and saints of India, the spiritual mummies and daddies of the twentieth-century world on the altar on the hotel landing, but says nothing. *Quienes son esas vergas?* retorts Mark in a faultless Mexican accident. Who are those tossers? Francisco looks at him and roars with laughter. *Y esas vergas que?* he repeats out loud and laughs all evening. You know, I say, looking at his hawk profile, his head like a mountain promontory, his stature like a pine tree, you would go down a *storm* on the Paris catwalk. He looks back at me speechless, and then a great smile breaks over his red rock face and something that feels like peace, like happiness, comes to us all in that moment.

Red root, white flower.

At Francisco's temascal, hand in hand, silently trooping around a fire of mesquite and juniper in a slow and reverent parade, I am seized with an irrepressible urge to skip. As I pull everyone at twice the speed there is a great shift in mood, and we all start whizzing and whooping in delight around the roaring flames on the cold November day. Francisco raises his eyebrows and carries on chanting solemnly into the night. Inside, though I do not know it, he is smiling.

You sit by the red root because you need to find your own medicine – your unshakeable root, your prickly thorns, your nourishing leaves, your sweet and intoxicating flowers; the way you can surprise the company and high-step like a deer. The talking was holding us back, but so were the old rituals. If you are modern you can't follow tribal traditions to get back to the land. We need a new dance that includes us all. We need to be fired with the sun, with all that colour and vibrancy and laughter you can feel in the deep blue caves of Hawaii, in the golden grass plains of Wyoming, in the moody beechwoods of England. Under the oak tree, Cyril and Aurelia want to show their gratitude with native American prayer feathers and corn. 'Oh, fuck off with your offerings!' I growl at them. 'The earth doesn't want you pussyfooting around her, treating her like your bloody mother! She wants us all to have a good time!' Everyone laughs. That's the spleen speaking to the mindset, what wild turkey brings to your door. A wild card in a stuck time.

The past was holding us to ransom, making us nervous and afraid. We needed to make an bold original move. I made this move in a canyon where bad things happened. I burst out of healing ceremonies and sweatlodges, broke circles to the goddess and the mountain, laughed at shamans in important hats, refused to dance to sacred drums. It was an irreverence I brought unwittingly from England. When the pilgrims left their native land on a ship named after the hawthorn tree, they left the lightness of the flowering thorn behind. They forgot about the singing and the dancing, the laughter that breaks up the atmosphere when humans get too righteous and mean. The way that Mark laughed at the corridor gurus in his impeccable Mexican accent. Without this lightness the spirit becomes grim and ritualistic, without the red root medicine the white flower parties become meaningless. Together we could start again on common ground, red and white, blood and lymph, following a wild track of flowers, the deer that dance across the world.

Where do you find this common ground? As the century swings open, it is a small town in Arizona, surrounded by boulders and bushes, beside a highway that stretches all the way down into Mexico.

It is a rough canyon where the deer brush held me in her gaze, a red hill where the strong arms of bearberry rocked me, a desert garden where the tubular ephedra slaked my thirst. It is a border road where the delicate wild cotton dances in the breeze and prickle-armed ocotillos stick out their red tongues and I could boldly reply to the border guard: *I am making a flower essence, what are you doing?* It is an empty highway where I stood beside the golden-flowering creosote and a 'hillbilly', 'redneck' man stopped and asked me gently: *Is everything all right, ma'am?* It is the morning I sat by a burned-out house beside the blazing coral bean and asked myself: *Am I on the edge of town, or is the town on the edge of me?* It is the afternoon at the wash where a troupe of wild quail ran gaily past me as I sat by the white-flowering desert broom as if I were an intricate part of the landscape, just like themselves. It is the evening when I walked towards the crucifixion thorn and the white cat and all her children and the tortoiseshell cat and all her children followed me into the desert. The evening as the sun went down and we sat together, one human, ten cats, a dark heavily spiked thorn bush full of fragrant flowers, a sickle moon in an indigo sky – one of those evenings when you can turn to the stranger who asks you with a full heart to say: yes, everything is all right. We are all here, and everything is all right.

When I finished my farewell tour of the speaking bushes, I put the little bottles of mother essence in a tobacco tin. I would travel with them always, and the bushes were always with me, in my heart, in the mother essence of myself, succussed, shaken, distilled, imprinted for eternity in all my living cells.

queen of the night
Bisbee, Arizona 2000/01

In Carmen's house there grows a queen of the night from the tropics in a pot; its huge arms extend over the floorboards of her large airy study. It flowers dramatically one night in September. On this night we sit with small candles and keep a vigil by the six large flowers, and afterwards leave all our adjoining doors open so that their extraordinary scent may reach us in our dreams. I have an uneasy night and am troubled when I wake up.

Irrevocable is the word that comes to me when I wake: a feeling of finality. I know that something represented by this house is over. It is dawn and I can hear the muffled footsteps of the illegal immigrants as they emerge from their hiding places and run down the street to catch their bus.

Nostalgia is a treacherous business. It comes like the memory of the kitchen of this house, with the sound of a screen door banging and a woman's voice singing. It is held in a certain line, a line someone once wrote, or that someone said to you, that brings the fragrance of a forgotten place within your heart. Just gone, just out of reach; something ineffable, unfathomable. Something over. Nostalgia takes all its power from the past. It is not a real past that it invokes, however, but an imagined one, a possibility that once existed. It didn't really happen in the past. It should have happened. Something should have happened.

I'm gonna build you a house in the bend down where the cottonwoods grow.

In her evocation to John Wayne this is the line, the nostalgia line, that pulls the writer Joan Didion all the way down into Mexico to watch him make his last movie. At a dinner with the dying actor and his wife, she basks in the radiance of the man who played so many pioneer heroes, of a time that was not really a time, when men built houses for women and made them feel at home in an alien land. A certain kind of America. Except this is not a house under the cottonwoods but a restaurant in Mexico City, in a different time, and no film is home. It's the illusion that makes-believe it *feels* like home, that holds you in a spell.

America is not a motherland, Carmen used to say. Only the name

America holds us like a spell, like a mantra we repeat to ourselves. To make ourselves feel at home.

There are some houses that hold you in their spell, that you return to year after year, and this was one of them. It was not built down by the cottonwoods but beside a chinaberry tree, and was originally a boarding house for the European miners who came here to dig for copper at the beginning of the last century. There were apricot trees too in a small courtyard full of pots and morning glories which you found if you went up a staircase and across a little metal footbridge. And when you went down the side alley there was a screen door, and if you pushed that screen door open you would find yourself in a kitchen.

The kitchen was large, bare-boarded, with red shelves full of books and icons, a big stove, and a central island with high stools around which everyone sat and talked. It was a lovely room and all manner of people have come here since Carmen and Peter restored it in the 1970s: poets, painters, mystics, travellers, herb people, crazy people. Exciting dialogues had taken place on the island as people came and went through the screen door, as they passed through the town. We had visited this kitchen for years, and now in 2000 were staying in one of the hotel's apartments. Something in me, however, couldn't settle in the hotel, something I felt that lurked underneath these talks was being skipped, some unquiet spirit that jarred our communications together. I kept running up into the red hills outside.

The truth is we will not say to each other what we really came to say in this kitchen, because Mark and I do not share the same past as this house, nor its inhabitants. We are from a different time and place. We will never speak the lines we wanted to out loud. Or perhaps we did say them, but no one took any notice. I think it happened once when we were praying for the rain in the drought times, but we were so busy thinking about the sky we didn't look at each other. It might have happened five years ago when we used to sing together, but we were so busy singing we didn't look at each other. And then the singing stopped. We just couldn't hold those harmonies anymore. There was always someone crying. Or arguing, or in a sulk, or one person laughing and one feeling uncomfortable. There was always something that made us look away.

Often we came at five and made coffee, waiting for Carmen to come back from the library. Sometimes Alex would be there cutting up carrots for the evening dinner or skinning chillies, and we would give him a hand, and we would talk, and he would roll tobacco in large perfectly made cigarettes, and we would all smoke them together. The tribe of cats would jump in and out of the window and Carmen would light a candle when she arrived, one of those lovely gaudy Mexican votive candles, and it would burn all evening on the island like a lighthouse in a stormy night.

I came because I loved to hear the lines about the 1960s. When Alex spent a decade driving a truck across America after he gave up his career as an artist in New York, how he once read out the contents of the Queens telephone directory at a Happening; when Carmen left her hometown in Wyoming and went to live in Haight Ashbury. I loved to hear about those times. About the crazy acid trips, the mystical hand-made films, the women with flowery dresses and bare feet, the tangerine-coloured dream.

Everywhere has its nostalgia, with its certain lines and sounds. In England this was a moment just before the Great War, a moment that is captured in lines that catch you by the throat. *The past is a foreign country. They do things differently there.* In America it is a song by Joan Baez about Bob Dylan, just after Vietnam, sung with a kind of crack in her voice. *We both could have died then and there.* It pulls you, that song, like all songs, like all hippy songs. But where does it pull you exactly?

Joan Didion's seminal book on America in the sixties, *Slouching Towards Bethlehem*, takes its title from Yeats' poem, 'The Second Coming'. Yeats, a metaphysical Celtic poet, writes of a spiritual breakdown where man (the falcon) has become separated from his spiritual self (the falconer), and how this separation will bear out its terrible consequence within the collective. The falling apart, the fall into matter that is not spiritualised, is a terrible fall indeed. There is no ascension after such a fall. No revocability. The book's title essay charts the phenomenon of a generation who broke with the tradition of home and hearth and went to live out a certain kind of innocence in San Francisco. She saw this expression of drug-swirling innocence as presaging a fall in America, a coming loss of freedom, a breaking apart of the whole.

Didion, writing on the edge of a nervous breakdown, on the edge of a hotel bed, on the edge of midnight with the fires burning on the skyline, is a master documenter of collective fragmentation. Even her own body becomes a metaphor for the age, as she charts with minute accuracy her physical and emotional experience of this shift, of her own lack of home.

On the Big Island in Hawaii Didion sits by the graveyards of the young dead in a volcano crater overlooking Honolulu. Thousands of twenty-year-old American boys who have died in the various wars wreaked upon the world: World War II, Korea, and now Vietnam. She is alone when she makes her visit; only the graveyard mowers with their mechanical scythes are there.

For some reason I think of myself in this kitchen when I re-read Didion's essays. Because what Didion felt or couldn't articulate exactly up there in the Hawaiian crater is now about to come further into focus. What she was saying is that underneath all the holiday consumerism, the real business of America was war. And what does it mean to live in a culture that is built on warheads, once the hula dances have stopped and the daiquiris run out and words like democracy and future and freedom begin to sound like threats? Underneath all her writing is the stirring of the rough beast waiting for its hour, and Didion, a great Cassandra, with her sensitive, neurotic, sometimes irritatingly flighty prose style, fends off the conclusion of the poem at every turn.

And it is this that the queen of the night has said is irrevocable. And something in me that has never trusted the diamonds and rust, never trusted the line about cottonwoods, never quite trusted the neurosis of anyone, not even my own, has started to pay attention.

The queen of the night in Arizona does not grow by this house but in the desert outside the town. You could miss this native queen, for she grows under the scraggy cover of the mesquite tree and, unless she is in flower, you could mistake her for a twig. And you might not even see her flower because she flowers only at night; and not only at night – she flowers only once in the year. What she does for the rest of the year is store huge amounts of water in her enormous tuber. The tuber sits underground and keeps a vast reservoir of energy.

The Southwestern queen of the night flowers in the height of the summer, like many of the succulent plants: the chollas, prickly pears, agaves and yuccas. All of them have these inner reservoirs and show their extraordinary colours in the fiercest and driest times. While all other desert dwellers are panting and groaning in the relentless heat, the cactus family are having a fiesta: rainbow magenta, fishhook pink, mammelaria yellow, barrel orange, saguaro white. The queen's flowers are luminous white, lotus-shaped, with a rosy tinge and delicate golden stamens. They are completely arresting, and their powerful scent travels far across the desert night floor.

The queen flowers just outside the room where I am sleeping this following year, in 2001, in a strawbale house in the desert, way out of town. 'Oh look!' Mimi says when she shows me the plants. 'The constellation of Leo.' We stare upwards. I have never seen this constellation before and my heart leaps up with excitement.

Later that night I make an essence. I go out at midnight and the white cat follows me. I put the bowl of water under the flower that vibrates her invisible energy into the darkness. The cat and I sit down beside her. It is beautiful, sitting here in the great hot night, under the star Regulus, the regal heart of the lion. The starry flower shines in the dark; they are all gleaming white: the stars, the flower, the cat. All of us in silent communication together. It's one of those moments you don't want to end, and I hold it as long as I can in my heart, and then I let it go. At daybreak I return to see the sunrise with the flower, and the white petals become tipped with gold. Soon it will fade. I wish it farewell. I bring the bowl back to the house, strain the water and make up the mother essence, just as the fierce morning heat arrives.

It's one of those moments you don't want to end. And yet it did end. For years I had come here. I had loved the flowers of this desert. I had loved the people of this town, and yet there was a split between us that was irrevocable. Some things need to end, says the flower, for others to begin.

What did Carmen's house represent, why did the memory of it catch me in the throat, bring tears to my eyes, a pain into my heart? Why when I remembered the flower did it bring me joy? Why did the flower visit feel so clear, so complete, mysterious, lived out, while our visits to the kitchen feel so incomplete? The house reminded me of a golden age which I had always longed for, a time where for one moment it seemed that love and peace and beauty could rule the world. An era which, when its 'flower power' had faded and its free expression had been forced underground, had been stored in the memories of people who still sang its songs and wrote its poetry, and kept a kitchen vigil to the spirit of those innocent times. It was a powerful nostalgia, but like all spells and mantras it could not bear the light of day, of our looking too deep into each other's eyes. There were marvellous conversations in this house, of spirit and soul, of art and music and poetry, and yet the dialogue that had to do with the future never happened. Because to live in that future means you cannot live in the past. Especially a past that is not your own.

At the end of the rainy season that year, just as the hotel queen was about to flower, we went up into the Huachuca foothills, Alex, Carmen, Mark and I. We walked to the edge of the hill and gazed over the golden lands of Arizona as they merged into Mexico below us. The warm wind rippled the grasses like an animal hide. Everywhere there was space and light. I stood by a craggy lightning-struck juniper and breathed in deep. Then we went down to have a lunch among the trees. We had made an English picnic for Carmen's birthday: there was chicken and salad and strawberries, and a jug of fresh lemonade. We sat at the table and Alex shinned like a boy up a sycamore and collected wild canyon grapes. And although we had known each other for many years, it felt in that moment as though there was nothing left to say. The wind blew softly through the Apache pines above our heads: 'I feel something bad is going to happen,' said Carmen suddenly, nervously. 'I feel it in the air.' It was September 9.

It's irrevocable, said the queen. *It's time to get real.*

creosote
Swan Road, Arizona 2001

I have a jar I keep in a wooden box in my room, and sometimes I take the jar out of the box and open it. As I do, an extraordinary scent permeates the room. It is a smell like no other, a scent that takes you, heart, body and soul to a red land, to the great Chihuahua desert after the rains. It takes you deep into the heartland of the chaparral, where the bitter-leaved, scaly-limbed, golden-flowered bush that emanates this perfume grows: the creosote bush.

The creosote is a formidable bush, known as *la gobernadora* because it inhibits the growth of all plants that grow around it and thus can command great areas. The bush is commonly called by the same name as its habitat: chaparral. But it is also secretly known as *la gobernadora* because when you step within its territory you know it is the plant that is in charge, with whose authority you do not quibble. As a physical medicine, its tough leathery leaves can heal almost anything. The chaparral's medicine lies in its slow combustion. As it takes hold of a territory the bush slows the combustion of everything around and thus inhibits the germination of other seeds. Its inhibiting nature has the same effect on alien organisms within the human body, and also works within its own form. It is an ancient plant that lives for a very, very long time indeed. There are stands of creosote that have been carbon-dated to thirteen thousand years. La Gobernadora is in charge because she has a formidable memory.

Mimi once told me that a sprig of creosote brought a woman she knew back from the brink of death. Memory can do that. And perhaps that is why I am here in Swan Road today, sitting by the creosote and digging my hands in the red earth, so I can remember everything. I breathe the warm air under a blue sky that already bears the tinge of winter. *If god had meant you to be in America you would be American,* we were told when we came back from Mexico. I sat beside the bush and thought of these people who had been here for a hundred years at the most, and wondered what gave them such authority.

At some point the moment you never want to pass comes to pass: you have wondered about this moment. How would you respond? This is the moment, I thought, as I walked into the immigration interrogation room at Phoenix airport. This is the moment you come to face the man that god has put in charge. The man in the uniform with the pale face, in this room without windows. In a bad time you don't get out of this room: you get your liver torn out. On the border of the bad times you get your visa torn in half. You get to be called an alien and told to pack your bags.

I sit in front of the pale man and look at him directly. He has all the power in this moment. He can put me on a plane, or not, and he toys with this power, as a cat will toy with a mouse. He is the good cop. Mark got the bad cop. He got a Mexican woman called Rose screaming at him on and off for two hours. This man is smooth-talking, reasonable. I resist succumbing to the relief, the feeling of being let off the hook. I follow the interrogation, point by point, answer the questions, and consider my options. I feel like opening my mouth and yelling, but something is being held in balance. Our fate is yet not decided. There is a small space, a possibility and I want that possibility. I want to have enough time to say goodbye.

'What are you doing in the United States?'

'I am a writer.'

The pale man laughs. He holds our travelling book in his hand. It was published in 1994, he tells me, as if to discount the fact, and asks me again what I am doing returning to Arizona?

'I am writing a book about plants.'

'What is it about Arizona?'

'I love the desert,' I say. 'And I have friends here. This is a B2 multiple-entry visa. What exactly is wrong?'

'You have done nothing wrong,' he tells me. 'You have to go back to your country, buy a house, get a job and be normal.'

'I already have a job, I'm a writer.'

The man is not listening. He does not live in a world where people are writers or consider wild plants, or return to places they love. He is filling in forms. I am a person of no consequence. An alien like all aliens. Not American. Not normal. Of no use to the Empire. Soon the form will be completed.

I wait and watch his every move.

'One day you can write about this,' he tells me.

I look at him and at his name plate which says Richard.

'Not about here, of course,' he adds hurriedly.

'You mean in Phoenix, Arizona?' I ask.

I wanted to say it was not paradise, this place I come back to. It was not a land of milk and honey, a god's domain of easy living and garden flowers. It was a territory of wild, bright spaces, mountains and sky. A place of thorns and rattlesnakes, where you could speak with people who thought there was more to this mysterious life than getting a job and a house and being normal. It was not paradise, but it was a place in which you could feel alive.

It was not hell either. But sometimes you could feel an antagonism between the people and see chain gangs working along the highway. When the wind blew from the south the sulphuric acid from the copper mine slag heaps stung your eyes and often, when you sat down by the devil's claw or the soaptree yucca or any of the plants that grew abundantly along the border, the patrol would stop and demand to see your passports. You are making us nervous, they would say, and wanted you to stop looking at flowers and go away. It felt like everyone wanted everyone to go away, even though there was space everywhere you looked. You woke up and there were helicopters at dawn searching for drug runners and refugees. You would find young men standing in the garden, lost and collapsing with thirst and exhaustion, looking for shelter. It was not hell, but it was a warrior land where you were challenged each day to be alive.

This is the moment. Do you have the courage in this moment to surrender?

You could yell, cry, shout about injustice, your innocence, take a haughty stance, threaten. But you don't. Something inhibits you.

Instead you grow slow and still and watch. You realise that in this room your independence, your integrity, your creativity, which you value above all things, have no value. In this moment you have no power, but you have memory. You know that beyond this room, beyond the history of men and mines, of native wars and border patrol, there is another Arizona. There is a bush that commands the badlands that can take all your ills away. It is unremarkable; you could pass it by as you drive along the highway. La Gobernadora is older than god, the god of the pale-faced Americans and all the other gods of the world. She is older than all these conflicts, older than this grief, older than all the aliens. She sits like a cat, perfectly contained in the heart of the red desert, and keeps her own counsel. In a bad time, you go to her.

When we finally arrive back in the desert in the dead of night, the tribe of cats will come where I lie in the straw bale house and surround me. All night their soft bodies will purr against mine and keep me warm. The constellations will turn above us. At times I will awake trembling and find one of them looking at me with her deep mysterious eyes. I will hear their sound in the darkness and fall back to sleep. By morning, I will awake and know what to do.

What you want in a difficult time is to act like a warrior. You want to be impeccable. I want to say goodbye in the few days now granted by my surrender. You can come back in six months, everyone told me: the lawyer, the state department, the man in the windowless room. I can come back in six months, I told myself, but part of me knew I would not. A door was closing. Bad times lay ahead.

We gave away everything we had collected over the years: books, thriftstore clothes, pots and pans, a wicker chair, the car. We sat with Mimi in the round house and poured the six Snake Sequence essences into bottles and packed them in boxes. We closed our post office box, visited people, swept the paths. In the cool mornings we sat under the cottonwood tree, under the elder and the mesquite. We sat on the roof and watched the sun come up with the cats sitting beside us. We sat overlooking the sky islands, San Jose, the Mule Mountains, the washes, and gulches where the medicine plants grew, all the speaking bushes that were silent and dark in the early light. And then on the last day I went to Swan Road.

Swan Road is a place we loved to go. Down a small dirt track off the road to the Junction there was a patch of ground where we used to sit as evening came, especially after the rains when it had become lush. There was a ring of the speaking bushes I had made essences with - ocotillo, desert broom, creosote - and you could sit by them and see around the great rim of the San José mountains, and yet feel sheltered from the vastness of the flatlands. It was a sort of desert room. The quail would come running in and out of the dry wash, talking to each other; ravens glided overhead croaking. It was a peaceful place and rarely disturbed by the border patrol. Now, after the monsoon, it was carpeted with marigolds and purple flowering datura; the devil's claw flowers had turned into green horned seed pods, the creosote flowers grown into fluffy grey seeds that caught the rays of the sun.

Last time I had come here I had brought a confused girl called

Meneka who had blown into Bisbee, into our lives, briefly, like a tumbleweed. She had found an injured cat in the road, but couldn't pay for its treatment at the vets. She was afraid the cat would die. So we gathered mud from underneath the creosote bushes for a wound pack. I knew creosote could cure almost any kind of desperation, so long as you spoke with the plant. Mimi had told the dying woman: go to the plant that speaks to you. The woman picked a tiny twig of creosote and it sparked new life in her. If you have courage, the creosote will speak to you of things that can overcome the greatest of shocks. To be refused entry to the land I had loved for twenty-two years was, at that time, the most shocking thing that could have happened.

'Now you have nothing to lose,' said the creosote quietly as I waited beneath her scaly arms, her seeds like small paws held in the breeze.

I waited by the bush for a long time in silence. And then a great sob broke from me as my heart broke open. I realised I would not be coming back. *You are an alien.* Alien as the young men from El Salvador I had once harboured in the desert garden, alien as the Mexican man and woman I had given a lift to in our car. We were all aliens, the people of the earth who came to live here. Our forms were stamped, our eyes were lasered, our fingerprints in files, in documents, on computers. I felt my broken heart open: it broke out across the land to include everyone that had been driven from it. It stretched back over the line of immigrants who were crossing the border. It stretched back past the train that had stopped in the middle of the desert in 1917 and thrown out all the striking coppermine workers, over the Apache nation hunted and driven out of these mountains until Geronimo surrendered in 1886. People driven out, made homeless, put on trains, planes, deportees, evacuees, refugees, torn up from their roots. In this heart-breaking moment, I knew what it is to be in exile from a place you love.

'Now you know,' said the creosote. 'Will you be strong enough, is your heart big enough, to contain the bitterness of this world?'

In that moment I knew there is nothing worse than not belonging to the earth, to be exiled from its beauty and its mysteriousness, unconnected to its power to drive away all ills, its medicine, to its long root, stretching back through time, anchoring us in a time and space in which everything can be seen and known and treasured for what it truly is.

'Who is in charge?' asked *la gobernadora*.

'You are.'

'We are,' she corrected me. 'Where do you want to be?'

'I want to be with you,' I said.

'You are always with me,' she said, 'because you are me. And now you can go.'

I poured the mother essence into the red earth, embraced the bush, and bid Swan Road farewell. I got into my desert-coloured car and drove back to Turtle Ranch. I did not look back.

The medicine of the creosote is bitter. Bitter, like all the heart plants. Only a heart that is bitter knows how to feel beyond its personal circumstance, to reach out for its fellows. A time when you have nothing to lose is the time when life opens up. When you are terrified of losing, you close down and do not see the bigger picture; you care only for yourself, your space, your desert. When you are terrified of losing you do not see that things that you counted on were not to be counted on, that friends, community, one's own talent or good nature, would not prevent this now-imminent banishment. It was a kind of innocence that went then. Creosote is a sobering bush: I knew that had circumstances been different, had it been a different time and place in history, I would have boarded a train that led all the way to the gulag and no one would have been able to stop it.

In the speaking bush years at the beginning of the millennium, the taste in my mouth was the taste of bitterness. Once you have learned to live with the bitterness of the heart, you take this medicine everywhere you go. It is the bitterness of the heart that will cleanse the world of all its grief and history, just so long as your heart can still love. So long as you can still sing your swan song, a song of everything you once loved and had to say goodbye to, and if you can remember the scent of the desert after the rains long after you have left it, and most of all, if you can remember who is really in charge.

There is a jar that sits in my room in a wooden box and today I have taken it out. Seven years have gone by since I distilled these leaves and flowers, and in this space of time many rains have fallen on the desert lands where these bushes grow, but I have not been there to see them. No one I once knew in the old mining town by the red hill is with me any more. But the plants are still with me, and I only have to remember and I am once again on the red hills running past the bearberry, sitting beside the wild flowering lilac, turning the bend at Swan Road. In the world beyond history there is an Arizona where we are always welcome. And in my long creosote memory, in the long count of my life, in my land-dreaming capacity, I can see that people always come and go, but the plants always remain. I can see that when the human dramas fade, when my heart recovers, what is left are the speaking bushes of the desert. What is left is Turtle Island. What is left are these words in my mouth, these rain-washed, bitter-scented words.

wormwood
Powis Castle, Wales 2002

Nobody knows whether the star in the Book of Revelations is in fact wormwood. But one thing is for sure, the plant itself is apocalyptic. Wormwood, the kingdom's most bitter plant, has brought the end-times to unwanted creatures throughout the ages: driven moths and insects from our drawers; putrefaction, worms and jaundice from our bodies; melancholia from our mind. And sometimes wormwood goes just a little further and starts chasing out bigger fish as well.

When we first return to England in those in-between travelling years I notice something strange: my gaze keeps going towards houses, rather than people. As we pass through villages and towns, my attention fixes itself on sash windows, the colour of the paint on the door, the flowering bush by the door; notices whether the roof is made from tile or thatch. Nice house! I find myself saying out loud without thinking. In the 1990s the houses of England are doing very well indeed. They have smart new conservatories and patios with hanging baskets, and clamber in their thousands all over the once-green fields, with their Georgian-style windows and the Swedish furniture inside. The talk is all about property, second homes and what everyone is doing with lofts and new kitchens. The houses stand in the centre of all this attention, proudly tended and cared for. It is hard to say the same for the people who live inside them. In fact, it is hard to know if there *are* any people living inside them. I walk down the streets of the villages and towns, past all these themed and preserved houses, and sometimes never hear a soul.

On our return from Arizona as the millennium turns I find myself strangely oppressed by these houses and the property conversations, by the clipped foreign bushes in the gardens. We find ourselves fleeing the prosperity of middle England and seeking sanctuary among the frugal green hills of Wales. We spend that winter in a tiny stone artisan's cottage in a remote valley and ask ourselves where we should go from here.

One day, we go to visit a large and powerful house called Powis Castle. This Big House is famous for two reasons: the first is that it houses the treasures that once belonged to the military leader of the

British Empire who was known as Clive of India. The second is a plant, a hybrid of wormwood and tree wormwood known as Artemesia Powis Castle. All down the terraces the vibrant silvery form of this bush can be seen, bringing its moonlight hue to the brightly coloured formal borders, to the clipped apple balustrades and the parklands of conifer and rhododendron.

Wales differs from England in many ways. The people are strikingly egalitarian. Your gaze looks towards its hills rather than its austere, slate-roofed houses. As we walk about the gardens of the National Trust property, the grandeur of the house appears at odds with the soft and subtle land, the flowers seem garish and oddly contorted. When we enter the café I notice everyone is moving around silently and very slowly, as if they were dead. My body has started to shake and my mouth clams up. The room feels freezing cold.

'I don't think it's about tea, do you, Charlie?' says Mark, as we stare at the scones and jam.

'Let's go home!' I say and walk quickly out of the door.

When I first bought an Artemesia 'Powis Castle' bush we were living in Oxford, next door to an American anthropologist called Sandy. She had worked among rural peoples in remote districts of Europe, studying their ways of life. Her favourite informant was an old wise woman who lived in the Basque country. She would often tell us about times she spent among the sheep herders in their mountain village. The Basque people are a fierce people, with a language and a mythology all of their own. One of these myths she learned from the old woman concerned houses.

In the village it was the houses that counted, not the people. Or rather the *indarra*, the spirit of the house, together with the *indarras* of the houses on either side. The *indarra* of the house on your left was about life, and on the right about death. Oh! we said, and went rather quiet (since that made her house our death and our house her life). It was these spirits that conducted everything in the village. Even the pews in the churches were named after them, rather than the families that resided within their stony walls.

That day I shuddered in Powis Castle, I remembered the *indarra*. The spirit of the house that rules the life and death of its inhabitants and neighbours. I went to look up Clive of India in the local library in Machynlleth. The house is proud of its past association. It did not, however, mention his apocalypse. On his return from Calcutta, where he had set about ruthlessly establishing colonial rule and amassing a great fortune, he died in mysterious circumstances: some say he cut his own throat, or shot himself; others that he was ritually murdered and buried at a crossroads. He was forty-nine years old and an opium addict (his jewel-encrusted opium pipe is one of the house's most prized possessions). Whatever had taken place was so dreadful his wife did not speak again. She did not utter another word for forty-two years.

In 2002 there was a film about a large house called *Gosford Park*. It is an upstairs, downstairs tale set in the typical Big House era of the twenties and has all the well-known ingredients – a weekend house party, evening dresses, shooting, maids, butlers, vistas, huge log fires and so on – and it would have been just another big house drama but for one fact. It was directed by Robert Altman, an American director famous for his ability to look behind the scenes and let everyone speak for themselves – the servants and the masters of the hidden worlds of fashion, ballet and party politics – all the shows that govern our strange and hostile histories.

In the centre of the drama, Ivor Novello sits at the piano in the English drawing room and sings about love. It's a new sound that comes from America. Some people shut their ears to this music, others linger on the stairs and listen. As he sings, the owner of the house is murdered and the truth of the past tumbles out of the mouths of the cook and the housekeeper, two sisters who have not spoken to each other for decades. As these sisters speak of their secret downstairs a balance is rectified. An old order passes.

One evening, returning from Wales, we go to see this film with the companions of our Oxford days and afterwards hold a discussion. It is an ordinary evening between five people gathered before a fire in a public house. But for one fact. Three of these people are working cooks, and one holds bitterness in her heart: the bitterness of the creosote bush and the dandelion flower.

What is your position in the house? I ask everyone. I declare I am a radical; down with the *ancien regime*! Mark stands beside the singer, who brings the sound of a new era that the aristocrats do not want. Miche and Arthur side with the servants. They think it is very important that form is observed, that the knives and forks go around the table in a particular way.

Shame on you, *citoyen!* I declare to Miche, who is half-French. *Vive la revolution!*

I turn to our youngest companion, who is also half-French. He does not say anything. He is the only one among us who has aristocratic blood.

What is The House at the end of the day? Is it a container for yourself, or for the spirits of the dead? Do we set the table for ourselves, observe the rules of knife and fork, or do we keep this form for an unseen relation, for a stranger who lived here a hundred years ago? Do you carry the rules of this house within you, even though you sleep in a small, bare room? Does this ancient house still run in your veins and haunt you?

How many dreams of houses have come to me in these travelling years? The houses I have known and those I do not know. The house that holds me in its heraldic grip. The mansion with its gargoyles, its dry fountains and formal hedges, its carved doors behind which strange rites are performed, where the great stairs run with blood; the house that is overgrown with vines, where the servants are still running the kitchen, though the owners have turned into statues long ago?

Since I came to Wales these houses have been disappearing from my dreams. One night I find myself in the dining room of a large house. It is the evening of summer solstice. The table is set with ornate dishes. There are six guests. I am the housekeeper, entering the room with a tray. *Is everything all right your side?* asks the owner of the house, and says he will come and see me. But we both know he won't. We both know that on my side everything is not right in the slightest. In the dream, as I move around the dining table with all its silverware, I tell everyone they can serve themselves. The owner of the house has golden hair and looks like our youngest companion.

Keep your children under control. Mark and I stand on the windy ramparts of Harlech Castle and look toward the Atlantic sea. All over the island the flinty buildings of Empire stand dominant on the round ancestral forms, on the old forts and burial mounds. These

252

places are cold: cathedrals, castles, towers, grand houses. We shiver as we stand there, though the day is warm. The land beyond is green and soft, the silvery snakes of the rivers flow into the sea, the flowers shine brightly upon the cliff ledge. The Atlantic breathes in and out as it moves ceaselessly towards us, towards the shore.

Maybe it is because I was born on midsummer's eve, at the zenith of the year, at the time of the greatest light, that I can now write of what it means to take the irrevocable step, the 52 steps along the downward path that lead us back toward the ancestral land, back down toward the sea. Maybe because the golden English oak stands so firmly behind me that I can embrace the dark holm, his brother, and let everything fall as I step through the solstice door, as the mood of the great year shifts, as the key slips irrevocably from major to minor, from sweetness into bitterness, from pleasure into duty.

Or maybe it is because I have loved form so truly and deeply that I can let it go. Maybe because I have known these old houses with their sun-striped lawns and faded walls, played among their borders of perfectly kept flowers with the thrush singing in the high trees, felt the poignancy of time as I have considered those kitchens and writing desks, the fragrance of larders and cupboards and those long afternoons, that I can now walk so fearlessly towards the unknown with these bitter plants in my hands. Or perhaps because I have known too well the shadows of these houses, borne witness to the cold indifference they harbour, the cruelty of their ways and shuddered enough times upon the stair, that when I first came across those books that questioned our privilege, as the night wind blew among the holm oaks, I knew that I should be searching for something else.

As I walked through the world's drawing rooms the loud boom of the men and the shrieking voices of their wives echoed up the stairs, spilled out into the dark garden. I sometimes leaned against their heavy coats in the hallway, and wondered if there were any other kind of passage open to me. Then one day among the clinking of sherry glasses I heard a man laughing and I knew I had chanced upon it. The laughing man told me about the time when he was my age, and he had walked out of his parent's house one midsummer morning with nothing but a violin under his arm. And maybe it was because I heard in his voice a love of nature and the spirit of adventure that my own heart vowed that one day I would follow in his tracks. The laughing man was a writer who had written some of the most lyrical prose ever composed about the English countryside. His name was Laurie Lee.

Absinthe is a fashionable city drink in 2002. Once banned for its destructive narcotic effect, famously ruining the lives of the demimonde in nineteenth-century Paris, it has made a comeback among the cognoscenti in the modern bars of London. It is a vermouth flavoured with wormwood, the name taken from the Anglo-Saxon *Wermut* which is sometimes translated as 'preserver of the mind'. One night we sat on the floor and drank the drink they call the 'green fairy'. There were three of us: our youngest companion, myself, Mark, in the small empty flat in Notting Hill. We were passing through the city. It was April; the cherries were still in bloom and a comet flew in the sky. This neighbourhood, in which I had lived the first thirty-five years of my life, had undergone a shift. It had become very smart indeed. Money had entered the once-bohemian *quartier*. All the old antique stores had changed hands. One of them now sold obscure liqueurs from Europe, firewaters flavoured with quince and bilberry, rare island whiskies and barrels of small vintage country wine. Walking by, my eyes lit upon the emerald-coloured absinthe. In the glass the drink becomes cloudy with water and tastes like anis. As it flows into our veins, it seems simply to have the inebriating effect any drink will have on three people relaxing at the end of the day.

But for one fact: instead of the nostalgia and *bonhomie* that usually comes with drinking, comes something else entirely. Mark starts to laugh a terrible laugh. The church tower opposite the flat had just collapsed. Some smart apartments were being built within the old church masonry, and that afternoon the stones of its tower had come tumbling down, revealing in that moment the shaky foundations of the new construction. I roar with laughter too. *This sinking city!* Mark yells gleefully, quoting the evening paper's headlines. And we both roll around the floor, laughing like a pair of hyenas.

Our companion looks at us, alarmed. He does not laugh. As our eyes meet across the room, I realise that however it appears, things are not right his side either, and that no matter what position we adopt within the *ancien regime*, each of us has a house that holds us hostage, rooms and corridors where terror grips us by the throat. Nostalgia houses, interior houses, dream houses, party houses, inherited houses, houses where an *indarra* rules instead of the person with a heart and soul. Some of our houses are large and some are small; some go back thousands of years. But all of them have a dark legacy in them, a conquistador, an unsolved murder and a woman who cannot speak, as all of them have a bush outside in the garden with a bitter scent, whose silvery form brings death to the worm and the melancholy mind, and life to those who live on the right hand side.

When you come back to England with the wild places inside you, with bitterness in your heart, you are not the same person you were. You have lived in a straw bale house, a round house built of adobe, in a hut thatched with banana leaves. You have lived up a mountain, in the desert, in a hard cot, on rice and beans. You no longer care for palaces or restaurants. The taste for excess has left your veins. When the tower falls down in the city you laugh. The Empire is falling. You hold to nothing. The taste of wormwood is now on your tongue.

You have returned from a country of the future, of space, to a country of the past indentured to time – whose unspoken secrets exert an influence more powerful over its subjects than any show of history. You see this secret invisible force, this *indarra*, wherever you look in the kingdom, in the houses, in the streets, in the people. It is a consequence of working with the desert plants, with the rattlesnake of Arizona. You can see this twisted force appearing before you like a dragon trapped upon a wheel. The power of the old forms holding sway.

The *indarra* dwells in the church tower, as it rings its unmelodious sounds, out of tune, out of synch, in the twilight hour. The *indarra* sits in the public house and toasts the hours of victory as the wars come and go, as her puppet shows and ancient dances are enacted outside on the green. The *indarra* sits at the head of the table and hits a hammer; the people appear and disappear before her pitiless gaze, leaving only their names behind, inscribed on the board in gold leaf, engraved in the silver cups, on the dull stones of the graveyard. The show goes on, repeating the *indarra*'s mantras and rituals, in the halls and chambers and cloisters. The vanished linger in their thousands around the houses, stare down from their portraits, waiting for the sweetness of justice, sucking the warmth of the living as they pass them by. If you are wise, you shudder. You walk out of the door one midsummer's day.

Who is in charge? The *indarra* is in charge. The people are following the form without question. Inside themselves they dream of changing the world, long for warmth and reciprocity, outwardly they repeat the sacred rituals of house and council chamber, keep the rules and regulations, do not move from their inferior and superior position. *That's the way to do it!* In their speech they talk of justice, freedom, power for all! and yet keep one other in chains. The *indarra* holds the world in her claws and reigns invincible, until those who have no taste for sweetness enter her court. The ones impervious to flattery, who no longer keep the form. *Serve yourself!* Those whose terrible unexpected laughter shakes the edifice of institutions.

You can laugh because you have left the sweetness of the pleasure-dome behind. Because the youngest and fairest of your companions left this morning and will not come again. You have long ago ceased to trust the cold and heartless rhetoric of Empire. You have lived through the worst and the best of times. Your account is empty, Your suitcases are stacked against the wall. It's the beginning of the third journey, the journey of the *nostoi*, those who return to their homelands and set straight what appears before their eyes.

Who will break the chains that everywhere bind us? Not those who seek the houses and the treasures of the world. Too many shadows run rampant in their veins. Release comes when you are devoid of ambition, when you no longer desire the glittering pleasures that bind us to fortune's wheel. When you gain in the desert years a taste for the great things the dark holm brings – creative work, spirit's duty, kinship with the earth. For liberation.

Below the window the Empire comes and goes in its shiny cars, its gorgeous dresses, in the coffee shops where the people are all on show. I watch them all go by. Sometimes I meet my former colleagues in the doorways of the galleries and boutiques. Sometimes they pass me by, stare through me, as if I do not exist. The parade looks one way, but it feels another. But you would have to know absinthe for that.

Absinthe colours the world green. The Impressionists of Paris painted their fellow absinthe drinkers staring ahead of them into empty space, as their café-dwelling lives collapsed all around them.

Even their canvasses took on a greenish tinge, like the pallor of death. The medicinal herb within the spirit acts as narcotic, stimulant, aphrodisiac, convulsant and hallucinogen. The light seen under its influence brings an immediate shift of attention. It was a shift that shaped the Montparnasse of Toulouse-Lautrec and Baudelaire and defined the bohemianism of all cities thereafter. But for all its looseness and apparent gaiety, the world absinthe inspired was bound by a strict and martial edge: first popularised by French soldiers fighting in Algeria who used it as an anti-malarial, it was banned by martial law for spoiling the élan vital of the trenches during the First World War. It brings finality, whatever way you cut it.

The ingredient that was held accountable for its demoralising effect was the psychoactive wormwood. When it was removed from the litany of herbs that flavoured the aperitif that included hyssop, lemon balm, fennel and anise (and sometimes also sweet flag, coriander, angelica, mint, chamomile and juniper) it become Pernod 51 and lost all its lore and reputation. After the war, the highballs and martinis of New York replaced the absinthe of the boulevards and the artists left the district to the haute bourgeoisie – a pattern that would be followed equally in all cities thereafter. Although hyssop and alcohol were later found to be far more dangerous ingredients, only the bitter wormwood brought the green fairy to the door.

Oscar Wilde, who knew about the perils of artifice as much as anyone, once wrote about the visions conjured up by this green spirit. After the first glass, he said, you saw what you wanted to see – your grand illusions; after the second you saw things that were not – all your demons; after the third you saw what was really there, 'and that was the most horrible of all'.

This is the third journey. Which, depending on your ability to deal with bitterness, is either the worst or the best of all journeys. Because you see, with a perfected clarity of mind, what is really there.

Bitterness comes from experience, the horrible crash with reality, the sobering moment, the shaking of your youthful idealism and illusion, the revelation of the parade. You can identify with these experiences, let them rankle in your breast, become a bitter-mouthed fool who weeps over their misfortune. Or you can find the wisdom in them all and become a moth-destroyer, a worm chaser, a dispeller of the dead. Someone who can look the indarra in the eye. You hope in these bitter years, in these shifting times, as you move around your former native land looking for a home, that you have the strength of mind, the staying power, to disentangle from the clutches of your ego and become the latter.

Wormwood falls within a section of the vast pantheon of composite flowers known as artemisias. All have a formidable purgative quality, a bitter taste and a silvery form. The most common artemesia, mugwort, grows everywhere in the world's wastegrounds and field margins and is recognised by the Chinese as the plant most configured like a human being. It is used to clear the meridians in the form of *moxa*, an archaic practice which burns the leaves to liberate the energy body of trapping blocks (*moksha* means liberation). In native America bundles of the desert artemisia, sagebrush, are burned to purify the space of sweat lodges and healing circles before a ceremony. The smoke cleanses the air of pestilence and the spirits of the dead. Modern smudge sticks, sometimes mixed with sweetgrass, are similarly used to clear negative influences from houses. In the law courts of England the Mediterranean artemisia, southernwood, was once placed in the dock to clear away the prisoners' stench and the threat of contamination by gaol fever. In 1917 the poet Edward Thomas wrote a prophetic poem about southernwood as he stood by the garden door watching his daughter shred its leaves and smell them, just before he returned to the trenches. He did not like the plant and yet he loved it. For, like all artemesias, it bears dreams and visions in its wake:

> No garden appears, no path, no hoar-green bush
> Of Lad's Love, or Old Man, no child beside,
> Neither father, nor mother, nor any playmate;
> Only an avenue, dark, nameless, without end.

All artemisias are named after Artemis, the fierce hunting bear-goddess of the moon. Even though wormwood is a sunflower and is cleansing and bitter in the manner of all solar plants, the territory it deals with falls under the aegis of the moon. Sister plant to St John's wort, artemisia hunts out all parasites that lurk beneath appearances and brings them to light: our unmentioned history, the underbelly of the world's glamour, everything our inflated rhetoric denies, keeps hidden in the shadows: the dark invisible forces we feel and yet do not wish to see. The souls who shuffle in the corridor. The prisoner who stands at the dock. The woman who does not speak in the house. The poet who will never return to his garden behind the tall damson hedge, and the small girl who stands by the door.

Who will set us free? The laughing men, the ones speaking about heart and soul, bringing the new sound back from America. Who will set us free? The sisters who open their mouths and speak to one another in the kitchen. All our attention has gone to the leaders and generals of Empire, but it is the silent women of the house who keep the secret, who hold the nightmare. The *indarra* does not care, so long as the form is observed. All eyes are on her treasure, so she does not hear in the stranger's ancestral apocalyptic laugh that now is the time of the dog's throw. She does not notice the girl in her bearcoat, in her dress of smoke and moonshine, as she turns and walks toward the door.

You hesitate as you stand before the door, as the sound of the midsummer beckons you. To proceed means to lose the house which has sheltered you for aeons. To go forward means to lose your innocence, all your aspirations and hopes, all the illusions of the outer world, and walk toward the wild lands, into the unknown territory of spirit. It's the moment you break from Empire.

'Once you go there is no re-admission,' said the black doorman at the Café de Paris. 'I know,' I said gaily as I went, though in truth I did not. I was thirty-five and carefree and about to leave for Mexico. I stand before the city I left that midsummer day in '91 and consider my options; the empty bottle of absinthe sits on the window, the long stones of a Welsh beach beside it. A sun falls between the tower blocks and bathes all the windows with fire. Behind me the suitcases lean against one wall, small sheepskins from Wales serving as beds in the empty apartment.

Whither shall we go on this third journey? What does my presence now signify in this place I used to know? The parade goes by along the sidewalks, and then disappears at either end. I gaze upon the neighbourhood I once knew as home, and the houses appear in the same places. But the bohemians have gone from the district and I am no longer the person I once was. I have slept in the Empire's prison, held my own among the canyons. I am looking at my old world in another light. The place appears neither resplendent with

259

former glory nor terrible with unexorcised demons, but exactly as it is: a pleasure dome that sucks the earth of all its joy and sweetness.

In the body, wormwood purges the excess of pleasure and expunges malignancy with a volatile oil known as *thujone*, which is also found in white cedar, tansy and sage. Its purgative effect in the invisible worlds is something only the inner eye can see and only the bitter heart can administer. The Empire crushes natural life in its demand for eternal pleasure and makes its subjects pay the price. Wormwood is its reckoner. Absinthe is called after its botanical name *artemisia absinthium*, derived from the Greek word *apsinthos* which means against sweetness. In the last testament the star *apsinthos* brings the end of the sugary world of Mammon and makes the waters of the earth bitter. With the clarity of mind conjured by the green fairy comes an awareness of an inevitable decline.

The tower collapses whether we hesitate at the door or not. After the zenith comes the fall. If we cannot wrench ourselves out of the hold of the *indarra*, the memory fails, the body collapses, the barbarians enter the city gates. And whether we understand this as an inner event, an individual destiny or karma, or outwardly as a revelation, an earth change or evolutionary shift, the severity of all our apocalypses will play out in direct proportion to our willingness to relinquish our own artificial and illusory worlds.

Nicholas Culpeper, radical apothecary of Spitalfields, is pithy and precise about most of the 360 plants he writes of in his famous herbal of 1653, but with wormwood he is lengthy. It contains the key to his astrological world-view of plants and his own significant place in history. His translation of the physician's pharmacopoeia has revealed all the secrets of the profession and secured a loyal readership among the people and the antipathy of the *ancien regime*. Unlike his contemporary, the royal physician William Harvey – and the scientist Isaac Newton who was to follow him – Culpeper did not see the human body as an organism made of mechanical systems. He understood it within the context of a living intelligent cosmos in which all conflicting forces were kept in a balance. Man was a fluid being influenced by invisible planetary energies, rather than a concrete machine which needed fixing when it 'failed'. Disease was caused by lack of balance and the righting of that balance fell under the auspices of a planet, whose energies were embodied in the native plants of England. The plants kept the natural complexity of life in order and the work of the herbalist was as much to encourage human nature and spirit as it was to cure the physical agues, inflammations and tumours that arose from their repression. 'Many times I find my patients disturbed by trouble of conscience and sorrow and I have to act the Divine before I can be a physician. In fact our greatest skill lies in the infusion of hopes, to induce confidence and peace of mind.'

Culpeper wrote at a time when the world of the apothecaries was clashing with the world of the physicians and was about to lose. An élite medical establishment was poised to take over from the midwife and the apothecary and put the human body at the disposal of the Empire. But in spite of its subsequent domination Culpeper, in the way of all creators, has the last word. His *Complete Herbal* has remained in print ever since it was first published. There is not one book about plants that does not refer to him at least once. I discover everything about wormwood from this herbal: in the botanical gardens in Oxford, I seek out the subtle difference between these artemisias, the feathery southernwood, the sea wormwood of the marsh, the bush-like common wormwood. I collect sagebrush in the deserts of Utah and New Mexico and purify my own house, though I have yet to find these wild artemisias in my native land. What I remember most about the plant is that it is governed by Mars, the planet of war, and 'remedies the evils choler can inflict upon the body of man'.

'Choler, temper, anger, scorpion bites, bruises caused by beating, throat, pox, he gives you no affliction but he gives you the cure. The eternal God when he made Mars, made him for public good, and the sons of men shall know it in the latter end of the world.'

Wormwood is the penultimate plant of the Complete Herbal. It contains the essence of Culpeper's work, a passionate exposition of the planetary influences within man and nature whose balance keeps us sane and sound. The herb cures the fears and furies of the mind, ends all the hostilities of Empire with its straight blade. When the body suffers from a surfeit of pleasure, Mars comes and rights it by antipathy with his sword. When antagonism rules the world, the Leveller comes and cures it by sympathy. Afflicted himself as a soldier in the Civil War by a wound that will end his life at the age of thirty-eight, Culpeper embodies the clear-cut and fiery qualities of Mars, attacking the ignorance of contemporary physicians and warmly urging his readers to attend to their own and their neighbours' good health. He is writing against time, against the time of his own life which is running out, and that of his ancient profession. And yet while the triumphant doctors of reason come and go, the dwellers of great houses and empires fade into obscurity and die strange deaths, Nicholas Culpeper remains in print, his heart beating among the flowers. In among the dry botanical facts of every guidebook, every dull treatise on herbs, he appears, flower soldier, with his sword of artemisia.

The bushy common wormwood is subtle, not so much a medicine person's plant as a plant of poets and seers. A warrior, bear-dreamers plant. One that brings a new light to old surroundings and sets the record straight. Under its influence Culpeper becomes visionary. Under its influence I see how to proceed. It speaks not of presence and space in the manner of the desert bushes, but of time, of what must pass and what will come to be.

The day we decide to live on the Suffolk coast is the day I find wild wormwood on the beach. Walking from the town of Aldeburgh I come across great roadside stands soaring into the sky. When I sit down beside their tall silvery leaved forms, I know I have arrived at my destination. We have been roaming westwards, but here on the eastern shore is where we will stay and make ourselves at home. I rub the scented leaves and small button flowers between my fingers and inhale their sharp camphory smell in the hot July day. The sky is pure blue above us, the glittering sea lapping beyond the dunes, the temple dome of the power station hovers like a mirage in the distance. The scent of wormwood lingers in the air.

The music did not just lead us out of the door; it was leading us to somewhere in all these travelling shifting years, beyond the falling tower, beyond the murder mystery and the exigencies of Empire. It was leading us towards this beach and the wild sea, back to a place where we once belonged and could begin again. I sat among the dry grasses on the warm ancestral stones and felt my journey turn. This is a seaplace I used to come to in my former years. Now my gaze is no longer directed at the houses on the skyline, but at the seaholly dancing with blue butterflies, the bright pink of the rosebay willow-herb, the sand martins flying over the stalks of fennel and artemisia.

In the town the people sit in the public house in their positions, talking-talking in their heads. They are the people who work in rooms without windows. The normal people with houses and jobs. They are eating fish when there are no fish left in the ocean, they are building houses over the land when the rivers have nowhere to run, they are advocating the culling of wild deer, chopping down the old trees, keeping the children under control. Bang! Slap! Wallop! goes the *indarra*'s hammer. *That's the way to do it!*

Outside lies a new territory, another England, the countryside of Laurie Lee. The larks are singing in the blue sky and the sea stretches outward toward the horizon. A gnarly apple tree thrusts its way upward through the pebbles. There is a sense of space and sky and light I have not felt since we came from America. From here I can return to my old country, neither prodigal nor victorious, but someone unexpected, without history, without illusion, appearing beside a silvery bush whose bitterness frees the spirits of this haunted earth and colours everything green.

VI
TREE DIALOGUES

Who are these forms that stand sentinel in our lives, at the end of our gardens, in our parks, gathering together in wood and copse and spinney, whose masses form the rainforests and pineforests of the world? Who do they keep watch over, the baobab scaled by the dark man collecting honey, the ceiba inhabited by harpy eagle and bat, the yew in the burial grounds? Who are these beings whose bodies cradle us in birth and death, provide fuel for our winter fires, give spring to our dancing feet, line our cabins, turn into bowls and the tables on which we eat, the paper on which we write our letters, our greatest thoughts and feelings, bound for years, long after we have departed? Who are these ancient bringers of wisdom, with their red and silvery bark, with their delicate blossom, with their sweet fruit, with their fragrant wood, with their cones and seedpods, those shapes we glimpse as we pass by in our trains and cars, fuelled by their fossilised forbears, who speak to us in places we no longer have words for? Whose disappearance, as one or in their thousands, brings us a grief we can hardly bear to acknowledge?

Trees are among the oldest inhabitants of the earth. To speak with them is to know our ancestors, to know who is in charge. Civilisations tell us 'superior' human beings in 'superior' countries are in control of the planet. However, the *driving force* of any individual or collective is not its *life-force*, nor what directs that life-force along the proper lines. To consider trees to be in charge of life on earth is to acknowledge that they know what being here requires in terms of presence, engagement and exchange.

Human beings are not like trees; we are not life-givers but connectors. At best we are creative symbionts with the earth, as the fly agaric mushroom is to the silver birch, bringing communication and interconnection with many life-forms, inventive network nodes in the great fabric of planetary consciousness.

As agents, we are not the all-wise and all-seeing. Our animal natures mean we are too much 'in the field' for broad and long-term vision. Civilisations have thwarted the creativity of our tasks and turned our symbiont relationships into selfish parasite activities. Instead of living in harmony with all our relations we live in a kind of survival panic or feeding frenzy on our host planet. Because we have the capability of mutating and destroying life forms, we think we are superior to them.

Trees live outside this artificially created mindset. They are primary life-givers and bring benefit to the planet in every cell of their bodies. Being rooted, they interconnect with life in a very different way from ourselves, holding atmosphere and weather patterns together, supporting soil, bringing rain, providing home and shelter for animal and insect kingdoms. They are the planets' great alchemists, converting direct sunlight and minerals into breath and food for all creatures. And they do this work with ease and assurance throughout their whole breathing, shedding, life-giving, shade-giving lives. In short, without trees we could none of us live.

It is for this reason that the ancient and native peoples have always held great reverence for trees and have sought their counsel in their own public and private affairs, knowing that if all things are in line with trees, their lives too will benefit. For many centuries in Europe councils were held under trees: the lime trees of France, the oaks of England, especially those trees that grew at vital crossing places on the ancient network of tracks that held the land in alignment with the sun. The trees in their longevity, both as life forms (some living for hundreds, even thousands of years) as well as their ancestral planetary presence, were recognised as the storehouses of a particular kind of memory. This chapter is based on experiences with a number of time-keeper trees and primarily takes place in lands where trees have been esteemed since archaic times as the dispensers of wisdom, justice, and right government.

It begins in Oxford in the autumn of 1999 where, having worked intensively with flowers in the plant communications practice during the summer, our attention shifted to the trees. We visited the crack willows and black poplars by the River Thames, sat beneath the great redwoods and London plane in University Parks, beneath the Persian ironwood and black pine of the Botanical Gardens. I collected crab apples, sloes, hawthorns and rosehips from the hedgerows, and made rose-scented tinctures and jellies. In my passionate pursuit of English apples, I began to climb apple trees, and then all trees – ash, birch, crab apples – the oaks of Shotover Hill. To sit in a tree is to know its energy and character in ways that are hard to describe. Your hands learn to recognise its bark, your body its structure, your eyes its shape; you can sense its inner nature, its warmth and presence, even in the depths of winter. By the time you jump down you are full of energy.

Back in the house during the *seeings*, the tree council took their places within two circles. An inner ring comprised nine native trees -- oak, yew, ash, black poplar, willow, alder, rowan, holly and beech, an outer ring a collection of smaller trees, such as hawthorn and hazel, and naturalised species, such as horse chestnut and sycamore. The inner heart ring was commanded by the generous and silent oak, the outer by the stately and severe silver birch. Each of these possessed a key, or way of seeing, which opened the doors of the trees – portals to certain knowledge. As I came to know this circle of trees, I saw how they worked together as a collective: the inner core trees for consultation and matters of the heart, the outer trees of the will that helped manifest these decisions in the world.

Engaging with the intelligence of trees was radically different from the work with the flowers. The territories they addressed had a far greater range and influence, and we often found ourselves in real-life situations in which their energies were dramatically revealed. Though the trees were singular, they always acted within a collective sphere, as they would in a forest. Working within their field, you looked in terms of the wildwood, across the planet into deep time. The pavement dandelion is quick. Your mind can assess its 'medicine' in a matter of minutes. The churchyard yew is slow. It speaks with the wisdom of centuries. Your whole being needs to pay attention as you absorb its influence, its presence in your life. A sprig of its fine needles and red-berries sits for a long time on your writing desk. One day it comes in a dream. At some point your knowledge of the tree is put to the test. Does the theory match the practice?

In 2001, on our return to Europe from America, we began an inquiry into the Celtic alphabet of trees. This was not an exercise in nostalgia or paganism, but an investigation into the balancing of natural cycles, in accordance with the archaic calender of the solar year. The tree alphabet begins at the winter solstice and the thirteen consonant trees (some of which are bushes and climbing plants) correspond to the annual thirteen moons. They revolve around the eight stations or doors that mark the dynamic relationship between the sun and earth during this year: the fire cross of the solstices and equinoxes (signified by the five vowel trees) and the birth-growth-harvest-death cycles of the diagonal cross, known traditionally as Imbolc, Beltane, Lughnasa and Samhain.

Thus we began our inquiry with mistletoe and silver birch in Oxford, continued with the firs, rowans, alders, hawthorns, oaks, hollies, crab apples and hazels of Wales, with the flowering gorse and willows of London, the dwarf blackthorns of Dungeness, the blackberry bush, heathers, white poplars, ivy, reed beds and ancient yews of Suffolk, with the forgotten elders of Ireland. We visited the circles of beech trees that crown the hills of southern England and several woods and forests: from Burnham Beeches to Box Hill to Tunstall Forest. Our lives became infused with trees. And we lit our festival fires with their twigs, cones and branches at all the stations of the year thereafter.

Three of the original key trees in this chapter are evergreens – holly, box, holm oak – which command the second 'dark' half of the solar year. This signals a time of maturity, in which the challenges and responsibilities of the spirit come to the fore; a time when you need to be able to stand up for yourself, speak out and be backed by your experience. By holding on to the young ascendant part of ourselves (the light half of the year, commanded by the deciduous

267

oak) we neglect our most potent fall. In this fall is our autumn and our winter – our fruit, our harvest, our nourishing dark. It is our link with the ancestors, with the mysteries, with our ability to let go and regenerate our lives. Without the qualities that these second half 'challenger' trees represent we never become elders, the vibrant spiky evergreen guardians of the land.

It was these initial investigations into the tree alphabet that fuelled all our later tree dialogues – with the evergreens of the ancient Mediterranean, with the world trees of many places, from the English oaks of Suffolk to the sacred peepal tree of India. And it also broadened the scope and context of all our plant-human communications. The tree council worked as a group of beings with diverse qualities. Its 'leaders' coordinated these energies as they possessed the innate skill of being able to hold many-things-at-one-time and speak as one-among-the-many.

The trees directed us to consider the government and spiritual structure of our social lives. With their size and their year-round presence, growing in harmony together in woods and forests, they naturally extend their energies outwards into the collective. Working with them challenged us to work together with people in groups, and face crucial issues concerning our collective future on the planet.

crack willow
The Thames, Oxford 1999

It is a city of willow trees. Along its winding rivers and canals the tribes of willow gather in all their shades: white willow, weeping willow, cricket bat willow, golden osier, grey sallow, goat willow, and most abundantly, crack willow. The wind is always in them. In the winter their bare branches shimmer with gold, and in the spring and summer their honey-coloured plumes and silvery green leaves are always waving. Underneath the earth their roots clasp the banks together and keep the waterways clear. Even the fences of the river gardens are made of their living forms.

When we came to Oxford that winter, it was not to the city of dreaming spires, but to a confluence of dreaming trees. As I went out and explored the neighbourhood these willows of the riverbanks and meadows became my reference point, my anchor in a new green world. I loved their whispering shade, their fissured trunks, their bendy forms that provided birds their nests and people their baskets. Meeting new acquaintances in the street, or along the canal, I would find myself looking up into the soaring branches of a crack willow, sheltering us in our communications.

These willows, I discovered, possessed extraordinary qualities: one was their ability to clean water; the other, to regenerate themselves. Their Latin name *salix* means to jump. The limbs of the crack willow, in particular, famously break and snap off, but wherever a part falls down seemingly dead, it sprouts roots and jumps up miraculously to life again. They are the ultimate trees of resurrection.

That first spring and summer of the plant practice, we worked almost exclusively with flowers. Then one October day, Mark and I visited an ancient beech wood in Gloucestershire. It was perched on top of a mound, and as I walked through its shady depth, following a path of glowing self-heal, I felt the intelligence of the trees all around me, as if I were being observed. Something in me shivered. That night a tree entered our *seeings* for the first time. I sensed a presence that I knew and yet did not know.

We are the council of trees. You need to collect the keys of the trees. I am Old Man Willow.

My heart leapt and I felt a thrill run through me that was almost a fear.

The crack willow stood at the edge of the seeing, the way it stands on the banks of the Thames, the Cherwell and the Isis, and all along the Oxford Canal. Unlike the images and feeling readouts of plants, the tree spoke clearly in words; its sober presence brought whole sentences to mind. The willow's theme was the practical use of imagination, which it referred to as dreaming.

Everything that happens on earth, the tree said, is dreamed first. To regenerate the earth, you need to regenerate it first in your imagination. The physical reality will follow. Because your imagination works within the living systems of earth, its nature is collective and interconnected. Therefore this dreaming takes time. And does not always happen in the way you imagine it will.

Why had my heart given such a start? What was shaken within me in the wood? That night someone told me about *The Wicker Man*, a 1960s film about an old Celtic rite that had resurfaced in modern day Britain: the burning of a sacrificial man. The basket that held the 'wicker' man was made out of bands of willow.

Modern people, proud of their great rationality and progress, often hold irrational terrors of being sacrificed – as children thrown into rivers, as young 'green' dismembered men, as wild women burned at the stake. These fears underlie many acts against 'nasty nature': the triumphant chopping down of trees, the suburban control of gardens. These fears, buried deep in our cellular memory, come to be confronted when you first hold a dialogue with trees. Trees, of course, do not control anyone. All the 'darkness' projected onto the wildwood comes from our own tribal history, in which human beings were once sacrificed for the fertility of the soil.

Old Man Willow brought a clear and sober intelligence which could confront these obstacles of the mind. He appeared and gave us instruction: negative memories and fears needed to be released in ourselves, otherwise they would continue to keep us alienated from the earth, and from the trees, our best allies, most of all. Dreaming connected us with the intelligence within the living systems of the planet.

How many of your dreams take place in nature, he asked, compared to constructed reality, in houses and rooms?

Dreaming was distinct from fantasy. Dreaming has no fixed outcome: you are tuning into and working with the living fabric, without knowing what will happen. Fantasy, on the other hand, is a controlled activity of the mind, based on the selfish desires of the ego: we construct illusions in order to satisfy our revenge, our greed, our sexual appetites. In order to *dream*, the fantasies and fears of the mind need to be rigorously dissolved. Only then will our imagination be free.

Oxford is an ancient university city, the seat of training for those who run empires and governments, the bastion of the Rational Mind. It has also inspired some of England's greatest works of imagination: *Alice in Wonderland, The Wind in the Willows*, the six 'Narnia' chronicles, *The Lord of the Rings* trilogy and in later times, Philip Pullman's trilogy *His Dark Materials*. All these tales centre on a young innocent hero or heroine who goes abroad into other dimensions to put a crooked thing straight.

The dreaming of trees began in Oxford because it was a place of dreamers. You are a dreamer, said Old Man Willow, and have no difficulty with the imaginative realms. Adults lack this relationship with the Otherworlds. You need to broaden your vision. Dreaming is not just for children.

'Something has got to move,' I thought, as sat under the two crack willows by the gate to Burgess Field. The afternoon winter sun bounded off the lake in Port Meadow and terns were swooping off its mica surface with their high-pitched cries. We had been in Oxford for almost a year, but it still felt as if we were living on the edge and needed to break through into the human collective in some way.

'I need a sign,' I said to myself, to the trees. *You need to get up and join in*, the crack willows replied.

'Hello, Charlotte! What are you doing?' called a voice behind me. I turned round. It was Su, wheeling a baby in a pram.

'I'm communicating with the willows,' I told her.

I was always meeting Su under willows, or finding her showing children how to make dreamcatchers from their branches, She was a community artist who lived above the local post office. She called herself the Queen of Trash, teaching people to transform 'rubbish' into art, and was famous for making banners for demonstrations and co-hosting an alternative performance night each week in the centre of town. She wore bright orange and red clothes and tore down the dignified streets of North Oxford on a bicycle trailer, in a whirlwind of tangerine. 'We're here to bring the love!' she would say as we passed each other by under the trees. We would have very intense discussions and then not see each other for weeks. Sometimes she was wary of me. Mostly I think because I had once said that cannabis stopped you dreaming.

'I'm coming to see you soon,' she said 'I've been straight for sixteen days. Can't stay now, I've got to listen to the last instalment of *The Handmaid's Tale* on the radio. It's so *grim*.'

'It's about liberation,' I said. 'And it's got a happy ending! The girl escapes from tyranny and goes free.'

'I do hope so!'

'Is this the baby you helped deliver last month in your friend's van?' I asked her.

Su grinned. 'Yeah, I'm taking him for a walk. His mum and dad met under a willow tree, so they named him Salix. Must go!'

As I walked home along the willow-lined towpath, I went past two signs calling for everyone to Join In a protest against the housing developments planned between the canal and the river Thames. These were the places where we had discovered many of our inquiry's flowers and trees. Wasteground lizards basked in the sun under bricks, deer slept in the afternoons, birds nested in the bushes, and a whole ecosystem flourished in its own right in the last wild green spaces left in the city. 'Right,' I said to myself, 'that's where I am going.'

Mark looked horrified when I told him. Still, the following Monday we set off to the neighbourhood pub where the meeting was to be held.

The meeting was organised by a group called Canal 21. Its name came from a directive called Local Agenda 21 which was created at the Earth Summit in Rio in 1992 to encourage small local groups to ecologically preserve the ways of community and neighbourhood. Originally it had been formed to establish ecological moorings for the barge-dwellers of the Oxford Canal and now it had become a protest group to raise awareness about the proposed buildings. The meeting had been called because the developer's plans were about to go forward to the council at the end of the following month.

Mark and I stood beneath a huge copper beech tree before we went into the pub gathering our resolve. *You need to broaden out,* said the tree. 'Here we go!' I said. In the dark back room, there was a lively interchange among funky-looking people with pints of beer – artists, activists, boaters – and a few wild-space lovers like ourselves hovering on the edge, not quite sure of the form. Su was in the middle of the crowd, laughing loudly. I took a deep breath and ordered two ciders from the bar.

The meetings are run according to the rainbow tradition, a man called Edward informed us as we sat down on variously coloured plastic chairs. He seemed older than the rest, in his fifties. This meant we spoke clockwise in a circle. Everyone had an equal say in whatever was discussed and conclusions were made within a group. I felt quite nervous, never having taken part in these kind of meetings before. Everyone was well versed in campaign lingo, rattling off terms like *greenfield* and *brownfield sites* and *on-* and *off-side* and referred to the architectural plans on the wall with consummate ease. When it was his turn, Mark exploded in a tirade against the wreckers of the lizard's territory. Everyone looked at him and smiled. It seemed to boost the energy of the evening. That left me.

'Why don't you do something that will catch everyone's attention?' I said.

'What do you mean?' asked Charles, an architecture lecturer who had designed an alternative redevelopment of the area.

'Well,' I said, thinking furiously on my feet. 'You know, if you wore a ... well, a green ribbon in support of the land. You could sell the ribbons on the streets, tie them round trees, and speak to people and the newspapers. That way the campaign would become a talking point.'

A circle of faces stared at me. Trust you, I thought to myself, to come up with a fashion detail!

But to my amazement the faces broke into smiles and everyone started talking animatedly. Edward was the last man to speak. As people had alternately ranted, exploded, droned on, been pithy, gone off in tangents, kept to the point, he sat with his eyes closed and listened. At the end of the meeting he spoke slowly and summed up everyone's views. The protest had waned in the last few weeks, but the idea of the green ribbon, he concluded, has resurrected it.

A campaign sprang to life.

Our house, strategically near 'the site', became a communications centre overnight. Canal 21 appeared at our door, and as if we had been doing this all our lives, we launched into writing and designing leaflets, posters, open letters, council letters, press releases, newspaper articles, websites, planning community days, 'art actions', more meetings. The willow leaf became our signature. I walked out and posted hundreds of flyers, putting up posters in shop windows and cafes and bookstores, and travelled all over Oxford to talk to other activists. At the turn of the millennium the city was a nexus of ecological protest groups. Everyone was up in rainbow-coloured arms on behalf of the earth.

'The Levellers used to wear green ribbons in their hats', said Emma, whose barge was moored under a weeping willow. 'Did you know that?'

'We're modern levellers, then,' I said and laughed.

I hadn't known. But I did know about timelines. The willows had once come as ancient and fierce interzone time-keepers in a dream, showing us how to 'wake up' and remember. Trees are storehouses of collective memory and remind us that we also hold this function. As our small group met by the riverbanks, in the back rooms, around fires, we became part of the timeline of the city. Three centuries earlier in a moment of high exultation, when the presses flew open, Oxford was a heart of radical activity and dissent in the land. In an intense fusion of spirituality and politics, green-ribboned levellers, ranters and diggers everywhere discussed how a liberated kingdom of England could belong to Everyman, rather than remain the sole property of the *ancien regime*.

It was the beginning of the English Revolution.

Our first revolutionary action was at 2am at the lunar eclipse when five of us met at Aristotle Bridge and erected a community noticeboard full of rainbow-coloured posters and wreathed in ivy. Bruce shinned up the willow trees and hung banners from their branches along the canal. After that small act in the small hours, our lives took a radically different course. Joining a campaign is a wake-up call. Your previously quiet and fixed world becomes fluid and full and loud. You find purpose and direction where none existed before. You take bold actions which your 'good' behaviour would not normally allow: acting up, trespassing, flyposting, marching into building sites. Once you were isolated and invisible, now you find yourself one-among-many, part of a group and emboldened to speak to any stranger regardless of their station. You plunge into the river.

The first time he took part in an action, Edward told me, he had arrived at an anti-road protest and saw a crowd of people running up a green hill in a great exultant wave. Something just broke inside and he ran to join them. He had never felt so alive, he said. The defence of the realm became his life. Edward was a peerless protester. He trespassed magnificently. He camped in the former common grounds under the cricket bat willows of Magdalen College; he walked naked in front of Buckingham Palace. Unlike the younger activists who had a hot-headed, energetic style, Edward was quiet and deliberate – neither 'fluffy' nor 'hard'. We stood together writing graffiti on a hoarding, paintbrushes in our hands. He painted a lizard wondering about mortgages. I wrote quotations from William Blake. Everyone put their coloured handprints on the temporary wall, like an aboriginal rock painting. Mark and Su talked merrily to the builders. The builders laughed. Something had broken inside.

Mark put on his black coat and walked out into the grey January cold and spoke to everyone in the neighbourhood. He spoke about feelings, what had been left out. I pulled on my gumboots and stood on the muddy towpath under the willows, selling green ribbons to everyone that went by. I spoke to policemen, security men, builders, surveyors. I berated the council on the telephone and held forth on the local radio. We stood up in meetings and stood by our fellows. The campaign was invigorating and challenging in the outer world, in the world of action, but sometimes inwardly, in the world of feelings, it was difficult. Sometimes we felt vulnerable, under attack by forces that were hard to name.

Willows are governed by the moon, the planet that moves the waters and the tides and flows, the fluidity of ourselves. The watery tree gives you the key to dreams, to imagination, to inspiration, and to the parts of ourselves that require an inner transformation. Like many moon-governed plants, its energy can decrystallise any rigid structure held in the human body. Its physical medicine, salicylic acid, the basis of aspirin (originally taken from white willow bark), encourages flow and releases the dammed-up energies that cause pain in our physical

275

heads and joints. It also provokes the same movement within the emotional body – so old, held-up, left-out feelings can be expressed, cleansed and regenerated. Our new radical activity challenged all kinds of *ancien regime* restrictions in ourselves, but it also stirred the muddy waters in the outer collective that needed to be made clear.

We found ourselves in a stagnant world. We felt fuzziness in our heads, an incoherence in the airwaves. People did not look you in the eye when you spoke with them. You couldn't see quite straight. It felt as if everything was going very slowly and you were wading through invisible treacle. You felt trapped under this city sky, as if everyone's thoughts and oppressions were bearing down on your head. Mind sets clashed, frequencies jammed, situations began to feel unreal and vaguely threatening. You felt nervous in your stomach. The atmosphere was disturbed. You woke up with nightmares. Often you felt you couldn't open your mouth.

In this confusion we learned to hold our own, to say what was actually going on, to find the meaning within the situation so that what was natural could prevail over the sense of grimness, *it's got to be done,* the sense that everything had already been decided. Mental decisions, the kinds of decisions developers make, are rarely questioned in the field. It was important to be clear. To keep still, keep asking questions, to keep in communication with the ground beneath our feet.

As the campaign mounted, so did the feelings of paranoia and hostility. There was a backlash against our publicity. The constructed world ruthlessly suppresses anyone who defends the living systems, by minimising and ridiculing their expression. It especially attacks protesters, most of whom do not hold powerful social positions. As a result, those who oppose their schemes can often find themselves subjected to the engineered negativity of the populace on whose behalf they are campaigning. This can have devastating results within the protest groups themselves. Even though we were all united in our hearts in defence of the land, there were terrible factions within the group. At the meetings tempers flew, tears flowed, quarrels often took place. The stress from these invisible forces was very hard to bear. We all felt it. In the weeks that followed, some people began to disappear.

All civilisations work by leaving out the feelings of the heart. When you take part in a campaign you don't leave these feelings out. However, unless you have been extremely smart, you will find yourself prey not only to your own untransformed emotions (some of which have got nothing to do with the matter in hand) but everyone else's. Those who work for the civilising world fuel this emotional and psychological oppression by encouraging the 'well behaved' status quo to scapegoat the 'badly behaved' protester. And it is also done in subtler ways.

The green ribbon campaign was initially a great success: our painted wall flourished, hands-off posters appeared in windows, green ribbons flowered in everyone's lapels. It united all the local small groups: the historical preservers of the area, the naturalists, the allotment holders, the boating community, the residents and all the visitors of the canal and the meadows. It provided a common ground and brought us together in ways that nothing else could. Suddenly everyone *belonged* in this wild urban territory we called home. Neighbours who had never spoken to each other were in daily communication. The feisty activists of East Oxford spoke to the outraged burghers of North Oxford. We went to each other's meetings, in halls, in pubs and gardens. What had not happened up until this time was a dialogue with the developers themselves, but as soon as the green ribbon appeared in the press, the company asked to meet all the groups separately. The meeting with Canal 21 took place in our house.

We voted on who should speak to the developers on behalf of everyone in the group. And so it was that Canal 21's founders Ceri and Su and myself sat one evening in late February in our living room opposite three men in suits, one of whom had started talking fast and very loudly at us as soon as he came through the door.

'We are going to run this meeting our way, ' I said, interrupting him. 'Sitting in a circle, rather than an us-and-them position. Then we will introduce ourselves, saying who we are and what our position is and how we feel about this development.'

The men looked surprised but nevertheless complied. I had designed the structure of the meeting to enable us to get as many points across as dynamically as possible: Ceri would speak for the boaters, Su for the local community, I would speak on behalf of the nature and the spirit of the place. I represent the willow trees, deer, birds, voles and the waterways, I told the men in suits. Since no one else considers them.

An eager young man wrote down all of my words.

The meeting was watertight and extremely energetic. Everyone spoke eloquently. The developers spoke about IT and traffic schemes and we spoke about wilderness and regeneration. But while I had concentrated on getting our message across, I had not considered why 'the other side' had called the meeting in the first place.

The mindset of the constructed world works within the fabric of life like a virus: it can replicate everything its host does to its own selfish advantage. I had assumed naively that these men had come to speak with us because they genuinely were concerned about the points we were raising. But they were not. They were no more concerned about what we had to say than the land they were working on. They had come to find out our objections, so their subsequent marketing activities could present their company as having these things 'sorted'; so they could use words like 'wildlife corridor' (by which they meant a strip of bushes through a housing estate) and thus ease the minds and conscience of the public about their destruction of the existing habitat.

The modern mind is educated to believe in the supremacy of the written word, so when it sees those slick marketed words it does not link them with any kind of earth-based reality. The authority of the writing assures us that 'they', the experts, have everything under control. Moreover, since we would like to believe 'they' have everything under control (wildlife has been informed and will now take another route) we allow 'them' to go ahead and do what they like. Even when it impinges on ourselves and our very real concrete lives.

Developers, like all business enterprises, are primarily concerned about their *image* and will employ vast resources to maintain a positive image in the public's mind. The reality of the situation is not their concern. The building of artificial systems is their concern. Those who bring attention to the negative effects these systems have upon the living systems of the earth are seen as a dangerous irritation, and the developers will use the power of shiny marketed words to divert attention away from their activities. Just so long as public opinion swings their way, or rather is neutral, and will let them carry on their enterprise either out of indifference or despair.

The despair of the residents was the main feeling we encountered when the campaign started. Speaking about the heart and soul of

278

things is what united everyone. The rigorous willow was waking up this heart and soul in us in order that we resonate with the feeling intelligence within all living things. Living according to the heart requires an even-paced, well-considered appreciation of all the factors involved in any action. You need to sit in a rainbow circle and be able at the end to sum everything up like Edward, and come to a fair conclusion. Local governments, developers, land owners, do not run things according to the heart but to the will – to satisfy their ego, their greed and their drive for power. As a result they are neither tapped into the living systems of the planet, nor themselves. They are busily constructing worlds in which the bearing of willow trees, water rats, the spirit of place, the soul of the neighbourhood are not considerations but irritations to be dismissed. Artificial systems all go as fast as thought and function by being as efficient and as machinelike as possible. They have the driving force of locusts and bypass the heart and soul at every turn. They hide this heartlessness from the public by offering words as substitutes that *sound* like heart and soul. And it was to find these key words that the developers came to speak with us:

'A Berkeley Home is one that people enjoy living in ... a home in *harmony* with its surroundings and right for the locality. Such homes are created by people with a *passion* for buildings ... people who know the needs of individuals and communities, who approach home-building with *commitment* and flair, who can add their own *creativity*. The result is a *quality* home – an asset not just to owners but to neighbours and the local *community* alike.'

Two days after our meeting the company put out a shiny brochure and posted it through the letterboxes of the neighbourhood. *Regeneration for the area!* it claimed. It used everything we had said in the meeting and co-opted our words for its own designs. At the end of the month a large public meeting with the city council took place at which both Su and Charles spoke, but it was clear that decisions had already been made behind the scenes, and this was merely a formality.

Outside the school in Summertown, Su sat down and sobbed. They are not listening, she said.

Silently in the wastelands of Oxford, the catkins of the goat and grey sallows dusted the dark night air with specks of golden pollen.

The solar path teaches you everything about life, and it does this in the way of initiation by breaking your innocence. Innocence is a dangerous commodity in the modern world. We would like life to be sweet when it patently is not. We would rather profess innocence than take responsibility. Instead of standing our ground as adults, we pretend we are little children who have done nothing wrong. We turn away. Innocence can take many forms. I have been innocent about words.

No one wanted this huge estate of replica houses all crammed together, with its garages and non-native garden bushes. No one wanted the tarmac, the street lighting, the cars, thousands more people with their machines and their machine minds, where once there had been empty space and free air. The site stretched right up the canal towards Wolvercote, and even after it was clear that the houses would be built I still walked the path, tying ribbons and notices along its length, replacing those that were waterlogged or torn by the builders. They seemed small and insignificant, our words printed on those pieces of coloured card, the meetings we held in the streets and gardens. But I knew it was important that we said these things. If you don't, you never find out what part you play in these events. Or do anything about that part.

Oxford is a city of writers: writers who champion the Empire and those who challenge it. The writers of the famous children's books sent innocents to change the world of shadows where everyone is a gargoyle, where the land is permanently frozen, held under a spell, where greed and power has thwarted the natural order of things. But children cannot save our world. To expect youth and innocence to save the day is no better than throwing children in the river, or putting a young man in a wicker basket and burning him on May Day eve. Only elders will save the day. If we have the courage to become them.

I walk down the towpath in the dusk and sit down among the great willows by the canal. At night you can smell the water in the air, and sometimes hear the owls in the trees. You have the world to yourself. Everyone has gone home. Canal 21 had fought to keep this wild path, to keep its mysterious dusk and dark. The developers wanted nice picturesque boats with geraniums next to their buildings. They wanted asphalt paths for joggers and powerwalkers, with street lamps and safety precautions. They didn't want these free-thinking boaters with their allotment gardens and woodstoves, this muddy path where you can watch the moon sail high among the trees, where you can keep in contact with the wildness of yourself. All spring I listen to the wind in the willows, hearing them creaking, cracking together in the night like the bones of old men. When I close my eyes I can hear the spirit of the trees roar through the land.

It began here, I said to Charles' group of architecture students. We were leading them through the wastegrounds, past these trees, past the green-ribboned fence, through all the building sites. We showed them the fields that would become a school playground, the tracks that would be fenced off, the wild gardens of mullein and dog rose that would become roads and houses. We walked past the giant hog-weeds now rising among the sycamores, towards Wolvercote past the acres of rubble and machines, until we reached the last of the canal boats. It was moored outside the main site. A dilapidated wooden vessel that had not been painted for a long while. It almost looked as if it were sinking. We must talk to Pierre, said Charles.

Pierre stood on the towpath in our midst, the fierce and independent captain of the old narrow boat. He told us about the dragon lines of Oxford, the rivers and the waterways that ran through the land and gave it its power and strength, and how to interfere with them as these developments do would bring about the stagnation of the city. As he talked of leys, I saw the sewage and water pipes running under the ground, the tarmac enclosing the land, thwarting its natural watercourses, the confusion and flooding it brought in its wake, the deadness to the spirit of the place. The young students, future employees of developers, shuffled awkwardly by the emerging stands of meadowsweet and bur-marigold. Pierre strode back towards his boat.

To be an elder means you have nothing to lose and nothing to gain by the shiny words of civilisation. It is to chart an independent course of action and to keep to it. It is to listen to what is really being said underneath all the talk and the PR, to know what the living systems are saying in the hearts of the people, in the wind that roars in the trees, in the water that runs through the land. You may believe people when they utter deep and meaningful words, but this does not actually mean they are deep or have meaning. I have believed these people. Maybe they believed themselves. But when I joined this campaign I realised that words are rarely the reality of the situation. People say things for all sorts of reasons and motives and often to cover up the fact they are compromising themselves. The developers we confronted, to whose hearts and good sense we appealed, were no different from anyone else. Their concerns were for how they appeared, how they might protect their interests, rather than how to engage in what was actually been said. When I looked at the brochure that came through the door I was shocked. I felt betrayed and a fool at the same time. The willows shook my world because I needed to wake up and know what was really going on when people used words. Because words were my business as a writer.

If you work on behalf of the living systems, you have to be as good as your word. You must not be a crow talker. You need to stand by what you say. What you say must have its root in the concrete world. What you imagine must be based in the real earth, as Old Man Willow in the seeing was the crack willow by Burgess Field. The artificial world is engineered by the written word which has no such root in reality, and no such allegiance. It affects the living systems, but has no regard for them. Those who write and speak for this world have no need of integrity. Men who are loyal to the company paycheque are not the same as men who are loyal in their hearts to the land.

As the groups began to disperse in the weeks that followed I realised that we would only go as far as our ability to act on the words we speak. If we say one thing and desire another, the desire will win out. If we are a campaigner but underneath desire a job from the very people we campaign against, or we entertain a fantasy of owning a big house ourselves, or if we are a resident who is concerned about the value of our property rather than the spirit of the neighbourhood, the world of materialism will always win because it knows that the words spoken by its detractors are not backed by reality. Moreover, those words can be taken and made to work for this constructed world because ultimately everything is for sale, including ourselves.

However, if one person speaks and is willing to act on what is said and is not for sale, something else takes place in the vast intelligence system that is the earth, that exists in everything, even in the wind that blows through the willow trees. This intelligence now 'knows' that this limit exists because it has been articulated and acted on. The words the constructed world uses now have less validity. You don't believe the spell it weaves. You tap into the intelligence of the living systems and you look into the hearts of people: you look for depth, tone, position, the feelings that lie beneath appearance of things. You start to take a different course of action.

'What shall we do now?' I asked Old Man Willow. *'Don't give them any more energy,'* he said. *'The more attention you pay them, the stronger they become. Battling against "them" feeds that world. When you stop there will be less energy to hold it up. You are dealing with a virtual reality, even though it doesn't look like it. Let them take responsibility, and they will not if you are providing the scapegoat. You need to know you are supported by the planet you are on. You will have to walk by.'*

It was not easy to walk by. When they said 'walk by' the willows did not mean walk by oblivious to what was happening: they meant walk by and keep an open heart, keep in communication. So I walked by the land where I had first seen the ladder of light in the St John's wort, where the periwinkle had told me to bury the hatchet, where I had gathered the honey-scented flowers of great mullein, where Mark had seen lizards basking in the sun. I walked through the fields of scarlet pimpernel and mellilot, along the railway tracks where the salad burnet and water-betony grew, through the fields of mugwort down by the canal. We joined forces with a local campaign for the preservation of a small oasis of wilderness, a patch of reed bed and scrubland known as The Trap Grounds. I walked its windy paths through dog rose and hawthorn, where great stands of hemp agrimony and goldenrod would flourish that summer and that I would never see. I walked by our community notice board that had been thrown into the canal by the security men. I heard the bulldozers move in, watched the trees come down.

One day I walked by the building site and asked the foreman whether he knew *Wind in the Willows*.

'Oh yes,' he said. He had a daughter who liked the tale.

'Ratty lives in that canal bank you are about to dig,' I told him. 'And those willows are the ones you are cutting down.'

'We are making green spaces,' he said, looking the other way, towards the muddy recreation ground.

And we looked at the empty municipal land, devoid of life and people, and were silent. And the wind blew softly through the long leaves of the trees.

'We would like you to comment on the amended plans,' said the company PR person on the telephone.

There was a space. 'I have nothing to say,' I replied.

'But we are asking all the groups in the area,' said the voice, almost pleading for my 'say' in the matter. 'We have made changes!'

'I have nothing to say,' I repeated, and put down the phone.

When you are young you think you can change 'the system' from within. You begin to work for the Empire and give it all your youthful energy and idealism and creativity, and then one day you realise that these beliefs *are* the system. The system always wins in the system. What you can change is yourself and the way you act. What you can do is take yourself out of the system, out of the battle you cannot win, and put your attention on life. The system attracts people because it is couched in the dramatic language of war. Powerless people everywhere love to fight *against* something. It gives an illusory sense of control and boosts the self-importance of the ego. Eventually, however, this egoic power struggle divides people against one another and enables whatever repressive regime there may be – political, empirical or religious – to take hold. When you are against nothing, something else happens.

Four months after the green ribbon campaign first sprang into life, the group began to drift apart. Fewer and fewer people came by the house. The plans were being amended but were going ahead. The ecological moorings were about to be secured. Our job was done. It felt as if the pressures of the world had driven us apart and nothing we hoped for had happened. But it had. During those months we had spoken together in a rainbow circle; in a moment of exultation the neighbourhood had communicated together in a great wave. And when Su had asked the developers on that February evening *'What is your dream?'* we all watched as something began to falter, as those who held all the cards, all the words, suddenly had nothing to say.

At the end of Canal 21, at the last meeting in the back-room of the neighbourhood pub, there were four of us: Su, Edward, Mark and myself. It was late May. Mark and I were about to leave for California, Edward was about to spend the summer in a remote hamlet in the mountains of Italy. Soon Su was going to be the only one left in Oxford. As we parted company Edward attached a green ribbon to the heart of the crucified Christ on the corner of St Margaret's Road. He smiled his enigmatic smile and disappeared into the night. I last saw him sitting in the home-made yurt he had erected illegally among the buttercups to hold a summer party on Port Meadow as the rain fell quietly all about him.

Its doorframe was made of a willow branch.

english oak
Staverton Thicks, Suffolk 2006

Odin, god of the north, hangs upside down for nine days and nine nights from the boughs of the great ash tree. He creates the first man from its trunk. Jehovah, god of the desert, roars from the mistletoe that flames like fire among the thorns of an acacia. His tribe has fallen by the wayside. In the rainforest the king of the Maya embodies the ceiba, night-flowering kapok of the three worlds, whose flower-shapes his people wear about their ears. Beneath the wild crab apple tree, the mysterious Q of their alphabet, the Celtic seers ask the question: *Where is wisdom to be found?* The world trees are the trees of life, doorways to the invisible realms of sky and earth, whose activities influence this middleworld of form. Without them we know nothing of ourselves. They connect the people with the spirit of the land.

At the apex of the solar year stands a tree that speaks for all that is great and noble in the misty islands of Britain: the English oak. Who speaks to us from within its mighty boughs? Whose face do we see laughing among its green leaves? We do not know. We have forgotten his name.

What we remember is that the oak is the monarch of the trees. We know that the presence of oaks signifies that a wood has reached its highest expression. Individual oaks can grow large and sturdy and live for over a thousand years. In their generous and mature embrace are kept all the creatures and the insects of the woodland. In their inner core they keep the memory of the deep forest. It is the tree that resonates with the human heart and pulls us all towards climax. The heart brings everything together, synthesises, records, holds balance. It remembers how things need to be in the wildwood, on the earth. When the heart is in charge, human beings are at their highest expression. You live in sovereignty in a united kingdom.

Arriving back from Australia a year before our plant inquiry, I began to visit an oak wood on the outskirts of Oxford. Frustrated by the roar of the ring road and the newly built estate where we were staying, I would pull on a pair of gumboots and strike out into the dark, windy weather, walk across the bridge and up into the woods on Shotover

Hill. It was cold after the heat of California and Australia but I found it invigorating. There was something in the wild grass pushing through, all that green, the rough coats of the animals, the colour of the stones, the fabric of the place that was exciting. It was like discovering Britain for the first time. I noticed everything: the toads clambering about the ponds, the singing of the blackbirds, the scent of foxes as I climbed the hill that overlooked the city. Most of all I liked to go at dusk and feel the presence of the wildwood – still, alert, the March wind roaring through its canopy. Sometimes I ran helter-skelter through the trees and would lean breathless against their trunks, feeling the rough bark against my hands. I felt at home in my own land in a way I hadn't since I was a child. Shotover Hill is an ancient wood, and rich in its understorey. Later I will discover wild raspberries, drifts of bluebells, yellow archangel, fly agaric mushrooms, and climb the large birches and crab apples. But most of all I will return because the old trees I love to stand beneath are English oaks and the oak was the first tree to come into my dreams.

It was a short dream but so vivid I awoke. I dreamed I went up to the wood at night and went inside a huge oak. There were passageways that led into the deep earth, and as I followed them I became aware that most of what was happening in Britain was underground. At the roots of the tree there were several men who came and stood in front of me. They had masks on their faces made of oak leaves. They were muscular and dark and had the same presence I had felt from the trees at Shotover. *Can you see us?* they ask. 'Yes,' I say, 'I can see you.' After our meeting these men began to emerge from the trees, out into the open air.

In the dreaming practice there is not much to say. Why did the oak come in my dream? What is it saying about the men who live in the roots of the trees of Britain, with their green-leaved faces, with their hearts of oak? In a land where most of life happens underground?

After this dream I sometimes see these men in the street. They are ordinary men, sometimes working on a building site, or in a garage, in a canal boat or walking down the lane with a stick.

I don't know these men, but whenever I walk by they turn and wave, and I wave back.

'What do you do?' I asked. I was on a hill outside Oxford, in a copse at evening, in the March of the following year. The man said:

'I plant oak trees.'

The man was not young, not like the young protesters who at this moment were gathering wood for the equinox fire, stacking the dead boughs into piles to burn through the night. He lived in a caravan and mended bicycles.

'I walk with a pack of acorns,' he said, 'and wherever I find a good place I plant an oak. What do you do?'

I looked at him in the shadows, his face half-revealed in the flickering firelight.

'I am a writer,' I said.

All around me people were gathering in the wood. Small tents had been put up between the trees, gaily painted protest banners hung from their boughs, a huge soup pot and kettle were on the fire. Everyone was talking and laughing. I am a stranger among strangers. I know nothing about protest, or about the equinox, or about the hills of Oxfordshire. But my heart is beating. I am remembering a name. It is a name from the books of my childhood and yet here it has come alive. I am returning to the wildwood of my memory, the only England I have ever wished to know.

Robin Hood, hero of the wildwood, hides in the mighty oak. He is a medieval outlaw, he is the Green Man, he is the spirit of the lands. He does not, like the doomed King Arthur, dwell in a fairy castle. He lives in the real greenwood with his merry men, with his Maid Marian, and protests against the Sheriff of Nottingham. He holds out for the return of the true king, *le coeur de lion*. The King of England, Richard the Lionheart, has been imprisoned in a tower in France and his dark brother has taken over the kingdom. It is a story from history. It is the myth of the oak kings. But it is also a mystery.

Robin Hood is hidden, hidden by his Lincoln green cap, by his mask of oak leaves. He is an underground hero who robs the rich to feed the poor. He *is* the King, of course, except that he does not wear the costume of kings. It is up to us to recognise him when we find him in a dream, by the fire, in ourselves.

What is the heart? This physical organ that beats inside my blood, the spirit core of myself that resonates in my breastbone? What does it mean to govern ourselves from the heart? This answer comes in glimpses, like flashes of sunlight, the way the English oak appears to me in glimpses during these years. In the heart you are warm and near to yourself and your fellows, all things cohere and have meaning. You are not living the separating life of the mind. You are not cold, autocratic, antagonistic, controlling, beyond suffering, cut off from life. You are not constantly on the lookout, like a predator bird.

Unlike the totemic birds of other nations, the national bird of England is not the mighty heraldic hawk or griffin vulture or eagle, but a small songbird, the robin. Robins are unusual, because unlike other song birds they sing all year long (except for a short respite in August). Both male and female robins sing. They sing in all weathers and at all times of the day. They even sing at night. In England they are well-loved. Perhaps because more than any other bird they feel kin to us, living alongside us in our gardens, in the country and in the town. Feisty, friendly, cheerful, bright-eyed, the robin red-breast is welcomed everywhere. He is the bird of the heart, and he has, for as long as we can remember, been a bird of the oak tree.

Here he is singing in an oak tree as I sit in Burnham Beeches in Buckinghamshire at the turn of the millennium, waiting in a clearing, in a woodsman's circle of tree stumps. A bright circle of spring light in the solemn wood. I feel the tree's presence behind me. I close my eyes. The oak is the most silent and mysterious of the trees, the last of the council I communicate with. To know the tree is to sit as he sits. In the command position.

In this position, as you connect with your own beating heart, you connect with the forces of the sun that radiate outwards in all directions, with the creative mysterious forces of life. The character of the oak is not defined like the other trees: he is not the warrior ash, nor is he an adviser, like the black poplar or willow. He is the king who holds the kingdom together. In his slow and steady presence you find out how it is to sit with the sun in the centre of yourself, so all situations naturally self-organise and proceed along the correct lines. You learn how to hold the heart's position within your individual being, which extends outwards into the collective. You do not dominate or submit, keep apart from your fellows, but sit in the centre and wait, so the solar 'rule' can radiate within you and everything in life can benefit.

The difficulty you face is that the sun within you is blind. In order to organise the connections between all things, in yourself, in the wildwood, within the kingdom, you don't see, you feel. You are working in the dark. You go entirely by instinct.

I have a crown of leaves on my head. To hold this weight requires balance, measure, grace, a full awareness of everything that surrounds me. Inside all dimensions are within me. Within this centre everything can be adjusted and aligned. I have no need to go anywhere. The integrity is inside of me, not on the outside of me. At one point, an irritation in my mind runs through my body and disjoints this equilibrium. The tree behind me speaks:

'You feel obliged to come up with the goods. You don't have to come up with anything. You can just be.'

I just am. There is a long silence as I sit in the glade, backed by the mysterious presence of the oak. The thought and the irritation disentangle themselves. The sunlight spreads like a carpet before my feet, the dark rings of sinuous beeches keep watch all around us. The song of the robin rings through the hallways of the wildwood.

'We are the same,' the oak says quietly. 'How does it feel to be with someone who is the same as you?'

My small heart roars. What does it feel like?

It feels like I am no longer alone.

The Dark Heart, a book about modern Britain and its outlawed underclass, begins in The Forest, a small scrap of the original forest of Nottingham, where now at a funfair two young boys wait to sell their bodies. It is a searing and disturbing book about social injustice, about the invisible quarter of the nation that lives on the poverty line. Its author, a journalist called Nick Davies, writes about a culture that no longer cares for its rag-and-bone children, that treats the men and women of the Forest, of the slumlands of Birmingham and the brothels of Bayswater, as mere objects, without feeling; that uses the poor to be the carriers of their own nightmares. It is not a new story, it is a very old story. How to end this story is the task of the solar heart.

Under the roots of the neighbourhood oak I sit and think about the kingdom I have returned to after so many years travelling. I think about the dark streets of Birmingham and Bayswater where I once lived. Mark and I talk about our childhoods in a nation where heartlessness rules. Mark comes from a poor house, I come from a rich house. *The Dark Heart* does not document the part the other three-quarters of the nation play in creating its shadow. It is commonly assumed that it is all right for people if they have money. The book argues that it cannot be, because if one quarter of the collective go down, everyone goes down. Money is not a measure, I tell Mark. If you have money, you are obliged to spend your life chasing the ever-demanding forms that it requires you to possess. Everyone feels obliged to come up with the goods. The truth of the matter is that everyone in the kingdom is for sale.

Mark and I sit underneath this oak at the crossroads, facing the downward curve of our lane, flanked by barley field and hedgerow, scarlet poppies and spindle tree. We lean our backs against its trunk. We wait for a word, a shift within our beings. We watch the sunrise and the moonrise. We wait in the winter chill, in the summer heat, in the spring when the leaves of the tree are young and green, late in the year when they flash gold and then tumble to the ground. In its bare branches at dusk the robin sings his sweet winter lament, and the tawny owls call one to another. The oak is solid, always there; it never changes; it stretches its straight dark limbs into skies of grey mackerel cloud, of serene washed blue, holds the fiery ball of the setting sun. We sit beside one another, by ourselves, and whatever difficulty we come with aligns itself within us and disappears. We are not alone.

The roots of the oak spread in all directions below us, mirroring its wide net of branches above. With these roots it is connected with all other oaks, with all other trees, with the hearts of everything in the land. This is the heart of the sun radiating throughout the land. Where the oak flourishes, everything flourishes – flowers, fruit, birds, insect life, people – life does not get better than the climax of the wood. The oak maintains this kind of life. Something that runs in our blood knows this when we sit with the oak. It is linked with the right order of things, something to do with the heart of the lion that is also our own heart, our best expression, something that knows that it is not right that the rich rob the poor and that the Sheriff holds us to ransom in our minds.

In the Celtic tree alphabet the letter of the oak is D, *duir*, which means door. According to Robert Graves, the Welsh word *derwydd*, origin of the word druid, means oak-seer. When the seer speaks with the oak he sits in the door and sees what is happening underground in the kingdom, beyond his five senses, under the surface of things.

The oak and the seer open the doorway so the command of the sun can shine on earth. In ancient Greece the people once sought Apollo's laurel for prophecy at Delphi, but Jupiter's oak at Sodona for the wisdom of right government. In modern Germany, to remind the populace of the right government, the visionary artist Joseph Beuys planted a thousand oak trees in the industrial city of Kassel, each accompanied by a mysterious block of basalt. 'In the future,' he said, 'Everyman will be king.'

When the wavy-leaved giant of the forest rules, right government comes to the planet. It is for this solar command that the green men of England, that Robin Hood waits. For the kingdom of the lion, for the rule of the lion-hearted king, for the return of the lion-hearted in the people who have lived for so long under the rule of the black-hearted sheriff.

Who is Robin Hood? He is ourselves.

The King is also ourselves.

In the high summer of 2006 Mark and I began a series of earth dialogues as a daily speaking practice. We held our dialogues in the dunes and shingle banks of the East Anglian coast where we now lived. The intent of the original earth dialogues was to go out with a group, to connect with the elements of a chosen territory, and then to build up a map between ourselves. These meetings had a different tenor. We would go down by the sea, connect with the physical place, and allow whatever arose within us to find expression. Afterwards we would swim in the sea. No longer in the hermetic room but immersed in the fabric of these wild places, the nature of our dialogues shifted. By the sea they became fluid, quicksilver, matched the mood and atmosphere of the day, the shift of the tides, its currents, whatever creatures or plants or people we encountered on the beach.

By late autumn when it became too cold to swim we went inland. The sea dialogues became tree dialogues. We held these in a grove of sweet chestnuts by the marsh, by the rowan trees on the common, the Scots pines on the river path, the hornbeams in the coppice wood. Whereas most of the tree work we did in Oxford was with singular trees, here it was always within a group. Usually we would sit with the trees by ourselves and then meet up and hold a conversation afterwards. Whatever took place in this conversation was an expression of the intelligence of the trees and the people working together, and the issues raised were those that fell within the tree's jurisdiction.

In the original council of trees the oak was always the leader, and yet I did not know the oak truly until I came to live in Suffolk. The oak is not a tree of cities or towns. It rules from the heart of the land. In Suffolk it commands the flatlands, marking the boundary and crossroads, its giant craggy forms appearing across the barley fields and the ploughed skylines and along the sanderling coast in small airy groves, among birch and Scots pine. But the trees we visited for our dialogue that October day were a group of oaks we did not know. They stood in a small ancient wood by the road between Iken and Woodbridge. It is known as Staverton Thicks.

As soon as you enter this wood you sense the presence of mature trees. The Thicks are dark and tangled, with a path that winds through large oaks and hollies that grow intertwined with one another. We walked in silence past these trees, skirted with smaller rowans and elders full of berries, and out into open grassland. Here the oaks had been planted centuries ago and formed an open grove, full of space and light. The trees in the grove were enormous, with wide girths and full crowns. Mark and I split up to find our separate trees. I went further down the grassy track, following the hoof-prints of deer, dented in the soft ground. A robin was singing above us, a clear, high, urgent song. Suddenly I stopped and turned to face a great oak near the path. There was a coil of barbed wire around its base, so instead of sitting down with my back to the trunk as I would normally do, I put my hand against the trunk and leaned into the tree. A wren cocked its eye at me from its bramble hideout and hopped into the oak. There was no one among the long grass and the trees except for us. The Thicks are surrounded by miles of estate farmland and conifer plantation that run between the coastal rivers of the Alde and the Ore. It is a quiet and empty land, except for the air traffic coming from the local airfield. As I stood under the tree the noise of the helicopters circling the skies suddenly became unbearable.

You fuckers have always been here! I said out loud, surprising myself and the stillness and the singing in the wood. As I spoke I realised I was not alone. I was standing not just by this tree, but among a grove of ancient oaks. It wasn't just me that was talking.

There was a big silence as I felt their collective presence, with their arms raised to the sky. As I stood there I became aware I was entering a time-line. I could hear modern army helicopters, but these were also Roman legions, Norman conquerors, alien forces. It was just a matter of theatre, of historical costumes, of technology. Beyond these 'shows' I saw that the oppression the sky invaders were exerting over the land had always been the same. What was causing the heartlessness of the people was this antagonism in the airwaves. It felt like a crushing pressure in my head. What was in the sky was also happening in our minds – the oppression of a mindset that did not originate from the earth or from our hearts. As I stood facing this noise and interference in the sky, something stirred from deep within me to challenge it. And as this stirred, the wood filled with other presences. I was remembering the hilltop in Oxfordshire, I was remembering the oakwood of Shotover. I was remembering the people. People I had known who had stood by trees, and people I have never known who had stood by trees. We were all there, waiting, it seemed, for an aeon by the tree in Staverton Thicks.

We are holding out, the oaks said finally.

My heart jumped.

'I am with you,' I said. 'I am always holding out.'

I am holding out that our hearts will return. I am holding out that the people of this green land will throw off our dark oppression. I am holding out that even though Mark and I are alone in this oak wood, we will all one day emerge from the underground and meet together. I am holding out that even though we are hidden and often alone, we know in our hearts, in our thousands, that we are together. No matter what house we come from, what work we do, where we dwell in the kingdom, we are already united: the men that walk the mountains, the men who swim the wild rivers and seas, who sleep in the branches of the trees and burrow among the roots to stop the machines from killing the wildwood; the lion-hearted who speak out loud, who call to account, who bear witness, the oak-seers, the acorn-bearers; the merry maids of England, who bring their lightness and beauty and laughter, who stand by the men, who walk beside them, who see them and keep the fire. I am holding out for us all standing here together, as the oaks hold the sky in their branches and their roots hold the earth. We are holding out. We are holding the land sovereign. And with one heart we say:

This planet does not belong to you.

VII
Radical Flowers

When we began the practice I found myself exploring a territory that is traditionally the preserve of men – nature, spirituality, mythology, mysteries, medicine. I followed their ancient tracks and found myself looking at an earth I did not recognise, governed by a mythological matriarch. Service to this moon-faced deity, Robert Graves wrote, was the basis of true poetry and life on earth. Driven underground by philosophers of the city-state this white goddess had become, like all suppressed women, furious and vengeful. She sat in her wild mountain nest littered with the bones of poets, in spite of their loyalty.

However, this was not the narrative I found among the flowers during those underworld years. The mysteries instruct us that without female wisdom neither love nor liberation nor return is possible. In female transformation lies the redemption of the world. Innana is stripped of all she possesses and left on a hook, Psyche is given impossible tasks. Persephone falls into Hades and rewards all those who visit her dark kingdom. Inside our female forms the lines of our lives are tangled into knots, and have not been straight for thousands of years.

The task I faced was to untangle these threads, to unhook myself, to sort the seeds whose names I no longer recognised. But just as I knew that one day Persephone will return to earth, I also knew that the fury that so cruelly distorted our world could only be transformed by the presence of another kind of female being. And that I was going to have to be that being, neither goddess nor harridan, but someone entirely new.

Returning to Oxfordshire on the eve of the plant practice, I walked out one summer afternoon and stood beside a herd of cows. A red kite swung above us and I felt myself take flight over the Chiltern Hills, over Wittenham Clumps, the vale of the White Horse, passing by its rounded forms and curves, following the shining river Thames. The land and sky shimmered together, and all at once I saw the constraints upon the land – the neat gardens, mown lawns, cropped fields and hedgerows – burst out of their constriction like so many snapping fasteners of a dress, revealing the real beauty of the place that lay beneath – a country full of light and blue air, like a young woman walking and singing, intense, intelligent, her dancing dress the colour of the glowing sun. It was the England of the sweet wild rose.

I saw that we had become like this indentured land, domesticated way beyond our natural selves, keeping everyone in our houses penned in with our cooking, cleaning, tidying. The matriarchs of Middle England stood with sharpened knives, their aprons smeared with blood and chocolate, before their chopping boards; they held the bodies of beasts and birds and fishes in their hands, heedless of their beauty, deaf to their cries, blind to the rainforests and flower meadows destroyed in their name. Lost in minarets of self-absorption, it was a dangerous power that they wielded. The unconscious will of the Empire exerting its absolute control.

In these acts no one saw how we enslaved whole geographies, whole peoples, whole biological kingdoms. How this pleasure and control suppressed our real female selves, how it affected the wild lands, the hearts of men and children; how there were no spaces left to dance in among the miles of tarmac, house and garden.

We needed to hold the world beloved in our hands. Outside the misty land of the wild rose lay waiting for our return, bathed in light. The great song of the heartland rippled sweetly down the river and ran in rings around the soft blue-tinted hills.

You have to start somewhere. I started here, in a borrowed kitchen, as evening came.

As I followed the flower path through England and America and slept in other women's houses, I led an outsider's life. I encountered people I would never have met had I remained in that self-absorbing kitchen, in my glamorous city world: sheltering illegal immigrants from El Salvador, campaigning with ecological activists in Oxford, being interrogated by the INS in Arizona, working in low-grade jobs in Suffolk. My story was a journey of descent: the story of a someone born into a powerful élite, but destined to undergo the patronisation, ridicule and hostility that élite imposes on 'the other' to keep its superior position.

Real-life experiences are what teach you empathy with your fellows and all creatures on earth. George Orwell, ashamed of his participation in the imperialist Burmese police force, went underground in the spikes of London and kitchens of Paris to learn a passionate equality that never left him. It never left me either. To become equal, I learned, is not a matter of the mind, of words we utter, or books we read: it requires a radical change of heart. The flowers in this chapter relate some of the life-changing encounters we have to undergo so that we might return to the heartland.

How you consider the female form is a key to how you perceive life and the planet. The earth – matter in its many dimensions – is a matrix, a web of interconnecting strands in which we as human beings play a certain role. When you enter this matrix, you are entering a female field. Whether you are male within this field or female makes no difference. How you act within its boundaries is what matters.

To perceive the earth in terms of a matriarchal deity is no more enlightened or human-friendly than if you understand it as the property of nations or patriarchal gods. In the first you are subject to 'its' power, in the second 'it' is subject to yours. Either way, you are not entering the earth's field with your free will. You and the flowers never meet. You stand in awe before the beech tree and adjectives tumble into your mind – regal, queenly, majestic. You fling your arms around its sinewy form, but there is no fellow feeling. It's a one-way performance. Still you are excluded from the dance.

To return requires a revolution of imagination, because only in other dimensions can you communicate on the same wavelength. Crossing into those dimensions is the big test. Once you cross that divide, life changes completely. You are on another planet. You are standing in big time, in touch with the creator-ancestors. This reconnection demands a high price, because you can't cling to your illusions of separation and all the convenience that brings.

Life won't be comfortable any more. That's the deal. It's why you hesitate in front of the door. Why people stay in their domestic prisons, assume the powers of deity in their kitchens. Why you don't go to meet the flower. You feel you will lose everything. And in many ways, you will. You will lose the life that is costing the earth its flowers, its fresh air and clean waters and costing you your heart and your freedom. The moment you stand before the door is the moment you decide whether you are here for the beer, or something else; when you decide whose side you are on. Whatever way you go through, your allegiance will lie outside the Empire.

The revolution the flowers bring is a quiet revolution. It is an inner event but it affects everything you do on the outside, every relationship you have. The shifts that occur on the flower path change the way you think and the actions you take and your engagement within the collective. All the plants I worked with in these years were directing my attention away from a dominant hierarchical structure and into a fair and inclusive solar organisation.

This organisation is based around the individual in communication with all their relations. These relations are not just with our fellow human beings, but with all our relations on the earth – seas, mountains, animals, birds, flowers and trees. To operate within this relationship requires a complete change of values. In effect, to live in this paradigm you have to become a different kind of human being. Not made differently but *powered* differently. This power is no longer resident in the nuclear forces – our wills fuelled by hate, fear, aggression – dictated to by outside broadcasts and our own rigid mentality, but fed by the dynamic energies of the sun and earth and wind and water in accordance with our natural beings, interpreted by all our seats of consciousness – our hearts and souls, our open minds, our free will.

This is easier said than done. We have been dictated to for millennia by the ruling élite. We are not used to thinking for ourselves or acting from our own initiative. We look for someone else to take responsibility and blame. We like to criticise, but we don't like to act. Mass controls, both political and religious, have been with us for a very long time and though we may dislike these controls they are enmeshed in the fabric of our daily lives. As female beings we are particularly distorted in our industrialised culture, hemmed in to conform by the fashion and entertainment business, by the fossil-fuelled dramas of our daily lives. To disentangle ourselves from their influence is a hard labour.

Why are these flowers radical? Because to align yourself with the living systems means you walk away from Empire and all its controls. You have to look not only at the ways you as an individual have been engineered to think and feel and perceive, but also to look at yourself as a social being within the collective. Because the flowers bring to light fundamental social injustices that need to be addressed. Because they help us see through the manufactured illusions and glamours that make us blind to the difficulties and suffering not only of ourselves but also those of our fellows.

This is no mean task: the institutionalisation of our social beings has been orchestrated since we were born. We do not like to think of ourselves as numbers and statistics. We do not like to think of ourselves as functions. Inside we are full of importance, with our mythological imaginings, our grand archetypal roles, our important entrances and exits from relationships and workplaces. We think our fellow actors are our best friends. One day, history knocks at the stage door and we find ourselves alone in a strange costume. Our dreams are full of the terror of this moment. Suddenly cast out, flung into prison, a loser, a number on a form. We wake and consolidate our position in the world. But the truth is we matter to no one, not even to ourselves.

It was not a big moment in history, the end of the second millennium – and yet, it was history. As we moved back to England and walked through empty seatowns and agricultural fields, I found out that though you imagine these exits and entrances to be so important, you are merely an actress, and like all actresses you are replaceable. When history comes and shakes the production, what your fellow actors really care about is the play. When you go down, they cling to their roles. For what is life without the play? That is what you learn. Once you know this you are free: free to act and get on with the business of transition, a business which operates outside the play.

When I stood beside these radical flowers in these topsy-turvy times, I realised what matters is not *caring*, what matters is *life*.

wild cotton
Dallas, Texas 2002

Off the road they call High Lonesome, the three of us once met under the wild cotton bushes that keep their secluded place deep in the sheltering wash. Most beautiful of the desert plants with scarlet leaves and white mallow flowers, she dances among her sisters, among the snakeroot and wild tobacco, salt bush and desert willow. *Gossypium thurberi*. We were at a loss for words that day when we beheld her – we, who were always such talkers.

Held patiently in the hands of Francisco Ozuna, *curandero* and one-time picker of commercial cotton in Mexico, whose lungs and eyes and hands had burned with the pesticides sprayed on that prodigious user of chemicals, the wild roots yield up their blood-red juice that will cure the failed libido of the farmer and his wife, whose womb is out of kilter. It has a sweet taste. It can bring children forth, or it can destroy them. Like all plants, it depends on how you use it. One day, he says to me, I will make a book and in it will be pictures of the hands of the workers of Mexico, the hands that hold the web of life. The warp and the weft. There will be no words.

Without rancour Mahatma Ghandi takes up his spindle to spin the native dyed cotton of India, refusing the colours and cloth that come from the satanic mills of England, dreaming not of his own Jerusalem but of an India with a united heart, of a simplicity coming from complexity. In his bare white room in Delhi I sit fifty years later, where his last footsteps etched in white paint lead into an empty garden. Above me a noisy technological show of his life is playing; chattering students press buttons on a computer and watch a simulated Mahatma cry tears, smile, be angry. No one comes down here. They should come down here. To be in a place where all the talking stops.

And here today in Dallas I am lying on a bench beside a little Mayan girl from Guatemala, in whose ancestral blood dance all the patterns and shining colours of the quetzal bird, the memory of the most beautiful fabrics of the world. She is a *maquilladora*, a worker of sewing machines, a sewer of factory jeans and anoraks, and like me she has just been refused entry into the Empire built on the slave trade of cottonpickers. Whose ugliness once tore the country apart.

It is May 1. On the greens of England this morning men and women are dancing the colours of the rainbow, weaving the fabric of life around a birch tree. Here in this Texas gaol words falter in our mouths, yet our physical beings, spun from the same loom, lie together, our breaths intermingling. We are *compadres, compañeras* in a stranger's realm. We have become snared in a web that has no colours in it, that has no dream of beauty, that has no use for a native weaver of cotton or a native weaver of words.

In London, among the fabrics of a department store one week from now, I will pick up a jade green towel but find that I cannot buy it. Because I have seen the cotton fields of Pima county that suck up eighty percent of the water table of Arizona, and I have walked under the cottonwood trees that are dying from thirst along the San Pedro river. Because on that day when we sat by the dry wash of High Lonesome the wild cotton held us in her embrace, her impeccable silence, and we were forced to confront in ourselves the ugliness of our own slavery, the false webs and stories we spin around ourselves, until we felt we held life instead in our hands and our blood-red roots sought tenure among the rocks. Because I have tasted those blood-red roots and because I once held the hand of Francisco Ozuna and slept in a deportee gaol in America. And because, with Ghandi, I have taken up a different spindle, and I dream another dream. And because I too have learned to live in a simple room, a room where all the talking stops.

elder
Dundalk, Ireland 2002

We went by way of Holyhead. As we walked toward the ferry, we passed through a gate made of the gnarled branches of two elder trees. The informing tree, I remarked to Mark, as we went on board. We were on our way to Dublin; our time in Wales was coming to an end. It was almost midsummer, and we were looking for a place to live. I remembered an Ireland that I saw through childhood sea holidays and reading James Joyce. Mark, who comes from an Irish immigrant lineage, harboured no such nostalgia.

The first flower I noticed in Ireland was not an elder but an orchid. Hundreds of pyramid orchids shone through the dark gloom of the port. 'Look at those orchids'! I cried to Andrew, who had met the boat and was now whisking us away northwards. But Andrew was not listening; he was informing us of the social schedule he had in mind for our stay.

When we arrived at his house there was a Jehovah's Witness in the garden in the rain cutting down an elder tree.

The following day, Andrew whisked us southwards us to visit a man who was planting an arboretum and who had an impressive garden in Co. Wicklow. 'I have orchids everywhere!' he declared when we arrived. 'Where are they? I asked. 'Oh, I had them mown last week,' he said, 'they were becoming untidy.' He showed us round his tree plantation. 'Oh, you have almost the whole Celtic alphabet here,' I remarked. He smiled in the proprietorial way of gardeners. 'And what trees are they?' he asked. 'The first tree is *beth*,' I said, 'the silver birch.' And as I reeled off the twelve names of the consonant trees, he informed me he had them all.

'And then there is number thirteen,' I said, '*Ruis*, the elder.'

'Oh no!' he said, 'I don't have that *weed*.'

Across the high rim of the world the silver birch, first tree of the Beth-Luis-Nion, skirts the emptiness of the land impervious to the silence, the cold and the extremes of light and dark. Through miles upon miles of the slim white-limbed trees the tribes of the far north move with their reindeer, seeking, tracking, making camp, as they have since the beginning of time. At their roots in autumn appears a scarlet toadstool, the ancient keeper of mysteries, sometimes known as fly agaric.

The birch is, above all things, female. To move through the mystery of the land is to know the territory is female. Most trees have a male presence: they stand like guardians, sentinels, warriors in the territory, but some are unequivocally female and appear in the alphabet at strategic points. All of them are in charge. The birch comes at the beginning of the year, and initiates all new starts. Everything begins with the birch: all woods in Europe begin with her vigorous saplings. She is nurse to all the great forests, the initiator of the living systems, the first tree to appear after the winter, after the ice age. Her twigs make the broom that sweeps and makes things clean, orderly for what lies ahead. First, she declares in all enterprises, sweep your space. Next, make clear delineations. Third, decide: what is the business of the day? Her switch keeps the discipline of what is required and what is not. Her astringent soapy bark and leaves purify the body of stagnant old things. Fresh scented, unequivocal, she makes all boundaries clear.

Those who do not love the birch call her an upstart, an opportunist, a tree of wastelands and scrub, as they call all female beings who appear in charge, who hold the vitality, rigour and authority of the land. They dislike this kind of sovereignty, and how it seems indifferent to their presence. They do not know that this tree, silvery, graceful, bendy as she is, is a stern and inflexible conductor because she keeps the time. Her body is the axis of the world, the maypole around which all colours weave their harmonious form. Without the birch there is no dance.

The elder, her sister, stands at the end of the year, unobtrusively within the human compound. She emerges among the ruins of houses, out of graves, on the edge of woods. Bony, scraggly, ghost-branched, broken-headed. She is the end of things, and yet, even in the coldest month, in the winter's depth, small dark-red leaves are sprouting within the joints of her twiggy fingers. Everything else in the wood has died back, except this ridged and swaying form.

On field margins, out of the ruined brickwork, the elder appears unannounced, unexpected, with her dark green foliage; she follows in the wake of people and animals, flourishing in what they refuse and leave behind: abandoned dwellings, deserted badger setts, rabbit warrens. She sprouts quickly and contains everything that has gone before her, the rhythms of come and go, of birth and growth and harvest, the songs of birds and the laughter of children. Each branch, each stem contains a pithy core which you can push quite easily to make a pipe or a peashooter. Inside this mysterious passage, in this hollow, the wind sings and makes music: the sound and rhythm that is stored in the bones of everything that has passed. Carved out of the elder's surprising hard pale wood come toys and combs and whistles. Out of her wood come pipes and violins. Without the elder there is no music. In modern Ireland, the elder is a weed. But in ancient Ireland, the elder is a sacred tree. She stands at the end of the wheel of time before the door of the winter solstice, held open by the red-barked yew of eternity and the birth of the silver fir.

In the churchyard of Holywell I met with an elder beneath the yews. She surprised me. A jolly being made of bones. Male trees are austere: they bring words of wisdom, they remind you of warriorship and government and right relation. Female trees have a different nature: they come close to you with their gnarly hawthorn faces, with their scented blossom breath and sweet juices, their washing-day crab apple whiteness, their dancing silvery forms of hazel and white poplar. You find yourself dancing and singing with them, gathering their berries, picnicking below their summer finery. 'Hello love, whatcha doing?' asked the elder tree, as she whisked me away into the dimensions of sky and earth and told me about her medicine of vindication. 'We have the last laugh,' she said. And dug me in the ribs.

Ruis, the elder, is the tree of death. Not death as it is commonly known: the death of the human wheel, the death of history and ghosts and sorrows. But the death of *life* that happily sheds its old forms in the grand ancestral cycle of the year. The death of the leaves which shed themselves from the tree, that tumble to the ground, rot down and become soil; the music and dance of ourselves, what we pass on, give up, let go, shed, so that life can come in again. The dead wood we cut out so there is space for new things to flourish and expand. Without death there is no treasure in life, no movement, no dance. Without elder nothing happens. We shrivel inside, dry out, flatten. Nothing new comes our way. All the generations suffer, our gardens do not grow, our corn dries up, everyone gets tired and fractious. Women lose their minds and forget where they are; children cannot sit still. Men lose themselves in machines. The world goes crazy and becomes fragmented. We cling to our dead old forms, to the clutter of our minds, and forget the treasure of life. We should be consulting with the elder: come and teach us how to die, how to let go, how we can start again, how we can flourish and sing among the ruins, play music with our bones and laugh our ancestral laugh – but we are not. We are cutting her down every day with a chainsaw and calling her a weed.

One day I go to visit Newgrange, now the most famous Neolithic burial mound in the world. Once it commanded the hill and the wind sang through its abandoned chambers. Now it has become a world heritage site, its stony face tidied up and fenced off. You have to take a shuttle bus with a tour guide who tells you what once happened here, and you are obliged to stare at the three rocks that command the entrance with their mysterious spirals like giant snakes. The guide does not know what they mean. In spite of these restrictions the centre of the mound is still an awesome space. As we sit in the dark our guide switches on a torch and talks some more about the different mark-stones. On one is etched a sheaf of corn. No one knows what that means either, she says, and falls silent. And then she turns off the light. We look through the winter solstice door. It is quite small inside the mound and you can sense people in the dark, strangers pressed together close, like animals, and in this silence you feel something unexpected. You feel suddenly how it was when the people came together and waited for the moment when the door of the great year swung open, when the sun came back to the earth and the darkness of Newgrange became full of sunlight, and your heart burst open with excitement. In the days when everyone lived according to the time of the sun and earth, and the elder was a sacred tree.

At midsummer the elder comes into her own. From the depths of her dark leaves and craggy limbs appear great panicles of scented blossom. They cover the tree like white plates and their heady fragrance drenches the warm evenings as you walk past in the lanes in the long late sunlight of high summer. In the cool rooms of astute households the blossoms ferment in flagons, lie carefully placed on trays in drying rooms and laundry cupboards. Elder is the crown of the hedgerow flowers, the last to bloom after all the thorns. Her flowers make the most delicious of all countryside drinks, cordials and wines, and the teas are highly prized as medicine.

Elder is a big medicine chest. All parts of the tree cure our maladies. The flowers allay our fevers and alleviate our allergies. Elderflower water cleanses the skin of our faces. The small dark antioxidant berries remedy our colds and 'flus. The bark makes a strong mouthwash, the root a purgative, the leaves a green salve for bruises and wounds. And maybe this is why, even as late as 1920, Mrs Grieve in her famous herbal noted that country people still used to doff their hats to an elder as they passed by, and did not care ever to cut her down or burn her wood.

She was addressed respectfully in the northern lands as Elder-muir, the Elder mother, and was loved because her sweet blossoms calmed all children's sleep. In the Hans Christian Anderson fairy story a young girl in a flowery dress appears from of a teapot full of elder blossoms to a child drinking tea for a chill. She tells the child the story of the revolving earth, about the time of the seasons and the time of human beings. How everything goes in a circle. In the story everyone is old and young at the same time. The elder changes her form in winter, spring and summer, but always she is herself, laughing with blossoms that crown her hair. 'Some people call me the Dryad, some call me Elder Mother,' she tells the little boy. 'But my real name is Memory.'

She is the one who makes us all welcome, and the one who wishes us farewell.

'Love you!' said Andrew.

'No, you don't!' retorted Mark, quick as a flash.

And they both laughed.

I am sitting beside Andrew at a supper party. This is not an Ireland I remember: a childhood Ireland of slate-floored sea-cottages, brown-coloured bars and a wild coast. The voices sound musical and sweet, and we are all singing here at Andrew's party in a circle. Most people are singing show tunes. Mark and I are singing *Passing by Woods on a Snowy Evening*, which is a folk-setting of Robert Frost's famous poem. But when everyone talks it sounds as if the country is as harsh and greedy as every other nation in the developed world. Ireland has become very different, I tell one woman. You have to make way for progress, she says, and stares ahead as if into thin air.

Andrew tells us about India, where he spends half the year working with a local community to reforest the land. I tell everyone about my experience at Dallas airport. Isn't that a shocking thing? I say. To be put into prison! But people do not think it is shocking. I am told 'you should have said this and that', and everyone chatters among themselves about what they would have done, or not. They talk about how marvellous it is these days that you can just get on these cheap aeroplanes and go to one city in Europe for lunch and another for dinner. I grow quiet at the end of the table. It's not that you want sympathy, or for others to get angry on your account. You want to say what happened, what happens on the other side of the tracks, what the flip-side of progress is, what the consequences are. Perhaps when we all realise what kind of world we live in, it might change. But most people do not want to hear this. They are quite happy with the world as it is. Everyone is rushing as far as they can away from the memory of those white-washed cottages, from those peat-fires; they want, in the manner of all vanquished people, what their oppressors have denied them all these years, and they do not care whom they step on in the process.

We were forgetting the ruin that will surely follow in our wake if we do not curb our appetite. Maybe if we recognised that we are all in the same boat, limited by the same earthly time, we would be treating each other – and life – in a more respectful way. We would all be sitting in Newgrange with bated breath at winter solstice, waiting for the sun to rise, and doffing our hats to a scraggly tree with fragrant blossoms that cures all our ills.

'My clients have got far more important things to be worried about than organic sunflower growers in Somerset!' The modern Celtic woman is a lawyer working for Monsanto and proud of it. Monsanto is an agribusiness corporation, an international producer of pesticides and genetically manipulated seeds. It is famous for bullying farmers by aggressive lawsuits. In alternative ecological circles it is known as Monsatan. We have started an almighty row over breakfast. The lawyer is telling us that the only proper way to treat the planet is to make it more comfortable for humans. Nature is to be controlled,

tamed, manipulated and put to our use. Nature is something repel-
lent in her mind, something that makes her face become contorted
and mean. Nature means girls who have too many babies and don't
go the right way for progress. Progress is what Ireland wants, so we
can all be flying to Brussels for lunch parties. Normally in other
people's houses. Mark and I are polite, but in that moment we are
not a bit polite. We have found our voices and launched ourselves
vociferously over the porridge, suggesting in more than clear terms
that it is nature that is in charge of life, and human beings better
remember it – or else! Suddenly the woman lawyer lunges towards
us, a ball of fury:

'Yous go and live on another planet!'

'No, you go!' we yell at her.

She backs off out of the kitchen and goes into the living room to
talk with the others.

Mark and I look at each other, quite astonished. It is the first time
we have shouted back at anyone for a very long time. And for the first
time in what seems like weeks, it stops raining and the sun comes out.

At summer solstice we made our own plans: we went down to the
sea and walked among the wild rocket and goosefoots. The beach was
sandy and littered with giant pebbles, the round, smooth, pale stones
that made the walls of Newgrange. The Irish Sea stretched quietly
before us. We drove on towards the Mountains of Mourne. If you
drive down by the Long Woman's Grave, the girl in the shop tells us,
you will come to a hill. Turn your engine off and freewheel down the
hill and you will see, in fact, that you will be going up.

I laughed. Everything, it seemed, had turned upside down. We
sang a song about winter solstice, when it was summer solstice; we
went up a hill that went downwards; we collected flowers from the
tree of death that, as it turned out, was all about life.

At Tara I climbed the mound where the high kings of Ireland had
once gathered, and sat with a young mother with five small children
dressed in the colours of the rainbow, who ran up and down. Below
us a wedding party was gathering. You could see for miles across the
green land, across rivers and fields and copses. It was lovely, but there
was something missing. Everything seemed pale and flat, lacking
in energy. It was like being at a house without a fire, or a kitchen
without a cook. Mark sat with his head bowed under an elder tree

in the churchyard. The blossom sprinkled the long grass like stars. 'I'm so tired here,' he said.

La Que Sabe, the One Who Knows, the Bone Woman, the Elder Mother, the thirteenth fairy with her thirteenth moon, lives out in the arroyos in the desert, out on the shoreline among the goosefoots, lingers among the old graves, on the edge of the dark wood. Except that I could not feel her presence in Tara, or Newgrange, or in any place we went. Where had she gone? Had she emigrated to Canada, gone to work in London, crossed the waters like my ancestors, like Mark's family? Or had she, unwisely, been uninvited to the party, and her flowering kingdom become hidden by briars?

'There is a plant in Ireland called sleepy grass,' I read out loud to Andrew in Dublin from a book on Celtic plant lore. 'It was said that if you felt tired in a certain place it was because someone from the famine had died there.' But Andrew is not listening; he has fallen asleep in his chair.

Outside, the traffic moves down thickly toward the Liffey, and it feels like a long time since I held *Ulysses* before me and read of Stephen Dedalus walking the shoreline, and even longer since I stood barefoot beside the burn with the heron waiting, and watched the shining water as it ran toward the western sea. It had felt in those moments as if a great door was opening.

Maybe it all began here in Ireland, in those days of my shining youth, in my sapling years, when I rowed across the dark lough with the wild swans flying behind me. Maybe Andrew did love us in South America in the travelling years, in our hawthorn season, in the years of our dancing and singing. But now it is a different time, a time of progression and fall. We came from Wales with our elderflower medicine and spoke of what is left out, what is not mentioned at parties. Andrew spoke about India and the local tribeswomen who are banished into the wilderness when they have their periods because they are 'unclean'. They had nowhere to go, he said. So he built them a shelter, and now they were reforesting the land together. He has given me a letter he wrote to me years ago that had been returned to him, Address Unknown. It's yours now, he said. I read it and felt the long gap of time that had passed between us and a wind that came and whisked us apart.

Nothing happens without the bones, without a proper farewell.

Frost knew that. It could have ended a long time before, but sometimes you have to go to the place and close the door. No hard feelings. In the poem the speaker stands by a lovely dark wood at snowfall, but he does not go in. That's when I realised we hadn't come to make a new start in Ireland. We had come to say goodbye.

We have promises to keep
And miles to go before we sleep
And miles to go before we sleep

opium poppy
Aldeburgh, Suffolk 2002/5

I am walking through Aldeburgh. This is a sea town I used to visit when I was young, a place I used to escape to from the city. I loved it with all the passion of the temporary exile. I loved the sense of freedom it afforded me in those stolen weeks of summer, with hollyhocks rising in the alleyways and the swifts screaming around the eaves at evening, the light sparkling on the early morning sea where I swam like a seal in its milky arms; the sense of having a world to myself, somewhere secure, comforting, for which I was not accountable. The small seaside place seemed to contain within its salty, coloured walls and passageways all the best parts of my childhood. I could replay them at will. I kept a ring of pebbles from its beach on my writing desk, and the sigh of the North Sea upon the shingle ran like a threnody through my early city life, like the haunting call of a curlew or a lapwing fluttering across the land. *Come back, come back!*

I am not in that time now as I walk round the stalls of the town's summer carnival. I no longer have the key to the cottage where I once stayed so happily. I have just arrived in the neighbouring town of Leiston. Twenty years later, this place has changed. No longer a backwater sailing and fishing town, it has become a destination resort for people with spending power, with city-style restaurants and shops and arts festivals. The once ad-hoc neighbourhood carnival has a slick marketed air and a shiny souvenir programme.

Some part of me has not realised this yet. Because the pastel-coloured houses appear the same, and the great shingle shelf still has its familiar curve, its salty haze, its wooden boats pulled up upon the beach. I am in the past, remembering a young man I once knew whose father spent all year making the fireworks for this carnival; how when his father died he lit all his remaining arsenal of rockets and bangers and Catherine wheels at the funeral, so his father's spirit could ascend toward the heavens in a great blaze of glory.

'Do you want to buy a carnival programme?' says a sharp voice, interrupting my reverie, in the manner of a shop assistant who suspects you might be shoplifting.

'No thank you,' I reply. 'I was just wondering what time the fireworks on the beach might be tonight.'

The owner of the sharp voice glowers at me with such a hostility I almost fall backwards.

'It's in the programme,' she says icily and turns her back on me. *You do not belong here. Get out!*

I feel as though I have been hit in the stomach with a mallet. Shaking like a leaf I walk away from the town, past the fishing boats, and find a place in the dunes where I can recover from the shock among the yellow toadflax and scented lady's bedstraw. As I sit down by these friendlier inhabitants, I notice a gaunt shape rising in front of me, an alien among these native shoreline plants. It is faded now, past blooming, and yet its form is unmistakable, tallish with pale crackling leaves and a huge ornate seed pod. A single opium poppy moving in the salt wind, shaking its head at me, scattering its thousand seeds.

It is almost a cliché to speak of ashes when you speak of the soul, and yet you cannot skip the ashy times, the time when you descend into the underworld and get your come-uppance, when the princess goes downstairs to work in the kitchen, when you stand in another man's shoes and are *bedonebyasyoudid*. Modern-day accounts of these liminal, alchemical times often speak eloquently about ashes, but they are rarely *of* ashes, written by authors who have deliberately gone down and out. There are few George Orwells reporting from the front line in the new millennium. All these soul-seeking, poet-quoting kitchen gurus are comfortable people, successful, sleek academics who talk as if they had never washed a saucepan in their lives. If they have, they are keeping awfully quiet about it.

On that day when I walked back home to Leiston from Aldeburgh, I felt a strange fury underneath my shaking, which I had not known before. It had been a shocking event and had shocked something awake in me. To be refused entry to a foreign country is one matter, but quite another to suffer the same indignity in your own. I had felt equanimous about weekend visitors before, but now I suddenly felt furious with the lot of them: the snooty voices, the monstrous big cars, the way at weekends all the Suffolk seatowns seemed to fill with these loud arrogant people, with their smart clothes and their properties, with their shiny programmes and marketing, the way you felt pushed off the pavements as they sailed by, not even seeing you. In that moment of pure anger I realised that I had no love for my own kind.

Leiston is not a gentrified town like Aldeburgh, with its festivals of poetry and culinary arts. It has quite a different fame as the host of the Sizewell Nuclear Power Station. It is the only industrial town in the area, where the engineering works of Garretts (now a museum) and the alternative school of Summerhill have given it a distinctive, radical edge. Leiston Common was a frequent meeting place for radical speakers in the past – most notably during the East Anglian bread riots and the Chartist movement – and the town briefly became the holiday resort for the British Communist Party. It is still outspoken. The local campaign for the shutting down of the power station is one of the most articulate in the land.

At the time of this encounter, Mark and I were living in a small terraced house in one of its back streets. Soon after I came across the opium poppy, I went to supper with someone I once knew in London in my journalism years. 'Slum clearance,' she tells me of the citizens of Leiston, and she finds people eating fish and chips in Aldeburgh quite disgusting. When I first come to Suffolk I am shocked by how many people of 'my' class are derogatory about 'commoners' and their eating habits. Fat people seem to obsess them. Fat poor people *offend* them in some way. The people who say these shameless things are often visitors from London, and I find myself in a strange position as an ex-visitor and non-local, too young to be a retiree and yet not in a very different position from a retiree, living in the strange limbo existence of all new incomers – living in a house but in no way relevant to the social fabric of the place.

In these ashy years, in this limbo time, I would sometimes be invited to parties by 'second home' owners and find myself in an England I no longer recognised. The owners of sharp loud voices would boom at me about the Empire: about how social workers have to teach deprived mothers how to play with their children properly; how their sons are teaching Bolivian *campesinos* how to grow vegetables properly. Between these proclamations of how We are managing Them, I also find myself listening to all kinds of stories about personal downfall and illness. I rarely find myself talking. I hold a glass of New World wine in my hand and feel oddly oppressed. Some of these people call themselves socialists. But they don't feel any different from right-wing people. And they are certainly not living a different lifestyle. It's then that I realise that the ignorant and deprived people they speak of are serving them in some way, and whether the superior people despised them or patronised them, it made no difference. The fact was that they fulfilled the same function: that of *lesser beings*.

As I stood dumb at these parties I began to notice a strange phenomenon: although the lesser beings were frequently classed as 'dysfunctional' – fat, lazy, sick, stupid, disadvantaged – the superior beings were not immune from these things themselves. They were on examination neither more svelte nor more healthy than anyone else. Their families did not seem to be any happier or more successful. And they knew almost nothing about growing the native potatoes I had once eaten in South America. In fact, several times on returning home, having listened to all those private confessions of failure, I found myself shaking for hours afterwards, or having nightmares about the houses or the people I had encountered. I realised that the lesser beings (of which I now discovered I had become one) were in place in order to suffer all the projections of these superior ones, so they did not have to look at or feel that we were actually all in the same boat, as *human beings*, that our stations of class or money made no difference to the fact that, whether we were on the winning or losing side, everyone was subject to the same brute forces of history. That we were, to put it bluntly, all suffering.

Suffering is what you learn about in the kitchen years. Suffering is what no one wants to do, and yet all of us must if we value our lives. The flower that knows about suffering beyond all other flowers is the flower I saw in the Aldeburgh dunes that day, shaking its seed-pod head, heralding the downward path which my own life was at that moment about to take.

Opium poppies are one of the world's most formidable painkillers. The latex excised from their large green seedpods has eased our suffering since the beginning of civilisation, and still does, as morphine and codeine. But it has also drugged us as laudanum and opium, fuelled the notorious Opium Wars of the nineteenth century, and still, in the form of heroin, serves to keep certain sections of society in their place, in the down-there place, while lining the pockets of barons and governments and tyrannising poor farmers wherever they grow – in Turkey, Afghanistan, India and China. The nightmare this pain-killing flower brings in its wake stalks the whole world. And in 2003 in Suffolk it is about to stalk me.

I have never taken heroin. Not wittingly, at least. At a 'hippy party' I once gave in my early life I unknowingly distributed small cakes of cannabis bound with opium as part of its retro theme. It had the most extraordinary effect. Several of my more anguished and uptight friends relaxed; others who were normally noisy and ebullient became mellow and thoughtful. At midnight a late guest arrived. 'What on earth is going on?' she asked me. 'What do you mean?' I asked. Everyone seemed very happy to me. 'No one is talking,' she said. Suddenly I looked around and realised we had all fallen into a kind of trance.

I never liked the trance of 'downers', so I never pursued narcotics in my city-dwelling years, but I met many who did: aristocratic junkies in London, homeless street musicians in Oxford, and a Frenchwoman travelling through Santiago who told me 'You can look at your finger all day and be in paradise'. Breaking the habit of heroin, even a temporary one, was the worst experience she had ever endured. It was like falling through a black hole, as if the horrors of the world were visiting her door. I didn't know heroin, but I knew what she was talking about.

Opium has been taken by writers since the Industrial Revolution – most famously by Coleridge, Baudelaire and Edgar Allen Poe. The poppy's presence haunts the pages of Romantic English literature as much as it once did the back streets of Manchester and Nottingham, where it was taken to relieve the terrible conditions of the cotton-mill workers. Thomas de Quincey, a journalist writing in 1820, gave the world its first candid document of many years' addiction to opium, describing both its pleasures and its pains in brilliant detail: from the sharpness it brought to his mind and the fabulous cities it constructed in his imagination, to dark memories of the prostitutes and the starving he once walked among in London's Oxford Street, and the Indian gods, Egyptian crocodiles and an ominous Chinaman known as The Malay who visited him in his dreams. These later nightmares plagued him. Like the poet George Crabbe, he was stalked by visions of outcasts of his own society, and sought in his own writing to find meaning for this suffering. Crabbe was a life-long opium addict. Keenly aware of his own social failure as a citizen of Aldeburgh, the poet wrote unswervingly of the social machine and the price it exacts from all those individuals who do not toe the line.

At one of the parties I was informed that the senior citizens of Aldeburgh were all now heroin addicts. I am not sure this is true, but there is a lot of heroin in Suffolk. The nearby market town of Saxmundham was reputed to have the worst drug addiction per capita in the country. Most people don't notice this as they drive by Saxmundham or Leiston or Lowestoft on the way to the more charming seaside towns. 'Well,' as one well-heeled woman told me at a lunch-party, 'they are not *really* Suffolk, are they?'

But they are Suffolk. Not the lovely magazine Suffolk of festivals and prize-winning beer and pretty weekend cottages, but Crabbe's Suffolk, the Suffolk of *Akenfield*, whose agricultural workers were once worn to the bone by manual labour, where the old and the useless of the village were kept in cupboards, and now are kept in bungalows and housing estates. The Suffolk which our minds bypass while we look for the view, always the lovely view.

I met many people in my kitchen years: some, like me, went to look for their souls among the saucepans and the soot, some had tumbled down there by accident in a moment of *katabasis*. But some had always lived in the kitchen, had been born with ashes in their mouths while others held high balls and parties upstairs at their expense. In the fairy stories where *doasyouwouldbedoneby* justice is done, the wicked sisters are sent down to experience the kitchen and the scullery maids inherit the kingdom. But this does not happen in real life. In England in the new millennium.

We don't need no education.
We don't need no thought control.
Teacher, leave those kids alone.

The year we left Leiston and moved up the coast, I found a host of opium poppies growing in a closed disused school near our cottage. The red-bricked classrooms were about to be converted into houses, but that year lay empty and abandoned. Where the schoolchildren had once sat at their desks a broken pipe had made a small lake of water, so that hares would come from the fields and drink there, and in the playground beyond the fence about a thousand poppies bloomed and swayed. All poppies love wastegrounds, disturbed soil,

316

mounds of rubble and ruin, and the opium poppy most of all. They live in the in-between places, in margins, on the outskirts, between the worlds. Standing waist-high among so many is an unnerving experience: their Otherness is palpable. It is something about their stiffness and their corpse-like colours – the petals flesh-pink or dead-white, but mostly a strange unearthly mauve, the leaves a glaucous pale green – the way they ruthlessly poke through the broken tarmac. It is an awesomely shaped flower, close-up. Staring into its strange-coloured ragged petals, into its array of golden stamens and its dark-spoked capsule, is like putting your head in a dragon's mouth.

The opium poppy has flourished among the rubble of humanity since antiquity. All fertile crescent civilisations came bearing the poppy in their hands. Descriptions of the 'plant of joy' appear in the first Sumerian texts. Depictions of the opium poppy are found in Egyptian frieze gardens, growing in a triad with yellow mandrake (another powerful old-world narcotic) and blue cornflower; seed pods of opium are among the nine circles of wild flowers that adorn one of the caskets encasing the boy-king Tutankhamun. Poppy seeds, like lotus seeds, are among the plant world's most enduring time-capsules. All their colours are arresting and otherworldly – the blue Tibetan poppy, the yellow Welsh poppy, the huge scarlet Oriental poppy, the glamorous orange poppies of California, the blood-red poppies of the English cornfield – and they were once known as the flowers of the underworld, the flowers of the mysteries. Before pesticides suppressed their germination they were found sprinkled throughout the cornfields of the civilised world, among the wheat and barley, shining in their strange and ominous ways, reminding the cities of the price they pay each time they sow a field, or build a house. Or go to war.

The presence of the poppy in the human world reminds us of our mortality and right balance with life, so long as we can understand the flowers in this way. As a physic, poppies depress the central nervous system and bring sleep and release. When the pain of a physical illness becomes too much to bear, the flowers that live between the worlds bring relief and usher people into the comforting arms of death. But it is another thing when their juice is used to deaden the pain of existence itself. When heroin puts you in a small room where nothing matters any more and your index finger looks like paradise.

317

When the Industrial Revolution turned life into a mechanical hell the poets fled to the hills, took opium, and wrote of England's green beauty and of its shadows. The mechanisation of production increased the misery of human existence in the towns and cities a thousandfold, as industrialisation does to all rural-based cultures, as it does now in the opium-growing countries, the lands of the Indian gods and the Malay. The Luddites, who risked death to fight against these life-destroying machines, are scorned by modern city-dwellers who live in an unnatural technologically dependent world. But this is not to look at how the machines of civilisation debase and malform the living systems of the planet, including the living systems of our selves.

No one who is happy takes heroin any more than they take any other painkiller: cannabis, cocaine, whisky or wine. You take these things because industrial existence has made life dull and monotonous and hard. Because it is unbearable without them. Living systems are multifaceted, complex and interconnected. All life has meaning within them. But industrial existence is mono-dimensional and meaningless. It reduces everyone to a function, a role, a statistic. What breaks the monotony and harshness of this life are the escapes into illusions and drugs. Orwell, writing about industrial culture in *The Road to Wigan Pier*, is struck by how the poorest workers will always reserve a certain amount of their hard-earned wages for football coupons, cigarettes, film tickets or cheap shiny clothes, even at the cost of being hungry. The manufacturing of illusion is big business in the industrial world, and so are its drugs. It cannot function without them. There are very few people in the modern world, rich or poor, who do not take an artificial substance to escape. Most people in England drink vast quantities of alcohol to deaden the pain of this life. Most of the younger population take some drug or chemical. I was no different when I lived in the city in the days when cocaine and champagne fuelled most of the fashion business.

But I am not living in that city any more. I am living down a country lane, a sober half-a-cider-sometimes-in-the-pub person working with a flower in an abandoned school yard, a flower whose ragged strange-coloured petals are shaking me to the core.

The opium poppy shook me from the beginning. I found one growing by a bus stop in front of a business school outside Oxford in 1999. A young pale drug addict was standing beside the purple flower, waiting for a bus. In the *seeing*, opium poppies showed me a world constructed of dragon-shaped energies. There were dragons in the clouds, dragons in the wind, dragons in the earth, dragons under the earth. These creatures underpinned the physical world. They were neutral but, like all energies when trapped and used for bad intent, they could also become malevolent and turn against their users. Opium-eaters used to call their habit 'chasing the dragon'. Heroin addicts still do.

When you chase this dragon with the flower, however, it doesn't take you away from pain – it takes you right down into it. It takes you down into the places where the creative energies of the earth have been trapped and used with bad intent, twisted by industrial revolutions, by businessman and governments, by the nightmares that haunt the young and pale and addicted. It shows you what price we pay for living life schooled in the monodimensional way. It takes you into the disturbed wastegrounds where it flourishes and makes you think about a culture where children are just another brick in the wall.

Standing next to a domestic science teacher called Gilly at a party at poppy time, she tells me that all the children in her class are impossible to teach because they live entirely in illusion: the boys want to be football stars, and the girls want to be pop singers. She tells us about two bright Portuguese students who qualify for a stream called 'Gifted and Talented'.

'What is going to happen to the others?' I ask.

Gilly doesn't reply. Her head has dropped. She is looking at her feet.

I met Dick and Jane at a lunch party. Jane worked in a real kitchen, as the head cook at a local boarding school. I was shocked by how little she earned and how hard she had to work. Dick worked as a psychiatric nurse, mostly with children from towns no visitor ever lived in. He dreaded going to Leiston. There was a notorious street there where he said *no one* ever grew up straight. Jane had lived in Suffolk all her life and now felt oppressed by the smallness of everything, by the place, by the people, by her work. She wanted to go travelling and have other experiences. As we stood with our barbecue plates in hand she pressed me to tell her how we had managed to leave everything and everyone behind. I was reluctant to say anything in those ashy times. I had said things before about travelling, about letting go, and when people had been inspired to do so I had sometimes been held to account when things did not turn out as they had hoped. Travelling means leaving, and most people don't want to leave, they want to escape. I had learned to keep my mouth shut.

'Did you ever regret it?' asked Jane.

'No,' I said. 'Not for one minute.'

My eyes flickered over the guests with their glasses of wine, talking to one another in loud and confident voices, and I felt us standing there quietly, two people out on a limb, on the other side of the tracks, and my heart couldn't hold back.

'Don't listen to anyone,' I told her. 'Just go!'

'What strange god are we serving?' Dick asked me suddenly, when we went to their house for supper. And we all fell silent then. I remembered that question the day I went to Ipswich to attend an induction course for charity workers. I had become a volunteer manager at a local arts centre and had been told that the only way I could be paid for my work was to go on a government scheme for cheap labour.

About thirty of us were there to learn about fire drills and how to file a complaint for sexual harassment. We all sat there in a grey office room filling in a variety of forms, our eyes glazed over with fatigue and boredom as the day ground on and on. I thought I was going to die of tiredness. I realised what the 'alternative' friends I once had in Oxford meant when they said they would rather be on the dole than be a wage slave. Because as if it were not bad enough to be working for a minimal wage, we had to be treated like slaves too. We were modern-day slaves, £4.95-an-hour people, rejects who had been put in a file containing those who were unable to get a job. Some people had worked all their lives and were receiving only £50 a week benefit. Some were young, some were disenfranchised, some were down on their luck or had been in hospital. All of us were very cheap but none of us were stupid. The smartly dressed young man in charge of accounts talked to us as if we were retarded and deserving of his derision. He had that nasty puritan control which all administrators have had since Rome. If we didn't fill in the right forms, the right way, on time, he was not going to pay us. 'Oh, you have 20/20,' he sneered, when I finished the 'Use of English' computer test long before the time was up. 'So I should bloody well think!' I snapped. 'I was a professional writer for years!'

It was an ashy time, the time of the losing throw, the dog's throw, but sometimes I showed my teeth. In fact, it was the kitchen that taught me that some people are really not nice, no matter which way you like to look at it. Working in the kitchen cures you of illusions about friendliness. You learn to see right through anyone's façade to whatever corporation or institution is running the show behind the scenes. Some of the most heartless people I ever met worked for charities.

At lunchtime while everyone else went to the pub, I sat next to a health care worker who was furious about going to interviews and never getting the job. 'They've appointed people already,' he fumed. 'And just want to use your ideas,' I laughed, recognising this tactic from my journalism days. However, for him it was no laughing matter. As we sat over our lunch he began to rant about Them and The System, and how hanging is Just Too Good for Them, and his face got all snarled up with hatred.

At that moment I had an extraordinary memory. I was in the private suite of a London hotel, looking into the face of another man all snarled up with hatred. He was one of the richest men in the world and I had, in another incongruous moment, just attended a dinner held for several oil magnates and their escorts. 'Every day I wake up and I curse the Jews. I hate them!' he is telling me. 'I own fifty orphans and when I visit them, they sit on my lap and they mean nothing to me. Nothing!'

How do you deal with these snarled-up power lines, these lines of hatred that fuel the world? Rich man, poor man, beggarman, thief. How can you amend such things?

First you need to see them. And you can only see them if you feel.

Years ago with the help of peyote I saw and felt how certain configurations of 'superior' entities – judges, queens, priests, gods – kept our imaginations and energy bodies in thrall, but how if you did not submit to these forms 'ruling' your consciousness you could liberate yourself as a human being. You needed two things in order to do this: one was a connection with nature, with the living systems of the earth; the second was a connection with the strength and integrity of your human heart. Since both of these have been ruthlessly suppressed by our industrialised culture, they require reactivating by individual effort.

Now, here in England, I was encountering these unkind forms in my daily working life, and found myself expected, like everyone else, to bow and scrape to their demands and take on their karmic loads. It was no longer a personal matter but a social one. The superior classes are educated to emulate these 'authority figures', much as the lower classes are bred to be receptacles for lower energies, like the untouchables of India. This is a very old system indeed, and has been remarked upon keenly by observant writers through the centuries, especially by poets like Crabbe who was himself mercilessly rejected by Aldeburgh. We think we live in egalitarian, democratic times but you only have to go downstairs into the kitchen to know firsthand that this is not the case.

When you are down there, scrubbing pots, hopping to, taking the flack, you begin to realise that this system only works if the feelings of people – the heart – are left out. It intimidates everyone into denying what they truly feel, in a kind of merciless self-censorship. What takes the place of the heart's feeling is the power of the will. Power becomes the singular goal of everyone, whether you live in the drawing room or work in the kitchen: it drives the whole social machine. Power is chiefly obtained from other people, from the daily proving of your superiority as a man, as a woman, as an administrator, as a politician, as a matriarch, as a guru... The more you adopt these positions of control and forego your heart and your humanity, the more power you feel. The more people you stamp on in your work, in your home, in your mind, the more power you feel. And, conversely, the more terrified you are of being stamped on yourself. The seeking of power becomes the unconscious objective of one's daily life. Unchecked, this becomes a totalitarian takeover of the human being; it allows all kinds of inhumanities to occur, both on an individual and on a collective level. You only have to look at history to find endless examples of the lengths human beings will go to to escape being in the down-there place, and the fate of those poor fellows who do not.

I knew all about the theory of these power systems, these hierarchies, from working with peyote and medicine plants like dandelion and monkshood. But the opium poppy was the hard and

322

bitter practice, when I came to feel what it is like to be in the down-there place, stamped on and derided in the social world. With this flower I realised that if you stay in the kitchen long enough, become wretched enough, everything that prevents you from feeling the pain of your situation – your illusions, your hope, your indignation – will be burned away, and you can see what is really there. In the end, when these things have become ashes, what remains is your heart. The heart works by including everything, and most especially those things that are left out. When you include your feelings, the world you see self-organises along the correct lines. You can release the dragon that is pinned on the wheels of history and progress, snarled up with hatred, and deliver it back whence it came – to the clouds, to the mountains, to the forests, and to the sea.

This is not politics, nor is it psychology; but it is the stuff of alchemy, the core of the solar path. The creative process by which you put into the smelter all the hard-edged, indoctrinated, mechanical parts of your own being – tyrant and slave – and submit them to the fiery furnace, to the salt of the sea and the darkness of night so that your soul, your inner being, can take shape along the lines of the life-giving sun and earth. In this alchemy what precipitates this sea-change is the planet Mercury, the one who travels between the worlds, the communicator. The role of Mercurius within the collective is taken by the writer, who was once a seer in connection with the dragon energies of the earth. In the ancient worlds the writer was the *pharmakon*, the poison and the cure, whose quicksilver presence changed everything and guided the collective back into a state of balance. Without Mercury, there is no alchemy.

Writers, those who see, true to this solar process of man, true to the dragon powers of nature, write of the iniquities they behold as they walk, following Dante into the inferno, into the underworld, through the kitchen and the drawing room, following their mercurial nature, the ones who can enter all systems, all worlds. All civilisations know this, which is why free-thinking writers are peculiarly oppressed by whatever empire they live in. When Mercury enters the system, he knows instinctively what is awry and what is required. He is the *phar-makon*, the one that doesn't fit the system, the one who makes good.

At the beginning of the Industrial Revolution, William Blake roared like a lion at the satanic mills, Wordsworth sang like a lark of the disappearing hills and lakes. Society took no notice. Society took their verses and turned them into hymns and schoolbooks. Everything they wrote is still true of England today, and all writers who keep walking the green hills as well as the streets of London still bring this to our attention. How can the writers be otherwise, since we are not yet in balance? It is not a comfortable position to be in. And yet it is what you are. I had been writing all my life, but until I gazed into the poppy's mouth I had not realised what was required of me, what I was really doing there in those parties, in that charity office in Ipswich, in that damned kitchen.

In the opium poppy years I was forced by circumstance out of my own small poppyland and into the nightmare of the world. Rudely awoken out of my lotus-eating reverie, I found myself in another Suffolk, a shadow Suffolk, no longer living in a delightful refuge but in a strangely feudal society, expected to take the rap of all freethinking serfs who live in a rented tied-cottage, with a secondhand car, whose overcoat has seen better days. I found myself in a countryside haunted by evictions, where marshes bore the scars of enclosure, woods haunted by the cruelty of poachers and gamekeepers, dark pub corners where the faces of the people were blurred in time – people who could have been sitting at that corner table for hundreds of years, where the unkind brick walls of maltings and manor houses compressed the living into ancient forms of master and slave, where women with screechy voices told me I was not welcome, get out, you do not belong. Sometimes I woke at night to hear myself screaming.

This ancient poppy had originally showed me the dragon lines, the elemental energies of the planet that get trapped and then are used badly. These are the lines of the will that play out their cruel power games within our own physical bodies and within the social structures of civilisations. If you do not feel sorry for yourself, get too mad, too depressed; if you don't burn yourself up, or give up; if you manage to avoid being crushed in these relentless games – you start to see through them. You realise that it is just a machine. Everyone running around suppressing and oppressing everyone. And that nobody is without suffering in this machine.

After years of shivering after parties, of bad dreams, of being ignored, dismissed, sacked, refused entry, I began to realise that none of this was personal. I was living out the consequences of a system, an authoritarian heartless institution that treated millions of people like this. Millions inured to bad conditions, to cruel treatment, deadened by opium, lost in illusions of sparkling fame and fortune, with their eyes full of shiny souvenir programmes, who do not complain of their experiences. However, these iniquities that I beheld burned like a fire in my heart. Suffering my own failures, without a reputation, patronised by schoolteachers, by counsellors, by managers, by ladies of the manor, I felt the humiliation suffered by all those around me – the dictatorship of a tiny heartless élite.

Eventually I saw what peyote had been trying to tell me up there on the mountain all those years ago; what the poppy was instructing me in the darkness to feel and see: that this dictatorship lives within our own consciousnesses. Inside our skulls lives a tiny heartless voice that dominates and enslaves our whole human existence, and by extension the whole world. If we do not give our energy to this mindset, it will collapse. It needs us, but we don't need it.

Janet and I sat filling envelopes with the programme of forthcoming events. A Sisyphean task, a giant mountain of paperwork which I had taken upstairs to complete in the lobby of the arts centre. Across from us, the tai chi class from the upstairs studio was having lunch. Suddenly I heard a great cry and looked up. A man had his head bowed over his soup plate and was sobbing, the instructor by his side, consoling him. I did not know this man but I knew he had recently come from the north, where he had given evidence against corruption at a university and was being hounded from all sides.

The man kept sobbing. Everyone else kept quiet, eating their soup. Janet, a former Bluebell dancer, kept filling the envelopes. *The show must go on.* What else can we do?

I do not know the man, and yet in one way I do know him. He is myself. I get up, and as I pass by, I put my hand on his back where his heart lies. *You are not alone,* I say, with my own fast-beating heart, in silence.

The return journey from the underworld goes widdershins, the way of the opium flower, against the flow, back to the source of life. It begins the moment you see in another the pain that is your own, the moment you stand in the abandoned poppy-filled schoolyard, where the bullies and the teachers once drilled the harsh facts of the monodimensional world into our heads. On this journey you walk deliberately down the highway that de Quincey called the cruel stepmother: you wait at the windy bus stop outside the school and travel the bus to Lowestoft, the branches of trees rattling against its windows; when you alight young men are swearing and fighting in the bus station, in the library, while the shoppers in the dusk flow by. The girls run past you screaming down the streets of Leiston on a Friday night. You fill in the forms at the Beccles job centre, and get your sums wrong. You look at the clever girl, the London writer that used to be you at a party on New Year's day, talking about how lovely Walberswick is to visit. 'Oh, no,' she says, 'I don't think I could actually ever *live* here.' You sit down and you listen and you feel: you hear the testimonies of the gamekeeper about the deer of Benacre disembowelled by gypsy dogs, shot with crossbows by Americans; of the young chefs who work eighteen hour shifts in the hotels of South-wold; of the overworked post office worker, telephone engineer and electrician, the men who keep the lines in Halesworth open, the men who sweep the floor. You put your hand on a fellow whistleblower's back. One day you make up your mind.

'How do you inherit the earth if you are from Hillingdon?' asked Dick. Jane and Dick were sitting in our garden among the clover and the dandelions. They had started to empty their house of its contents, all their books and records and pictures, everything that had once defined their lives. 'You and I have changed places,' said Jane.

Sometimes you change places, tie another woman's apron around your waist, and live in Leiston where once you lived in Aldeburgh. Sometimes, though you were born with a silver spoon in your mouth, you get to taste what life is like on the other side of the tracks.

In these ashy times, like Dante in the underworld, you find yourself in places where you see everything but can do nothing. You can't even speak. This is because you are in a place where you need to witness and understand. You need to know exactly what it *feels* like to be in these places. If you were allowed to use your natural 'high-born' abilities, you would of course be yelling, scoring points, fighting and disagreeing like everyone else at the party, but that would be to miss the experience of what it feels like to be patronised and humiliated.

To be held in an energetic place where others can score points on you, where they can push you down so that they can feel as if they are up above it all.

The way through patronisation and humiliation is not to become another bully. It is to access the intelligence and fair play of the heart. It is to find the places in our own spirits where they are stuck, and find ways out. Because, then and only then, can life for human beings evolve. The solar path is exacting on this point. Our world is cruel because we lack empathy with our fellows. The only way we learn how to respond with the heart is by experiencing what others feel and then coming to other conclusions. George Orwell learned this when he slept with the tramps and worked in the hotel kitchens, stood freezing in the Spanish trenches for months. I learned it by enduring parties; by being treated as an undesirable alien, as a social reject; by living in towns which the visitors by-passed; by working in the kitchens; by trespassing into a schoolyard and speaking to a flower whose sap makes your blood run cold.

There is nothing romantic about being poor: living in the slum-lands of Birmingham cured me of that when I was nineteen. But you need to know that poverty is going on, and what it is like to have doors that were once open shut in your face. This is not just a question of money, of possessions. You can have shoes and a car and still be poor. It is the emotional experience that goes with being poor, what it does to your sense of self, your power of reasoning, what it does to your imagination, to your heart; the feeling that you will never get out, never be free, that everyone is in some way against you, suspects you, detests you, holds you accountable for imaginary crimes. What it feels like to be on the run, without anywhere to hide; what it feels like to be boxed in and to have no way of escape. Or rather to have ones that, if you thought about it, you would wish not to go down.

No one wants to live their life like this and yet millions of people do. And even more millions live in fear of being in such a position, so they will do everything they can to avoid it, even trample on the heads of those that are already there, or dismiss their presence entirely. When you go deliberately into that box, you find out first-hand what the injustice of this so-called civilisation feels like. To stand next to the opium poppy is to feel the antagonism of the world and the hatred that fuels it. It is to feel the heartlessness of the Oxford business school and the pale boy wandering around the bus stop. It is to know that though suffering emotional pain is the consequence for everyone in this civilisation, rich or poor, the poor have a far worse fate. If you are a dysfunctional, unwanted, surplus number of the collective, you are on the lowest rung of the pecking order and everyone feels justified in despising you. You are a leech on society, you are fat, you steal, you have too many babies, and most of all, your children take too many drugs. So not only do you have to deal with living life on the edge with very little money and very little hope, you have to live with everyone else's judgement about your very existence. De Quincey, years after his starvation in the London streets and his addiction when he lived in Wordsworth's cottage, was haunted by the things he had once witnessed. Once you have seen it you can't unsee it. What happens next is to know why you have seen it, and what you need to do.

There is always something you can do. It is a move on the solar path that you were born to make. You make this move by knowing what kind of country you are living in, what kind of person you are – or in my case, what kind of writer. At the end of *Down and Out in Paris and London,* Orwell writes that he won't enjoy eating in smart restaurants any more. I don't either. You don't need to despise people for working in a kitchen, for being poor or fat or ugly. You need to be down there yourself. You need to know what it is like to live on £50 a week and to be treated like a criminal. You need to walk through the towns you don't think are Suffolk and have your own feelings. Then you can proceed. What you can't do is not know. Everyone thinks that the horrors of the world are perpetrated by ghastly cruel sadists. And this is true, there are sadists. But there are also millions of people who are not sadists but who don't care about their fellows, who go about their lives doing ordinary things, inured against what is happening day after day. Stuck in the small heroin place, the opium place, avoiding what is staring them in the face, escaping into illusions, chasing dreams. To make the move you need to wake up out of this dream, this nightmare, and realise what part you are playing. And then do something about that part. That is how you inherit the earth, whether you are born in Hillingdon, Aldeburgh or Ravenscourt Park.

After emptying their house of its contents, Dick and Jane went to Thailand and Australia. They had spent most of their lives in this part of Suffolk. No one they had worked with or known in all those years understood why they decided to go travelling, or came back three months later in order to sell their house and leave for good. Occasionally we would pass each other by in the lanes and laugh at the way everything turned out. 'Most of my life was governed by fear. I am looking at things very differently now,' Dick said to Mark as our paths crossed one day down by the river.

And then one winter's day they were gone.

I am in Aldeburgh three years later in a hotel lobby, talking to a poet whose radical lines I can still remember from the days when I was young and loved poetry. His name is Adrian Mitchell. He is just about to give a talk entitled *Who Killed Dylan Thomas?* that is going to change everything. That is going to change me from the person who adjusts the microphone on this literary stage to the person who can stand boldly before it and say what it is like to work in the kitchen and not be able to open your mouth.

The kitchen years are about to end: the years when I adjusted microphones and radiators, stuffed envelopes, poured wine, knew the insides of buildings like my own body and the needs of people better than they knew themselves. These are the years in which I failed because I was someone who believed in editorial and who could not write advertising copy, marketing copy or the kinds of prose shiny souvenir programmes are made of; where line managers tell me 'we don't want to know what you think', and charity trustees tell me that I am 'just A.N. Other'. These are the years in which I wear badges that declare I am A.N. Other event manager, venue manager, safety officer, press officer, and spend hours counting the small change. The years I serve a strange god. Here at this poetry festival I have been talking to poets who are sent into prisons and mental asylums, who are laughed at by schoolchildren; poets who cannot speak, who cry in supermarkets, who are not listened to any more than I am listened to myself. Poets who wake up in the midst of terror and make an oath of loyalty to the kitchen table, who praise radishes and olive trees when the times are bad.

'Poets put themselves on the line, and every time they speak part of them dies!' roars Adrian Mitchell.

'Time held me as I lay green and dying,' recites Dylan Thomas, 'though I sang in my chains like the sea.'

In the festival's open writing seminar a line from the Cad Goddeu, *The Battle of Trees*, is inscribed on the blackboard. The great riddle of the Welsh bard, known as Taliesin after the mythical twice-born Taliesin, is there to inspire us to write a poem about the houses of ourselves. *I have been an eagle*, writes the sixth-century bard, *a spotted snake on the hill. I have been a house*, write the participants of the creative writing seminar. *Just another brick in the wall.* What kind of house are you? asks the teacher. *Who but I can call the cattle of Tethra home?* I write, as I remember the lines of the poet-seers who knew the names of the trees, the secret of the unhewn dolmen and the circling of the stars above our shining earth.

Who indeed but you?

Who indeed but ourselves?

I put down my pencil. I have solved the riddle, posed but not answered by the poet. It was the Empire that killed Dylan Thomas, the System that took the script and neglected the man. It is the system that always shoots the messenger, the *pharmakon*, rather than listen to what he has to say. Or that binds him to a cage: the gulag that bound Osip Mandlestam, the madhouse that held Christopher Smart, the Tower that held Walter Raleigh, the prison treadmill that broke Oscar Wilde, the trenches that killed Edward Thomas and Wilfred Owen, the fascism that killed Garcia Lorca – the civilisation of the western world. What poet, what visionary, what philosopher has not seen and written of this heartless authoritarian machine even as they gave their blood to oil its wheels?

'The 'Je' is very important,' said the speaker, talking of Rimbaud and Baudlelaire. The 'I' of the poet is the 'I' of the heart as it faces the machine, and sings though it binds him to the wheel. This is not the 'je' of the ego, the 'I' who lives in a house like all other houses, another brick in the wall. This is the Promethean 'je' of the creator, who is the salmon, the wave on the sea and the furze on the hill. The system demands that you sacrifice your natural creative energies to keep it going, that you fit into its unkind geometry. To do this you would have to relinquish the 'I' that is the heart in the living systems, the green fuse that drives the flower, the 'I' who knows the ways of the sun and the earth and how to converse with the dead. You cannot do this. You are the *pharmakon*, the quicksilver one who never fits, who never stops moving. Life keeps going because of you.

How do you break this machine? You destroy it from within, with the power of your heart and your imagination. You forge something anew. You become aware there is something more important in your creative act than all your rightful sorrow, your woundedness, your reputation – even more important than your carefully wrought prose or poetry. You find something down there in the kitchen in those years: something primordial, something buried in deep time. You were working with it all the time, your clothes stained with ashes, your face blackened with soot. The treasure was in your hands. You were so busy being outraged at the injustices of the world, offended by the arrogant ways of the drawing room people, so intent on re-entering the ballroom in your finery to great acclaim. And then one day you realise: you are in charge of the fire.

That's when the world stops. That's when my world stopped. Who but I knew the way back, the path that leads to the sea? The *Cad Goddeu* is a pied fragment, a struggle for words: the battle for Britain waged between two tribes, the native and the invader, between the gods Bel and Bran, between the light and the dark half of the year. The trees are letters, the armies, two kinds of alphabets, signifying different bands of knowledge. That which is written and that which is not. In the battle the sun-followers of Gwydion (he who knows, speaker of poetry) find the secret name of Bran, god of the underworld, disclosed in the boughs of an alder tree. The nature and spirit language of which this poem is made is the language of poets, the language of water and fire, the elements of life: the kettle of water you set on the stove. It is the alphabet of dragons.

Once in these lands the poets did not have to beg for money. They did not live on the outskirts of society like town foxes, scorned like Dylan Thomas by the BBC, or like Elizabeth Jennings by Oxford City Council. They did not have to crawl to the Suffolk aristocracy like George Crabbe or teach Suffolk matrons how to write, as they do now, to provide material for high-brow shows and the school curriculum. They held a high office, acknowledged for their great abilities as metaphysical guides, those who held up a mirror to our souls, witnesses to correct procedures, rememberers of our shining conscience, our hearts, our roots, those who knew the way through the briars of this world, along the green trackways, all the way down to the roaring sea, beacons that shone in the dark. They were so regarded because in their ways of walking this world, along those trackways most people never get to see, they were recognised as the keepers of the cosmic fire.

To know the way of dragons is to know who keeps the fire, and why that fire is kept. Who but the poet can light our way home, as he faces all eternity? Who but I could stand on the edge, be thrown out into the empty dunelands, and return? At the Aldeburgh poetry festival I hung up my apron for the last time, and went out of the kitchen door. I did not go upstairs, as I had once imagined. I went outside into the fresh salt air, walking toward the shingle shore, toward the curlew river, moving far and deep into the lapwing's land.

lady's smock
Sizewell Belts, Suffolk 2006

I am walking down the lane at midnight, following the call across the still, black land. At the curve of the hawthorns, with all the sleeping houses behind me, I pause to listen for its direction and then press further into the darkness. A crimson slice of moon hangs just above the wood before me as I walk, the air faint with the smell of invisible horses in the field and the dew-soaked grass. The warm damp breath of land and the eddies of a colder wind weave alternately across my skin. Everything feels close and urgent in the way of the night. The great oaks loom above me as I pass, stars hanging between their branches. *Come nearer, come nearer!* I move toward the dell, where the nightingale is singing among the blackthorn. His song pierces the darkness with each note: deep into the core of the night. *Here, here,* he sings. *Deeper, nearer, closer!* His song enters my chest. I wait by the thicket, listening, the blood singing in my ears. At dawn the song of the thrush will awaken me. *We are here, we are here, are you?* the birds call out.

This midnight, this morning, this Maytime, I am here.

But it was not always so.

The girl in the dress is beautiful, but it's a bad business she is in. It is a bad business we are all in today in America, as we pour our creativity and she her youth and vulnerability into fabricating an image to uphold the Empire. This is a Japanese girl as fragile as a flower with a blue tattoo on her arm, wearing the dress that the business wives of Fifth Avenue will wear next season, that the actresses of Hollywood will flaunt, that the cheap boutiques of the world will copy in their millions. A dress stitched by a thousand girls, bent over machines that suck the energy from the earth's rivers and give them chemical dyes in return, in the name of 'human' power. Oh yes, it is a bad business and a heartless business. And maybe this is why we have all decided to wait to take another picture of this girl, standing with her girlfriend without any clothes on. It is not on the schedule but something in us has begun to rebel.

On this day in 1994 in New York I know this is a revolution

because, as we all wait for three hours in her studio apartment, there is a picture of Venus on the kitchen wall, standing naked on the half-shell with a man in a business suit beside her. Something is happening here on the last day that I work for the fashion business. It's the day I take off my magazine byline and write a poem instead. The poem is called: *Venus is Not for Sale.*

> *glamour is not the same as beauty*
> *beauty is true and natural*
> *and glamour is a vampire with a painted face*

There is a power to beauty that belongs to beauty alone. It cannot be manufactured by man or Empire. It is the rebellious beauty of the heart. You can substitute beauty with glamour, with an artificial shine, but it will never be the real thing. You can project all manner of archetypes onto a woman's face or form, make her a madonna, a diva, a supermodel, but she will never become Queen of the May. Because, no matter how delicately or finely formed, no matter how many pay her homage, she will not hold within her being the brilliant unsurpassable energy of the morning and evening star.

Venus, the earth's mysterious sister, appears in the morning and evening, shining brilliantly in the sky during the month of May. You cannot look at her directly, as her surface is veiled by cloud. The veil hides a planet of volcanoes. No man or machine can land on her fiery body without being blown apart. In the painting Venus appears out of the sea, naked, balanced on the half-shell. You gaze into her pale, vacant face and fall at her feet in adoration. But this is a manufactured Venus. The real Venus is active and fiery, not static and pale. When she comes naked into the world she brings revolution and May Day parades. She does not bring consent. When you work with the wild flowers that emit her presence in the month of May, you know that artificial glamour has no power in or of itself. It is an object that can be adored and worshipped. But real beauty cannot be possessed; it can only be beheld. And only those whose hearts can match its fiery revolutionary nature can really know the love for which Venus is also famed.

> *It will not be printed*
> *our one rebel moment*
> *still we wait three hours*

334

Beauty emits the high frequency that you feel in all living things. Its power arrives suddenly, unexpected, and yet you look for it everywhere. You get up at midnight to witness it. You feel it in the high intensity of a hummingbird or a butterfly wing as it brushes past and startles you; you can see it in the colour of the bee orchid or a cherry tree in full bloom, the scent of a jasmine flower at dusk. It is almost oppressive, that moment: unbearable, as if this colour, this taste, this sound were pushing all the unkind things within your being out into the light. The frequency Venus brings has dramatic transformative powers. Sometimes you turn away from that beauty. But if you hold that moment you undergo a kind of alchemy, as you shift from the base mindset of the world into the high frequency of the heart. This alchemy begins by pressurising the lowest elements down into their base material, forcing the beast out of the matter. Once Venus has forced everything ugly out of its hiding place, it can go about its radical makeover.

This is why all empires are threatened by real beauty. The Empire does not want to change, it wants to hold on to its power. It is terrified to experience its own ugliness, its lack of heart, its human vulnerability. It will do anything to prevent discovery. It blocks beauty's dangerous alchemy by mutating the natural forms of earth, by copying, grafting, manipulating its components, bringing them under the control and ownership of its corporations and then attracting the people's attention to the tamed and tortured and hybridised. It does this by highlighting and praising the monsterish elements of life, by making the mind and emotional body dependent on end-of-the world dramas, by entertaining us with circuses and freakshows, by fostering envy and possessiveness, a 'lifestyle' epitomised by grand and showy garden flowers, by young girls adorned in monster costumes. Meanwhile, it does everything in its power to destroy the real thing. This is why wild flowers are mown down and poisoned, why native peoples who celebrate the beauty of the earth are so oppressed. Why the developed world appears ever more ugly and flaunts its power in ever-increasing images of artifice. It is working hard to prevent every shred of beauty from appearing.

Fairy stories are full of vicious stepmothers who plot to kill the natural and beautiful daughters of the earth. If we read these cautionary tales correctly, rather than dismissing them as children's stories, they would show us how to preserve our beauty and our humanity, how to be resourceful in the face of these predators and privateers, how to wake up out of our enchantments, how to grow up, get smart, seek out the older wisdoms that still live in the wild places, forests and mountains, in gnarled old elders and hermits. How to start transforming ourselves.

While the planet, regardless, keeps pushing up more and more radical beauty each spring.

Lady's smock is not a garden flower; it is a wild flower that grows by streams and in damp pastures. Neither grand, nor rare, nor scented, it is an undistinguished member of the humble cabbage family and shares with many of its other relatives – honesty, dame's violet, sweet Alison, candytuft and all cresses – a clear simplicity of form and peppery sharp-tasting leaves. However, it was once regarded with awe by country people, and even modern wild flower guides will tell you that it belongs to the Queen of the Fairies and that it is unlucky to pick it. Like many wild flowers that bear the signature of the ancient matriarchal goddess, the 'smock' was later said to belong to the madonna of the patriarchal churches. But whatever mythology or religion claims her for their own, the flower remains loyal to the lady of the house. And its power, like that of the earth, resides in its particular quality of being female.

When I first saw its simple slender form appearing outside the window, my heart leapt. It was the first wild flower to come to the Oxford garden. There were daffodils and lilacs in abundance, a budding mock orange against the wall, but none of these cultivated plants had startled my heart like the appearance of this pale quiet form among the long dewy grass. To grow a flower is to master its every move, but when a wild flower arrives, it comes of its own accord. You can invite and entice, but you can never *make* a wild plant come to your garden, as anyone who has *tried* to grow a daisy lawn will tell you. To be truly female you need to understand the wild in this way. You need know about the moon and the planet Venus, the mood and breath of the sea, about flowers that appear because a place pleases them. You need to be able to sense their delicate and primal energies, their simplicity and peppery temperaments. You need to learn to love these qualities in yourself. If you do not, you will be at the mercy of what the Empire tells you is female. A 'woman' who is told every way to grow, to serve and please whomsoever is in control.

Cultivated and domesticated within the garden, women let themselves be managed, trained, groomed, snipped, pruned and espaliered. Outside its perimeter they inhabit their true form, go where they please, keep their medicine and their wild beauty intact. Church flower ladies, grateful wives who clutch roses, horticultural matrons who brandish garden rakes and declare war on dandelions are not necessarily *female* as far as the living systems of the planet are concerned. In fact, the ancient fairy stories teach us to be wary of such characters.

'Neither to be pitied or praised!' declares Robert Graves about the women who do not emulate the lady of the house.

As for the lady herself, and the flower who bears her name? She doesn't see them. They have not yet arrived on her planet.

You look at the flower. Its clear simple stem, its delicate leaves, the washed pink and white petals, its tight buds, how it rises delicately out of the boggy soil, out of the brackish water, pure and clean. All around the flower spring is at its height. Light is everywhere. The blackbird sings his carol in the wood, the wren his high shrill notes, the sing-song of the chaffinch saws the air. The sunlight falls through the branches. The perfume of the lily rises.

I have come to see the sweet-scented lily of the valley. It flowers in small white bells out of sheaves of green leaves under a ring of beech trees in a quiet corner by a pond. You walk to the wood from the common, through a watermeadow fringed with willow and alder, following a path of rising white foxgloves. The scent of pine and bluebell and white lily beckon you. But I am stopped in my tracks: in the meadow there is a host of lady's smock, sprinkling the coarse wetland grass with its elegant white and pink form. This one flower has summoned me and I have sunk to my knees to attend.

Listen, she commands.

I close my eyes. The whole world is singing. It is the peak moment of May when everything pushes towards the sky, grows green, increases, becomes intensely alive. The moment when the earth begins to dance. Out of the spangled watermeadow, through woods of rhododendrons and glowing bluebells, down the lanes ribboning in all directions, brimming with hawthorn and cow parsley and out towards the lupin-scented shoreline. There is light and colour everywhere. At that moment a great surge of energy rushes through my body and the blood roars in my ears, and when I open my eyes everything is green, vibrant, pristine, radiant. The world has taken off its grey coat. That's when I realised that the beauty is all on the inside.

This is your work, says the flower simply. *This is what the earth requires. It needs to be seen as beautiful. The female being needs to be in charge. That is you and the earth and us. Remember this moment.*

This is the moment you find yourself making a wish. You wish that this life on earth will flourish forever. As you wish, you realise you are here to love this life, this moment when you are as beautiful as the flowers. The moment appears like the wild card, like the May: your ears blow, the rainbow appears after the rainstorm, the light flashes across the river, the nightingale sings across the dark land. In this moment, everything is changed.

That's when you remember: you are in charge of the dream.

This is the trance that Piers Vitebsky wrote about. High on the reaches of the larch forests of the world, the anthropologist goes to live among the wild reindeer brigades of Siberia. They are a people whose lives follow the deer, and like every other native tribe they are being torn apart and shredded by the Empire, whose most silent and deadly weapon is glamour.

When the Soviet government issued cheap factory frocks among the Evenki women, they forgot everything about reindeer and started squabbling among themselves. Kept within the village boundary where once they had camped within the forests and the wild snowy wastes, their prodigious skills reduced to the function of administrators, they placed all their attention on baubles. Without the women to wait for them in the taiga, without their skills, their firelight, their laughter and stories, without the dreaming of deer in their wombs, the men lost their way. A thread snapped and the connection to the wild world began to disappear. It is a cautionary tale about Empire, related to an island people who have already spent an aeon eyeing each other suspiciously in the mirror, holding cheap and expensive garments in their hands, who have forgotten entirely what it means to be female. What it means to hold the dream of the earth intact within their hearts.

338

This is the tale of a trance where there should have been a dream. The Japanese model in New York wears the dress that the women of the western world want to possess. The blank-faced girl who has all the men at her feet in adoration. The girl with a tattoo on her arm.

We want to possess what she has – all that attention – but nobody wants to *be* the girl in the picture; not even she does. I know this because when we stopped working that day, some of us began to talk to each other in a way we would not normally have done. We spoke to each other of our experiences of the world. 'Nothing exists on the outside any more, does it?' said the stylist suddenly. And the girl, whose name was Jenny, told me that she liked riding her motorbike in the Pasadena hills and reading poetry and stories with happy endings. What she really wanted was to go back home. Outside the window, the Statue of Liberty raised one arm to the sky.

Along the latitudes of the northern lands a woman lies buried in a white silk blouse and red woollen skirt with a box of hemp flowers. She has been sleeping under the frost for two thousand years. Her arms are tattooed with blue reindeer, her horses and her mirror sleep beside her. Some say she is a storyteller and a medicine woman, others a Sythian princess. Her discoverers call her simply: Lady.

The women stare at the magazine and do not see the girl buried beneath the dress. They only resent her slim body, her smooth oval face, wanting what she wears. As they turn the page their eyes are glazed over, transfixed.

Jenny folds one arm around her sister's waist and they stand naked before the camera at the end of the day. We stand before them.

Silently, the reindeer move across the tundra.

It seems I have spent an aeon listening to these women talking about daddy, about god, twisting their bodies into the designs of Chinese and Indian holy men, jabbing their faces with pencils from Paris and chopping their hair this way and that, tearing badly behaved English flowers out of their gardens. I have spent a lifetime listening to their dissatisfaction and their disturbance as the world espaliers their natural form, tells them beauty is in how they look at themselves in the mirror – and at each other, askance – rather than how they look deeply at everything with the fire of life in their hearts. I have spoken a mountain of words in those endless afternoons, pleading with these sisters of mine as they stare into space, their minds elsewhere, trying to break their trance – which is also my own.

I am waiting for them to recognise me. To open the door and see me.

But they will not open the door.

Sometimes I let slip my cloak of rushes, flashed a violet eye in the winter darkness, let go a ripple of blue in the spring woods; breathed out a scent of honeysuckle as the women passed by. Still they did not notice. How charming, lovely! they said absentmindedly and carried on walking and talking, thinking of last year's argument or next week's meal. Each week they gave me their garments, torn and shredded, fouled and stinking. I refreshed and mended them, handed them back scented with lavender and roses, strengthened with nettle leaves, washed in rainwater and sunlight, oiled with primrose and hemp seeds. They did not thank me. It was, after all, expected.

What did I expect in return? What did any of us expect? As we stood in the city libraries, behind the shop till, with our berets pulled down, our mackintosh collars turned up against the wind as we stood waiting by the bus stop. Who was supposed to pay attention to us? Were we waiting for our sisters to notice us as we went sorrowfully about our thankless tasks? For the beauty and knowledge we held inside us? The women of the Empire gaze at the view outside the room as they throw the ugliness, the ghosts of their lives towards us. *I am suffering!* they shout. *You! Take this pain away from me. Wash it clean!*

Here I come, I said, with my reindeer medicine. Here I am with my hornbeam arms, sinewy and hard; my rough coat made of dandelions, my wild hair matted like sea-grass, with the strength of the deep frost within me. Feel me! I said. It is not what we look like, it's what we feel inside that matters. Beauty is in what we love, what the wishes of our hearts are. Do you remember?

But the women of Empire remember nothing. They remain enclosed within the garden, guarding their medicine cabinets, fingering the hem of last season's skirts. They do not like what they see. Something wild and unbidden in their houses. Something that brought the rainbow after the storm, the light and the sound of transformation. Suddenly I realised that I had run out of time. Already the fires were flickering on the skyline. The deer had gone before me.

So I walked away, out of the village, following the tracks they left along the snowline. I walked toward the burning reedbed, toward the bluebell wood, toward the nightingale singing at midnight. I had arrived at a place where I could go no further. I had awoken at dawn and looked in front of me, and saw that the future had vanished. There was only a stormy darkness before my eyes. When I was utterly naked, holding nothing, not even the price of a new dress in my hands, only then could I turn away from the trance of the world, from the ugliness of my sisters, and set myself free. It was my own small revolution.

What else can you do in such moment? When there is nothing left, when all life is dying around you, when the chips are down, the sea is coming in, when your hope is gone, when your dreams of a life have withered, what other course of action is there but to love?

To put on your lady's smock in the dark and sing?

heather
Dunwich Heath, Suffolk 2006

At the turning point, halfway through a conventional life, you realise that a deep integral part of yourself has always walked in another direction. And though you may have wandered far away from this core self, become lost in alien lands, that part is always calling you home.

When I was eight years old I took a journey each day across the city of London. It began in Newton Road, Bayswater, then went to St Saviour's hall in Knightsbridge and back again. Wearing small boots of sheepskin I set out alone in the snow and fog of winter and came in the bright afternoons of summer with a boater swinging down my back. This return journey to and from school belonged entirely to me. Boarding the number 52 bus, I sailed aloft on the upper deck through the tops of the Hyde Park trees, through cherry blossom and plane leaves, through conkers and chestnut candles and, on embarking at Scotch Corner, plunged into the teeming streets of Knightsbridge. In this riverine flow I took no notice of the men in coats and women in smart dresses. My eyes noticed other things – the sweet kiosks that loomed full of coloured lights in the dusk, the grape-sellers from Spain at the street corners, the onion-sellers from Brittany cycling by. I heard the sounds of the rag-and-bone man calling out, and the organ-grinder. All these things delighted me.

But sometimes I stood in my tracks and was disturbed by what crossed my path – the old matchseller with shaky hands, the naked woman who stood screaming at the window, the female tramp asleep on the bench beside the Victoria and Albert Museum, her coat thick with newspapers. Who were these people? Where did they come from? What did their suffering mean?

One afternoon, walking to the bus stop, I saw some large women in long skirts darting in among the crowd that flowed past Harrods. The people they approached shrank away from them, or scuffled alarmed in their purses. I stood intrigued, wondering who they were. Then one of the women loomed up in front of me. I was excited and nervous at the same time. She bent her large frame down and put something in my hands. 'There you are my darling, for luck.' I looked down. In my hands, wrapped up in a piece of silver foil, was a sprig of purple heather.

In the Celtic tree alphabet, heather forms the O of midsummer, the vowel of the solstice *ohn*, and like the golden gorse of spring equinox it is associated with bees. It is the queen bee of all the alphabet.

Bees visit a myriad wild flowers, but some they seek out more than others – rosebay willowherb, sycamore, bramble, crab apple, dandelion. Heather is one of their most coveted flowers and the honey made from its deep purple bloom is particular and commands the highest price in the marketplace. Its jelly-like thickness requires it to be pressed out of the comb, giving it a signature bubbled appearance in the jar. Its high protein content often makes it ferment and taste alcoholic. Most honeys are light and amber-coloured, easy on the tongue – those made from the abundant nectar of white clover and limeflowers, for example – but heather honey is dark, full of pollen, its taste not to everyone's liking. When you open the lid, its fragrance exudes far into the room.

In 1924 the philosopher and seer Rudolph Steiner gave six lectures on honeybees. He told his audience of beekeepers that the bee colony indicates the most highly developed organisation known to man – a collective in perfect tune and synchronicity with the solar system. The queen bee, he asserted, is a creature of the sun and emanates the full force of love through the high vibration of the planet Venus. It is to keep connected to this solar power that her workers (all female) return loyally to her colony with all the sweetness from the flower realms of the earth. The male attendants, grounded in the vibration of the earth, keep the sound; the female workers, intermediaries between sun and earth, the dance. Inside the vibrant, warm, fragrant hive the queen produces the future generations, thousands upon thousands of embryo bees. She dwells in the core of the hive like the sun in the solar system, like the heart in our human bodies. In the centre of this universe she radiates an immense rainbow-coloured light which only bees and human seers, like Steiner, can see. It is the light that illuminates all the world.

Sometimes on a September day you can see this light as you stand among the purple haze of ling on the Suffolk coast and watch the waves running to the shore: it fills your head and intoxicates you. In this light the bees go out and collect the nectar from the heather and bring it back to store in the hive's hexagonal cells. As they return they dance the position of the flowers and pass this map on to their fellow workers, orienting their figure of eight with the path of the sun. All the sweetness of the summer months is stored this way. Honey is one of the most extraordinary substances in nature, and until hives were constructed (by the Egyptian empire), great stealth and skill was required from human beings to obtain it in the wild.

Steiner was concerned about the future of the honey bee. He had seen that the increased interference by beekeepers in the life of the hive to try to increase honey production was destabilising its equilibrium, and that honeybee populations would suffer. And by extension, ourselves. The fate of the honey bee, one of the earth's great pollinators, was intrinsically tied up with the fate of human beings.

In the modern mechanised world, Steiner observed, the organisation of the human body was often weak and cold. Honey affected our constitutions by bringing warmth to cold places and strength to the weak. Steiner recommended a spoonful of honey each day as a cure, just as (Manuka) honey is now taken, principally for arthritis and stomach ulcers. But these were simple physical remedies. What brought us towards our higher development was the activation of our 'Venusian' consciousness, our own honey song and dance.

Inspired by these lectures, Joseph Beuys, the radical German artist and performer, made an installation in 1977 in the art show 'Documenta 6' in the industrial town of Kassel. It was called *Honey Pump in the Workplace*. Two ships' engines pumped fat and honey through a network of clear tubing that circulated around the large exhibition hall like arteries and veins around a human body. In the centre of this network was a space in which a programme of discussions took place.

These seminars, lectures and demonstrations, he explained, were 'an expression of the principle of the free intelligence university working in the bloodstream of society.'

During the war, as a Luftwaffe pilot, Beuys had crashed into the snow-bound steppes of the Crimea and had been rescued by Tartar nomads. He had been wrapped in fat and felt to keep him alive. It was an encounter that informed all his work. Many of his installations juxtaposed the vibrant dynamics of nature with an industrialized culture that produced cold-blooded human beings, incapable of empathy or mystery. The warmth and movement of natural substances (in this case fat and honey) that related to the warmth and movement of our blood, activated the higher centres of our consciousness: thought became imagination, feeling became inspiration, will, intuition. In short, the alchemical presence of honey provided the warmth and vibrancy in which our materialistically hardened thoughts softened, and heart-felt communication could take place.

Warmth of feeling, as well as the unimpeded movement of the mind and will, were necessary for the 'free intelligence university' to work. Many of Beuys' actions were followed by group conversations to discuss their meaning, and in *Honey Pump* these discussions were expanded over the whole period of 'Documenta 6'. They were seen as key steps towards creating a social organisation as a work of art, a collective that would be oriented, like the beehive, to the sun. He was, like all creators, laying down a map for the future development of human beings. It was a vision he maintained to the end of his life.

When I was eight years old I sometimes went through the doors of the great department store where my grandmother worked, to visit her for tea. I had a passion for the lime and raspberry milkshakes in the Fountain Room. Like all children, my desire for sweet things was giant. But below the Fountain Room with its artificial syrups, its fluted glasses and twirling straws, lay something I treasured more deeply and secretly. Among the opulent shelves of the Food Hall there lay a small box. In it were six jars containing the Honeys of the World – eucalyptus from Australia, orange blossom from Mexico, clover from New Zealand. I would hold that box and long in my heart to taste the nectar of their flowers.

The sweetest honey comes from the dry lands. When I am grown I will taste the honeys of those countries I only dreamed about as a child: the treacly honey of the desert acacia, the sharp flavour of lavender from the Provençal garrigue, the thyme honey of the Greek island. But already, at eight, I know that nothing quite captures that dryness, that utter reckless wildness of the moor and the mountain as heather, the greatest honey of the British Isles.

There are three native heathers that grow on the heaths of Suffolk: the bell, the cross-leaved and the ling. The first two bloom in summer and are the heathers of the summer solstice. But it is the third that is the best known, that is treasured by bees and their keepers as it spreads its purple coat all over the wild lands of Britain, over the hills of Scotland and Wales, across the moorlands of the north, and here along the East Anglian seaboard in August. In some places, you can see the surname *Ling* carved on the ancient gravestones of coastal Suffolk. The word comes from Anglo-Saxon, meaning 'fire'.

Before enclosure, ling was a vital plant in the life of commoners on these heaths. The flowers of the heather not only provided honey and ale, but its branches were used for thatch, baskets, brooms, ropes and bedding, its roots for nails. It grew alongside the bracken and gorse that provided litter and fuel, the oaks that gave acorns for pigs, and the grasses for geese, cattle and sheep. In the seventeenth century a quarter of England was 'waste': that is, wild land that was collectively used by the people, rather than the property of individuals. Today this is now less than one third of one per cent.

When I come to Suffolk I start to walk the cinder tracks that crossed these ancient heaths – across Dunwich, Tunstall, Blaxhall, across the heathy commons of Leiston, Westleton and Warbleswick. These territories are quite different, I discover, from any other of Suffolk's coastal woods, fens, meadows. Even though they are managed by councils and the National Trust, their relationship is still with the people.

In a weekly wild flower exhibition I coordinate during one summer, a sprig of heather sits in a jam jar on the windowsills of the Southwold Museum and I find myself uncharacteristically veering away from botany:

> 'In 1624 Sir Robert Brooke, landowner, set up a boarding house for men and dogs to drive out commoners' cattle from Walberswick common, in order that the land could be enclosed for his own use. A terrible fight took place in which four men lost their lives and the place was named Bloody Marsh. These men were resisting an enclosure of land by force which began with the arrival of Norman kings who claimed the wild forests, and was completed by Parliament who claimed the rest of the wild land for agriculture.'

All civilisations have to raid and enclose for the benefit of their rulers. That is the 'nature' of all parasitic systems. What suffers under its cruel and contemptuous rule are the natural host systems – the wild lands and the hearts of the people. The pauperism suffered by the dwellers of the Suffolk Sanderlings as a result of enclosure was the worst in all England. They suffered the kind of poverty and despair found among all relocated native peoples in Australia, Africa, Indonesia and the Americas today, all the lands that the heirs of the Norman conquerors went on to raid – and still do in their present corporate form, in every rainforest, every last marsh and mountain of the world.

As I crossed the commons, heaths and warrens, I found myself walking a time-line that stretched across the world. Through the golden yellow of the gorse and the purple ling, past the history of the rabbit (also a legacy of the Normans) and the blackfaced sheep who keep the heaths from reverting into forest, I walked a time-line that mapped the struggle for human liberty. The commons were the meeting places of the people – resisting medieval peasants, the East Anglian bread riots, Chartists. I watched activists gathering at the nuclear power station of Sizewell, heard the guns of the landowners all around me.

I followed the sheep tracks through bracken and birch and entered the kingdom of the adder, the lizard, the linnet and the glowworm. There I lay among the bright green moss and the tiny toadstools, ate blackberries under a rowan tree, waited until dusk for the whirring of the nightjar as the moon rose and lit the seashell track all the way down to the singing sea, toward a different heritage we share under the starlit sky.

When I walk across Dunwich Heath in 2006, I take a different route. I walk from Eastbridge across the marshes, with dykes full of marshmallow, the broom bushes rattling their pods, and approach the heath from the dunes. It is early September and the ling is at its height. As I turn onto the main track I suddenly feel intensely irritated. Mean thoughts enter my mind. I start looking most suspiciously at the two people coming towards me.

For goodness sake, Charlotte! I say to myself. *You are here to see the heather!* But somehow I can't concentrate on the heather, as I feel overwhelmed with negative thinking. The people walking by don't look any more agreeable than I do. We are all scowling like mad, wishing we had the path to ourselves. What a crew! I think to myself, and avert my gaze to the ground. *Oh, it's the track!* I realise, and immediately I step off it and plunge into the unmapped heather. As soon as I do, all the fury inside me disappears.

Released from my inner turmoil, the heath opens its arms. Everywhere there are purple flowers and sky. I head towards Minsmere making my own path, high-stepping through the bushes, following the line of fire-breaks. No one is in view. The ling is dotted with bristly low gorse and young Scots pine, the sky full of racing clouds. I feel intensely free. The sun pours down on us all. As I climb the hill red deer appear as if from nowhere. Their heads emerge from the heather one by one, until the whole herd stands and watches me as I stumble by, off-track, lost but at home.

Home is a place the heather leads you. Sometimes without realising, I go through the heather and get lost. Even when I know the track, I lose my sense of direction and find myself somewhere else. Or I come across someone who asks me the way, or who has lost their dog. Dreaming of heather I find myself at a crossroads, watching people going down paths across the common. All of the paths are dead ends. Are you alive? I ask one woman, but she is dead. Another appears and tells me: We have saved the Romany girl! She is found! But this evangelist is no more alive than anyone else.

In 1998 another German visionary walks across Dunwich Heath and gets lost. He is walking a time-line that goes in the opposite direction to a radical future. His name is W.G. Sebald and he is on his way to visit the translator of his first work. Michael Hamburger, who lives in the village of Middleton on the other side of the heath. Sebald is collecting material for a book that will make his name. It is called *The Rings of Saturn*. The book is about a walk, a particular walk in time in which, if you do not follow the clues, you will find yourself walking into a trap.

History is doomed to repeat itself. It is like the rings of Saturn, an exploded moon whose form fascinates everyone who gazes at its coloured detritus which whirls endlessly round and round. Out of this meaninglessness, at certain points in time, appear writers and philosophers who have walked along this Suffolk coast. Some of them are aristocrats, eccentrics who break the mould. Sebald recounts their stories as their houses and their histories are washed away by the ceaseless waves of the North Sea, which he calls the German Ocean.

Sebald becomes confused on Dunwich Heath, oppressed by its lack of signposts, finds the purple ling dingy and oppressive. He is walking in the dog days of August, when everything is dying down and becomes stagnant, a time when even the birds have ceased to sing.

Afterwards he dreams of the heath as the figures of myth and history enact their meaningless dramas of horror on the shore. The heath in his dream becomes a labyrinth. In many ways the book itself is a labyrinth: one in which the readers are given a thread woven by the silk weavers of Norwich, cultured by the peasants of China; a thread that leads us not *out* of its convoluted passages, but *towards* the Minotaur, the beast who will one day feed upon us as Saturn once ate his own children. In this, Sebald is no Ariadne. He is writing from the position of Daedelus, the mythical constructor of prisons.

The labyrinth of Crete, created by Daedelus, was a remnant of the Minoan culture that was washed away by a great tidal wave caused by the eruption of Santorini in the Aegean. At the centre of this culture was the goddess of the honeybee, known as the mistress of the house. Ceremonial dances were performed in her honour by women dressed in skirts shaped like beehives, while men cavorted and leapt over wild bulls.

Of all nectar-loving insects, including wild bees, the honeybee is particular. Instead of flitting from one type of flower to another, it works one flower at a time. When bees return to the hive they dance on the floor of the hexagonal honeycomb, making a 'map' of how to return to these flowers. The Minoan dances, orientated to the sun, were a map that showed how to reach this place within and return, and thus keep our relationship with the earth in harmony. The arena of these intricate dances was once known as Ariadne's dancing floor.

When this female-based culture disappeared, the heroic male culture of Greece turned its labyrinthine dance into a fortress. In its centre they kept the demonised bull, the Minotaur, totem of the star Venus, and turned the mistress of the house (later their bull-slaying hero's accomplice) into a spider. The world constructed in their wake was a prison.

Labyrinths are seen everywhere in Europe and the Middle East. They live on the rocky shores of the northern lands of Finland and

Norway. They appear, like spiderwebs, on desert rocks and baskets in Arizona and Nevada. On the floors of medieval French churches, in the ancient Celtic dances of the summer solstice. Some of them are traps, a way of holding spirits, but some lead towards the sun in the centre of all things. Some of them take you home.

The heather takes you off the path when you are going down the wrong track, along the lines of Empire. The Minoan labyrinth was a prison, but beneath this labyrinth is a map. The rings of Saturn go meaninglessly round and round. You get confused. You find yourself in a maze, overwhelmed by choices, stuck in your mind. But the map leads you to the centre, towards the heart. In the centre of the hive sits the queen bee. At the zenith of the solar year she presides over the harvest months of July and August, season of all heathers, beloved food plant of the bee. In the centre of her being is the sun, organising everything in our lives for our highest development.

When you lose track of history among the heather, that's when you find her dancing floor.

There is a patch of heather at my feet, a smell of honey in the air, warmth on my face. Dragonflies rest on the stems of the small bushes, their folded azure wings glint in the sunlight. One lands on me, swivelling its eyes, and polishes its pincers. Its forelegs sink down, in three precise jerks. We sit there in the small windless patch. Over our heads the clouds race and scud.

'You see that patch of sky,' said my grandmother in the English garden of yew hedges. 'It's enough to make a pair of sailor's trousers. Soon the sky will be all blue.'

'You see the hole in the clouds,' said Karen in the Andean valley of immortality. 'That's the whole. So long as we pay it attention.'

You see that patch of heather in this last corner of wilderness in the world? That's enough to remember your wildness. When you go there, when you find the honey, you will know you have found your way home.

It's our last stand. Our last rebellion.

Why are the flowers radical, why is the honey-scented heather radical? Because when you speak with the queen bee who is yourself, you stand in the centre of the universe. When you bring harmony to bear at the centre of your being, you become the lady of the house. You have gone out to visit the flowers, and at the turning point you have come back to the core. This dance of the self, aligned with the sun, is the dance the old order does not want to happen. For when we begin this dance, the prison will collapse and their rule will end. We will have come home to ourselves. And once you are home no one can persuade you to leave.

Something within us knows this, even though we are born into places quite opposite to our natures. No matter how much our house has told us we should have such and such manners and our school that we should think in such and such way, always we take a path that is uniquely our own. I lived in a road named after the cold-blooded scientist whose mechanistic rules still dominate our consciousness and attended a school in a church hall whose autocratic, cold-blooded god still lays claim to our souls, and yet my dance took place outside these labyrinths. Because I was born with the taste of honey on my tongue.

I have long since forgotten the lessons I learned in these places, but of the times I boarded the number 52 bus and sailed through the tops of the trees, when I considered the fate of the matchman, tasted the sweet grapes of Spain and a large woman put a small bunch of gypsy heather in my hand, I remember everything. For that is the path my life took: the path that led to quite different conclusions about the world than the one described by my parents and teachers.

Your own path is always radical, because it leads away from the mind and walks towards the heart. It returns to its place of origin, like the salmon, against all odds. It's radical because it puts you in the centre and commands that you create a warmth and a vibrancy so that all in your house can speak in harmony; a position that can co-ordinate the flight paths of 50,000 bees pollinating a million flowers that become seeds and fruit for all living beings and keep the whole world turning. No institution, no school or god or family, can teach you to take up that position. Only the heart will lead you there. Only the heart will lead you home, your own foolish and fiery child's heart. It has to be that way, because it is a path of love.

VIII
FLOWERMIND

Each flower contains a universe. In their seeds and pollen their unique structure appears like a small galaxy. The variety of forms appears endless. In the hands of Empire, these seeds become property – hybridised, mutated, made to work for profit. In nature they belong to no one but themselves. To consider the seeds of flowers is to consider ourselves: who we belong to, where we originate, why we are here. To apprehend our own mysterious universe, which for a fleeting moment flowers among other universes, leaving a seed trail in our wake. A unique dance we do once and once only, in this unique form we call ourselves, on a unique dancing floor called Earth.

In the practice years, when I set out to discover the language of the heart, I was shocked to find that the rational mind had all the vocabulary. Faced by the beautiful intelligence of the planet that spread like a witty intricate work before my inner eye, I could find no words to describe it. In our dialogues we forged a technology, so we could describe the world beyond its forms and outwit its domination of the rational mind. We did this by connecting with the intelligences of wild flowers, and engaging in lively acts of imagination. As we did we found ourselves breaking free in ways we had not anticipated. As Sartre said: 'Imagination is not an empirical power added to consciousness but the whole of consciousness as it realises its freedom.'

The concept of flowermind came one day in Arizona in 2001, while I was making a flower essence with a tumbleweed known as Russian thistle. Tumbleweeds are famous for uprooting themselves and whirling along the desert floor, scattering their seeds. In America they are considered 'aliens' and 'wasteland weeds'. However, they are formidable nitrogen fixers and go wherever they are needed to regenerate the soil. When I dreamed of them I saw a circle of neurologists peering inside my brain, seeing how the pathways could be altered for the benefit of my whole being.

'What are you doing?' I asked them, horrified.

'We are not *doing* anything,' they replied. 'We are just looking. *You* are doing.'

Flowermind was about perception. It was about working with the intelligence of a flower so that you might see where else to go than along the tramlines of your habitual thoughts. When our lines of thinking go down well-tried grooves, we come to fixed and known conclusions. When we explore other pathways, our perception of the world alters. We start to imagine other possibilities. The flowers assist this process: first by liberating us from fixed and 'educated' thinking, and secondly by showing us other avenues of consciousness. Thoughts by their nature are like objects, like known familiar furniture that belongs to the past. We are condemned to repeat the past by thinking them. By exercising our imagination outside those well-travelled tramlines and adventuring into the wild lands, we can access the unknown qualities of ourselves and also the earth. We learn the art and skill of direct perception. Some desert flowers that appeared that summer were the pathfinders in this last part of the inquiry.

But the main flowermind crew we found in Wales.

The wind has been roaring for days, rain lashing against the pane. We drive down flooded lanes through the green, hawthorns thrown into extraordinary shapes, sheep huddled in the lee of the hill. A dark wet light is everywhere. This little house is like a crucible, making us whole again after a difficult time. We dream intensely, deeply in the roots of ourselves. In the wild winter we begin our lives again. We carry on the practice. We let everything go. Outside the plants appear, the snowdrops in the churchyard, columbine and foxgloves by the side of the road. I climb the green hill and sit among the rowan trees and remember the red hill and all the mountains I once climbed. We visit an ancient forest that appears from under the sea, restore ourselves among a people who feel egalitarian and welcome us. Each morning and evening a man walks down the lane to visit his cow and her calf in a small field of buttercups. Sometimes I meet him and we talk about the weather, about the herb robert that grows on the wayside.

As summer came certain flowers caught our eye on the wayside – red valerian on a stone wall, twayblade orchid in the dune grass, yellow rattle on the clifftop. In what will turn out to be our last sequence of *seeings* we recognise that these flowers deal specifically with direct perception and the restrictive mind. Often they are flowers with a particular intense 'fast' vibration. Brightly coloured like viper's bugloss, intricately shaped like columbine or bee orchid. They sharpen our senses, like the tuning fork-shaped centaury flower, or piercing eyebright, imperceptibly lighten our mood like the 'laughter-bringer' scarlet pimpernel.

Where other plants brought medicine to the body, these flowers addressed our consciousness. They opened our minds so we could dwell upon the bigger picture. All of them looked upwards, into the sky, to the stars. What were they looking for? They were looking to the future.

It is hard to see the future because our minds only think about a future time that is based on past events. To perceive the future with our imaginations means we need to reconfigure how we understand time. Human thinking takes place in a timeless world, where everything can be changed at whim. On the physical earth time is the measure present in all things: it begins with our birth and ends with our death. The mind-life of our civilisation separates us from this awareness, and as a result we are not rooted in the moving fabric of life. We are homeless, whirling without direction. Like a tumbleweed.

The first of the 52 plants, *epazote*, the Mexican wormseed, and *Salsola kali*, the Russian thistle, both belong to the goosefoot family. Among the world's first flowering plants, goosefoots are the primal vegetables that appeared at the sea's edge. Their strong green bodies provide human beings not only with building-block foods, but also with a link to our ancestral selves, the root that allows us to foresee a future.

In Mexico in 2001, ten years after my first goosefoot encounter, I attended a lecture on cosmic time in San Migeul de Allende. It took place in a room where an artist was painting a mural of Quetzalcoatl, the feathered serpent of the morning star, who was banished from the Mesoamerican pantheon because he had no taste for sacrifice. The Aztecs and the Maya are famous for their intricate calendars of cosmic time, which revolve around the axis of Venus. When the conquistadors came they forced everyone to live their lives according to linear time – the time of the clock – rather than original or ancestral time, thus making their rigorous balancing of past and present unnecessary. Now became this monodimensonal moment, not a 'now' in which all time and all dimensions are held.

In linear time there are no cosmic consequences. But in Mexican culture, the lecturer from Florida informed us, the creation of the world comes from death, from the bones of the ancestors. There are always consequences. When someone in the audience asks about the ancestors he looks nervous and starts to backtrack. It is all right to talk as if education has got them under control, but not as if they were still here. Not as if they were real. The conquest destroyed the ancestors, he repeated, several times.

But we all knew, even though we could not say this to each other, that the conquest had done nothing of the sort. We were in Mexico, after all, not the United States.

We get nervous because at some point the plant sets its seed. At some point you have to pay. At some point the ancestors say the past is not in balance with the present and if you don't do something about it, they will. All ancient peoples know this and make the balance in their own ways, whatever the conquest says.

When you take yourself back to the beginning, you root yourself in the business of the planet. You take responsibility for your presence here. When native peoples sing of their ancestors, they remember their origin, their original bargain with life and death.

The mind does not like to think of death and the ancestors. It likes to keep its options open at all times, entertaining itself with grandiose fantasies and theories, and never letting any of its thoughts go. But the body lives with the reality of death at all times. It knows we are on a planet governed and limited by time. The plants remind us of this earthly time as the flowers appear and disappear before our eyes, as the trees grow and branch out, as their leaves rot down.

Death allows change to happen: lets go of the old and lets in the new. Without the death of microbes there is no soil, and without soil no plant can grow, and therefore no creature, including ourselves, can exist. Our mind-based culture, however, distracts us from this knowledge, and as a result change does not happen as it should. We endorse spiritual systems that tell us we can live in a timeless place in our minds, where we are all one and there is no separation. We listen to broadcasts telling us we can be young forever, and nothing we do has consequence. But the flowermind leads us to see that the earth is a place where change happens, and if we could see ourselves in the bigger cycles of time, we would most assuredly want to change.

One of the crucial shifts, therefore, is the one that takes place in our minds. The modern citymind thinks it is immortal; flowermind knows it lives in time. The citymind only considers itself; flowermind considers all factors. Like this mind in our own feeling bodies, the cities on our planet are cut off from the ecosystems of the planet. This separation is the primary cause of the environmental crisis on the earth. The solar path of flowers challenges human beings to imagine other possibilities for us all. This future cannot be borne of a mind that shifts its allegiance according to the power structures of civilisation. It can only be borne of a consciousness that feels at home on the earth.

How does this mind change its allegiance?

It changed at the beginning of the dreaming practice as we travelled through Australia. This journey changed our direction and led us to return home. It was partly our dialogue about dreams, the way our attention was turned towards our interior lives, to face our childhoods, relationships, houses, our history that kept us so aggressive and so restless. But it was also the place itself, its searing light, its vast unknown nature, the bone-slow tempo at which everything happened. I caught a glimpse of something in the parks, under the eucalyptus trees that grew by the sea. I saw how everyone gathered under their shade, sharing picnics, from whatever country of origin; and later in the rainforest, where we swam naked, how there was a peace and

356

silence between us all – the men, women, children – as the hot wind shivered through the slender groups of gums.

As the cities of my memory and my recollections of people slipped away, these aboriginal-shaped gatherings appeared before me. Out of the blue. Then I realised I was looking at the future: the future of the people and the land. The *dreamings* were freeing up my mind so I could see it. And there was just space after that. Space and silence became part of our lives.

But mostly it changed in the plant practice, with these brightly coloured flowers that spoke to us about the future: the buddleia that brought two hundred butterflies one day in our Suffolk garden. The lotus, marigold and hibiscus that appeared in our last voyage abroad in India. The vervain flowers of Dr Bach's garden in Oxfordshire, the golden columbine of the Arizona canyons. The mysterious white flowers in California in 2000 that gleamed in the green shade. A pool where I lay naked under the willow trees. One of those small bubbling mineral pools where you can sit with others among the rocks, under the stars, feeling relaxed, intelligent, at home.

Imagining the future, the writer Tom Robbins once wrote that the next age would be The Age of Flowers. Human beings possessed three kinds of brain: the reptile, the mammal – the midbrain – and the flower-powered neocortex. In the Age of Flowers the ancient fight between the mammal and dinosaur brains would cede to the visionary leadership of the neocortex. The neocortex fits like a swimming cap over our heads and it receives its impulses and information directly from the sun. All inspiration happens in this part of our brain. I imagined it there like the swimming cap of flowers people once wore in the '60s. Certain flowers lighting up certain parts of our minds.

Flowermind was the intelligence of our neocortex that could communicate with the high frequency of the earth and could recognise the signals of the sun and translate them. It opened like the flower trumpets of datura to the starry skies of Arizona, like the Very Large Array, and brought dreams and *seeings* and our imaginations into play. However, sometimes it was hard to receive these transmissions. The brain can be distorted by images of ugliness and brutality, by repeating cruel thoughts. We live hemmed in cities far away from nature. We look at the prison and we dream of the prison. We keep ourselves in squares and boxes, our eyes trained on pixels, encased in a kind of geometry.

The natural mind, however, is clear and fluid like these pools. It gazes upward into a sky that goes on forever, pristine, serene as the blue Pacific sea that day in California. When you look at beauty, into that expansive blue, into the shapes and colours of the flowers, and keep looking, that geometry starts to reform along the wavy lines of nature, and the snares and bars that hold you captive disappear. Your mind opens up and you can let other images and ideas appear.

And then something else happens on the outside: you can start to let down your guard with others. Suddenly you can sit, as you once did with these strangers and a small snake, in a pool in the flowery glade. You can talk with ease about many things, even difficult things, and there is no hostility, no competition between you.

Yerba Mansa was the mysterious plant's name: *mansa* meaning soft and yielding. What kind of life does the flowermind imagine? A future marked by its gentleness.

Flowermind showed how to forge communications of a kinder nature, fostered an ability to see in a more highly tuned way, unconcerned with fighting, jostling for position, for control and possession. You need all three brains to be fully human. You need the dragon alphabet and your free will, you need your creaturehood and warmth, but your inspiration comes from another kingdom entirely. Flowermind allows us to tell another story and imagine another future. Once you are rooted, aligned with the sun, you are in earth time, working within the fabric of life itself. All things are possible. This is the return which every flower calls us to remember. Life is in our hands, in our hearts, just where it was when everything began, long ago.

magnolia
Quaker House, Mexico City 2001

I am in a corner in a café in Mexico City. Disorientated after months of desert solitude, cut off from the activity outside the window, I watch the traffic whirl around the roundabout, the hands of men in suits flying in gestures over cups of coffee, the street acrobats climbing on each others' shoulders and tumbling down. What am I doing here? The city presses towards me in a welter of noise and confusion. I want to rush away, push everything from me and retreat back into my hotel room.

Then, out of the blue air, a bee zigzags past my table. *Oh, this is not the time to be sitting here!* I exclaim, and without thinking, walk out of the café and merge with the crowd flowing past. Swept up among the people I find myself on a bus, alighting on an unknown crowded street, entering the metro, being handed a ticket and finally arriving at a large indoor market. I stand still: all around me swirl colours, bright cloth, the scent of chocolate, fresh *tortillas*, wet coriander, women moving in checkered aprons, avenues full of swinging light bulbs, the raucous sound of a mariachi band. Something deep within me stirs, like a sleeping animal awakening. *Oh! Mexico!* I laugh, as I remember, as everything floods back, and my isolation breaks and falls around me like a shattered shell.

Suddenly I am here.

We are staying in the Quaker House, a hostel in an unknown quarter of the city. The rooms are spare and inexpensive and there is a lounge upstairs where you can meet your fellow travellers across plastic blue tables. But there is something unbearable and repressive in its atmosphere and so I have retreated to the light and airy library, a former artist's studio, to read the impenetrable prose of Madame Blavatsky. Surrounded by the works of saints and missionaries, I read about the root races and the destiny of man, about the masters and the masterplan. Occasionally I stare out of the large north window and am astonished by the giant white flowers of the street trees that stand immaculately among the fumes and chaos of the district. 'Oh, they are magnolias!' I say out loud to myself, to the empty library. And for the second time that day, my heart begins to beat unaccountably.

The *Magnolia grandiflora* is an impressive tree. The leaves dark and shiny, the flowers pale and waxy, and the whole tree so silent and still that it feels as though no wind could shake it from its roots. And yet when you see it there in the side streets of the city something stirs within you which you can barely name. In Mexican folk medicine the buds of this magnolia tree form part of a powerful heart tonic. *Flor de corazón* stirs the place where life has stopped and doesn't make sense any more.

On Sunday at the Quaker meeting in this library an explosion will take place: a young man will rage about the 'Right to Bear Arms' and no one will able to stop him. This is shortly after the bombings in New York. None of us yet know how this event will affect our lives. But something in this man's behaviour will show us how the world will start to go crazy. Not exactly to plan.

The Quakers are famous peacemakers and people of conscience. Among the theocracies of early America, only the Quakers of Pennsylvania kept true to their dissenter roots. In Arizona during the 1980s this conscience led to a remarkable act of civil disobedience. Quaker groups formed an underground network and smuggled people fleeing the atrocities in Guatemala and El Salvador across the Mexican-US border. It was an act of dissent against the government's participation in those authoritarian regimes.

I am here because the founder of this network, known as the Sanctuary Movement, wrote a book about his experiences which I have just read. His name is Jim Corbett, and he lived in a place called Cascabel (Rattlesnake) on the edge of the Sonoran desert. It is the beginning of saguaro country.

Corbett was an unusual Quaker. A cow rancher and philosopher, he rescued a tract of wilderness in Cascabel from developers by forming a community ownership, the Saguaro-Juniper covenant. It's a radical document and reads like a blueprint for the future.

'Native plants and animals on the land have a right to life with a minimum of human disturbance. Nothing – no rock or water – have a right ever to be rented, sold or extracted as mere commodities.'

Goatwalking is part autobiography, part manual, part treatise on right relationship with the land. Travelling with goats allowed Corbett to guide refugees across the untracked desert and inspired a community practice of hallowing the earth, based on the wandering life of the early Hebrews.

When they fled from Egypt into Palestine, the Hebrews created a new way of being with the land that Corbett calls *cimarrón*, a Mexican term for feral cattle. No longer hunters or gatherers from an archaic world, but ex-slaves from Empire, this group of people lived a semi-nomadic life among the hills, herding sheep and goats, which was distinct from the settled civilisation that considers itself the owner and ruler of nature. They were, as Corbett saw them, co-creating associates. To remind themselves of this covenant, they kept certain living laws – in which keeping the Sabbath was paramount. It was a day when you ceased to be busy, bending the world to your will.

To become *cimarrón*, you walk away from busyness, from possessiveness, from the worship of owner-masters. You live in a place in which you become errant, living life as if everything were shared rather than owned. The Sabbath reminded people of the wilderness from which they came, and kept their daily working lives in balance. To keep this focus required 'attentive stillness to meet and know the land as an active presence.'

'Attentive stillness' is the mood of the tree outside the house. It's the mood of saguaro country when you sit there for a long time in contemplation. You are not declaring war on the neighbourhood. You are not seeing a flawed creation that needs to be fixed. You are activating your ability to tune into the land, to remember the agreement you made when you originally broke from Empire.

I had never met Corbett among the saguaros of Cascabel, but I had a lot of time for his integrity. I had a lot of time for American nonconformists and their acts of civil disobedience. But something on this Sabbath was putting this to the test. Free speech is one of the Quakers' greatest tenets. In their meetings anyone who is inspired can speak. In the library the man ranted and raged and everyone listened. When someone tried to intercede, he was advised not to criticise. The man raved on. Afterwards, shocked and alarmed, the people began to question themselves, to consider whether Quakers should indeed be allowed to bear arms.

'They said what?' I exclaimed when Mark returned to our small room. It felt as if the ethos underpinning America had just been blown apart.

There is a borderline in the mind. Once crossed it leads towards fragmentation. On the other side of the line harmony becomes dissonance, sense becomes nonsense. The personality that was once simply neurotic slips into psychosis and situations that were negotiable suddenly become unnegotiable. The hold on reality slips. The interconnecting relationships that make sense of the world are severed and all hell breaks loose. This can happen in the mind, it can happen in your life and in the world. Suddenly something breaks. A line is crossed and though life may appear to be the same, it is not – on an internal level. The wiring has gone and no one knows any more how to reach inside and fix it.

No one could control the man in the Quaker House. The world's rage was running through him and no amount of tolerance could deal with the forces that had been unleashed.

'It was like a collective spirit of trauma let loose,' Mark said as we slipped outside into the dusk, and headed towards the restaurant. 'As if there were invisible forces running through him that were saying, "We are going to get arms into the Quaker place, so we will never have peace." It was terrifying, as if, had he had a gun, he would open fire.'

When we returned we saw the man, who had been in a street fight, wild-eyed and sobbing among the blue tables of the dining room. Everyone left him alone.

What regains order in a time of hostility is not peacetalking, but a love for life that beats irrepressibly in the heart. Without the inner command of the heart the outer world becomes meaningless, and the mind and personality fragment. The medicine of the heart brings coherence into play. You hold the flower of the magnolia in your hands. It shines like a lantern. Its presence brings back time, pace, rhythm, feeling; your feet touch the ground and you find your centre, a stillness in the middle of emotional and physical confusion. Within the still core of the heart, the whirling world self-organises around you. The ability to hold a still place within chaos is the key that opens the door. Through the door comes change and new creation. Without this key you do not break through, you break down. You are condemned to repeat the past and all its unbearable hostilities. None of us can enter the future.

When I lost myself in the crowd in Mexico City, I found myself. Although it is as cruel and overcrowded as any other city in the world, there is enough heart in the people and the culture for self-organisation to occur. There is the stillness and balance that *Magnolia grandiflora* brings you within its dust-laden streets. When the mind fragments and there is no heart in the people and the culture, you find yourself alone in an alien city square stalked by pure terror. Everyone is the enemy.

The trouble is, you want it your way, and you have been allowed to have it your way – or at least that is how it looks from a certain distance. You don't see it that way. I don't see it either. We are peeking out of our windows, looking at the parade that passes us by, everyone else seeming successful and happy and busy with their lives, thinking that life didn't treat us as it ought to have. The truth of the matter is we have become little Alexanders: dissatisfied conquerors all. When we don't get our way we ruin everything that crosses our path, good or bad. *If I can't be Caesar I'll be no-one*, as John Fowles writes in his essay on *The Tree*. We are spoiled because the city has promised us everything, but in reality has given us only this timid heart and this small street to live in, these people who infuriate and disappoint us. I will go out, we say, to new lands and ransack the world!

When you go in pursuit of these new worlds, this land of milk and honey, this American dream, you think the old world won't exist for you any more. The trouble is, you carry that old neighbourhood within you, and you live out all its ancient consequences. When the nonconformists arrived in New England, they found themselves reconstructing the old England they imagined they had left behind: they established their own lucrative slave-trade, embarked on a ruthless genocide of the native peoples, ransacked the natural forests and oceans in acts of unparalleled greed. Among their own kind they kept a strict and oppressive regime. In spite of the ideals of democracy and their own dissenter origins, the ritual hierarchies of masters and servants were observed in Massachusetts and Virginia as unjustly as anywhere else in the world.

Travelling in Africa, the English journalist Norman Lewis noted, in his astute and measured way, that when the emancipated slaves of America returned to their native shores, they did not revert to their old leisurely lifestyles in the bush. They started to build mansions in the style of their cotton-growing overlords and to behave like them among their own people. In spite of the *cimarrón* covenant of the early Hebrews of Palestine and the early socialism their descendants established with the collective kibbutz, modern Israel has become one of the most repressive military dictatorships in the world.

Domination sows the seeds of revenge hard within us, and only the straight and the true can resist their germination. When you have been controlled your first impulse is not to gain freedom, but to seek retribution. You want what your oppressors stole by conquest, and set about getting your own back. Generations later we stand in our control towers, looking out into city streets, restless and vengeful inside, incapable of seeing the double-thinking consequences of our actions: the emancipated tyrants; the warmongering Quaker; the survivors of ghettos constructing walls; the traveller trapped in a corner in Mexico City.

Some radical act needs to happen for us to reverse this process. Even as the military and economic powers of the United States and its allies begin to avenge themselves on the whole planet after the bombing of the World Trade Centre, a movement known as *The Great Turning* was beginning. To turn means to 'walk away from the king', to deliberately disengage oneself from the clutches of a 5000-year-old Empire. It is an act of dissension that seeks, on a personal and social level, to expand beyond the bullying schoolboy imperialism of modern culture, in order to see life in terms of consequence, how every action we take affects our fellows and all living systems. It is to actively shift from a childish 'my' world to an adult 'our' world, from Empire to Earth Community, inspired by what Quakers might once have called the imperative of conscience.

Sometimes I dream about my old city and the way it makes us go crazy, not according to plan. On a London bus I dream that a boy I once knew is saying goodbye to a girl. On the surface they appear happy and free, but underneath their faces are twisted in anguish. They share an ancient history between them, but lack the words to speak of it. The man is pushed around by hostile forces that surround him like a grid, and keep him trapped. There is a vast wilderness outside this grid, where his spirit lives, but he does not see it. I cannot speak with this boy, this man, in the dream, though I know every inch of the land.

When I awake I feel troubled. Once we had been able to meet

and talk freely. Now in the city streets people have become stiff and defensive. We are saying words to one another, but not speaking from experience. As we issue broadcasts about our lives – Everything is under control! Business as usual! – we sit inside a tower of silence. I realise that it is not just individuals who are autistic. We are beginning to live in an autistic world.

Autism creates an isolation so extreme within a human being that relationship is not possible, and there is no connection with the world outside. Cold-hearted, self-obsessed, the autistic boy and the autistic nation live in their own élite mind-spheres, constructing fabulous cities and complex systems. These they protect at all costs, insisting that everyone must obey their strange rules and rituals, or they pay with acts of fury and destruction. In the autistic state there is no empathy; all other beings must be subjected to an implacable will – human populations, ecosystems, ocean and mineral kingdoms. Everything outside your state is hostile. You build walls and watch towers, enclose yourself in ever-increasing circles of defence.

In 2001, the empire of the United States was entering an extreme state of control. It had no relationship with the peoples of the world, except insofar as they served its own corporate interests and its fantasy of global domination. When the 'objects' it sought to control retaliated, it went berserk.

Soon after the meeting we left Mexico City and travelled north, through rocky lands of agave and flowering cosmos, through small towns with jacaranda trees and ornate white churches, and we alighted from the bus at a colonial town where once we had lived. Although we had planned to visit Oaxaca, to go to the jungle, to the desert, to journey towards the ocean at Puerto Angel – those places which had brought such delight in our travelling years – we did none of these things. Something stopped us. Instead, we found rooms in an old hotel, and we waited. One morning we went to visit an orchid house which housed a collection of these rare, exotic flowers, built by an American *émigré*. We sat on the benches in the courtyard in the early sun of a brilliant September in silence. Everything was still. The morning glories opened their small sky-blue universes and embraced the walls of the town. Three thousand orchids stood behind us, immovable in the freshness of the morning. It felt that this peace and tranquillity would last forever. In that moment I realised that life in America was never going to be the same again.

In this stillness you knew, though no one else was telling you, that the heart was going to have to take charge. If a future was to happen, we would, unequivocally, have to learn to love that old neighbourhood and each other. The country I had visited so freely and gaily for twenty-two years had started to rearrange the planet like some autistic boy his room, and who was now going crazy because other people didn't agree to his rules.

In the stillness of the morning I realised it was not going to be the same again in Mexico, either. Already I couldn't just board a small plane and arrive in Oaxaca Square, as once I had, with the scent of gardenias at dusk. In so many squares, in fact – Merida, Tuxtla, Villahermosa, San Cristobal. To feel the evening stretch out in front of me, a towel laid out to dry upon the balcony, Mark standing smiling before the camera, the world at our feet. Already I could not board that night bus bound for the coast and drink coconut milk and take off my clothes beside the waves of La Playa de Amor. I was here, waiting in a resolute morning, anticipating the small betrayals that were to follow, the loss of all the people that I once knew in America. Our way of walking carefree in the world would not survive the fallout of that now famous event; tested against reality our fragile friendships would not hold.

In times of chaos, everything not held irrevocably by the heart fragments, and will press on all sides for everything to go down with it. One man from New York raving, holding a room full of sane and sober men hostage. In such a time you cannot rush around the world and seek delight: you have to hold to the moment, serve the experience, face what lies ahead. In a restless time you need to be still, to secure a foothold in whatever place you find yourself. In a present in which the past and the future have been erased, you need to remember, to look forward. Already you have decided to hold fast, to turn, and the tree, the flower, the place, this morning keep you in your decision. In a time of meaninglessness you set about forging meaning, you sit in attentive stillness and become an active presence in the land, in the garden with the orchids behind you.

Once we had called this attention with flowers *location in time and space*. Among the roses of the botanical gardens in Oxford it was a theory, a way of connecting with the living earth; in the orchid house in San Miguel it had become an imperative, a radical move from Empire. During our voyages with the hallucinogenic mushrooms of England and Mexico equally there came a point in which we found ourselves facing a howling darkness.

Here is the line: shall I be pushed across it, or do I stand fast?

We have learned to like theories, the ideas of democracy, of love, of freedom, and we play with these things in our minds as if they were arbitrary, as if we had a choice. And perhaps at one time we could fool ourselves that we had a choice. But now we realise that we do not. Or rather, we do have a choice: a real one that is stark, one of integrity. In a state of fragmentation you need a sense of the concrete, of real things. You need to keep close to your spirit, to keep your heart aflame. In a time of tyranny, an act of disobedience may be necessary. In such moments of extremity, you learn not to hold to the grandiose abstractions of the mind, to your textbook ideologies. It is the things of the real world that you hold dear: the small move, the valuable encounter, the fragrance of the morning, the memory of place, the flower as it opens, as its petals fall to the ground, the island that taught you everything about silence, the cat who showed you how to leave, the man who still walks by your side, sits with you under a tree, however hard the wind blows.

We have called life by grand and abstract names, and hold it at arm's length with our technology and our minds, but the reality of life is not so. We prefer the marketing, the distraction of our destination rather than the place, the earth, itself; the idea of communication, rather than the speaking to each other and listening. And though each of us carries the weight of Empire in our own way, this line we face demands a decision from us all. It bears consequences we cannot see. In the night, as the autumn winds shift around the town, as I sit in the garden in Mexico, I feel these consequences. And so you realise, though you had hoped it would last forever, that the world you once roamed in and loved was coming to an end.

When the excesses of control become too much, chaos happens: you burst out of your restriction. In this moment you are faced with the line and with the decision: enter the darkness, or find your heart. In the darkness you lose your way, but the heart will call you home. At home you mind your own business. You do not ransack the world

367

minding everyone else's business. To break through means you have to walk out of your tight corner and become errant, become *cimarrón*, find what is missing, no longer bending the world to your will. You realise that to go forward you can't be on your own, you have to dismantle the walls of silence that lie between you, and face the ancient history you share. To live in attentive stillness, you have to get to the land, the heartland, the wilderness. You have to remember the Sabbath, walk with goats across the desert, make a covenant with the land. Move from Empire to Earth Community.

To live together in the collective there has to be relationship, fellow-feeling. Communication between us cannot shut down. The heart is the only power within us that can break the tyranny of mind-control. But to find the heart, you have to lose the one thing you believe is more precious than anything: your isolation.

Inside the mind there is a hostile god telling you that you are different and alone. But you are neither different, nor alone. You have been condemned to repeat history and become the very thing you once exiled yourself from. The Hebrews have become Egyptians, constructing watchtowers, oppressing their slaves, building ghettos. The Christians have become Romans, treating the world as their bloody arena. Everywhere there is a consolidation of power, of élite, of privilege, of masters and the master races. The god's voice dictates the minutes of every meeting, burns down the world in his thunder-bolts and ire. What do you and I have? Nothing, except the diktat that enslaves us and keeps us apart.

To discover the heart and re-enter the living systems, you have to let go of the god that rules the mind. You have to let go of your house rules, your temple rituals, your position of absolute control. You have to enter a state of chaos, lose your grip and when nothing makes sense any more, let life carry you like a river downstream. You have to experience feelings: feelings of discomfort, disorientation; get swept up into different situations without controlling anything, until someone, a stranger, hands you a ticket and you find yourself in a place you remembered from long ago – a dark warm place of laughter, music, colour, scented with tuberose and mango, where you are among your planetary fellows, separate no longer. That's the moment when, on a rainy afternoon in September 2001, you put aside the book in the library that tells you there is a masterplan for the human race, and instead look out into the street and see a dark still tree with white flowers standing there. And a feeling that all manner of thing will be well comes quietly, miraculously, out of nowhere.

sea kale
Heritage coast, Suffolk 2007

I came because of Derek Jarman. I had read his journals and noticed the flash of wild flowers in the text, between his struggles with the elements that howled through his shingle garden and to keep his own tenuous thread to life. He had come in search of bluebells and found instead the bleak Dungeness shoreline and the sea-kale that grew beside the nuclear power station. It was a singular territory that he made his own: wind-broken, austere, at the end of the line. There was in his shout for life as it ebbed away, a defiant love that grabbed my heart. The wild flowers of Kent weave themselves like a garland about his wasting body. The sea-kale, the *Crambe maritima*, appears at his head like a crown.

It was 2002. We had, like the artist, driven out of the city at bluebell time and found the crambe just emerging in the great shingle banks of Dungeness. The crinkly purple leaves were pushing through the stones. We walked past the black fisherman's hut and its now-deserted garden, sat among the flowering dwarf blackthorns and crab apples and thought about ourselves at the end of our long journey. As we drove away I looked back, and the familiar mosaic of marsh and sky and sea sparked something in me. It was the memory of somewhere I used to know.

Months later in Wales, a vision flashed across my mind's eye. I was standing outside a gallery in a sea town. Inside there was an exhibition of wild flowers that formed a kind of maze, or a clock. With a jolt I realised that the show was my own. I went upstairs to where Mark sat typing up our practice notes, surrounded by quilts. It was late June, but still damp and cold. Outside the rain fell everywhere quietly in the valley, sliding down roofs, held in the leaves of the alchemilla growing between the dark grey slates. We need to go back to the coast, I said. We need to go to Suffolk.

Nigredo

The best way to encounter rhododendrons is to trespass into a great estate in late May, just after the rain has fallen, and stumble upon them by surprise. The best way to behold a horse chestnut is to enter a park in early morning as they tower before you in a great skirt of flowers. There are all manner of ways to sit beneath a hawthorn, but when the tree is in her splendour, you have to back off and get the full whammy of the rose as it tumbles full tilt into your chest. You resist falling to your knees in front of all these plants because you are modern; words like 'goddess' occur to you nonetheless. These are the big flowers, mega-bushes, the lady-of-the house heart trees of May. They need a whole-body approach.

There is only one position to commune with the sea-kale of the Suffolk coast and that is lying down, preferably on a blue day when there is a slight mist – one of those almost-summer days when you take off your shoes and put your feet in the cold sea that laps quietly against the stones. There are few people on the beach. It's a week-day. A boat moves across the horizon. You lie beside a big flowering individual, sheltered at ground level from the sea-breeze, immersed almost immediately in the aroma of pungent cabbage-flowers. It is an exorbitant scent, with something a whiff of urine about it. And yet, you can't ever quite get enough of that smell. Your head is crowned by large crinkly leaves. The plant is almost five feet across and embraces your body in its presence. Immediately you enter a state of calm: the shingle holds your form. The sea sighs against the shore, the larks are singing. The rest of the beach disappears, people and boat. You are in sea-kale time, big time, huge, ancient as stones and sea.

On Kessingland beach the great crambes have arisen slowly and inexorably. Along the shingle banks of Norfolk, Suffolk and Kent their forms appear, dark-leaved, deeply rooted among the grey and tan pebbles, with their curly leaves and stalks, great sprays of huge strange-scented flowers. Here in the wild eastern sea garden they are surrounded by mats of magenta sea peas and luminous sea-poppy. Tree lupins and red valerian appear around the fisherman's boats, the silvery prickly leaves of sea holly beside their winches, platoons of great lettuce and sea beets among the pebbles, wild radishes on the cliffs.

Lying by the sea kale, you don't want to move. There is nowhere else you want to go. With these roots sunk deep into the shifting shore, you feel you can deal with anything. It is said that *Crambe maritima* can detoxify anything.

Can this wild plant detoxify the world and give us our roots back?

Can it give us our hearts back? Kessingland is a strange place to ask this question, and yet it is where I have come at a turning point.

One thing I know: when you find the place at the end of the line, you don't move from there. It has taken you a lifetime to get there. To get back to the place where you began.

You do not come back to the same place. You do not find the child who danced on the ribbed sand, ran wild among the dunes and the sea holly. You do not see the girl leaning her head on the shoulder of her dancing partner, standing before a sea of phosphorescence. You do not go back to hear the sound of the swifts screaming around the eaves at dusk, to the sound of the sailboats rattling their stays on the river, to stand in the hollyhock garden with the friends that came and went on their bicycles, with their picnics and bottles of wine. These moments were markers, markers of a life that has now fallen like sand through your hands. But the land is still there. That is where I belong, you say. And one day, when there is nowhere else to go, you go back. The people have gone now, and the child, the girl that was you, but something remains. You don't go back to the same place, but you do go back.

It's a place which costs nothing to go to, and yet it has cost you everything, this struggle through the harsh pebbles to find yourself on an empty beach on a summer's day, as a misty calm sea, flowers arising, gaunt windblown forms of elder and sea buckhorn behind you, passageways of blackthorn on the cliff, curved by the wind. I look down the coast with all its estuaries, across mud flat and fen, towards my stopping places – Aldeburgh, Felixstowe, Sandwich Bay – and I chart my own life as I came slowly northwards, slow as a red-sailed barge that once made its way up the eastern rivers, stacked with salt and barley.

I remember a Jesuit who quit his monk's cell and walked instead into the mountains. Afterwards he wrote that no human being can touch you where it really matters. We let our entire lives be shaped by the people who we think should love us completely, should tell us that we matter, and yet they cannot. Because no one can love us until we love our own self, and that self is something mysterious, indefinable, ungovernable, so *other* that we can only reach it in the rigour of our own inner solitudes, in the depths of ourselves, in the wild places. And when we find that self, we realise that we did not come to be loved for what we think we should be, but for something else entirely. We came to love our own nature, which can only be found in wild nature itself. This is not a nature that is accessible in any other way than through our own living form, our own presence within the territory, by our being with this otherness. It is a question entirely of relationship. As, indeed, love always is.

So I did not come back to the sea to recapture a self I had lost – the shore-dancing child, or the schoolgirl who sat under the holm oaks, or the young journalist who escaped to the sea town where the curlew called over the shining river – but rather to remember an unknown part of myself that, in spite of all adversity, in spite of everything that had conspired to vanquish us, had always stood by through the city years, through the travelling times, the ashy times. It was to know that the being who had sent up her medicine flowers, her sentinel trees, her bitter bushes to stand watch over those girls, was the same being as myself.

I had started at midnight with a book in my hand, a book written by a man who had taken his name from one of the rivers which runs through this waterland of heath, birch copse, fen, marsh. The book was called *England, Your England*. You return to this territory because your heart has always lived there. You can, like George Orwell, like all writers, take a stand against Empire, but you have to have somewhere you love to do that from. Somewhere tough enough, resilient enough, fluid enough to withstand the storm that now advances towards you. And you need a root that can hold you as an anchor within that place, so that you can hear the larks singing and know why they sing, why you make your pilgrimage to the sea kale today.

The urge to return is powerful. Something in us longs for redemption. We cut the forest down and yet long for the tree to forgive us, to let us back into paradise. We hunt the wild things, destroy their shelter, and yet search out for the one that licks our hand, the lion that comes out of the savannah to remember us. We long for that lion to be our friend. In our longing, in our desire for redemption, we ignore the paradise that is before our eyes. So desperate are we for love, we forget to love. Love would redeem everything, which is to say it would turn it around, bring everything back. Free love, no holds barred, no conditions, no limits, love. When you love, that's when the planet starts taking off its old clothes and shows you what it's really about underneath. You start seeing what you once saw in San Pedro in Ecuador all those years ago, what the dolphins and the whales once showed you of the ocean in your dreams. When you return and love the place at the end of the line, you forget about redemption. You realise it's not about redemption. It's about transcendence.

Albedo

In Yoxford village hall, a woman called Rose is telling me about the multitude of flower workshops she has attended around the country. Everything, she says, is connected to something else. Though the lines of her conversation never seem to arrive at any destination. Rose is not so interested in the flowers as flowers, but as signs. Once she sat by a *Crambe maritima* and wondered *what it all meant* and as she was driving home her eyes caught the words *crown cleaners*. It was the name of a laundry.

'Which power plants did you study?' I ask her. She can't remember. The thing is to keep moving. 'I just use my pendulum over the catalogues,' she says.

In the hall there are pendulum swingers everywhere. A belly dancer encourages women of all shapes and sizes to shimmy like a snake. An astrologer advises us to keep inside our eggs and protect ourselves. At several stalls therapists minister to heads and feet, a herbalist sells burdock root and dandelion leaves, a girl stands surrounded by scarves made of spun silk, like the gossamer wings of a dragonfly. 'Is this hand-made by the people?' I ask. The girl stares at me with a faraway look, and does not know the answer.

The bazaar is for a village school in the Himalayas, so that people can learn the facts and figures of Empire and be like we are, enclosed in imaginary eggs, ruled by geometric forms, wiggling about like reptiles, swinging pendulums over catalogues, over the sacred trees and power plants of the world, forgetting their names, looking for a sign. Trying to get to that comfortable place where nothing happens.

I go outside and sit in the field opposite the village hall, among a host of scarlet poppies. Over the fields, along the stony beach of Sizewell, the flowers of the *Crambe maritima* swell into green fruits that seem like small bunches of seaweed. The plants dig their roots deep into the shingle shore, hold tenure, in preparation for the winter storms. The waves increase upon the shore.

By the sea the rules of the mind start to be erased. Something else begins to be remembered.

I am walking northwards, on my way home. At Walberswick on a peerless day, I set out to swim. The sea is bone-cold and serene. My body moves through the water, making ripples as it passes. In the marshes beside me there are small round gardens of sea-aster and sea-rocket. The samphire is turning red. It's autumn and only the ragged leaves of the crambe are left.

In alchemy there are three processes, each governed by a planet: at the beginning comes Mercury to quicken the black *materia* of our lives. In the nigredo our base material begins its work of transformation into gold. At the end is the *rubedo*, the reddening, commanded by the fire of the sun. In between there is the whitening, known as the *albedo*. It is ruled by the moon. Its element is salt. Salt is what remembers us, brings us back to the beginning, so we can start again.

Once, in the beginning, we were creatures of the sea and salt wave. The tide-shifting moon brings us the memory of our origin – our belonging, our natural rhythm, our fluidity. We know nothing of alchemy, yet something instinctive, primordial, running at a different axis to our dryland selves, calls us to return to the sea. And just as salt is essential to our physical bodies, so is the influence of salt water to our intelligence and feeling. To immerse yourself brings back the relationship with the living systems. Over-stimulated and exhausted by electricity and artificial light, the sea restores our magnetism, our creaturehood, our intuitions, our dreams, everything that is left out by a dry mind-body-fixated civilisation. Stiff routines and thought-patterns are broken up by the roar and movement of the surf, and our inspiration returns. Standing on the shore half-naked with our fellows, floating like seals and porpoises, we remember the starry matrix, the ocean from which we came. At night as the waves sigh in and out and the Milky Way floats above the horizon, something huge, indefinable, mysterious is all about us and a space opens up where only mechanical thoughts, worries, furies exist in our daily selves.

We come to the sea to remember ourselves. Though our civilisation tells us we are the result of dry bones and dust, no laboratory or church shapes how we feel. Our ancestor moon feels fluid, cosmic, moody, ecstatic, uncontained, powerful, alive. We are succoured by her presence and by her nourishing salty plants.

Down by the sea, among the shingle and the sand-dune and the salt marsh, grow the plants of our primordial memory. Our ancestor vegetables – the leaves and roots of wild carrot, wild cabbage, sea beet, sea pea, sea rocket, oraches and samphire – that feed us, and the medicines that restore us – centaury and eyebright flowers, sea buckthorn berries, sea holly root, scurvy grasses. Greatest among them all is the crown that cleans our minds, that restores the kingdom when you lie beside her on a summer's day, with one boat passing. *Crambe maritima*, the heart of the sea.

Rubedo

When the conqueror of the ancient world asked the feral philosopher Diogenes, *What can I give you?* Diogenes replied: *Get out of my sunlight.* This is because Diogenes, the first cynic (from *cynos*, meaning 'dog') knew everything about the dog's throw and spent his life looking for another real human being to converse with. This is the lot of sages, seers and poets. History does not tell us if he succeeded. But then we live in a world that worships Alexander.

Another thing history does not tell us: you do not return when you expect to, in the spring with the hawthorn flowers, or at midsummer with the rose, but when the barley is being cut, at the time of the fall, in the heat of the dog days, as the broad haze of sun burnishes the land. You arrive at the seashore with wild carrot and valerian when the harebell and the rowanberries shine in the heathlands.

When I went down to the shore to greet the sunrise that August day, the day of the losing throw, I repeated to myself a phrase that struck me as I had awoken at dawn:

'This time it will not be me that loses.'

When the sun emerged out of a milky sea that morning I noticed first its colours, then the light, then the warmth that suffused every-thing. The sun flashed its double-sun rainbow over the earth: gold, pink, green, blue, magenta, filling its seapath with liquid gold and solarising the land with a lambent fire.

Today is the day they once called *lughnasa*, the light of the sun, the time of gathering, of barley and salt and the people from the land. It is the door that follows the zenith, the time we consider our fall.

The losing throw happens because in the Empire – the one that invented the word *lughnasa* and the one that invented the concept of the losing throw – someone always has to lose. Something has to be sacrificed. But in the mysteries of fall you learn to let go of that which you no longer need in order that new things can live. Like fruit that falls from the trees. To be in life is to live with death, with letting go. That way no-one loses. Everyone gains: you, your fellow man, the earth. Down in the underworld at the end of the line you learn this, among the sooty saucepans, from the ashy years. The Empire demands that we sacrifice our living beings to keep an old show going. It demands that we hand over our hard-won harvest, even though we starve. But one day we make a stand. We don't move away. We are not going to lose. We are not going anywhere. Our roots run too deep in the land. The sea has remembered us.

The scent of fennel impregnates the air, reminding me of the vacant lots we saw, climbing up the staircase in the desert town. You learn to live in real time, out of the time of the Empire. You don't believe its magic formula. You don't even believe your own.

History is famous for repeating itself, for knowing everything, but one thing it does not know: when you return, something shifts in time. You arrive at the shoreline, go through the fennel door with a familiar musty scent in your nostrils: sharp, aniseed-flavoured, the scent of golden fennel flowers mixed with salt air. As you brush by its stalky umbellifer presence on your way through to the sea at dawn, you pause, trying to sense what this scent reminds you of, something that is elusive. You cannot recapture it: and yet some part of you knows.

The part that knows is the part that is returning: your mysterious ancestor, she who stood by all these years: your unknown universe, living in form and time. The stalk of fennel in its giant form once formed the pine-cone-topped *thrysus* that spearheaded the mystery rites in Eleusis, so people could experience death-in-life and thus the infinity that lives in the depths of themselves. In the time of fall, they fell like plants into the dark land, into the underworld, and discovered the sun that lives ever-burning inside them. To find the way home, they had to let go of everything they had gained in their ascendancy. It was how they learned to live as real human beings, in

377

alignment with the sun, the earth and all the planets, and do the work of transformation, which is the challenge of all human beings. A challenge kept in obscurity by civilisation.

We no longer live in the time of gods or half-gods, when philosophers walked the streets carrying lanterns in their hands. We do not know what happened in those mystery rites and maybe we don't care to know. But here is the fennel with its mysterious scent and the passage that leads to the sea on a summer's day. The passage the ancient philosophers once knew as the solar path, that still is the only way to proceed if we want to live as real human beings together.

No one can walk this alchemical path of flowers except for ourselves. It is not by proxy that we are here. Children cannot run through these tall plants for us, nor can I send my best friend, our enemy, or any god we may or may not believe in. It is a self-only task: the task of being alive.

Today I was emerging out of the darkness into the sunlight. I found myself down by the seashore, like Diogenes with his lamp, waiting for the real human beings to arrive.

During that first year when we began our plant practice I went out and hunted the flowers, learned all their names, gathered their leaves, made medicine, looked at their energies, kept a log. The second year, we went into the territories with our companions, carrying glass jars, and held dialogues in the wastegrounds. The third, I took a camera and notebook, painted desert, mountain, river, sea. At night I tracked the medicine flowers in my dreams. The fourth, I walked the flower paths, mapped a neighbourhood of lanes and oak trees. The fifth, I took the plant knowledge into the community, kept a jar of wild flowers at my desk for a working year. The sixth year, we began a dialogue with the wild places, held tree dialogues, sea dialogues, watched the doors of the year as the sun rose over the waves.

The seventh year, I began the book.

After the seventh year you stop counting: the plants have become part of your life. There was a moment in the beginning when they were everything, where their appearances and their meanings absorbed you like a child is absorbed completely by a game. You were sensitive to their every nuance, colour and form. They appeared in your dreams as new universes, as lithe and mysterious beings. The trees whispered to you as you walked past; every leaf was a medicine, a language. But with your entry into this new world came a fear of its terrible disappearance. You suffered the fate of every nature lover in a time of unravelling. You clung to the roadside appearance of valerian and cowslip; in the city you had eyes only for the buddleia and dandelion. You chafed at the lack of snowdrops and orchids, lamented the disappearance of the wastelands. When the cutters came you roared down the lane brandishing your fist, wept, wrote letters, spoke out at every opportunity. Eventually, you learned to grow still, made strategies, knew that when one wasteground disappeared another would appear. You did not close your heart, but you did not let it bleed either. You placed your hands on the severed stem of the great burdock and addressed its roots: *We are not all so*, you say. The plants already knew this, but you needed to say it anyway. It was your move, the sound you made in the fabric. The hand you held between the worlds of plant and human beings. Without each other, we went nowhere.

In time you learned to become like the plants, bearing neither grudge nor malice, but not forgetting your treatment. To those who noticed you shared all your benefit, to those who turned away, you were indifferent. It is a simple measure of heart, a 50/50 matter of exchange. Above all, you learned that nothing remains exactly as it was. As you sit by the flowers each season, sometimes a door opens, and sometimes it does not. 'It's a good great willowherb year,' you say, as the ditches in the lanes shimmer with translucent pink and green, and you notice how the primroses remained a long while on the bank though the damsons and wild plums did not fruit. Somewhere along the flower track, you learn to hold fast to your integrity, and to make communications between the plants and the people where there were none before. You start to imagine a future in which the wild places can restore themselves in all their original beauty. You hold an ash twig in your hand and say: *With this twig I can recreate the world.* This future, this power of creation, gives you an edge over Empire, which lost sight of these things long ago.

That winter the sea rose up. The wind ran against the tide and the estuaries flooded their banks. In the village halls everyone began to speak about how to protect their land. Small bands of people collected together, stacked sandbags against the river wall, spoke out for the birds and the spirit of the land.

Just a few cows, said the grey-suited men in the village hall, refusing to mend the broken banks as the government announced its retreat back to the metropolis. 'What about the fishermen?' I asked. 'It's not economic,' he replied. The cows in the watermeadows didn't count. The birds didn't count. The land didn't count. The people in the coastal seatowns didn't count. Only the populations in the industrial towns would be secured. The oil prices began to rise.

'They are going to take everything!' said Charlie.

I am talking with a man I once knew when I lived in Notting Hill and we were both young. He is talking about the fish in the ocean, which he has spent his life defending, and a book he has written called *The End of the Line*. His name is Charles Clover and he lives down the coast, beside the estuary of Blackwater. I am telling him what is happening down by the sea's mouth. The Empire is abandoning the defences of the rivers and their harbours along the territory of the sea kale – the Blyth, the Ore, the Alde, the Deben. As we talk, a kestrel outside hovers on the breeze. All eyes watch the activities of Empire. The Empire does not care, does not listen, protects its own interest at all costs. It is business as usual in the hotels in town, down at the pier. *The show must go on!* The beach keeps winning prizes, but stormy weather keeps the visitors away.

As I watch a grey mullet swim in a tank at Southwold harbour, its ancient eye lines up against mine. It is a million years old. How old am I?

At night I begin dreaming of floods, of strange horizontal waves that come and go over the land, that no-one takes notice of. Then one day they come for real.

I am walking: walking past the pier and the sea wall, the breaches in the river, the burnt reeds; I am walking down by the sea-aster gardens, past the four men who are watching intently for the bearded tits on the late sea-asters. A small boy shouts, exultant: *I have found a crab!* There is a rainbow in the sky. A cat sits in the window of the pub surrounded by flood water, and looks out toward us. It looks like the end of the world, and yet there is beauty everywhere.

After the flood, we will start to walk down the edge of the kingdom. We will walk from Lowestoft where sad-eyed men sing about love, past the statue of Neptune, towards the tower of Aldeburgh. We will walk from November to the following August. We will stand on the beaches making a protest to the government, lie by the sea kale, watching an adder slither through the sea peas as the police and protesters outwit each other at the power station. We will swim in still seas and high waves. The sea will become glass-green, pewter, azure, opal, bruised, mad with foam, tipped with fire, running to shore, swirling at my feet, leaping. The sky will race with clouds, the wind blow sharp or warm, hail will spatter on our heads. The sands will shine silver, the cliffs flash gold, rays pour down on the land. I will pocket treasures from the beach – sea coal, sea peat, a glass bead, a worn kitchen tile, an oyster shell, flint, heather root, a guillemot feather – hold their forms in my hand, keep a collection on my writing desk. The sand martins will depart and return to their cliff dwellings, the barnacle geese to the marshes. In the mornings, standing at my window, I will see the sea like a band on the horizon, gleaming like a mirror. *It's a good day,* I will say to Mark. *Let's go out.*

Everything is changing, shifting as we walk out, following the track of sea-kale as it disperses its green seeds. You keep walking; the flowers are guiding you as they appear at your feet: bird's foot trefoil, sea campion, thrift, scabious, houndstongue. The world is falling about my ears. We are walking the wild edge of the kingdom, at the end of the line. Across the sea on the mesas, the Hopi keep the balance of the world by keeping themselves in balance, at a time when the Empire is set against them. What is going down in the kiva, in the kingdom, is going down in the world. Down on the shoreline, what you find at the end of the line is your heart. You don't have money or reputation. It is too late for these things. What matters is that you hold tenure, that you treasure the spirit of place that the Empire considers worthless. It's your art, your skill, what you bring back from your medicine years. Because you realise it's the only thing worth living for.

At the end of the journey, among the Aldeburgh dunes, I sat by the half-buried apple tree with its rough leaves, by the wormwood and the willowherb, remembering those who came here before me and struggled within the stony crucible of this wild shore: the writers who slept on the tip of the shingle banks, who kept the wind out of the garden, who swim across the broad rivers and cold rough seas, who love the *Crambe maritima*. One thing you find at the end of the line, at the edge of the narrow land, the place that keeps you alive.

England, my England.

Out to sea there is a sandbar, I am told by a diver for treasure. There are seals there. The sandbars appear and then disappear. When summer comes you can swim out to them and feel the cross-currents move around your feet. You can feel how everything moves and is fluid, not as it seems. In your imagination you trace seahenges, songlines. The great waves of the full moon race to the shore like waves of undulating light. In a flash of sunlight the sea now is deep gray, the colour of mullet, becomes luminescent turquoise. You are standing beside all oceans, in Africa, in all time. The white flowers of the sea kale gardens dazzle, the perfume of heather rises, the larks ascend above you, an exultation of larks. The sea goes in and out, like our breath. We are in the kingdom of the crambe, a selkie people, an island people, a people returned, starting again. Nothing is as you imagine it is.

England, our England.

The sun is rising down at Southwold. It is 5am August 1, a year after I moved through the fennel gate. 2008. There are thick clouds everywhere in the sky. Gulls are waiting on the empty beach, a warm wind comes up from the south, the sand is damp from the night rain. The sea is choppy, white-flecked at low tide, the shoreline is edged with bright stones and bladderwrack.

The sun is rising before us though we cannot see it. We turn to go home, but then something makes us turn back. The sea is calling. *There's a light!* says Mark. We stand on the dunes among the marram grass and watch the sky. All around us the clouds are tinged with light, suffused with pink. On the horizon in the face of a cloud the eyes suddenly blaze. I laugh, *It's coming!* Then the head breaks apart and the sun bursts through, a dazzling ring of white light around it, and a bolt of fire shines through the waves.

I run down the beach into the warm sea and start to swim down the golden path that leads all the way to the sun.

Appendix 1: The 52 Flowers

I GERMINATION

epazote *notting hill, london*
passion flower *mérida, mexico*
liberty cap *high wycombe, buckinghamshire*
red geranium *santa fe, new mexico*
juniper, saguaro, cottonwood *bisbee, arizona*
eucalyptus *sydney, australia*
wild plums *great milton, oxfordshire*

II BUSH SCHOOL

morning glory *deia, majorca 1993*
peyote *real de catorce, mexico 1993*
san pedro *vilcabamba, ecuador 1993*
blue mushroom *norwich, norfolk 2003*
hemp *reydon, suffolk 2007*

III PLANT COMMUNICATIONS

dandelion *port meadow, oxford*
agrimony *botanical gardens, oxford*
st johns wort *railway junction, oxford*
sycamore *cowley road, oxford*
alder *city canal, oxford*
moschatel *marsh lane, suffolk*
suffocated clover *southwold, suffolk*

IV MEDICINE ROOT

hemlock *port meadow, oxford*
monkshood *botanical gardens, oxford*
californian poppy *southmoor road, oxford*
pine *santa catalina mountains, california*
poison ivy *santa barbara, california*
tronadora *bisbee, arizona*

V SPEAKING BUSH

bearberry *bisbee, arizona*
snakebroom *warren, arizona*
red root *highway 90, arizona*
queen of the night *bisbee junction, arizona*
agave *san miguel de allende, mexico*
creosote *swan road, arizona*
wormwood *powis castle, wales*

VI TREE DIALOGUES

crack willow *the thames, oxford*
holly *holywell churchyard, oxford*
holm oak *alpes-maritimes, france*
box *gorges du verdon, france*
peepal *sarnath, india*
english oak *staverton thicks, suffolk*

VII RADICAL FLOWERS

wild cotton *dallas, texas*
japanese cherry *south kensington, london*
elder *dundalk, ireland*
opium poppy *aldeburgh, suffolk*
lilies *halesworth, suffolk*
lady's smock *leiston, suffolk*
heather *dunwich heath, suffolk*

VIII FLOWERMIND

yerba mansa *highway 101, california*
columbine *french joe canyon, arizona*
magnolia *mexico city*
vervain *brightwell-cum-sotwell, oxfordshire*
lotus, hibiscus, marigold *rishikesh, india*
buddleia *reydon, suffolk*
sea kale *minsmere, suffolk*

Appendix 2: A glossary of terms

The plant practice took several forms of interaction that included *visiting, seeings, dynamic dialogues* and *energetic readouts* and *dynamic dialogues*. During 1999-2000 about 100 *seeings* were undertaken and formed the principle "lexicon" of our dialogue with plants. Thereafter the practice focused on *visiting* and *energetic readouts*, especially in our shared explorations with others.

Visiting Active engagement with a plant in the field. The intents of visiting are threefold: to acquaint yourself with the plant's energy configuration, to initiate a communication and to gather material for the *dynamic dialogue* or *seeing* that follows.

The first action is *sitting down alongside with*, a physical and emotional tuning into the plant's energy field. Entering a state of attentive stillness *with* the plant. Awareness of what happening around and within you – words that come out of the blue, memories that surface, feelings and changes of energy. This action requires reciprocity. You are not going to "get information" but entering the plant's field, as you might visit a friend's house, noticing its atmosphere, design and effect on your being.

The second action is *locating the self in time and space*. This includes feeling your feet on the earth, tuning into your heartbeat and breath, relaxing, becoming an active and alert participant in your surroundings rather than a passive bystander. Placing yourself within the territory in order to expand your perception and release yourself from the past and future of the mind. Connecting with the intelligence of all the living forms around you, your own heart, in the here and now.

Seeing A method of communicating in other dimensions. Providing a set and setting – quiet space, concentration, time – in which you can perceive images and messages to and from other life forms. A *seeing* gives a visual and feeling demonstration of a plant's workings – an energetic configuration of its qualities and how they relate to the human world. Access to these shared imaginal realms requires flexibility and imagination on the part of the seer.

The *seeings* require feeling to work. If your thinking mind holds control over your perception, your feelings will not be able to access your seeing faculty -the inner eye and heart. You will be prevented from seeing a composite picture because the thinking mind, which works in duality and mechanical or sequential "trains" of thought, cannot make sense of a visit's multidimensional information. The heart however is able to assimilate many kinds of input at once and organise it into a coherent and meaningful whole.

Dynamic Dialogue An intentional dialogue that is consciously building creative links with the plant world. Held between two or more people in an agreed space and time after a seeing, visiting or dream.

Energetic Readout Energetic messages that demonstrate an encounter with a plant being. During our joint flower work we conducted these readouts in a simple and formal way, agreeing to a time and place in which there would be no interruptions from the outside world. In this hermetic space (usually around a table or in a small circle) we would take it in turns to speak of our experiences, to ask questions, make notes. Sometimes we placed a sprig of the flower or tree in the middle of our discussions, or drank a tea of its leaves.

A readout gives a composite picture of what has been felt, thought, exchanged in the territory during the *visiting*. This includes a physical description – your response to the shape of the plant – and its effect. *How* you speak about your encounter is as important as *what* you say. Your mood, energy, the way you move, are all indicative of the plant's innate character and qualities merged with your own. Readouts are co-operative engagements. Everyone who takes part is there to ask questions and encourage whoever is speaking.

Dreams The exploration of dreams is a key way of discovering the energy fields and intelligence of plants and how they interact with human beings. In the practice plants appeared in our dreams spontaneously, or on invitation. They came as themselves, as abstract patterns, or in figurative form. Often their influence was felt within the scenario of the dream itself. In the *dynamic dialogue* we would explore this territory, noting our positions, feelings, actions taken during the dream. If, for example, the plant was directing us in finding our way out of a certain situation, this was its medicine, its action upon our physical, emotional or mental states. Some plants operate more than others in the dream world and have a strong influence on our imaginations. Mugwort, a traditional dreaming plant, came in the form of a naked young woman who appeared before Mark and myself in a prison cell. "I have beautiful breasts," she informed me. When I paid attention to her form we found ourselves outside the gaol.

Tree dialogues A intentional entering into the tree's *field* and discourse with others within that field. Keeping aware that whatever transpires within that dialogue is linked with the tree's emanation and intelligence. Where plant *seeings* often address the alignment of our individual souls and bodies, *tree dialogues* address the governance and spiritual structure of our social lives. Since early times trees have been meeting places where justice was meted out and important decisions made. They marked strategic points on the pathways across the land, that demonstrated right relationship with the earth and sun. Thus within their emanations many human events were aligned in accordance with the harmony of the cosmos. By their nature and as a result of our ancestral relationship with them, *tree dialogues* will often bring to the fore crucial issues to do with the collective and our place within it.

Two Ravens Press is the most remote literary publisher in the UK, operating from a working croft by the sea, right at the end of the most westerly road on the Isle of Lewis in the Outer Hebrides. Our approach to publishing is as radical as our location: Two Ravens Press is run by two writers with a passion for language and for books that are non-formulaic and that take risks. We publish cutting-edge and innovative contemporary fiction, nonfiction and poetry.

Visit our website for comprehensive information on all of our books and authors – and for much more:

- browse all Two Ravens Press books (print books and e-books too) by category or by author, and purchase them online at an average 20% discount on retail price, post & packing-free (in the UK, and for a small fee overseas)

- there is a separate page for each book, including summaries, extracts and reviews, and a page for each of our authors, including interviews, biographies and photographs.

www.tworavenspress.com

EarthLines is a lavishly illustrated, full-colour A4-sized quarterly magazine of around 64 pages, dedicated to high quality writing on nature, place and the environment. Our focus is on writing which explores the relationship between people and the natural world, and encourages reconnection. We want to help forge a new ecoliterature that is truly responsive to, and that deeply and meaningfully engages with, the challenges we face. That doesn't just acknowledge, but that actively embraces all the contradictions and discomforts inherent in our relationship with the natural world – those contradictions which surface in all of our genuine attempts to reconnect.

- Visit the *EarthLines* website to find out more and to subscribe.

- Read our blog at http://earthlinesmagazine.wordpress.com

- Join us on Facebook – just search for 'EarthLines'

www.earthlines.org.uk